THE BROWNSON–HECKER CORRESPONDENCE

Courtesy of Helena W. Odiorne

George P. A. Healy portrait of Orestes A. Brownson, 1863

Courtesy of the Paulist Center, Boston

Healy portrait of Isaac T. Hecker, c. 1870

NOTRE DAME STUDIES
IN AMERICAN CATHOLICISM

Number 1

The Brownson–Hecker Correspondence

EDITED AND INTRODUCED BY
Joseph F. Gower and
Richard M. Leliaert

UNIVERSITY OF NOTRE DAME PRESS
NOTRE DAME LONDON

Library of Congress Cataloging in Publication Data

Brownson, Orestes Augustus, 1803–1876.
The Brownson-Hecker correspondence.

(Notre Dame studies in American Catholicism; no. 1)
Includes bibliographical references.
1. Brownson, Orestes Augustus, 1803–1876.
2. Hecker, Isaac Thomas, 1819–1888. 3. Converts, Catholic—Correspondence. 4. Philosophers—United States—Correspondence. I. Hecker, Isaac Thomas, 1819–1888. II. Gower, Joseph F., 1945– III. Leliaert, Richard M., 1940–
IV. Title. V. Series.
B908.B64A4 1978 230′.2′0922 76-20160
ISBN 0-268-00656-3

Manufactured in the United States of America

Contents

Preface

Orestes Augustus Brownson (1803–1876) and Isaac Thomas Hecker (1819–1888) are deservedly ranked among the principal figures of their time. Their outstanding contributions to the religious and intellectual history of nineteenth-century America have long been recognized. Recent interest in this country's distinctive Catholic tradition has focused renewed attention on the central roles these two American-born converts to Catholicism played in the formation of that tradition. Almost from the moment they embraced the Catholic religion in 1844, Brownson and Hecker set out to demonstrate that the Roman Catholic faith was essentially harmonious with American life. The apologetical trend emerging within American Catholicism was substantially advanced by their combined efforts. The letters they exchanged between the years 1841 to 1872, therefore, present us with important primary source material that is useful not only for deeper insight into their rich personal lives, but for a greater understanding of the history of the Catholic Church in the United States as well. It is within this wider historical and theological context that the worth and significance of the Brownson-Hecker correspondence are situated.

Because these collected letters have their own coherent story to tell, the editors desire them to be read in their entirety as a single corpus, independent of any imposed interpretation. By providing selective assistance, however, we hope to facilitate a more comprehensive grasp of the correspondence. Thus, in addition to transcribing and editing the manuscripts in order to make them available to a wider audience, we have prepared an Introduction and have also attached identifying notes. It was not the intention of the editors to compose elaborate biographies of the two men nor to provide detailed analyses of their writings. Since such tasks have been ably undertaken elsewhere, we encourage the readers to consult the pertinent secondary literature, and we strenuously recommend that the works of Brownson and Hecker themselves be read and studied. In accord with our limited aim, the Introduction traces the general outlines of the correspondents' careers while discussing the main features of their religious thought and those issues which relate to the content of the correspondence.

Regrettably, not every letter transferred between these men has survived; perusal of the correspondence in sequence reveals unmistakable gaps. Nevertheless, we are confident that this first printed collection of these 178 documents—consisting of 171 original autograph letters, 5 drafts, 1 fragment, and 1 telegram—represents the complete and critical edition of the extant Brownson-Hecker correspondence.

We have divided the body of documents into three sections, reflecting distinguishable phases in the relationship between the two correspondents. Each division opens with a short prelude to the specific period. Throughout the text, brief factual notes are furnished to justify dating and to identify persons, writings, events, or places mentioned in the communications. The Appendix contains the three extant autograph letters to Orestes Brownson from Isaac Hecker's brothers: two from John Hecker and one from George V. Hecker. Finally, to help in locating references this volume closes with an Index of persons.

As a collaborative undertaking, the co-editors together assume responsibility for this present volume—with its shortcomings and defects. Even though they jointly shared the burdens of researching, annotating, and introducing *The Brownson-Hecker Correspondence*, the one central division of labor should be pointed out. The chore of transcribing and editing the letters of Isaac T. Hecker was allotted to Joseph F. Gower, whereas to Richard M. Leliaert fell the job of copying and editing the letters of Orestes A. Brownson.

Acknowledgments

"We must bear in mind," Brownson boldly declared, "that scholars are trained for the public good, not for their private advantage." This sage admonition aptly characterizes the disposition with which this collaborative editorial project was conceived and executed. Moreover, it realistically accords with the generous spirit manifested by so many persons who contributed to this publication of the Brownson-Hecker correspondence. To these considerate persons the editors owe a debt of gratitude.

We are indebted to descendants of the Brownson family and to the Paulists, whose help and encouragement enabled us to proceed with this edition. We are especially obligated to Father Lawrence V. McDonnell, C.S.P., archivist of the Paulist Fathers, and Helen D. Curran, his assistant, for the immeasurable cooperation and courtesy afforded us. We are equally grateful for the far-reaching help and geniality extended by the staff at the Archives of the University of Notre Dame—by the archivist, Father Thomas E. Blantz, C.S.C.; associate archivist, Mercedes Muenz; assistant archivists Lawrence J. Bradley, C. Thomas Buonaiuto, Peter J. Lombardo, and Wendy Clauson Schlereth.

From the earliest stage of researching the director of the University of Notre Dame Press, James R. Langford, prudently made many sound recommendations. Its executive editor, Ann Rice, was extraordinarily conscientious as she warmly and patiently suggested numerous improvements. Support and valuable advice were given by Professors Jay P. Dolan and Philip Gleason of Notre Dame's Department of History. Counsel in legal matters was ably imparted by Larry Bradley and Philip J. Faccenda. The House Council of the Crosier House of Studies in Fort Wayne, Indiana, together with Father Joseph Hennen, O.S.C., and Father Charles Kunkel, O.S.C., kindly provided financial assistance so helpful for completion of the work. Furthermore, the editors earnestly appreciate the publishing subsidy awarded by the Center for the Study of American Catholicism at the University of Notre Dame.

The exacting business of compiling data for the annotations was made easier by the expert assistance dispensed by librarians and archivists in this country and abroad. Particular expressions of appreciation are in order for the following: Frank Clark, head of the Notre Dame microfilm department; Brother Barnabas D. Hipkins, C.SS.R., archivist at the Archives of the American Redemptorist Fathers in Brooklyn, New York; E. d'Hondt, librarian of the Faculty of Theology at the Catholic University of Louvain, Belgium; James J. Mahoney, executive secretary of the U.S. Catholic Historical Society, Dunwoodie, New York; Anne-Marie Salgat, librarian at the St. Mark's Library of the General Theological Seminary, New York; Alan Seaburg, curator of manuscripts at the Andover-Harvard Theological Library, Cambridge, Massachusetts; Rev. Joseph J. Shea, S.J., archivist at the College of the Holy Cross, Worcester, Massachusetts; Sister Marguerita Smith, associate archivist of the Archdiocese of New York, Dunwoodie; Caroline T. Spicer, reference librarian at the Cornell University Library, Ithaca, New York; and William W. Whalen, assistant at the Harvard University Archives, Cambridge, Massachusetts.

We also wish to thank the library staffs at the American Antiquarian Society, Worcester; Catholic University of America and Library of Congress in Washington, D.C.; Catholic Theological Union, Lutheran School of Theology, Meadville-Lombard Theological School, and University of Chicago, all in Chicago; Graduate Theological Union and Pacific School of Religion in Berkeley, California; St. Charles Seminary and St. Joseph's College in Philadelphia; University of Notre Dame; University of Scranton; and Western Reserve Historical Society in Cleveland.

Likewise we are grateful to certain colleagues and friends who contributed in some manner to the production of this work: Robert T. Cardinale, James E. Dolinsky, James Hennesey, S.J., Robert F. Hueston, Norlene M. Kunkel, Mary Augustine Kwitchen, O.S.F., James J. Neville, S.J., William H. Osterle, George Patterson, James J.

Rashid, and David Wright, O.P. The members of the Crosier community in Chicago were always gracious and hospitable. Much of the typing was done by Julia Baugher, Helen LaDow and Margie Nichols. Lastly, we express our heartfelt thankfulness to our parents, Joseph and Marion Gower and Lucy and Maurice Leliaert, for their constant encouragement.

History of the Correspondence

It would surely be beneficial to the readers if certain remarks were made at the very outset about the provenance and history of the collected Brownson-Hecker correspondence. Fortunately, both men were faithful letter writers and exercised much care in preserving correspondence. Upon the death of Orestes A. Brownson on 17 April 1876, his private library and papers passed into the custody of his son Henry F. Brownson[1] of Detroit, who had been personally commissioned to safeguard his father's reputation and honor. Soon after, the younger Brownson undertook the twofold task of producing a twenty-volume edition of Brownson's *Works*[2] and a three-volume biography.[3] Henry Brownson's biography made ample use of Father Hecker's letters to the elder Brownson. In 1900 Henry donated his father's library and papers to the University of Notre Dame through the agency of Professor James F. Edwards.[4] Since then the Brownson Papers have been meticulously stored and calendared in the University of Notre Dame Archives. Hecker's original letters to Brownson, therefore, are located at Notre Dame, Indiana.

After Isaac T. Hecker's death on 22 December 1888, his associate and loyal disciple Father Walter Elliott, C.S.P.,[5] assumed the task of protecting Hecker's papers and placing them within the Archives of the Paulist Fathers in New York City where they have likewise been carefully stored and calendared. Father Elliott himself felt authorized to compose a biography of Hecker, which first appeared in the pages of *The Catholic World* and later in book form under the title *The Life of Father Hecker*.[6] Strangely enough, however, these two earliest biographers of Brownson and Hecker, Henry F. Brownson and Walter Elliott, did not share with each other the letters in their possession. The original Brownson letters to Hecker still remain in the Archives of the Paulist Fathers.

The desired mutual sharing had to wait until 1938 when Father Thomas T. McAvoy, C.S.C.,[7] archivist of the University of Notre Dame, and Father Joseph I. Malloy, C.S.P.,[8] archivist of the Congregation of St. Paul, agreed to exchange photostats of the pertinent Brownson-Hecker material in their respective depositories. One year later, Arthur M. Schlesinger, Jr., in his biography of Brownson,[9] showed an awareness of the significance of this correspondence for understanding the relationship between Brownson and Hecker. The first major and critical use of these letters was in Vincent F. Holden's doctoral dissertation[10] on the early years of Isaac Hecker. Subsequent biographers of both correspondents had recourse, in varying degrees, to the important documents. In this respect we might mention the works of Doran Whalen, Theodore Maynard, Katherine Burton, Joseph McSorley, and another by Vincent F. Holden.[11] An essay by Wilfrid Parsons[12] was devoted almost entirely to a discussion of these letters.

A landmark in the history of the correspondence occurred in June 1965, when the University of Notre Dame Archives received a grant from the National Historical Publications Commission to prepare a microfilm edition of the Brownson Papers. This laborious project—which even included photostats of manuscript items from other collections such as that of the Paulists—was directed by Thomas McAvoy with the assistance of Lawrence J. Bradley as manuscripts preparator. Upon its completion in April 1966, this extensive production consisted of nineteen rolls of microfilm and was made available for purchase; later a supplementary roll was added. Many researchers have found this publication, with its accompanying *Guide to the Microfilm Edition of the Orestes Augustus Brownson Papers* written by Dr. Bradley,[13] to be an invaluable resource.

In recent years a number of doctoral dissertations in various disciplines as well as several scholarly monographs have appeared which to some extent relied upon the letters exchanged between Hecker and Brownson. Among the published studies are those by Americo D. Lapati, Per Sveino, Hugh Marshall, Leonard Gilhooley, and the diligently researched biography of Brownson by Thomas R. Ryan that was issued during the centenary of Brownson's death.[14]

The editors, like so many others interested in American Catholic studies, are grateful for the way in which this revealing set of correspondence has been collected, handled, and preserved. Whoever wishes to inspect the original manuscripts can do so in the appropriate depositories. More accessible is the microfilm facsimile of the unedited Brownson Papers. Those rolls of microfilm relevant to our present edition are the following: for Brownson's letters to Hecker, roll nine; for Hecker's letters to Brownson: the years 1841–42, roll one; the years 1843–49, roll two; the years 1850–54, roll three; the years 1855–59, roll four; the years 1860–62, roll five; the years 1863–70, roll six; and the years 1871–72, roll seven. Exceptions to these groupings are found in the notes. For the letters in the Appendix consult roll two. It may be noted, however, that the present edition also contains certain significant documents omitted from the microfilm publication.

NOTES

1. Henry Francis Brownson (1835–1913), Brownson's fourth son and principal biographer, author and editor, U.S. Army major, leader in Catholic lay movements.

2. *The Works of Orestes A. Brownson,* collected and edited by H. F. Brownson, twenty volumes (Detroit: Thorndike Nourse, 1882–87; reprint ed. New York: AMS Press, 1966).

3. *Orestes A. Brownson's Early Life, 1803–1844* (Detroit: H. F. Brownson, 1898); *Orestes A. Brownson's Middle Life, 1845–1855* (Detroit: H. F. Brownson, 1899); *Orestes A. Brownson's Latter Life, 1856–1876* (Detroit: H. F. Brownson, 1900).

4. James Farnham Edwards (1850–1911), history professor at the University of Notre Dame, director of its Lemonnier Library 1874–1911, foremost collector of Catholic Americana.

5. Walter Elliott, C.S.P. (1842–1928), author and missionary preacher, ordained Paulist priest 1872, founder of the Catholic Missionary Union 1893.

6. *The Catholic World,* LI (April 1890) through LIV (November 1891); *The Life of Father Hecker* (New York: The Columbus Press, 1891; reprint ed. New York: Arno Press, 1972). A French translation by Countess de Revilliax was entitled *La Vie du Père Hecker* (Paris, 1897).

7. Thomas Timothy McAvoy, C.S.C. (1903–1969), author, educator and historian, archivist of the University of Notre Dame, 1929–69.

8. Joseph Ignatius Malloy, C.S.P. (1889–1959), author, archivist for the Paulist community 1937–52.

9. Arthur M. Schlesinger, Jr., *Orestes A. Brownson: A Pilgrim's Progress* (Boston: Little, Brown and Company, 1939), reissued as *A Pilgrim's Progress: Orestes A. Brownson* (Boston: Little, Brown and Company, 1966).

10. *The Early Years of Isaac Thomas Hecker, 1819–1844* (Washington, D.C.: Catholic University of America Press, 1939) by Vincent Francis Holden (1911–1972), author and historian, archivist of the Paulist Fathers 1952–72.

11. For those interested in the history of Brownson-Hecker scholarship the following information is provided: Doran Whalen, pseudonym of Sister Rose Gertrude Whalen, C.S.C. (1882–1958), educator and author; *Granite for God's House: The Life of Orestes Augustus Brownson* (New York: Sheed & Ward, 1941). Theodore Maynard (1890–1956), author and historian, Catholic convert 1913; *Orestes Brownson: Yankee, Radical, Catholic* (New York: Macmillan, 1943; reprint ed. New York: Hafner Publishing Company, 1971). Katherine Burton (1890–1969), author and Catholic convert 1930; *Celestial Homespun: The Life of Isaac Thomas Hecker* (London and New York: Longmans, Green & Co., 1943). Joseph McSorley, C.S.P. (1874–1963), author and historian, superior general of the Paulists 1924–29; *Father Hecker and His Friends: Studies and Reminiscences* (St. Louis: B. Herder Book Co., 1952); reissued as *Isaac Hecker and His Friends* (New York: Paulist Press, 1972). Vincent F. Holden, C.S.P., *The Yankee Paul: Isaac Thomas Hecker* (Milwaukee: Bruce, 1958).

12. Wilfrid Parsons, S.J. (1887–1958), author and educator, editor of *America* 1925–36; "Brownson, Hecker and Hewit," *The Catholic World*, CLIII (July 1941), 396–408.

13. (Notre Dame, Ind.: University of Notre Dame Archives, 1966).

14. Americo D. Lapati, *Orestes A. Brownson* (New Haven, Conn.: College & University Press, 1965). Per Sveino, *Orestes A. Brownson's Road to Catholicism* (New York: Humanities Press, 1970). Hugh Marshall, S.T., *Orestes Brownson and the American Republic: An Historical Perspective* (Washington, D.C.: Catholic University of America Press, 1971). Leonard Gilhooley, *Contradiction and Dilemma: Orestes Brownson and the American Idea* (New York: Fordham University Press, 1972). Thomas R. Ryan, C.PP.S., *Orestes A. Brownson: A Definitive Biography* (Huntington, Ind.: Our Sunday Visitor Press, 1976).

Editorial Policy and Procedures

In the matter of editorial policy and procedures, the editors have, on the one hand, decided against the complete modernization of the texts; on the other hand, the accessibility of the microfilm of the Brownson Papers has freed them from giving an absolutely literal rendition. Motivated to provide an accurate yet readable version of the Brownson-Hecker correspondence, the editors have taken a middle course and with some deviations have observed the directions for the "expanded method" of editing manuscripts as specified by the *Harvard Guide to American History*.[1] Therefore, the text of each document is printed as it was written, according to the following guidelines and exceptions.

(1) The grammar, spelling, and capitalization are reproduced exactly. While a misspelled proper name is correctly rendered in the notes, the first occurrence in a letter of a misspelled word is followed by the term *sic* placed within brackets (thus: [*sic*]). Though as much of the original punctuation as possible has been retained, there are instances (determined by the sense of the text) where punctuation has been altered or added in brackets by the editors. The first word of every sentence is capitalized, and missing ending punctuation is sometimes silently supplied. In several places dashes have been silently changed into modern punctuation forms. Furthermore, without notice, apostrophes have been placed in possessives where they were lacking. When it was difficult to conclude whether there was capitalization or not, we resolved the question as best we could.

The early Hecker letters (as well as those in the Appendix) are almost completely devoid of punctuation, thus necessitating many editorial improvements. In the Brownson letters some superfluous commas have been either removed or transformed into periods. Because Brownson was inconsistent in capitalization, we have elected to capitalize certain words throughout his letters, e.g., 'Providence'.

(2) Indentation, spacing, and alignment of the datelines, salutations, closings, signatures, and postscriptions have all been regularized for the sake of typographical appearance. Paragraph indentation has been provided where a new paragraph was clearly signaled.

Where necessary for readability, omitted words or letters in the text are printed in Roman type inserted in brackets. All other editorial interpolations are printed in italicized type also enclosed in brackets (thus: [*illegible*]). Uncertain or ambiguous readings are followed by a bracketed question mark in italics (thus: [*?*]).

Abbreviations are retained, but those not in common use today are spelled out within brackets when they first appear in a letter (thus: F [ather]). The one exception is C.W., for *The Catholic World,* which recurs with great frequency in the third section of the correspondence.

The forms of the ampersand are printed as & and &c. Superscripts and interlineations are lowered to the line of the text. Cancelled words and passages are omitted, but if they are considered instructive they are placed in the notes. Obvious slips of the pen are silently corrected, while underlined words are rendered in italics.

(3) Each document has been assigned a heading that consists of a number, an identifying description, and a date. When the editors provide, approximate, or change a date—either in part or in whole—that determination is presented in the heading in brackets. Hence, the dating for an undated, partially dated or wrongly dated letter is fixed as nearly as possible by the editors in the heading and is justified as much as necessary in the notes.

The dateline is placed at the upper right corner of each letter; it contains the dating information, if any is given, as found in the manuscript. Postmarks receive mention in the notes only when they have a bearing on a questionable date.

(4) In annotating the correspondence, the editors use two kinds of notes which are placed immediately after the text of each document. When a heading is marked with an asterisk that is keyed to an asterisked note, this indicates where a letter has been previously published in its entirety or almost in its entirety (other than in the microfilm edition or in dissertations). This same practice is used to signal when a document has been omitted from the microfilm publication or erroneously calendared. For instance, the heading of Letter 74, 23

August 1855, has an asterisked note which reads as follows: *Microfilm, roll three (calendared 23 August 1853).

(5) In all other cases the usual form of annotation is adopted; that is, by means of numbered notes keyed to superscript numerals in the text. These notes are designed to be as concise yet as thorough as necessary, while avoiding repetition whenever possible. The editors make entries for persons, literary works, places, events, etc., which are considered essential to clarify the text. No entries are provided for persons and subjects that are very well known. The first reference to an individual person is annotated with a brief biographical sketch; subsequent references are usually not annotated, except when it is deemed helpful. Regarding persons named *only* in the Introduction, an appropriate note will be given there. If a person or literary piece could not be identified, no note is furnished.

Most numbered notes do not cite secondary materials or authorities nor do they catalogue the diverse sources from which the information was gathered. The editors have consulted standard reference works such as the *Dictionary of American Biography,* the *Dictionary of National Biography,* the *Catholic Encyclopedia,* and the *New Catholic Encyclopedia,* to list a few. In addition, the editors have had recourse to many uncommon sources, such as other manuscripts, rare books, nineteenth-century periodicals and journals, and various documents in archives and libraries.

(6) To shorten the notes, these abbreviations are employed:

APF	Archives of the Paulist Fathers
BEL	H. F. Brownson. *Brownson's Early Life*
BLL	H. F. Brownson. *Brownson's Latter Life*
BML	H. F. Brownson. *Brownson's Middle Life*
BosQR	*Boston Quarterly Review*
BP	Brownson Papers
BrQR	*Brownson's Quarterly Review*
CW	*The Catholic World*
EY	V. F. Holden. *The Early Years of Isaac Thomas Hecker*
FH&F	J. McSorley. *Father Hecker and His Friends*
HP	Hecker Papers

LFH	W. Elliott. *The Life of Father Hecker*
Microfilm	Microfilm edition of the O. A. Brownson Papers
OAB	T. R. Ryan. *Orestes A. Brownson*
UNDA	University of Notre Dame Archives
YP	V. F. Holden. *The Yankee Paul*

NOTE

1. Frank Burt Freidel, ed., *Harvard Guide to American History* (Cambridge, Mass: Belknap Press of Harvard University Press, 1974), I, 27–31.

Introduction

In 1844 Orestes A. Brownson and Isaac Hecker formally entered the complex saga of the Roman Catholic Church in the United States, for in August of that year Hecker was received into the Church by John McCloskey, coadjutor bishop of New York, and the following October Brownson was baptized by John B. Fitzpatrick, coadjutor bishop of Boston. Though in time these two converts were among the most dominant figures on the American Catholic theological and ecclesiastical scene, their roads to that destination were fraught with intellectual turmoil and spiritual unrest. Expressing the perplexities both he and Brownson encountered in their personal quest for religious understanding and a church affiliation which would speak to their deepest concerns, Hecker lamented to his family: "alas, how sad it is to be always a seeker without ever being a finder."[1]

It can rightly be said that this collected correspondence documents the odyssey of two seekers who became finders. Despite certain notable differences in age, experience, personality, and learning, Orestes Brownson and Isaac Hecker were able to forge an excellent relationship that endured for over thirty-five years. This Introduction examines their life stories by focusing on the Brownson-Hecker relationship as it is reflected in the letters they wrote to each other. It must begin, however, with an overview of the years preceding their friendship.

Brownson's Early Years

While reviewing the experiences of the previous decade, in 1840 Brownson summed up his career as follows: "It has been with us a leading object to bring out . . . the great fact, that Jesus was a social reformer, that the aim of his mission was to establish equality on earth, as well as to secure salvation to the soul hereafter."[2] Long before he met Isaac Hecker or contemplated joining the Catholic Church, Brownson's life was shaped by a preoccupation with religious issues and a passion for social justice. According to his autobiography, *The Convert,* his spiritual quest extended as far back as he could remember. It was a most extraordinary journey that involved a steady but courageous trek through Presbyterianism, Universalism, radical humanism, Unitarianism, and Transcendentalism, up to the founding of his own Society for Christian Union and Progress. Concurrently, he embraced various causes aimed at securing greater justice for America's working classes against the rising powerful business and capitalist interests.

Orestes A. Brownson was born in Stockbridge, Vermont, on 16 September 1803. He never knew his father, Sylvester, who died shortly after Orestes' birth. Because his mother, the former Relief Metcalf, was too poor to support all her children, at the age of six young Orestes was separated from his two older brothers, Daniel and Oran; his older sister, Thorina; and his twin sister, Daphne,[3] and was sent to live with an older couple on a farm near Royalton, Vermont. Although Brownson's guardians were of a Calvinist-Congregationalist background, they seldom attended church services. He was not baptized during these years nor did he officially belong to any sect or denomination. Yet he read the Bible conscientiously, and his guardians instilled in him traditional Calvinist values, teaching him to "be frugal and industrious, to speak the truth, . . . to keep the Sabbath, and never to let the sun go down on [his] wrath."[4]

When he was fourteen, after eight lonely years of separation from his family, Brownson's mother reclaimed him and moved the entire family to Ballston Spa, New York (north of Albany). During his adolescence he was exposed to the frenetic religious agitation of upstate New York, where he encountered various sectarians, atheists, and "nothingarians" (those who held no particular religion). Then at the age of nineteen, still "in a labyrinth of doubt with no Ariadne's thread to guide [him] out to the light of day," Brownson walked into a Presbyterian church in Ballston one sunny September morning. There he experienced a resurgence of hope, and one month later, in October of 1822, he was baptized in that church. Elated by this newly discovered spiritual peace and security, young Brownson set out to lead the rigorous life of a professing Christian.

Wishing to grow in the knowledge of God and Jesus Christ, he also resolved to pursue his studies with a view to the Christian ministry. But contrary to his high expectations, the tranquility and certitude he desired were not sustained by his association with the Ballston Presbyterians. Explaining this dissatisfaction to the pastor, Brownson confessed that he felt confined by the absence of intellectual freedom, the exclusive spirit of the congregation, and "the harsh doctrines of Calvin"—especially those of double predestination and unconditional election and damnation.[5] To him these doctrines were both unjust and unreasonable; he could not accept the belief that God predestined some to salvation and others to damnation. If the Bible taught these doctrines, then it could not have been divinely inspired. Even though Brownson did not totally reject the authority of the Scriptures, he relied more upon reason as the rule for their interpretation.

Still driven by an urgency to believe in God but unsure where to turn, he became attracted to the Universalists, whose glowing picture of the divine goodness and whose struggles for the rights of man enlisted his sympathy. In sharp distinction to Calvinism, Universalism held out the possibility of universal salvation and denied eternal damnation. In 1825, while working as a schoolteacher, Brownson applied to the Universalist Association for a license as a preacher. Having been accepted, he underwent ministerial tutoring and was ordained on 15 June 1826 at Jaffrey, New Hampshire. Also at this time he was appointed editor of *The Gospel Advocate,* a respected theological journal of the Universalist denomination. In the following year Brownson married Sally Healy, one of his former students from Elbridge, New York.

The Reverend Brownson regarded the Universalist doctrine of eventual universal salvation after death much more palatable than "the harsh doctrines of Calvin." Yet, this position too was not without its own theological difficulties. For if all persons would ultimately be saved, what need was there for a savior? Moreover, if God forgives unconditionally, the foundations of morality would seem to be undermined, since sin would go unpunished. Faced with these intellectual problems, he was lead to repudiate entirely the authority of the Bible and soon found himself drifting into radical humanism and agnosticism.

Frustrated by the inconsistencies of liberal Christianity, late in 1829 Orestes Brownson left Universalism and aligned his efforts with the aims of the Workingmen's Party in New York state. He fell under the sway of the revolutionary social theories that were being promulgated by Frances (Fanny) Wright[6] and Robert Dale Owen. As an editor for Owen's journal *The Free Enquirer,* Brownson helped disseminate their novel reform program and educational views. Soon, however, he became disheartened by the Owen-Wright utopian scheme and separated from the Workingmen's Party. Throughout this decade and into the next, Brownson's concern for the cause of the laboring class remained constant.

During the 1830–31 period, Brownson resumed preaching as an independent, but in 1832 he became publisher and editor of *The Philanthropist* at Ithaca, New York, now intending to defend his understanding of Unitarian Christianity against the bondage of Presbyterian influence. His interest in Unitarianism stemmed from a "reconversion to Christianity" which sprang from reading William Ellery Channing's famous sermon "Likeness to God." In contrast to Calvinism's stress on the wide gap between God and man, Channing's emphasis on man's having been created in God's image and likeness rendered Brownson favorably disposed to Unitarianism. Then in the summer of 1832 he received a Unitarian pastorate in Walpole, New Hampshire. Two years later he accepted another pastorate in Canton, Massachusetts, with George Ripley preaching his installation sermon. During these years Brownson taught himself French and made frequent trips to Boston, where, thanks to Dr. Channing, he met the leading intellectuals. Soon he was contributing articles to Unitarian journals such as *The Christian Register, The Christian Examiner, The Unitarian,* and the short-lived *Boston Observer and Religious Intelligencer.*

Brownson's writings criticized the Unitarian clergymen for their dry preaching, their indifference to the problems of the working people, and their lifeless rationalism in theology. To stimulate their thinking, he adapted ideas from such French philosophers as Claude Henri de Saint-Simon,[7] Benjamin Constant,[8] and Victor Cousin. Saint

Simon's "New Christianity," which de-emphasized worship and dogma in favor of the morality and social equality demanded by the Christian law of brotherly love, served as an antidote to Unitarianism's social conservatism. A new order of social relations, embodied in the rising Christian democracy, would supersede Unitarianism, unless it ceased its identification with the wealthy class. Echoing Constant, Brownson protested the Unitarians' excessive intellectualism and asserted that religion and morality were grounded not in the human intellect, but rather in "an interior sentiment" possessed by everyone. The religious sentiment was the source of spiritual intuition and neighborly love. This universal sentiment, the very basis of religion, became embodied in different historical forms. Cousin's Universal or Absolute Reason, which Brownson identified with God, was independent of, yet present within, every person.

Brownson's study of Constant and Cousin made him receptive to the romanticism of the New England Transcendentalists. "So far as Transcendentalism is understood to be the recognition in man of the capacity of knowing truth intuitively," he wrote, "or of attaining to a scientific knowledge of an order of existence transcending the reach of the senses, and of which we can have no sensible experience, we are Transcendentalists."[9] He regarded the Transcendental Movement as a necessary alternative to the overly objective, historical, and rational approach to religion advocated by scholarly Unitarians like Andrews Norton.[10] Still, Brownson was also very wary of the subjective tendencies in Transcendentalism which held the danger of substituting a "lawless fancy for an enlightened understanding." Objecting in particular to the thought of Ralph Waldo Emerson, he insisted that we became moral by obeying the commands of a power transcending and independent of ourselves rather than by obeying the inner demands of our nature.

In 1836, Orestes Brownson moved to Chelsea, near Boston, to engage in an experimental ministry to the working classes of Boston. That same year he also spelled out his socio-religious vision of a new order in the book *New Views of Christianity, Society, and the Church.*[11] He envisioned a "Church of the Future" which would transcend the overly spiritual or sacramental concerns of Catholicism, the material or earthly emphasis of Protestantism, as well as the weaknesses of New England Puritanism and Unitarianism. The mission of Christ, the God-Man, was to reconcile earth and heaven, spirit and matter. The unity and the progress of the human race would occur at Christ's second coming, when Christ would be "truly incarnated in universal humanity," making God and man one.

While writing *New Views,* Brownson fully understood that the time was not ripe for so utopian an ideal to be actualized. Yet in the hope of raising the consciousness of the populace, he took practical steps toward its realization. His "Discourse on the Wants of the Times" signaled the founding of his own Society for Christian Union and Progress in Boston on 29 May 1836. This society was designed to rescue laborers alienated from the established churches by providing nondenominational worship each Sunday. It would encourage free inquiry into religious truth, the practice of a more genuine morality, and amelioration of the lot of the poor and oppressed. When he became editor of the *Boston Reformer,* Brownson tried to make this latter goal more attainable by advocating universal public education and the establishment of manual labor schools.

In 1838 Brownson began his well-respected *Boston Quarterly Review.* Stating its purpose in a letter to Martin Van Buren, the Democratic president of the United States, he wrote: "I wish . . . to say that this Review is established for the purpose of enlisting Literature, Religion, and Philosophy on the side of Democracy."[12] For Brownson, democracy was primarily a spiritual movement, a social and philosophical doctrine, rather than just the tenets of a political party or even the ideals of popular government understood as majority rule. Democracy meant "the movement of the masses towards a better social condition than has heretofore existed," and it also comprised the more perfect application of Christian principles to man's social and political relations.

The task of democracy was to put an end to privilege and to the moneyed interests of America, symbolized by the Whig political party. Brownson knew the realities of politico-economic power as well as the need for practical measures to achieve greater justice for the lower classes. Hence he felt compelled to associate himself with the Democratic Party as the best vehicle for realizing his dreams. In July 1840 he published his provocative essay "The Laboring Classes" to promote the re-election of Martin Van Buren and to aid the cause of the Democrats against the Whigs and their candidate, William Henry Harrison. "No one can observe the signs of the times with much care," he declared as he remembered the terrible economic Panic of 1837, "without perceiving that a crisis as to the relation of wealth and labor is approaching."[13] The struggle between wealth and labor, however, was inherent in all of America's social structures—particularly the wage system—and could not be resolved except by a revolutionary alteration of those structures.

If social evils arose from man-made institutions, then the appropriate social remedies had either to reform or eliminate these corrupt institutions. First among these institutions to be reformed was the Christian church as symbolized in its priests. Contrary to Christ's gospel, which called us to establish justice and God's kingdom on earth, the gospel of the priests turned people's eyes toward heaven with an elusive promise of eternal happiness. The next step involved the right exercise, but not the overthrow, of civil government. Government needed to limit its own powers, to protect the workers from wealthy interests by fair legislation, and to virtually eliminate the banking system. Finally, Brownson called for the abolition of all monopoly and of all privilege, especially the inheritance of property: "as we have abolished hereditary monarchy and hereditary nobility, we must complete the work by abolishing hereditary property."[14]

To his dismay the 1840 election resulted in a Whig victory. A deeply disappointed Brownson was forced to rethink the sociopolitical elements of his religious vision. No longer did he have faith in the ability of human nature to achieve the good. Individual and social reform would not spring from mere human effort but only from a power higher than the people. Politically, this necessitated a constitutional republic that was rooted in the divine will and that favored states' rights so as to protect the rights of minorities.[15] Philosophically, this meant adapting Plato's doctrine of ideas and adjusting Pierre Leroux's "doctrine of communion," which held that man lived by communion with a reality other than himself, "the Not-Me." More precisely, man communed with nature through property, with other persons through the family and the state, and with God through the church. Theologically, the church, as Christ's organic extension in space and time, was the sole medium of God's saving grace. Human nature could institute nothing higher than itself; hence only a divine power mediated through Christ's church was capable of effecting the progress of humankind.

Quite clearly the adverse reaction to his astute analysis of America's economic problems together with the election defeat marked an important turning point in Orestes Brownson's intellectual life. The gradual change which had come about in his political thought had altered his theological perspective as well. Now, with the Democrats out of power, he lost his politically sponsored stewardship at the United States Marine Hospital in Chelsea. In 1839 he had ceased preaching and his *Review* was beginning to decline in circulation. In 1841, therefore, he resorted to lecturing as a way of supplementing his meager income. It was during a lecture tour through New York City that Brownson became better acquainted with the man who would become a life-long friend and fellow religious wayfarer.

Hecker's Early Life

The parents of Isaac Hecker were emigrants from Germany. They met, married, and raised their five children in New York City, where Isaac, their youngest, was born on 18 December 1819. John Hecker, Isaac's father, was a skilled metal worker, but little is known about him. On the other hand, much is known about his mother, Susan Caroline Friend Hecker, the leading figure and dominant personality of the family. Her cheerful manner, sympathetic ways, and honest qualities had enduring effects on her offspring. Although the family originally was Lutheran, Mrs. Hecker became a devout Methodist, and Isaac regularly attended services with his mother but never actually held membership in the Methodist Church.

Despite his rather modest beginnings, Isaac Hecker benefitted from the love and affection of a tight-knit family. He was able to attend the primary grades in school before financial demands made it necessary for him to take an unskilled job with a newspaper and then to be apprenticed to a foundry. His older brothers, John and George, became excellent bakers and eventually opened their own shop, where Isaac was invited to work to learn the craft of baking. Their native inventiveness and business acumen enabled their baking business to prosper, and in 1842 John and George also became millers and established the Croton Flour Mill. By 1843 the brothers formed a partnership and the enterprise, which later became known as the Hecker Flour Company, boasted the ownership of five shops in addition to the mill.

The prosperity that the Hecker family was beginning to enjoy was certainly not typical of working persons in this period of American history. On the contrary, for many it was a time of great hardship. The advent of the new industrialism worsened the imbalance in the distribution of the national wealth and made even more pronounced the dismal contrast between rich and poor. The three Hecker brothers, knowing the situation firsthand, sought to improve conditions for the workers and the immigrants. In the mid-1830s, they became active with the Loco-Focos, a group of radical Democrats who strongly opposed state banks as well as the Bank of the United States and paper currency. In their rejection of all monopoly and in their call for equal rights, the Loco-Focos considered themselves the authentic embodiment of Jeffersonian political philosophy.

In 1836 the New York City Loco-Focos joined with other labor groups in the state to form the Equal Rights Party. Their efforts for social reform, however, were stymied by the severe economic Panic of 1837. The collapse of the financial market through drastic speculation and the suspension of payment on paper money, together with the ensuing failure of businesses and the huge rise in unemployment, ushered in both economic disaster and great societal unrest. John Hecker was vice-president of the Equal Rights Party at the time it was trying to deal with this crisis. He and the Loco-Focos gave priority to the passage of the Independent or Sub-Treasury Bill, which would permit the federal government to take charge of its own funds and take them out of the hands of state and private banks. President Martin Van Buren convoked a special session of Congress in September 1837 to pass the bill, and the New York Tammany Democrats allied themselves with the Equal Rights Party in supporting the measure. But when it was proposed that this alliance should back a united ticket in the coming November election, only discord resulted. This dissension caused a split in the ranks of the Loco-Focos themselves into the "Buffaloes," favoring compromise with Tammany, and the "Rumps," committed to the pure ideals of Loco-Focoism. The Heckers were aligned with the purist group, but in the ensuing election they saw the Democrats lose to the Whigs. The gradual demise of the Loco-Focos as an integral movement followed.

In 1837 Isaac Hecker was only eighteen and unable to vote. Yet his involvement in radical politics and his experience in the Old Seventh Ward of Manhattan provided him with practical knowledge of the American political processes. This early commitment to civic duty and responsible reform would become one of his life-long concerns. He looked upon Loco-Focoism as an instance of Christian democracy, dedicated to the cause of humanity and equality.

Isaac Hecker's interest in social improvement continued into the next decade. He kept abreast of many of the current ideas as they were aired by lecturers who spoke in the public forums of New York City. He was also attracted to the stimulating sermons of Orville Dewey at the Unitarian Church of the Messiah. In March of 1841, however, the prominent Boston reformer Orestes A. Brownson came to lecture in New York City. On 4 March he spoke at the Stuyvesant Institute on "The Democracy of Christ" and the following evening gave an address in Clinton Hall on "The Reform Spirit of the Age." So impressed was Hecker with Brownson's oratory that even in his old age he recalled the themes of Brownson's first lectures in New York. About them he wrote: "The life and teachings of our Saviour Jesus Christ were brought into use and the upshot of the lecturer's thesis was that Christ was the big Democrat and the Gospel was the true Democratic platform."[16]

At this juncture in his career Brownson was stressing the positive role of religion for the progress of civilization and the reform of society. He advocated the establishment of a Christian state based on the principles of the gospel. Hecker and his two brothers approved of what they heard and turned to the speaker as the one person capable of invigorating the progressive movement in New York City. Since they were eager to hear more, they volunteered to act as his agents for future lectures. In this capacity they arranged for Brownson to deliver the Fourth of July oration at Washington Hall. Once again the speaker struck chords that were congenial to the labor advocates as he proclaimed: "The principles involved in the American Revolution were but the application of those political associations involved in the principles taught by Jesus Christ."[17]

Following this talk, the Heckers met with their "client" to discuss his teachings and also to work out a schedule for more addresses. The three brothers wished to arrange a full series of lectures at the New York Lyceum. When the Lyceum refused, they resolved to sponsor the events on their own and accordingly hired a hall and provided the public notices. This event occasioned the first extant letter from the Heckers to Brownson, dated 14 November 1841. Brownson selected as his topic "Civilization and Human Progress," presented in four lectures—17, 19, and 25 January and 2 February 1842. In these discourses he ranged over human history and claimed that societal progress depended upon "extrinsic influences," meaning the communication of divine revelation through certain "providential men." His thinking was directed toward formulating the correct philosophical framework for a properly ordered society. Such questions and the objectives of the reform movements occupied Brownson during his stay in New York, where he was the guest of the Hecker family at their Rutgers Street home. This visit and many future ones provided opportunities for the development of an amiable companionship between Isaac Hecker and Orestes A. Brownson.

The Brownson–Hecker Meeting

All of Hecker's biographers agree on the decisive importance of his relationship with Brownson. Walter Elliott writes: "One thing that becomes evident in studying this period of Isaac Hecker's life is the fact that his acquaintance with Dr. Brownson marks a turning-point in his views, his opinions, his whole attitude of mind toward our Lord Jesus Christ."[18] Vincent Holden concurs: "More than any other person, Brownson was Hecker's director during his early years. He was Hecker's constant adviser and friend."[19] And Joseph McSorley notes that Hecker knew Brownson longer and more intimately than any other of Brownson's friends.[20]

Since Hecker's meeting Brownson was such a crucial turning point in his life, it is important to fix the date of their meeting as accurately as possible. However, conflicting dates have been assigned for their initial meeting, and no one of them can be judged absolutely certain. Vincent Holden maintained "it is quite clear that Hecker was not intimately acquainted with Brownson before the close of the year 1841."[21] Further he specified that the Hecker brothers originally met Brownson when he was on his first lecture visit to New York City in early March of 1841. This proposed date approximates the time of the first letter in this collection, 14 November 1841, and the letter itself betrays a formality which implies that the senders ("Hecker and Br[o]th[er]") were not on intimate terms with the recipient ("Mr. Brownson").

The second possible date of this meeting was advanced by Henry F. Brownson, who suggested that his father's introductory encounter with the Heckers occurred in the summer of 1837 when the Reverend Brownson was invited by William Henry Channing to come to New York City for the purpose of exchanging pulpits.[22] Major Brownson believed that his father accepted the invitation and also that the Heckers were present in the congregation. We have found no conclusive evidence to confirm these suppositions.

The third contending date has greater authority because it stems from Isaac Hecker himself. In the year before he died he dictated an essay dealing with his early experiences with Brownson. Hecker stated that Brownson first came to Manhattan "somewhere about 1834" when he was still a member of the Workingmen's Party.[23] This was accepted by Walter Elliott, who gave it wide currency in his biography of Father Hecker.[24] Lending support to this dating is the indefinite comment found in the next to last letter of this present volume. In Letter 173, 30 January [1872] Hecker writes to Brownson of "the high esteem and sincere friendship which I have borne for you now nearly forty years. . . ." Another reference supporting his having met Brownson sometime during the 1830s was his assertion made in 1876 that his friendship with Dr. Brownson had endured for forty years.[25]

The consistency, if not the precision, of Hecker's references lends credence to a pre-1841 date as the time of his initial meeting with Brownson. However, we do not believe that they became well acquainted until 1841. Furthermore, there is no evidence that they corresponded prior to the date of the first extant letter in this collection. In 1841 Orestes Brownson was thirty-seven years old, and Isaac Hecker was twenty-one. Both were then engaged in social and political activities. They were entering a period of transition in which their lives were to merge in ways remarkable and significant.

Road to Rome: 1842–1844

The Boston editor's keen intellect and vast learning greatly impressed the young baker. Following Brownson's promptings, Hecker became an avid reader of the *Boston Quarterly Review* and in short order was drawn headlong into the bewildering world of theoretical speculation. Knowing Hecker spoke German at home, the journalist recommended that Isaac read the philosophical writings of Kant, Fichte, and Hegel. Since he was ill prepared for this, Hecker became quite confused and fell into a type of skepticism.

The year 1842 was similarly perplexing for Brownson as he confronted questions of pantheism and epistemological subjectivism. Retreating further from Transcendentalist positions, he appropriated the synthetic philosophy of Leroux's *L'Humanité,* from which he concluded that societal amelioration could only be effected through special divine interventions in history. In June of this year he composed his famous open letter to Dr. William Ellery Channing, *The Mediatorial Life of Jesus,*[26] wherein Brownson affirmed the belief that Jesus Christ was the sole mediator between God and man. Now he began to search for the agency or institution that perpetuated in history Christ's mediatorial activity.

While Brownson was once again verging on orthodox Christianity, Hecker at this time was caught up in a series of transforming ecstatic experiences, which, in view of his intellectual bewilderment, caused him much mental anguish. He was then also attending the church services conducted by William Henry Channing. Overwhelmed by mysterious feelings of dependency on God, and unable to work, he became absorbed in contemplation and was at the same time plagued by bouts of nervous depression and physical illness. Fortunately, Brownson was lecturing in New York in early December 1842. This visit afforded Hecker the chance of discussing his upsetting spiritual condition with his respected friend. In order to continue their conversation, the lecturer invited the troubled man to visit him in New England.

Hecker's trip to Massachusetts was to prove extremely determinative for his intellectual formation and religious maturation. He was warmly welcomed by Mr. and Mrs. Brownson and their six children[27] in their Mt. Bellington home in Chelsea, a suburb of Boston. In the fashion of master and disciple the two men talked over the religious problems so disturbing Hecker; Brownson related how Leroux's writings helped him establish the objectivity of operations of the mind. Because he felt that Hecker would benefit from rest and serious study, Brownson recommended a sojourn at Brook Farm, the utopian commune founded by the Transcendentalist George Ripley.

Acting on this advice, Hecker joined the Brook Farm community in January of 1843 as a partial boarder who helped out as a baker. His intention was to learn some Latin and French while also studying theoretical issues. During these eight months away from home, Isaac Hecker associated with the leading intellectual and literary figures of America. At Brook Farm he acquired an insider's knowledge of the Transcendental Movement as he conversed with Emerson, Parker, and John Dwight,[28] as well as with fellow students such as Deborah ("Ora") Gannett and George Curtis. The latter nicknamed Isaac "Ernest the Seeker." Besides following Ripley's lectures on Kant and Spinoza, the eager student read the romantic literature of Goethe, Schlegel,[29] and Jean-Paul Richter.[30]

Despite these fine acquaintances, Hecker's dependency upon his Chelsea friend did not diminish. Occasionally, Brownson would come to Brook Farm to see his son Orestes, who was a student there, and would also consult with Isaac. More frequently, Hecker paid visits to Brownson and accompanied him to his Sunday preaching services. When together, they continually discussed theological issues. In particular, Brownson was preoccupied with the question of the church and Hecker was taken by the traditional tone of his recent writings. In a series of articles on "The Mission of Jesus" appearing in *The Christian World,* Brownson applied his version of the doctrine of communion to Christianity. What he was advocating was a Christian union movement—a "Catholicity without the papacy." The two seekers closely followed the Oxford Movement and delved into church history. Hecker was intrigued by reading *Symbolik* by the Catholic Tübingen theologian Johann-Adam Möhler. Commenting on Brownson's shift from his 1840 essay, Hecker observed: "Brownson, like Paul (I make the comparison with reverence), who was the chief in opposing the Church and her priests, is now in the midst of her enemies, battling alone against them, amidst the laughs of his former friends and the jeers of his enemies, for the Church."[31] For his own part, Hecker was becoming attracted to the Catholic Church, though resolving his personal religious quandary was far more pressing than church membership.

While he was pleased by the intellectual stimulation of the cultured company at Brook Farm, Hecker's spiritual quest was still unsatisfied, and so he determined to leave the Farm and join the newly founded ascetic community at Harvard Village, Massachusetts. Founded by Bronson Alcott and Charles Lane, Fruitlands was dedicated to the interior transformation of the individual through self-denial and mortification. Hecker was taken by the residents' Christlike spirit, and over Brownson's objection, he joined the community in July. But his stay was brief, for after fifteen days he judged the experiment to be insufficient and departed for his New York home. Since Brownson never was keen on these communities, being especially critical of Fourierism,[32] he was glad that Hecker had abandoned these "humbugs."

Life had continued along normal lines in the Hecker household, and the Hecker Flour Company was doing well. The family grew interested in religious affairs, and John Hecker joined the Episcopal Church. The brothers also remained active in politics and took a prominent role in backing the ill-fated candidacy of John C. Calhoun in the 1844 presidential race. Looking upon Calhoun as the candidate better disposed to the working class, the old "Rump" faction of the Loco-Focos determined to support him over Martin Van Buren. This matter occasioned a spurt of letters from John and Isaac Hecker to Brownson, who was fascinated by Calhoun's theory of "concurrent majorities," and for some time had been a prime mover in the Calhoun campaign in the North. The Heckers enlisted the journalist's help in preparing addresses, but Brownson declined the offer to edit a pro-Calhoun newspaper, wishing instead to recommence his own review, which had been merged with *The Democratic Review* in 1842. As it turned out, the Democrat James K. Polk was elected the eleventh president of the United States.

At this stage it was religion rather than politics that was of paramount importance to Orestes Brownson and Isaac Hecker. Yet in no way did their passion for social reform abate. On the contrary, they now perceived the internal connection between the church question and societal advancement. Holding that the true church was embodied neither in the Anglican nor Roman communion, Brownson was promoting an "ecumenical" conception of the church to be realized in a new catholic organism. Writing to Hecker, he declared: "I shall come out boldly for the Church on the principles you and I have so often discussed, and independent of, but not in opposition to, existing organizations" (Letter 11, 3 October 1843). In response Hecker expressed his emerging belief that the church was the "soul centre of all life, and reform. . . ." The correspondence of this period reveals a curious recommendation made by Brownson that Hecker should affiliate with the Episcopal Church. Yet this advice was immediately rejected as inconsistent, since Brownson himself had no intention of so acting.[33]

Catholic Conversions

During these months Orestes Brownson was preparing a series of essays for his own journal, which he revived in January 1844 under the title *Brownson's Quarterly Review*.[34] Consolidating his recent study of church history and elucidating his evolving ecclesiological notions, these essays dealt with topics such as the church and reform, church unity and social amelioration. In gradual steps he was making a case for the true church of Christ understood as an organic, visible, objective, and historical instrument of divine mediatorship. To some readers it appeared that his thought was drifting Romeward or at least tilting to the Tractarians of the Oxford Movement.

In many ways Isaac Hecker's mind was mirroring Brownson's direction. While working only part-time in his brothers' business, he continued to study and devote time to prayer and meditation. Although his exhilaration with human reform schemes diminished, he nonetheless kept in touch with his comrades in the progressive movements. Seeking to ascertain the appropriate historical agency of supernatural life, he examined various denominations, eventually determining that he would choose between Rome and Canterbury. Accordingly, he had interviews with such Episcopal clergymen as Samuel Seabury and Benjamin Haight and also had an audience with John J. Hughes, the Roman Catholic bishop of New York.

After further months of reflection, Hecker reached a momentous personal decision; he resolved to give up his life to the service of the church of God. "The step I contemplate of taking," he communicated to Brownson that March, "is to devote my whole energies and time for the purpose of becoming a laborer in the cause of the Church." While Brownson approved the choice of career, he reminded his confidant that he must select a church. Hecker, however, preferred to postpone that decision and await the results of the Oxford Movement. To prepare for the ministry, he considered being tutored by a Rev. William Norris, an Episcopal priest, but finally chose to pursue classical studies under George Bradford in Concord, Massachusetts. Because he suspected that Brownson, who had retreated far from Transcendentalism, might oppose this locale, Hecker assured him he would not be overly influenced by Concord's Transcendentalist atmosphere.

In mid-April, Hecker arrived in New England and went directly to consult with Brownson. Since the philosopher was on the verge of settling his own conflict about church affiliation, Hecker discovered his friend in an agitated state. After stopping off at Brook Farm and the Shaker Village, Hecker took up residence in the Concord home of Henry David Thoreau. He intended to spend his days learning Greek and Latin under Bradford and reading literary and theological works, including *The Catechism of the Council of Trent,*[35] but as the weeks passed by, Hecker found himself unable to study seriously. So overcome was he by mystical states that his activities were mostly restricted to prayer and contemplation. Uncertain what to do about this situation but knowing he must submit to whatever was God's will, Hecker wanted to share his experiences with his sage advisor. He set down his feelings on paper, then refrained from posting the intimate epistle. Instead on 25 May he went to Boston to see the editor. Brownson, however, was not able to converse because he had an appointment with Benedict Fenwick, the Catholic bishop of Boston, for the purpose of discussing his possible conversion to the Church of Rome. Within seven days Brownson had made the decision to become a Catholic and was entrusted to Bishop Bernard Fitzpatrick for instructions in the faith. Perhaps the most important letter Brownson ever sent to his young friend was the one of 6 June 1844 (Letter 25), in which he announced his resolution. Calling the Catholic Church "the appointed medium of salvation," he urges Hecker to enter the Church. "You cannot be an Anglican, you must be a Catholic, or a mystic."

This news did not come unexpectedly, but the correspondent's pejorative remarks about Hecker's mystical nature greatly disturbed the recipient. Although logic and argument brought the older man to Rome, the younger man was jolted that his loving guide failed to recognize that it was a profound spiritual thirst that was leading him to the identical goal. Nevertheless, this letter forced Hecker to confront the grave challenge. On 8 June he was received by Bishop Fenwick, who then referred him to Bishop Fitzpatrick. Thereafter Isaac Hecker made up his mind to convert to Catholicism. Now he was persuaded that it alone was capable of satisfying his deepest needs and highest aspirations, that it alone was for him the church of Christ.

Once the word of Hecker's intention to become a Catholic was known in Concord, it seems that Thoreau and Emerson reacted negatively, but the Ripleys received the news with warmth and understanding. In 1847 Sophia Ripley herself was to embrace Catholicism. On the advice of Bishop Fitzpatrick, Hecker traveled to the Jesuit College of the Holy Cross at nearby Worcester to observe the intellectual life and piety of his chosen co-religionists. Then he returned to New York and made contact with the coadjutor bishop of the New York Diocese. Bishop John McCloskey, who was to become Hecker's close friend, spiritual director, and confessor, soon realized how far advanced the catechumen was in the preparations for Church membership. He shortened the usual course of instruction and aided the young man in acquiring books on Catholic theology. Then on 2 August Isaac Hecker was baptized in old St. Patrick's Cathedral on Mott Street.

In July 1844 Brownson made his own convictions known in print; he wrote:

> We have no wish to disguise the fact, nor could we, if we would—that our ecclesiastical, theological, and philosophical studies have brought us to the full conclusion, that, either the Church in communion with the See of Rome is the one holy catholic apostolic church, or the one holy catholic does not exist.[36]

His actual entrance into the Roman Catholic Church did not take place until 20 October 1844. During the preceding months, he studied theology under Bishop Fitzpatrick, who strongly disapproved of Brownson's original doctrine of life and communion and instructed the candidate in the traditional Scholastic apologetic. Moreover, the bishop encouraged the scholarly editor to continue his *Review* as an aggressive instrument of Catholic defense. Dr. Brownson's conversion was looked upon by other bishops as the inauguration of a new era for Catholic America.

Now a Catholic, Isaac Hecker was eager to direct his life in the service of the Church. Hoping to benefit from greater Catholic influences, he contemplated a pilgrimage to Europe with Henry Thoreau. After this plan fell through, he recommenced the study of the classical languages by enrolling at the Cornelius Institute, a school designed to prepare candidates for the Christian ministry. In the meanwhile, his brother George also converted and they both were confirmed in May of 1845.

Bishop McCloskey guided Isaac as he tried to decide on the course of his religious vocation. McCloskey favored that he join the Jesuits, Fitzpatrick the Dominicans, Hughes the secular clergy, and Brownson even suggested the Carthusians. The Seminary of St. Sulpice in Paris or the Urban College[37] in Rome appealed to Hecker as suitable places of study. But in July he settled upon the Redemptorist order, since he was impressed by the manner in which this community combined the active and contemplative aspects of the priesthood. Once accepted by the visiting provincial, Hecker, along with two converts from the Oxford Movement in America, Clarence Walworth and James McMaster, sailed on 1 August 1845 for the novitiate in Belgium as the first native-born Americans to enter the Redemptorists. Brownson expressed approval of Isaac's choice but cautioned him about his tendency to mysticism and further expressed that he would regret his extended absence.

After a voyage of twenty-five days the three aspirants landed in England en route to the novitiate at St. Trond, Belgium (the American foundations of this order were attached to the Belgian province). The novitiate was to last one year, in which time the novice would be instructed in the rule of the community and nurtured in the religious life. There Hecker found that rigorous discipline he wanted, but McMaster, realizing the religious life was not his vocation, returned home to embark on a fiery career in journalism. The novitiate provided Isaac the chance to read the mystical writers, whose descriptions of religious experiences he easily appropriated. Only a few letters were exchanged during these years, but we are fortunate to have the one written from the Redemptorist house of studies in Wittem, Holland (Letter 45 [1 November 1846]), in which Hecker tries to explain his mystical experiences to his fellow pilgrim in the faith.

Just as his spiritual condition hindered his educational progress in Concord, so too at the seminary in Holland did Brother Isaac Thomas Hecker find himself unable to adjust to the regulated curriculum. His Redemptorist directors, however, recognized his advanced development and proposed a program of private theological study. Then he was sent to Clapham, London, and after finishing the necessary priestly formation, he was ordained on 23 October 1848 by Bishop Nicholas Wiseman. During these years in Europe, Hecker caught a glimpse of what would be the focus of his missionary career: "I believe that Providence calls me . . . to America to convert a certain class of persons amongst whom I found myself before my conversion."[38]

The Missionary Years: 1851–1864

Now a priest at the age of thirty, Isaac Hecker was assigned to the apostolate peculiar to the Congregation of the Most Holy Redeemer, namely, the conducting of parish missions and retreats. When in 1850 the United States was designated an independent Redemptorist province, its first provincial was Bernard Hafkenscheid, the famous Dutch preacher. At this time the principal work of the community was that of staffing parishes and giving missions for German-speaking immigrants. Father Hafkenscheid determined to broaden the community's apostolate to include outreach efforts for English-speaking Catholics. To initiate this plan he enlisted Walworth and Hecker as well as another native-born priest, Augustine F. Hewit. Although the son of a Congregationalist minister, Hewit had been an Episcopalian deacon before he embraced Catholicism in 1846.

Around mid-century the parish mission had become an integral part of Church life both here and in Europe. Appropriately understood as a form of Roman Catholic revivalism, its purpose was to effect spiritual renewal or conversion.[39] Each mission lasted for several days and provided an exceptional occasion for religious rejuvenation, brought about through a coordinated series of liturgical events and pious practices—all of them centering around the delivery of intensely emotional sermons.

Soon after Hecker's return to this country, he and the other members of Father Bernard's band of revivalists conducted a mission at St. Joseph's Church in Greenwich Village which "marked the beginning of organized and systematic missions for English-speaking parishes in the United States."[40] The success of this bold experiment far exceeded all expectations, and quickly other missionary orders, such as the Jesuits, formed comparable bands. Yet, there was a great demand for the Redemptorist preachers by bishops and pastors throughout the East and Midwest. In the manner of itinerant evangelists, Hafkenscheid's corps of specialists traveled the land reviving the waning faith among English-speaking Catholics. Walworth gained a reputation for his eloquent, fervent sermons, Hewit for his clear dogmatic presentations, while Hecker himself became skilled at delivering effective instructional lessons. Scattered among his epistles to Brownson are informative references to these labors. Letter 49, 15 May 1851, wherein Father Hecker describes in detail the group's apostolic activities at Loretto, Pennsylvania, is invaluable for understanding the inner workings of a rural parish mission.

The 1850s represented a period of missionary intensity for both Brownson and Hecker, and it is unfortunate that so few of Brownson's letters from this decade have survived. It was not until the summer of 1851 when the two friends were able to reunite, but their years apart did not diminish their high regard for each other. Expressing his indebtedness to Hecker for his very conversion, and also that of his wife, the publicist requested the young priest's advice in regulating his spiritual life. They both, however, were eager to get about their common business of collaborating in the advancement of the Roman Catholic cause in the United States.

While Hecker was being trained in Europe, Brownson had established himself as the towering Catholic writer in this country, despite the presence of other illustrious journalists such as Henry Major.[41] In addition to his literary undertakings, the reviewer lectured extensively. With regularity he made tours to New York, Philadelphia, and Baltimore, and at times he visited western and southern cities and even Montreal. Among the topics commonly treated were "Catholicity and Civilization," "Civil and Religious Liberty," and "The Compatibility between Democracy and Catholicism." Although Brownson was not preaching parish missions as was Father Hecker, he was nevertheless very much engaged in missionary tasks as he set forth the Church's teachings and defended its rights in the public forum. For these reasons the middle phase of the Brownson-Hecker relationship may aptly be designated the missionary years.

The Redemptorists' successes persuaded Hecker of the pivotal importance of the parish mission as the way of infusing new zeal into the Catholic population. Through such efforts the Catholic people would develop in their faith and devotion, and this in turn would produce a great impact on their non-Catholic countrymen, whom Hecker judged to be fundamentally religious. Writing to Brownson, he summed up the goal of his priestly labors as that of inaugurating a new age of faith on this continent, an age characterized by an effusion of spiritual enthusiasm, nurtured by Catholic asceticism. Hecker concluded that the era of immigration was nearing its end and that the future of the Church would be entrusted to the native-born youth. Testifying to the enormous growth of the Catholic minority was the fact that when the First Plenary Council of Baltimore convened in 1852, the Roman Church was the largest denomination in the United States.

Hecker's optimistic view of the national religious situation was somewhat at odds with the assessment reached by Dr. Brownson. During the ten years after his conversion Brownson had embarked on a deliberate course to protect the Church from its vicious opponents. When the Native-American evangelicals reacted to the soaring Catholic immigration of the mid-nineteenth century, it was quite clear that the Church was in a state of siege. Threatened by the flow of newcomers from abroad, the nativists, who organized the Know-Nothing Party, felt the aliens would undermine the security and prosperity of the country. Consequently, their objections to the Roman Church were not merely theological but also social, political, and economic. It was in this combative environment that Brownson emerged as the stalwart champion who ably defended his co-religionists against violent hostility.

As early as 1845, Brownson repudiated the original line of thought which brought him into the Church and took up instead the more conventional style of controversy.[42] Abandoning the philosophical doctrine of communion, he adopted, under the direction of Bishop Fitzpatrick, the traditional historical approach that continued the Counter-Reformation pattern of demonstrating that the Catholic Church was the necessary witness to and infallible interpreter of revelation. A representative piece from his *Review* during its early Catholic period was "The Church against No-Church," wherein he argued that the Roman Catholic Church alone was essential for salvation and outside of it was only "no-churchism."[43] Some essays exhibiting this apologetical method were gathered in the book *Essays and Reviews*.[44]

Brownson's writings had a militant tenor which intentionally put Protestants on the defensive. Not only did he contend that Catholicism was compatible with American institutions, he claimed that it was absolutely necessary to sustain popular liberty. Stressing the priority of authority and stability in the political realm, he reacted negatively to the disorder sweeping Europe. On the one hand, he denounced the Hungarian revolution led by Louis Kossuth for its renunciation of all legitimate authority; on the other hand, he worried about the ascent of political absolutism in the coup d'etat of Louis Napoleon.

Along with this political conservatism there was a thoroughgoing ultramontanism to his thought. The editor even went so far as to affirm the theory of the indirect power of the pope to depose a temporal ruler who directly violated the laws of God. When taking up timely issues, he provoked much furor both within and outside the Catholic community. It was his wish to give a balanced appraisal of Native-Americanism. Thus he judged the nativist movement as contradictory to our true national ideals, yet he sympathized with its demand that immigrants affirm allegiance to their adopted country. To encourage the process of acculturation Brownson recommended that the Catholic immigrants, particularly the Irish, foresake their foreign customs and traditions. He provoked further controversy in taking up the school question. Although he opposed state control of education and recognized the abuses of the public schools, Brownson, nevertheless, found the Catholic parochial system of his day to be defective. Perceiving his views as anti-Irish, many members of the hierarchy were infuriated, and Bishop Michael O'Connor of Pittsburgh and Bishop John Purcell[45] of Cincinnati publicly denounced them. Curiously some bishops who opposed Brownson's political opinions supported his sustained theological critique of the theory of the development of doctrine as it was elaborated by his contemporary English convert John Henry Newman.

The Convert Apostolate

Unlike his mentor, Father Hecker never lost confidence in the philosophical argumentation which conducted him to the doors of the Catholic Church. Therefore, when he plunged into the waters of theological apologetics, he was determined not to copy Brownson's mistake but rather to appropriate the dynamics of his own conversion experience. By building on this foundation, he began in 1854 to compose a non-traditional treatise designed to attract those non-Catholics who were inclined to mysticism and asceticism. This category included his one-time associates among the New England Unitarians and Transcendentalists as well as many others who had given up on Puritanism. His purpose was to exhibit the basic drives of the human heart and demonstrate that they could be fully satisfied only by Catholicism. Employing an anthropological rather than a historical method, Hecker's approach signaled the emergence of a ''new apologetics'' within the tradition of American Catholicism.[46]

In a letter to Brownson of 14 September 1854 (Letter 63), the budding apologist summarized the contents of his book: ''My object in view is to bring minds similarly constituted as my own to similar convictions & results, by the same process as I passed through. The leading idea is to expose the wants of the heart and demand their proper objects, rather than a logical defense of the Church.'' Describing human nature as essentially open to God's self-communication, in *Questions of the Soul* Hecker depicted the inner exigencies of the soul as orientated toward an incarnational and historical revelation; in order for these wants to be met the sacramental channels of divine grace and an infallible teaching authority were required.[47]

Since this irenic work was issued during a phase of fierce nativist reaction to Romanism, it created a minor public sensation. Catholic reviewers received it very favorably, while the Protestant critics were less complimentary. According to Dr. Brownson, *Questions of the Soul* was one of the few original, truly American books whose refreshing, innovative model of controversy represented a high point in our national Catholic literature. Besides this notice, the April 1855 number of his *Quarterly* contained an article on ''Liberalism and Socialism'' wherein the editor further recognized the need for a less polemical and less strident style in addressing those outside the Church. From then up to 1864 we can detect a decided change in Brownson's theological perspective—a change in accord with Hecker's more liberal stance.

Bolstered by the appreciation of his first book, Isaac Hecker set out to write a companion volume purporting to demonstrate the true value the Church accords to human reason. Intending to reach those persons who had fallen back on simple nature, the starting point for this second treatise was the Transcendentalist principle that human nature aspires to God. To Brownson, Hecker explained that he planned "to show how the dogmas of the Church answer in a way, to the demands of the intellect, as the sacraments do to the wants of the heart" (Letter 69, 27 March 1855). Even though *Aspirations of Nature* was not completed until 1857, Brownson unreservedly approved its outline.

These writings formed only part of a plan to implement his cherished ideal of an organized movement for the conversion of the United States. He became involved with a small number of priests and laymen committed to reconciling the Catholic faith with the American nationality. They sought to propagate their views through the *Freeman's Journal and Catholic Register,* edited by James McMaster in New York. Prominent in this group were the learned clergymen Jeremiah W. Cummings and Ambrose Manahan and the eminent laymen Dr. Levi Silliman Ives and George Hecker. (It should be pointed out that George Hecker was a most generous benefactor of Catholic causes. On numerous occasions he monetarily assisted his brother's ministry. Moreover, he frequently contributed to financially distressed individuals such as Brownson, McMaster, and Henry Hewit, M.D.—Father Hewit's brother who also converted to Rome.) Looking upon Orestes Brownson as the champion of Catholicism, this circle invited him to join its literary efforts. Brownson welcomed the chance to leave Boston, which had grown "too Irish" for his tastes, and before the close of 1855 he relocated his family and periodical in Manhattan.

In the more progressive atmosphere of New York City, Brownson's writings began to manifest detectable sympathy with the sociopolitical outlook of certain European liberal Catholics like the French author Count Charles Montalembert and the Italian statesman and philosopher whose works greatly influenced Brownson's philosophical theology, Vincenzo Gioberti.[48] Reflective of Brownson's altered posture was his famous essay "The Mission of America," in which he declared that the providential destiny of this country was to give modern civilization a more Christian social order.[49] Yet, this mission could be fulfilled only through Catholicism, and as a prerequisite to this development, Catholic citizens would have to cast off their foreign ways and totally embrace the good aspects of American culture. In one letter Brownson credits Hecker as having been "the godfather" of these thoughts.

In obvious contrast to his earlier Catholic phase, the lay theologian was backing off from the old-fashioned polemics and was pursuing now a conciliatory program. Brownson's awareness of this shift is indicated in his judgment, rendered in 1856, that Father Hecker's new apologetical strategy was superior to his own logical method. During the next year Brownson issued his religious autobiography, *The Convert.* There he elucidated his doctrine of communion in order to spell out the process by which he reasoned himself to the Catholic faith. Once again he realized the worth of that original doctrine for expounding the rational elements of Catholic theology. In Hecker's estimation *The Convert* was his friend's most important publication. As it happened, the editor's optimistic sentiments and nationalist feelings provoked the anger of the powerful Irish-born prelate John Hughes, who openly rebuked him. To avoid further clashes with the outspoken archbishop, Brownson moved across the Hudson River to Elizabeth, New Jersey, to enjoy the more congenial Newark Diocese headed by Bishop James R. Bayley, who was himself a convert.

The Paulist Fathers

Just as Brownson was occupied throughout these years with his journalistic duties, Hecker was engrossed in his missionary endeavors. In 1853 Father Bernard's tenure as provincial ended, and he was assigned to Ireland. His successor was the Bavarian-born priest George Ruland, who wished to make the parochial ministry to German Catholic immigrants again the community's top priority. Nevertheless, the celebrated American Redemptorists continued to present missions in English-speaking parishes. In 1856 this small band was augmented by two other converts from the Episcopal Church: George Deshon, a graduate of West Point, and Francis A. Baker, who had served as an Episcopalian rector in Baltimore.

For several months the missioners were engaged in extended tours of the southern states, where their preaching attracted the attention of many non-Catholics.[50] To deal with this unusual interest, they altered their schedules so as to present lectures specifically geared for Protestants. On one occasion, in Norfolk, Virginia, Hecker delivered a lecture on the popular objections against Catholicism. This talk was so well received that he interpreted it as the turning point of his missionary career, for it confirmed his convictions about the convert apostolate. Likewise its favorable results persuaded his confreres of the vast potential which such a ministry held if it were properly coordinated. In Letter 78 (12 April 1856) we have an account of Hecker's excitement with this bold experiment.

Even though the new provincial superior favored a different course, these five convert priests concluded that their service to the Church in America resided in the foundation of a mission house to be staffed by English-speaking Redemptorists. This proposal for a special apostolate was given life in the spring of 1857 when Bishop Bayley invited them to establish such a religious house in Newark. However, when Clarence Walworth relayed the request to Father Ruland, not only was it rejected but the superior communicated his displeasure to the congregation's headquarters in Rome. Viewing these missioners as a divisive force in the community, he accused them of laxity and nationalism.

When they learned of Ruland's actions the dismayed priests were anxious to correct so flagrant a misrepresentation of their attitudes and to gain serious consideration for their proposal. After much discussion Isaac Hecker volunteered to plead their case before the rector major of the Redemptorist Fathers. Yet when he requested leave for the journey to Rome, permission was denied. This action triggered a controversy over the interpretation of a community document regarding the right of direct access to the superior general. Believing the journey to be both legal and in the best interests of the order, Father Hecker departed for Europe on 5 August 1857. Before leaving he obtained letters of recommendation from the foremost members of the hierarchy and also from outstanding laymen including Ives, Brownson, and Louis B. Binsse.[51] Once again George Hecker provided the necessary funds.

Isaac Hecker could not have foreseen how violent a storm awaited him in Rome. When he arrived in Rome and presented himself to Nicholas Mauron, the rector major, he was told that his journey was illegal and in violation of the vows of obedience and poverty. Without the benefit of a hearing, Hecker was expelled from the Redemptorist order. Distressed and shocked by this precipitant action, he looked for help in overturning the verdict. Assistance was forthcoming from the Sacred Congregation of the Propagation of the Faith, whose jurisdiction included the Church in America, since it was classified as a missionary territory. The Propaganda's prefect, Cardinal Alessandro Barnabò, and its secretary, Archbishop Gaetano Bedini, sympathized with the dismissed priest and instructed him to prepare a legal brief laying out the grounds for an appeal. Thirty days later, when Father Mauron was still unwilling to reverse his decision, Hecker proceeded to draw up a petition to be submitted to Pope Pius IX.[52]

Soon he realized that his stay in Rome would be of long duration. Thus he determined to take advantage of the opportunity to inform the Vatican officials about the state of Catholic affairs in the New World. At first he considered having Brownson's "Mission of America" essay translated into Italian, but he chose instead to write an article for the influential magazine *Civiltà Cattolica*. Appearing in two installments in late 1857, this piece—"The Present and Future Prospects of the Catholic Faith in North America"—surveyed various social and religious movements in this country which pointed to the dissolution of Protestantism, while making a case for the receptivity of the American people to Catholicism. Central to this presentation was an analysis of the democratic political system which claimed that its underlying conception of human nature corresponded to Catholic teachings.[53] Although it was anonymous, this glowing account of the growth and prosperity of the Church in the United States enhanced Hecker's prestige among Roman churchmen.

During his absence, his fellow missionaries obediently carried on their duties. In November Hecker's *Aspirations of Nature* was finally released in New York, and the apologist was hopeful that its favorable acceptance would support the struggle for an English-speaking house and would substantiate his appraisal of the convert apostolate. In particular Hecker felt that a commendatory review from Brownson would count for much because Brownson was highly regarded in Rome. But to Hecker's amazement this expectation was misplaced.[54] Instead, his comrade published a reproachful criticism which seemed to undercut not only Hecker's personal defense but the basic premises of his "new apologetic" as well. Disagreeing that Transcendentalism signified the flow of our country's religious history, Brownson contradicted the author's claims about the spiritual and moral qualities of the national character. In a damaging fashion he depreciated the convert movement by insinuating that it was tinged by a feeling of accomodation motivated by a desire to recast the Church in an American mold. Cautioning against a too hasty foisting of our nationality on the Catholic immigrants, the Yankee reviewer pleaded for more direct guidance from the episcopate, particularly the Irish-born prelates.

Although he stopped short of labeling the book unorthodox, Brownson severely censured its interpretation of the effects of original sin and dismissed outright Hecker's immanentist assumption that our nature aspired to God. There was a twofold purpose at work in the theology of *Aspirations of Nature:* one was to vindicate the rights of human nature and the powers of reason against the Calvinists and Jansenists, the other was to assert the necessity of grace and revelation against the rationalists and naturalists. To accomplish these purposes, Hecker had undertaken a detailed comparison of the Protestant and Catholic anthropological doctrines.

While arguing the Catholic position regarding the basic goodness of human nature, Isaac Hecker interpreted the Council of Trent as teaching that by his transgression Adam lost the holiness and justice wherein he was constituted. These absolutely gratuitous gifts of sanctifying grace and original integrity were not due Adam by nature (*indebita naturae*). So when Adam fell from his elevated state, they were forfeited. Because of original sin, he argued, we are now born in a state of privation with respect to supernatural justice and integrity; yet our nature has not been intrinsically debased. On the contrary, it remains essentially good and still in possession of its natural abilities and rights (*debita naturae*).

Given the popular audience Father Hecker was addressing, his terminology was not always technically precise. Such imprecision led

Brownson to imply that Hecker endorsed the theory of the "state of pure nature" (*status naturae purae*). This was a much debated theory formulated by post-Tridentine Scholastic theologians to explain the distinction between the natural and supernatural orders. While trying to safeguard the utter gratuitousness of man's elevation to grace, this concept with its corollary of a natural beatitude also safeguarded the logical possibility that God could have chosen to create man in a state of pure nature without calling him in fact to supernatural vision.

Even though Brownson admitted that Hecker only mentioned the *status naturae purae* as a possibility, he accused him of overestimating the human capacity to do good after the Fall. Describing himself as an Augustinian theologian, the lay editor calculated the consequences of the Fall to be far more extensive than the loss of the *indebita*. Although he did not hold with the Calvinist view that our nature was essentially corrupted, he firmly insisted that it suffered a positive injury. Original sin so weakened and wounded human nature that it inevitably, though not necessarily, committed sin. Apart from grace, the intellect was darkened and the passions disordered.

Coming from such an intimate colleague, the timing of so adverse a critique served to dishearten the embattled Redemptorist. It is uncertain what brought about this sudden lapse of affection, though it seems that the editor wished to distance himself from the priest's ecclesiastical problems. Perceptively, Hecker was taken by the resemblance between these negative comments (excluding those about original sin) and the charges leveled earlier against Brownson himself by Archbishop Hughes. The author was willing to forgive his old confidant's ill treatment and advised his associates to do likewise. That the philosopher would play a major role in the movement to convert the United States remained one of Hecker's constant hopes. The seven items that touch on these events are among the most revealing in this entire collection. We draw special attention to Brownson's Letter 82, 29 September 1857, along with its rather interesting variant.

Resuming with the events in Rome, the Hecker case was brought to the attention of Pius IX, who passed it on to normal channels. Soon Cardinal Barnabò recognized that the litigation to win reinstatement would not succeed and he proposed that the young priest consider realizing his apostolic ideals outside the ranks of the Order of St. Alphonsus. This meant considering the formation of an entirely new congregation devoted exclusively to the conversion of the American people. On their own, Hecker's confreres formulated a canonical request for separation from the Redemptorists, intending to perform missionary work as an independent band. Now, the issue was transformed from a dispute between a subject and a superior to a question of the welfare of the Church in the United States.

As his four confreres solicited support on this side of the Atlantic, Father Hecker submitted another petition for the review of his dismissal. From the coordination of their efforts there quickly flowed an outpouring of approval from the national hierarchy, whose letters carried much weight with the Roman authorities. Curiously, the statements sent by Francis Kenrick and Martin Spalding were more enthusiastic than the one from John Hughes. Moreover, an effective intercession was made by the Canadian bishop Thomas Connolly,[55] and the respected Redemptorist Frederick de Held also lent his help. Then, at long last, on 6 March 1858 and with the blessing of the pope, the Congregation of Bishops and Regulars dispensed Baker, Deshon, Hecker, Hewit, and Walworth from their religious vows, thereby releasing them to continue their sacerdotal ministry under the supervision of a local diocese.

After seven arduous months in the Eternal City, Isaac T. Hecker arrived home in May to join his companions in the serious business of organizing the first Catholic order for men to originate in America. Living in George Hecker's residence, the group contemplated the shape this new society should take. As Hecker envisioned it, this association would fuse together the Catholic faith with the American culture, being primarily committed to the conversion apostolate. The others, however, were less eager to make so drastic a departure from their priestly pasts and favored instead a more general objective, stated as the carrying on of the missions in the spirit of St. Alphonsus. They agreed to make New York City their headquarters, but their ministry was to be nationwide. Stressing personal responsibility, all members except one preferred to unite, like the Oratorians, on the basis of promises rather than vows. To Clarence Walworth this voluntary principle was unacceptable, and he withdrew to assume a pastorate in the Albany Diocese. The four remaining members entered into an agreement with Archbishop Hughes formally founding the Missionary Society of St. Paul the Apostle on 10 July 1858 under the leadership of Father Hecker.

The formation of the Paulist Fathers was greeted with a generous response, since these men were so well known by laity and clergy across the land. Even though the demand for their missionary service was unabated, the Paulists were required to establish a parish where they built their residence, or "convent," as they called it. This was located in a poor area on the West Side of Manhattan known as "Shantyopolis," which was populated by immigrants from Ireland. Opening in late 1859, St. Paul's Church was to undergo successive enlargements, culminating with the impressive structure now occupying the same address. Noted for its liturgical ceremonies and music, the parish was soon recognized as one of the most vibrant in the city. Its many societies and its Sunday school were judged the models of their kind within the archdiocese.

Yet, of all the conspicuous features of the Church of St. Paul the Apostle, the one that most clearly set it off from other parishes was its distinctive style of pulpit address. To the extent that these convert priests were gifted mission preachers, so too did they excel at parochial preaching. Attuned to the needs of their congregants, these pastoral discourses were characterized by simplicity and clarity. They promoted growth in the Christian life through the performance of religious and ethical duties.

Beginning in 1861, selected homilies were published in a popular series. Their specific theological themes generally coincided with Hecker's anthropological perspective. For instance, in an 1863 sermon on sanctification entitled "The Saint of Our Day," Hecker called for a redefinition of the meaning of Christian perfection in the nineteenth century.[56] Moving beyond the ascetical restrictions of his Redemptorist days, he widened the sphere of holiness. Not surprisingly, Dr. Brownson heard in this echoes of what he considered to be a mistaken understanding of the effects of original sin. As the correspondence indicates, this lingering dispute was to resurface at a future date, driving a wedge between the Paulists and the lay theologian.

Apostolic ingenuity marked the formative years of the Congregation of St. Paul. Parish and mission obligations kept the small group quite busy. The community's first recruits were also convert priests—Robert Tillotson and Alfred Young. On Easter Monday 1861, Clarence Walworth rejoined his former associates and became an active mission preacher, but, due to illness, he again departed in July 1865 and took charge of St. Mary's Church in Albany. Genuine tragedy hit the small band in April 1865 when Father Baker died of typhus fever. Afterwards the Paulists suspended the missions until other members were acquired in 1872. Nevertheless, Hecker pushed on with his outreach efforts and inaugurated the practice of lecturing to Protestant audiences on themes like "The Church and the Republic" and "Why I Became a Catholic."

Meanwhile Brownson increasingly pursued his more liberal course showing affinity with those European Catholics who championed liberty and democracy; his fascination with the thought of Vincenzo Gioberti also endured. A number of his inflammatory articles generated complaints from bishops. And when he suggested in the "Rights of the Temporal"[57] that the lessening of the temporal power of the papacy might augment its spiritual authority, the publicist was secretly reported to Rome, but no denunciation was forthcoming.

Growing fatigued by the storms of ecclesiastical polemics and the mounting hostility of the hierarchy, in his January 1864 issue Brownson announced his resolve to eschew theological topics, concentrating instead on subjects that were "national and secular, devoted to philosophy, science, politics, literature, and the general interests of civilization, especially American civilization." Even this National Series did not free him from the meshes of criticism. Some charged that he wantonly accused the Jesuits of indifference to civic affairs, while others objected to his treatment of the pope's dominion over the Papal States.

It seems that the proximity between Hecker and Brownson during these years precluded the need for much written communication. They were in regular personal contact, and Brownson scheduled a monthly overnight stay at the Paulist rectory. Notable in the entire correspondence is the attachment the two men had, not only for one another, but for each other's family as well. A spirit of gentle concern and benevolence permeates their letters.

Hecker's solicitous attitude toward the Brownson children was evident as he counseled the sons regarding their vocations and as he encouraged Sarah's literary talents.[58]

The paucity of letters in this period deprives us of what was, no doubt, an interesting exchange of views regarding the War between the States. To Hecker, a resolute unionist, the war represented a step toward the eventual unification of the nation under Catholic influences. In the *Quarterly Review* Brownson unfalteringly defended the Union as he bitterly denounced the South's rebellion. Formerly an inveterate opponent of abolitionism, he now reversed himself, calling for the immediate abolition of Negro slavery as the only means of preserving the United States. So critical was Brownson of President Lincoln's conduct of the war and his plans for reconstruction that he supported the nomination of General John Frémont[59] in the campaign of 1864.

The war also forced the editor to reconsider his political theory. No longer could he hold that sovereignty was vested in the states separately, but rather it was vested in the states only within the federal union. Expounding the doctrine that the American democracy was a "territorial democracy," Brownson collected his articles conveying a theological-political vision in a book which some consider his best work, *The American Republic: Its Constitution, Tendencies and Destiny*.[60]

Even though these were years of intense controversy for him, the public strife was nothing when compared with the personal tragedy that befell the Brownson family. Sally and Orestes Brownson were troubled at the news that their son Henry was wounded in battle; then a profound sadness overwhelmed them in 1864 upon learning that their other soldier sons—Edward and William—were killed. Given these tragic events and his painful chronic infirmities, it is not surprising that Dr. Brownson was beset by emotional depression. All these factors taken together resulted in the discontinuance of *Brownson's Quarterly Review* that October; it closed with a deferential statement of submission to "the judgment of the Church, as pronounced by the Holy See." Now, without his journal and restricted in his lecturing, the Brownson household faced severe financial hardship. This difficulty was partially alleviated when lay and clerical friends, led by Isaac and George Hecker and Jeremiah Cummings, hurried to his aid by organizing an insurance annuity that would pay Brownson $1,000 yearly.

Once more Orestes Brownson was to modify his intellectual outlook. Subsequent to the 8 December 1864 publication of Pope Pius IX's encyclical *Quanta Cura* with its attendant Syllabus of Errors, Brownson determined to become an unquestioned champion of Roman Catholic orthodoxy. Obediently, he accepted the condemnations of political and theological liberalism, though in no way did he regard these papal censures as touching on his own positions. However, he did revert to the conservative stance of his earliest post-conversion period. Insofar as he curtailed his alliance with liberal Catholics, so too he retracted his conciliatory attitude toward the value systems of nineteenth-century culture. Committed to an unmitigated defense of the papal teachings, Dr. Brownson set out to engage in battle with all the evils of the times: infidelity, political liberalism, Protestantism, and any attempt to accomodate the Church to the contemporary *Weltgeist*.

In sharp contrast, Isaac Hecker was more consistent in his outlook regarding the positive possibilities for the Church in the modern age. If these two apologists were to diverge in their theological convictions, that did not entail the splitting of their common bond of loyalty. In fact, Brownson's first writing after the cessation of his *Review* was a lengthy pamphlet counteracting Octavius Brooks Frothingham's criticism of Hecker's message and the Paulist vision of a Catholic America.

The Catholic World Years: 1865–1872

So persuaded was Hecker of his missionary vision that during the immediate postbellum period he undertook decisive steps to secure its implementation. For several years he had been convinced of the vast potential of a learned monthly magazine for promoting the Catholic cause in the United States. Therefore, in April of 1865 he boldly launched *The Catholic World: A Monthly Eclectic Magazine of General Literature and Science*. Assisted by the talented John Hassard as associate editor and the indefatigable Lawrence Kehoe as publisher and business manager, Hecker functioned as editor-in-chief. At first this literary organ was intended to be a vehicle for translations and reprints, but within a year it was transformed into a medium of original articles and reviews. Brownson contributed translations before becoming one of its foremost writers of original essays. By the time he stopped working for *The Catholic World*, in 1872, the noted reviewer had contributed over seventy articles, some of them his finest. Letters pertaining to this magazine fill much of the third section of the collected correspondence.

In a short time *The Catholic World* had gained a reputation for a high literary tone and a strict standard of scholarship. It cultivated an appreciative following among Catholics and Protestants. Over the years many of the finest American Catholic authors were invited to contribute to its pages, among them Agnes Repplier, William Seton, and John Talbot Smith.[61] It has been said that the issues of its first thirty years furnish the most complete record of the growth of Catholic letters in America. As a principal instrument of the Paulist ministry, *The Catholic World* reflected Father Hecker's irenic practice of presenting Catholic doctrine in a way that would be comprehensible and appealing to his fellow citizens, yet it would still defend the Church by engaging its opponents in honest dialogue. In fact a good number of articles were written in reply to charges or misstatements by the anti-Catholic press, such as those made in *Harper's Weekly, The New Englander,* and *The Church Review*. Although the editorial policy required that the articles be unsigned, it would be a mistake to assume that they all were anonymous. For, despite Brownson's frequent complaints about this custom, many an astute reader could readily identify his style and argument.

The success of *The Catholic World* prompted the Paulist Fathers to expand further into the "apostolate of the press." In 1866 Hecker announced the formation of the Catholic Publication Society as a national agency for the distribution and publication of Catholic literature, primarily inexpensive four-page tracts. Thousands of copies were printed. Some of these popular tracts caught the attention of evangelical commentators; in particular the tract *Is It Honest?* sparked a heated discussion in which Brownson gladly entered with his old apologetic fervor. A steady backer of Hecker's journalistic initiatives was his friend Archbishop Martin J. Spalding, who in 1866 invited him to address the Second Plenary Council of Baltimore. There the Paulist superior gained the approval of the hierarchy for his work with the Catholic press. Hecker and Hewit even traveled abroad to form contacts with European tract societies, but unfortunately the Catholic Publication Society never attained its full promise. Nevertheless, another remarkable venture in mass instruction was undertaken in 1870 when Hecker established an illustrated magazine for children. Welcomed as a resource for the incipient Sunday school movement, *The Young Catholic* acquired a circulation of over 50,000 within its first year.

Theological Divergence

During these years Orestes Brownson supported his family not only by writing for the Paulist periodical, but he also contributed to *The Ave Maria,* the new Catholic magazine established by Notre Dame's Father Edward Sorin. Moreover, he acted as editor for *The Tablet,* a weekly run by the Sadlier publishing firm in New York. Working under the supervision of another was difficult for a man who had conducted his own journal for over a score of years. His letters tell how he felt constrained by Hecker's editorial directions and how he resented corrections to his essays by Hewit and Hecker. Augustine Hewit, C.S.P., served as managing editor for *The Catholic World,* and Hecker's respect for Hewit brought him to name his companion as the magazine's ecclesiastical censor. In addition Hewit supplied many articles on theological and philosophical topics. In his roles as censor and editor Hewit was to become embroiled in a set of scholarly conflicts with his friend and fellow convert, Dr. Brownson.

We have already discussed the long-standing quarrel between the Paulists and Brownson over the question of original sin. This debate broke out with renewed vigor in 1868 in a round of speculative squabbling that was triggered by Hewit's writings on the subject. It should be mentioned that Augustine Hewit's education in patristic studies and Thomistic philosophy gave him a theological perspective different from that of Brownson. The latter considered himself an

Augustinian thinker and understood the consequences of the Fall of Adam to entail the loss of sanctifying grace and the preternatural gifts. The negative effects of the Fall were felt in the natural order as well as in the supernatural order. In contrast, Hewit, like Hecker, held that the loss suffered by the Fall pertained to the supernatural gifts (*indebita*), whereas our nature still retained its natural endowments and powers (*debita*).

The major point of contention between Brownson and Hewit centered on the somewhat ambiguous papal condemnations of the positions expounded by two controversial figures in the history of theology, Baius and Jansen. To summarize the problem, it was alleged that Baius and Jansen held in common the belief that God was unable to withhold from man the supernatural gifts connected with original justice. In other words, they affirmed that grace was due to Adam by right; hence *indebita* were confused with *debita*. Following from this was the outright rejection of the "state of pure nature."

Brownson and Hewit disagreed in their interpretations of the propositions condemning Baianism in 1567 and then Jansenism in 1653. According to Brownson, what was judged heretical was the belief that original justice was due to man by nature. But he found acceptable as an Augustinian position the notion that original justice was conferred on Adam because of a certain fittingness on the part of God—though surely not as something owed Adam. Because he believed that mankind was always under a supernatural providence, the layman rejected the "state of pure nature" theory.

From Hewit's angle of vision, Brownson failed to distinguish sufficiently his position from the condemned theses. Moreover, in line with the Thomist school, Hewit looked upon the *status naturae purae* hypothesis as being necessary to account for the gratuitousness of man's participation in grace. Their argument extended to further charges and countercharges. Brownson accused Hewit of denying both the reality of *genera* and *species* as well as Adam's place as the physical head of the human race. Expectedly, Hewit defended himself against these indictments.

The high degree of intellectual divergence between Isaac Hecker and Orestes Brownson regarding the reconciliation of the Catholic faith with nineteenth-century culture becomes obvious as we read the letters written from 1868 onwards. While the priest was consistent in his moderately liberal outlook, the layman grew more rigidly conservative. Renouncing any form of "latitudinarian Catholicity," Brownson advocated an uncompromising cast of mind that would fearlessly battle "the spirit of the age." Under the leadership of the pope, the visible locus of divine authority, the Church of Rome was to confront head-on the evils of modern civilization. Brownson's articles in *The Catholic World* criticized the works of Spencer, Draper, and Huxley, seeing in them the emergence of scientific materialism. Among the other topics about which he voiced disapproving verdicts were spiritualism and the women's suffrage movement. In Letter 121, 5 March 1869, Brownson disparages the movement for female suffrage and eligibility: "I took upon the present movement as the most dangerous that has ever been attempted in our country."

When it was announced that Pope Pius IX was convoking an ecumenical council, the Paulist superior hoped to attend, since it was to be the first general council in which Americans would take part. The calling of the First Council of the Vatican was to him a signal of a new era in the Church's history—one to be affected by the American experience. Appointed as procurator for a non-attending bishop, Father Hecker arrived in Rome in November 1869. While en route to the council, he was informed about a group organizing opposition to the definition of the doctrine of papal infallibility, and prior to the council Hecker became associated with the anti-infallibilist faction led by Bishop Félix Dupanloup of Orléans.[62] Hecker felt that such a definition was inopportune and he believed this sentiment would prevail.

In Hecker's absence, Hewit was placed in charge of *The Catholic World,* but Hewit and Brownson, who both favored the infallibility definition, were instructed not to deal with the disputed subject. Hecker took measures to supply news about the council, and when the scholarly theologian Rev. Dr. James Corcoran[63] could not oblige, the Paulist turned to James Gibbons and Patrick Lynch, two young prelates.

While at the council Hecker was named personal theologian to Archbishop Spalding of Baltimore. He came into frequent contact with numerous bishops and theologians, and was especially taken by the interest the Europeans showed for the state of religion in the

United States. Struck by the coincidence of holding the council when Europe was undergoing great political turmoil, Hecker decided that the moment had arrived to make a case recommending the American arrangement of church-state relations. He requested an article on this topic from Dr. Brownson and even provided an extensive outline. In the lengthy Letter 139, 30 January 1870, he suggests the following line of thought:

> In our own country, where the church exists in her entire independence from State control, yet all her rights acknowledged and protected by the laws of the country, where her right to hold property, of establishing colleges, schools, charitable associations, etc. and to govern and administer her affairs according to her own laws and customs; it is here she is putting forth an energy and making conquests which vie with the zeal & success of the early ages of Christianity.

Brownson did accept the task, but the traditional tenor he hit in his "Church and State" was not what Hecker had intended. This fact only highlighted the distance between these two theologians regarding the harmony between the Roman Catholic Church and the republican form of government as well as the meaning of America's mission. In Letter 142, 25 August 1870, Brownson openly confessed: "Catholicity is theoretically compatible with democracy, as you and I would explain democracy, but practically, there is, in my judgment, no compatibility between them."

Growing less sanguine with age and illness, Orestes Brownson no longer shared Isaac Hecker's confidence about the triumph of Catholicism in this country. He was now convinced that the Church's progress and expansion would result from increased immigration and not from the convert apostolate. Strictly interpreting the Catholic dictum "outside the Church there is no salvation," the reviewer came to reduce all of Protestantism to the utter exaltation of the principle of private judgment; this amounted to what he called "theological atheism." Brownson's guns were directed against the entire Protestant spectrum as is seen in his articles on Charles Hodge, Henry Ward Beecher, Ferdinand Ewer, and others. His serious differences with Hecker and Hewit were spelled out in a letter of 1871 to his son:

> The only trouble I have grows out of the fact that Father Hewit is not sound on the question of original sin, and does not believe that it is necessary to be in communion with the Church in order to be saved. He holds that Protestants may be saved by invincible ignorance, and that original sin was no sin at all except the individual sin of Adam, and that our nature was not wounded at all by it. Father Hecker agrees with him on these points, and is in fact a semi-pelagian without knowing it.[64]

Their Final Years

Despite the parting of their intellectual paths, both Hecker and Brownson continued to treasure their friendship, and as leading Catholic spokesmen they were still cooperating in certain common enterprises. These activities were quietly encouraged by their mutual colleague John McCloskey, who succeeded John J. Hughes as archbishop of New York after his death on 3 January 1864. For instance, when Isaac Hecker joined the serious efforts of Archbishop McCloskey and Bishop Bernard McQuaid[65] to secure public funding for parochial schools, Orestes Brownson responded to the editor's request for timely and forceful arguments favoring a denominational system.[66]

Furthermore, they both supported the establishment of the Catholic Union.[67] Prompted by the 1870 occupation of Rome by Victor Emmanuel, this movement was modeled on similar European associations and was devoted to defending the temporal power of the papacy. Backed by the hierarchy and clergy, the Catholic Union of New York was headed by the noted convert-scientist Professor Henry J. Anderson, assisted by the prominent attorneys Charles O'Conor and Richard H. Clarke.[68] Hecker viewed the movement as a vehicle for advancing Church causes by uniting lay and clerical energies in educational and charitable projects. He especially hoped that it would start a daily newspaper and then organize a national Catholic Congress, following the example of the Belgian congresses.

But by now the intellectual differences between the two friends had created a tension in their working relationship which was painful to both of them. Their disagreements about apologetical methods and their differing approaches to the modern age bore important practical implications. At times the older man felt the younger was patronizing and inconsiderate, and so he contemplated separating from *The Catholic World* in order to write some planned books or to revive *Brownson's Quarterly Review*. Hecker, however, persuaded him to continue. Brownson was also contributing to *The Tablet,* and he accepted the invitation of Monsignor Michael Corrigan[69] to lecture at Seton Hall College in South Orange, New Jersey.

The calm was to be short-lived. Another clash between Father Hewit and Brownson erupted in 1871 when the censor for *The Catholic World* altered one of Brownson's philosophical essays. The quarrel again stemmed from the difference in their theological orientations, and the dispute focused on the epistemological question whether God was known by analogy (a Thomist position) or by intuition (an Augustinian position). The precise difficulty had to do with Brownson's understanding of the ontologistic system of his philosophical mentor, Vincenzo Gioberti.[70] Detecting in Gioberti's writing the danger of pantheism, the Holy See had censured some of his views in 1861. What was condemned was the doctrine that human knowledge is made possible through a direct, even if nonexplicit, vision of the divine essence.

The matter was further complicated by the papal condemnation in 1866 of seven ontologistic theses held by certain professors at Louvain University, Belgium. Again we find that Brownson and Hewit disagreed on how to interpret these two ecclesiastical condemnations. Hewit worried that the layman's views fell under the official ban, whereas Brownson claimed that the Paulist misunderstood him and Gioberti. Even though he employed Gioberti's technical phrase, "*Ens creat existentias*" (Being creates existences), Brownson insisted that he avoided the pantheistic error, since he carefully distinguished between cognition and intuition, as well as between the creator and creatures. The wrangling came to a climax early in 1872 when, with Hecker's approval, Hewit rejected for publication Brownson's two philosophical pieces titled "Ontologism and Ontology" and "Reason and Revelation."

For some time Dr. Brownson had been piqued by Hewit's editorial actions and was dissatisfied with Hecker's theological policies. After the rejection of his articles in January of 1872, he decided that he could no longer suffer under their restraints and that what little physical energy he had left should be put to other uses. The final exchange of letters terminating the professional association of Brownson and Hecker also signaled the decline of their personal contact with one another. In hopes of reversing Brownson's decision to withdraw from *The Catholic World* Father Hecker, in his letter of 30 January [1872] (Letter 173), acknowledges his high esteem for his venerable colleague and implores him to persevere in serving the Catholic Church in America by writing "in refutation of the calumnies of the enemies of the Church" and "in applying Catholic principles to the social and political questions of the day." Brownson was adamant in his resolve, however, and as graciously as possible submitted his resignation to the Paulist editor. His final letter to Hecker, which is also the last item of their collected correspondence (Letter 174, 31 January 1872), closes with these kind words: "I thank you for the many proofs of your friendship you have given me, and I assure you that my feelings towards you have undergone no change. And I trust our intercourse is not to be interrupted, but is to continue as cordial and friendly as ever."

When in the same year the journalist also stopped writing for *The Ave Maria,* Father Sorin invited him to retire at the University of Notre Dame. But Brownson refused, for he was determined to revive his *Quarterly Review*. The "Last Series," which appeared in January 1873, was in large part a response to a request his beloved wife, Sally, had made before her death the previous April. Intending to place himself *rectus in curia,* the editor disclaimed ever having been a liberal Catholic. The revived *Review* was greeted with acclaim by his admirers, among them James R. Bayley, who had recently succeeded Martin J. Spalding as archbishop of Baltimore. Because of his overall poor health, Brownson was not always capable of producing new articles; thus he reprinted ones from earlier editions. Still, some fine essays were written dealing with familiar topics such as church and state, religion and science. In particular, he focused on enhancing the authority of the papacy in articles like "Papal Infallibility and Civil Allegiance."[71]

The death of his wife had been a severe blow for the aged editor, and since his daughter was now married, he lacked sustaining emotional support. Unable to cope with his mounting financial and physical problems, in October 1875 he issued his valedictory number of the *Quarterly Review*. That same autumn he left New Jersey for Detroit, Michigan, in order to reside with his son Henry, and it was there that he died on 17 April 1876. Ten years after his death, his remains were transferred to a permanent vault in the Sacred Heart Church at the University of Notre Dame.

At the time of Brownson's break with *The Catholic World*, Isaac Hecker himself was in declining health—a condition that endured for the next sixteen years. Like his colleague, Hecker was now compelled to restrict his active ministry and to lessen his participation in the projects of his flourishing religious order. The Paulists were receiving new members and were recommencing their missionary tours. Needing rest and tranquility, the Paulist superior resided at the community's Lake George, New York, vacation house and then spent several months in the South. Following the counsel of his physicians, he traveled to Europe, staying there from the summer of 1873 to the fall of 1875.

Since Hecker was not well enough to resume his official responsibilities, most of the congregation's business was delegated to Augustine Hewit. After Hecker's return to New York and while he was living under the care of his brother George, the bed-ridden editor made a final attempt to re-establish contact with Orestes Brownson in Detroit. Father Hecker instructed an associate to request an article from the celebrated reviewer, yet Brownson's deteriorating strength prohibited him from obliging.[72]

Upon hearing of the death of Brownson, Hecker immediately sent his condolences to Henry F. Brownson, saying: 'I owe more perhaps to your father than to any other man in my early life. My friendship and sense of gratitude to him has never been affected by any event during the last forty years.''[73] A Solemn High Requiem Mass was sung in the Church of St. Paul in New York with Father Hewit preaching the funeral sermon. He also wrote the obituary in *The Catholic World* honoring Dr. Brownson.[74]

Despite Hecker's limited energy, he was able to write and to supervise the editorial work of the Paulist periodical. His writings extended his apologetical stance and expanded the posture of openness to modernity; some essays were devoted to reconciling Roman Catholic religious thought with the political and cultural changes occurring in the United States and in Europe. At this time the renowned convert was truly an international figure, and his influence was felt beyond the range of American Catholicism. A number of his important magazine articles were collected in the volume *The Church and the Age*.[75] Also he dictated five insightful essays assessing Dr. Brownson's career. In answer to the question, what was Brownson's predominant passion, Hecker replied: "love of truth, devotion to principle. . . . This was all his glory and all his trouble; all his quarrels, friendships, aversions, perplexities, triumphs, labors—all to be traced to love of truth."[76]

When James Gibbons became archbishop of Baltimore and when Leo XIII[77] assumed the papal throne, Hecker's optimism for the success of his apostolate was reinforced. Through various personal contacts he impressed the significance of his missionary vision upon his younger associates. In the role of an elder churchman, the infirm priest was present at the Third Plenary Council of Baltimore in 1884. But, the years of struggle and labor finally took their toll, and on 22 December 1888, Isaac Thomas Hecker died in the company of his fellow Paulists. As it turned out, the biography of Hecker composed by Walter Elliott, C.S.P., was to become one factor among many others which sparked the controversy during the 1890s that has been called the Americanist crisis.

"The correspondence between Hecker and Brownson," Joseph McSorley once remarked, "would fill a fair-sized volume."[78] Heartily agreeing with his judgment, the editors have prepared this present edition. We have endeavored in this Introduction to sketch a broad context for understanding the lives and thought of Orestes Brownson and Isaac Hecker so as to provide a historical and theological framework which renders their correspondence meaningful.

NOTES

1. Hecker to his family, 19 April 1844 (HP, APF).
2. "The Laboring Classes," *BosQR*, III (October 1840), 432.

3. Not very much information is available about Brownson's immediate family: Sylvester Augustus Brownson (c. 1768–c. 1803); Relief Metcalf Brownson (d. 1865?); the eldest son, Daniel, distinguished himself as an orator; Oran converted to Catholicism from Mormonism while in Ireland c. 1860; Thorina Brownson Dean (d. 1875); and Daphne Augusta Brownson Ludington (1803–1892).

4. *The Convert; Or, Leaves from My Experience* (New York: D. & J. Sadlier, 1857), p. 2.

5. Brownson to Bernard Whitman, 13 June 1831, Rare Book Room, University of Notre Dame.

6. Frances Wright (1795–1852), Scottish-born reformer and author, founder of the Nashoba (Tenn.) community 1825.

7. Claude Henri de Rouvroy Saint-Simon (1760–1825), French social philosopher.

8. Benjamin Constant (1767–1830), French philosopher and political theorist.

9. "Two Articles from the *Princeton Review,*" *BosQR,* III (July 1840), 322–23.

10. Andrews Norton (1786–1853), conservative Unitarian author, professor of sacred literature at Harvard Divinity School 1819–30.

11. *New Views of Christianity, Society and the Church* (Boston: C. C. Little and J. Brown, 1836).

12. Brownson to Martin Van Buren, 2 April 1838, Library of Congress, Washington, D.C. (photostat BP, UNDA).

13. "The Laboring Classes," *BosQR,* III (October 1840), 366.

14. Ibid., p. 393.

15. See Richard M. Leliaert, "The Religious Significance of Democracy in the Thought of Orestes A. Brownson," *The Review of Politics,* XXXVIII (January 1976), 3–26.

16. "Dr. Brownson and the Workingman's Party Fifty Years Ago," *CW,* XLV (May 1887), 205.

17. "Oration of O. A. Brownson Delivered at Washington Hall, July 5, 1841," p. 4, Harvard College Library, Cambridge, Mass.

18. Elliott, *LFH,* p. 26.

19. Holden, *EY,* p. 45.

20. McSorley, *FH&F,* p. 215.

21. Holden, *EY,* pp. 52–55; also see his *YP,* pp. 16–17. Ryan follows Holden, see *OAB,* pp. 217–23.

22. Brownson, *BEL,* pp. 159–60; also see W. H. Channing to Brownson, 5 June 1837 (BP, UNDA).

23. Hecker wrote: "My first acquaintance with Dr. Brownson was when he came to New York and delivered a course of lectures in favor of the principles and aims of this party. This was somewhere about 1834." "Dr. Brownson and the Workingman's Party Fifty Years Ago," *CW,* XLV (May 1887), 202.

24. Elliott, *LFH,* pp. 15–22.

25. Hecker to Henry F. Brownson, 17 April 1876 (UNDA).

26. *The Mediatorial Life of Jesus* (Boston: C. C. Little and J. Brown, 1842).

27. In all the Brownsons were to have eight children; the only two not mentioned in the correspondence are George Brownson (1840–1849), who died of scarlet fever, and Charles Joseph Maria Brownson (1845–1851).

28. John Sullivan Dwight (1813–1893), music editor and critic, graduate of Harvard Divinity School 1836, professor at Brook Farm.

29. August Wilhelm von Schlegel (1767–1845), German author and champion of romanticism.

30. Johann Paul Friedrich Richter (1763–1825), popular German author who wrote under the name "Jean-Paul."

31. Hecker to his brothers, 1 March 1843 (HP, APF); quoted in Holden, *YP*, p. 53.

32. Fourierism, or phalansterianism, is the theory of utopian socialism proposed by Charles Fourier (1772–1837) that advocated the reorganization of society into cooperative economic units called phalanxes.

33. See Letters 13 and 14. About this incident Hecker later wrote: "In his *Convert* Dr. Brownson says that he had a high appreciation of the Tractarian movement, and I have a letter from him somewhere, written at this time, of which he was afterwards always heartily ashamed. In it he advised me to join the Episcopal Church, if I could do so with a good conscience." "Dr. Brownson in Boston," *CW*, XLV (July 1887), 472.

34. Since the numbering of the twenty-four volumes of *BrQR* changed so frequently, in making our annotations we have chosen to cite its month and year, with the article's title and pagination. Brownson divided the periodical as follows: First Series, volumes I–III (1844–46); New Series, volumes I–VI (1847–52); Third Series, volumes I–XI (1853–63); National Series, volume I (1864); and Last Series, volumes I–III (1873–75).

35. *The Catechism of the Council of Trent,* English trans. by Rev. Jeremy Donovan (Dublin: R. Coyne, 1829; first American ed. Baltimore: James Myres, 1833).

36. "Sparks on Episcopacy," *BrQR,* July 1844, p. 386.

37. The Urban College of the Propaganda was a Roman seminary founded in 1627 by Pope Urban VIII (1568–1644). It was under the direction of the Sacred Congregation of the Propaganda and trained candidates for the priesthood from mission lands.

38. Hecker to Mon. T. R. Père [Rev. Michael Heilig, C.SS.R.], 30 May 1848 (copy in HP, APF).

39. See the recent important work by Jay P. Dolan, *Catholic Revivalism: The American Experience, 1830–1900* (Notre Dame, Ind.: University of Notre Dame Press, 1978); also see Dolan's *The Immigrant Church: New York's Irish and German Catholics, 1815–1865* (Baltimore: Johns Hopkins University Press, 1975).

40. Holden, *YP,* p. 160. Also see Michael J. Curley, *The Provincial Story: A History of the Baltimore Province of the Congregation of the Most Holy Redeemer* (New York: Redemptorist Fathers, 1963), pp. 115–17.

41. Henry Major (1819?–1873), former Episcopalian priest, Catholic convert 1846, editor of *The Catholic Herald* of Philadelphia 1847–55.

42. About this change in Brownson's theology, Hecker recalled in his old age: "And when, shortly after my conversion I went to Europe, all the letters I wrote to him were filled with complaints that he had given up his first principles, or at any rate ignored them." "Dr. Brownson and Bishop Fitzpatrick," *CW,* XLV (April 1887), 7. Other than this remark, there is no evidence for the existence of these letters.

43. "The Church against No-Church," *BrQR,* April 1845, pp. 137–93.

44. *Essays and Reviews, Chiefly on Theology, Politics and Socialism* (New York: D. & J. Sadlier 1852; reprint ed. New York: Arno Press, 1972).

45. John Baptist Purcell (1800–1883), Irish-born, graduate of the Seminary of St. Sulpice, Paris, second bishop of Cincinnati 1833, its first archbishop 1850.

46. For Hecker's theology see Joseph F. Gower, "The 'New Apologetics' of Isaac Thomas Hecker (1819–1888): Catholicity and American Culture" (Ph.D. diss., University of Notre Dame, 1978).

47. *Questions of the Soul* (New York: D. Appleton & Co., 1855; reprint ed. with Introduction by Joseph F. Gower, New York: Arno Press, 1978).

48. See Richard M. Leliaert, O.S.C., "Orestes A. Brownson (1803–1876): Theological Perspectives on his Search for the Meaning of God, Christology, and the Development of Doctrine" (Ph.D. diss., Graduate Theological Union, 1974).

49. *BrQR,* December 1856, pp. 409–43.

50. Information about these missions can be gathered from "Chronicle of the English Missions given by the Redemptorist Fathers in the United States of North America, April 6, 1851 to March 28, 1858," Redemptorist Archives of the Baltimore Province, Brooklyn, N.Y. And also "Chronicle of the Missions given by the Congregation of Missionary Priests of St. Paul the Apostle, commenced April 18, 1858" (APF).

51. Louis Bancel Binsse (d. 1885), New York businessman and Catholic spokesman, consul general for the Papal States to the U.S. 1850–70, president of the Catholic Union 1884.

52. Pope Pius IX (Giovanni Maria Mastai Ferretti) (1792–1878), Italian churchman, archbishop of Imola 1832–46, named cardinal 1840, elected pope 1846.

53. See Joseph F. Gower, "Democracy as a Theological Problem in Isaac Hecker's Apologetics," in Thomas M. McFadden, ed., *America in Theological Perspective* (New York: Seabury Press, 1976), pp. 37–55.

54. "Aspirations of Nature," *BrQR,* October 1857, pp. 459–503.

55. Thomas Louis Connolly (1815–1876), Irish-born, Roman-trained bishop of St. John's, New Brunswick, 1852; archbishop of Halifax, Nova Scotia, 1859.

56. *Sermons Preached at the Church of St. Paul the Apostle, New York, During the year 1863* (New York: D. & J. Sadlier, 1864; reprint ed. with Introduction by Joseph F. Gower, New York: Arno Press, 1978), pp. 58–70.

57. *BrQR,* October 1860, pp. 462–96.

58. Hecker's letter to Sarah Brownson of 19 January 1865 is placed with his letters to Brownson in the microfilm edition, roll six; it is a brief note about the publication of her novel *At Anchor.*

59. John Charles Frémont (1813–1890), military and political leader, Republican candidate for president 1856, nominated by radical Republicans against Lincoln but withdrew in September 1864.

60. *The American Republic* (New York: P. O'Shea, 1866; reprint eds. Clifton, N.J.: Augustus M. Kelley, 1972, and New Haven, Conn.: College and University Press, 1972).

61. Agnes Repplier (1855–1950), essayist and biographer; John Talbot Smith (1855–1923), priest of New York, author and historian; William Seton (1835–1905), novelist and scientist, a grandson of Elizabeth Ann Bayley Seton (1774–1821) who was canonized a saint in 1975.

62. For a partial estimate of Hecker's role at the Vatican Council see Josef L. Altholtz, Damien McElrath, and James C. Holland, eds., *The Correspondence of Lord Acton and Richard Simpson,* III (Cambridge: at the University Press, 1975), 281–88, 291.

63. James Andrew Corcoran (1820–1889), graduate of the Propaganda College, author and seminary professor, founding editor of *The American Catholic Quarterly Review* 1876.

64. Brownson to Henry F. Brownson, 25 March 1871 (UNDA).

65. Bernard Michael McQuaid (1823–1909), president of Seton Hall College and Seminary 1856, first bishop of Rochester, N.Y., 1868, author and advocate of Catholic education.

66. See Joseph F. Gower, "A 'Test-Question' for Religious Liberty: Isaac Hecker on Education," *Notre Dame Journal of Education,* 7 (Spring 1976), 28–43; and also James M. McDonnell, "Orestes A. Brownson: Catholic Schools, Public Schools and Education—A Centennial Reappraisal," ibid. (Summer 1976), pp. 101–22.

67. Contemplated as early as 1868, the Catholic Union of New York was formally instituted in May 1871. The plan was to organize nationally with branches or "circles" in every diocese. In addition to calling for the establishment of a daily Catholic newspaper and the convocation of a congress, it supported the founding of a national Catholic university and sponsored various lectures and religious celebrations. The New York Circle of the Catholic Union opposed proselytizing in public institutions and fought for legislation providing freedom of worship for inmates in state-run asylums, hospitals, and prisons. It seems that this circle was active for years before merging with the Catholic Club of the City of New York (1888), formerly the Xavier [College] Union.

68. Richard Henry Clarke, Jr. (1827–1911), New York lawyer, Catholic leader and author.

69. Michael Augustine Corrigan (1839–1902), Roman educated, president of Seton Hall College 1868, bishop of Newark 1873, coadjutor bishop of New York 1881, then third archbishop 1886.

70. See Richard M. Leliaert, "Brownson's Approach to God: The Catholic Period," *The Thomist,* XL (October 1976), 571–607; also see Thomas T. McAvoy, "Brownson's Ontologism," *The Catholic Historical Review,* XXVIII (October 1942), 376–81.

71. "Papal Infallibility and Civil Allegiance," *BrQR,* January 1875, pp. 105–21.

72. John MacCarthy to Brownson, 15 January 1876 (BP, UNDA).

73. Hecker to Henry F. Brownson, 17 April 1876 (UNDA).

74. "Dr. Brownson," *CW*, XXIII (June 1876), 366–77.

75. *The Church and the Age. An Exposition of the Catholic Church in View of the Needs and Aspirations of the Present Age* (New York: Catholic Publication Society, 1887).

76. "Dr. Brownson and Catholicity," *CW*, XLVI (November 1887), 234. For the other articles, see *CW*, XLV (April 1887), 1–7; (May 1887), 200–8; (July 1887), 466–72; and XLVI (October 1887), 1–11.

77. Pope Leo XIII (Gioacchino Vincenzo Pecci) (1810–1903), Italian churchman, archbishop of Perugia 1846–78, named cardinal 1853, elected pope 1878.

78. McSorley, *FH&F*, p. 289, n. 1.

The Correspondence

PART ONE

1841–1846

The opening letters of the correspondence span the period from the early acquaintance of Orestes A. Brownson and Isaac Hecker to their first two years as Catholic converts. When they met in New York City, both men were involved with questions of social reform and political action; consequently, the items in this section abound with references to contemporary events, figures, and movements.

Since Brownson was sixteen years Hecker's senior, the prominent Boston publicist exercised much formative influence over the young Manhattan baker. In tracing the direction he gave to Hecker's intellectual and religious development, these letters vividly disclose how they each interacted with the Transcendental Movement in New England. As Hecker was seeking peace of mind by taking up residence at the utopian communes of Brook Farm and Fruitlands, Brownson was forging an independent philosophical position under the sway of Pierre Leroux's doctrine of communion.

Their shared personal struggles and common interests led them to a deepening concern for religious matters. Brownson's spiritual journey was one of disciplined inquiry and logic, whereas Hecker was driven by mystical longings and existential needs. Yet, together they were drawn to confront the question of church membership, having restricted their choice between the Anglican and Roman Churches. Then, dramatically, in the summer of 1844 they decided to embrace Roman Catholicism. Thereafter Brownson determined to serve the immigrant Church by conducting his *Quarterly Review* as an instrument of Catholic defense, while Hecker committed himself to a religious vocation with the Redemptorist order.

1

HECKER TO BROWNSON • 14 NOVEMBER 1841*

New York November 14, 1841

Mr Brownson

We were much pleased to receive a note from you through your Radical Friend Mr Partridge,[1] we would be gratified to receive a letter from you at any time, we have felt often like writing to you before this, the only excuse we have is our bussiness [*sic*] not calling us to correspond with any one makes it a task for us to write, we are often compelled to do it out of duty to our friends and if oftener it would be greatley [*sic*] to our advantage.

We have done but little in furthering the object we spoke of last summer, that is to get you to come here and deliver a Course of Lectures, we had an interview with the President[2] of the N.Y. Lyceum[3] at the time they were making arrangments [*sic*] for their lectures. He said the peculiar opinions held by yourself are so unpopuler [*sic*] that they would be an injury to the course in a pecuniary point of view, it was in that view they invited every man that was to lecture before the Society. We have since then spoken to some of our friends about it[;] they seem all anxious that you should come but it appears it is left without any concerted action.

The friends of Reform as we look at it are poor and few in number at present in NY, we do not expect much from them. It is the Subject you may select for your lectures that will call an audience; we have no faith in the lecture going people of N.Y. except upon some peculiar subject or occasion[.]

We will be able to get a Hall and give publicity to any subject which you have or may select[.] The time for the lectures[4] we think would be best after the Holidays[.]

Whatever you make up your mind to do–we are always ready to co-operate with hearty cheer so long as it makes a stir[,] a shaking amongst the People. In fact if we would think of any other than the ordinary course to persue [*sic*] so as to excite enthusiasm we would do it with all our might[.] We hate the beaten track.

We send you a copy of Dr Dewey's[5] two last sermons[6] which we had the pleasure of hearing prior to his departure to Europe.[7]

Dr Rev Dewey we suppose is gone to meet the german Saviour so as to preach the Gospel of design at Boston to those German transcendentel [*sic*] mystics. Look out now you metaphysicians get your Cognition faculty in order so as to envisage him a Priori a Posteriori by intuition subjectively in your understandings[.]

From Your Friends

Hecker & Br[o] th[er][8] 56 Rutgers St.

*Holden, *EY,* pp. 48–49.

1. Possibly a Mr. Parsons of Buffalo, N.Y., is meant since he brought Brownson messages from others; see Letter 2, n. 3.

2. Isaac Townsend Smith (1812–1906), a New York City merchant.

3. The New York Lyceum was instituted in 1838, incorporated 1840, for the moral and intellectual growth of young men.

4. Four lectures on "Civilization and Human Progress" were delivered by Brownson at Clinton Hall in New York City on 17, 19, 25 January and 2 February 1842.

5. Orville Dewey (1794–1882), Unitarian preacher and author, pastor of the Second Congregational Church (later the Church of the Messiah) in New York City 1835–48.

6. Either two sermons from Dewey's *Discourses on Human Life* (New York, 1841) published before his departure for Europe or his sermon "On the Uses of the Communion, and the Propriety of a General Attendance Upon It," published at Boston in November 1841.

7. Dewey sailed for Le Havre, France, on 8 October 1841 and returned from Europe in August 1843.

8. This is the only letter signed with the trade name the Heckers used in business. Holden (*EY,* pp. 49–50) renders this 'Hecker and Brothers' and judges Isaac to be the author. The editors believe the handwriting to be that of George Hecker, though it is uncertain whether 'Brth.' should be rendered as Hecker & Brother or Hecker & Brothers. Their firm was first Hecker & Brother and became Hecker & Brothers by 1843 (Holden, *YP,* p. 10). Since Isaac was probably involved in composing this letter in any case, the editors have included it in the main correspondence with that reservation.

2

BROWNSON TO HECKER • 28 NOVEMBER 1842

Chelsea Nov. 28, 1842.

My good Friends,

For such I trust you are even yet. I write to say to you that I shall be in New-York, Providence permitting on Tuesday morning the 6th of the coming

December. I propose to Lecture[1] at The Tabernacle on that evening, and am to Lecture at Brooklyn on Thursday evening following, and must leave Friday for home. Mr. M'Kenzie[2] has written me to lecture before the Mechanic's Institute.[3] I have put off answering him until this time, hoping I should be able to stay longer in the city, and could fix upon some more eligible time to lecture. But I can find no time but Wednesday evening, the 7th. If you see him or Mr. Eaton,[4] say that, if it is their wish, I will speak on that evening. If you should see Mr. Gordon,[5] connected with the Mercantile Library Association,[6] [tell him] that he may say to Mr. Van Cott[7] that I shall choose for my subject in Brooklyn, "The Law of the Progress of Humanity."[8]

You have been so kind to me, and one good turn always deserving another, that I shall do myself the pleasure, and impose upon you the burden of making my home with you while I stay, not withstanding one or two requests from some other friends in the city to stop with them. It would [not] be New-York, if I stopped any where else. I shall come by way of Norwich [Conn.].

Yours very truly

O. A. Brownson

1. A lecture on "Government, its origin, organization, and end."

2. William Lyon Mackenzie (1795–1861), Canadian newspaper editor and politician, played a leading role in Canadian uprisings against Great Britain 1837–38.

3. An institute incorporated in 1833 to establish lecture series, schools, and a library-museum for New York's mechanical workers. A letter from Mackenzie to Brownson, dated 8 November 1842, mentioned a "Mr. Parsons of Buffalo" as the bearer of the invitation to lecture before the Institute (BP, UNDA).

4. Perhaps Brownson meant a "Mr. Ewbank" mentioned in Mackenzie's letter (see n. 3 above).

5. Cuthbert G. Gordon, corresponding secretary of the Mercantile Library Association, who wrote Brownson on 30 November 1842 BP, UNDA).

6. An Association organized in 1821 for the moral and intellectual benefit of the mercantile community; its library numbered 24,000 volumes by 1842.

7. Joshua M. Van Cott, prominent Brooklyn citizen who served on the lecture committee of the Hamilton Literary Association; he was expecting Brownson to repeat his December 6 lecture on "Government . . . " in Brooklyn (see n. 1 above).

8. Delivered before the Hamilton Literary Association of Brooklyn on 8 December 1842.

3

HECKER TO BROWNSON • 19 DECEMBER 1842

New York Dec 19, 1842

Friend Brownson

When I made you the promise of visiting you there was nothing that I then perceived would prevent me from fullfilling [*sic*] it. But the Sunday following I called to see Dr Channing[1] and as I was quite unwell he proposed to me to call on Dr Buchannan[2] because he or Mr Inman[,][3] a person who is with him[,] pretends to have the power to discover any disease of the system or any tendency the mind may have to excessive excitement of perticuler [*sic*] organs. I accepted the offer and Channing was to call on Buchanning [*sic*] to see what time we could meet, it so happened that Channing was not able to see him until last Saturday and the time was fixed for this morning[,] Monday. I called to see Channing this morning and found him unwell he could not go this morning but promises to go [to]morrow. You have my excuse here length and breadth for not fullfilling [*sic*] my promise. That I regret to make this excuse no one more than yourself knows. It was my ernest [*sic*] wish to be in Boston within last week as you perhaps anticipated but it has not so happened.

My faith in this intended experiment is very little yet I feel it my duty that if there is any medicinal remedy I ought to try it because living out a complaint[,] if I may say so[,] is not only a very slow process but at the same time wretched and rather unpleasant living. I do not suppose the meeting with Buchannan will prevent me making the visit this week. The health of our Family is the same as when you left.

That [which] we wish most to utter and it is to[o] often the better part of our natures we leave untouched by our timidity and mistrust I am led to say in closing this letter.

My good wishes for thee and all thine.

Freundt [*sic*]

Isaac

1. William Henry Channing (1810–1884), nephew of Dr. William Ellery Channing; Unitarian clergyman 1838–41, newspaper editor and social reformer, founder of the New York Christian Union in 1843 as a "free religious society".

2. Possibly Joseph Rodes Buchanan (1814–1899), psychometrist, author, and physician.

3. Possibly Henry Inman (1801–1845), a New York artist and portrait painter, a friend of Orville Dewey's (see Letter 1, n. 5).

4

HECKER TO BROWNSON • [23 JUNE 1843]*

[*Undated*] [1]
Friday half past 3 o'clock

Dear Friend

I have returned this afternoon from Alcott's[2] and am as much pleased with the people and spirit there as I anticipated. I met a Mr Bower[3] on visit there and in returning he gave me the "Reasons"[4] which you will find with this, after I had read them I remarked that you had put forth similar views. He wished me for to let you see them which I promised, would you please to preserve them until I see you again.

I do not know but that my mind will lead me to make at least a trial at Fruitland as they call their place. Mr Alcott[5] seemed very desirous that I should come and perhaps may. I made a visit to the Shakers[6] while there and a lesson of Self-denial I did receive from them. I had an intimate and interesting conversation with them.

I go to Brook Farm[7] this afternoon.

Your Son

Isaac Hecker

*Brownson, *BEL,* p. 504 (no date given). Microfilm, roll two (calendared [1843]).

1. The date of 23 June 1843 is given on the basis of a letter written by Hecker to his family dated 24 June 1843 wherein he stated: "I have returned last evening from my visit" to Alcott's Fruitlands (HP, APF).

2. Fruitlands, Transcendentalist ascetical community, near the village of Harvard, Mass., established by A. Bronson Alcott and Charles Lane in June of 1843.

3. Samuel Bower of Andover, Mass., a member of the Fruitlands community recently returned from England.

4. Possibly the *Maxims* (London, 1826) or another of the spiritual-pedagogical writings of James Pierrepont Greaves (1777–1842), English Transcendentalist and educational reformer. Greaves's library was brought to Fruitlands

by Charles Lane, his chief disciple, who edited *The Golden Sayings of Mr. Greaves* (1844?).

5. Amos Bronson Alcott (1799–1888), prominent Transcendentalist philosopher and educator; founded the Temple School in Boston, 1834.

6. The Shaker Village consisted of a small group of Shaking Quakers inspired by "Mother" Ann Lee Stanley (1736–1784), English-born millennialist prophetess; in 1787 her disciple Rev. Joseph Meacham (1742–1796) organized the United Society of Believers in Christ's Second Appearing, near the village of Harvard, Mass.

7. The Brook Farm Institute of Agriculture and Education, an experimental Transcendentalist commune in social reform and education founded by George Ripley in 1841 at West Roxbury, Mass.

5

HECKER TO BROWNSON • 30 AUGUST 1843*

New York Aug 30, '43

Dear Friend

My brother[1] having addressed to you a letter[2] as regards you[r] writing an address for the mass meeting that is to be held in the Park[,][3] under the impression I believe that it was to be held at a later date than is the fact. He with many others thought that the convention of the Delegates at Syracuse[4] was to be held on the 15teenth and instead of the 15teenth it is to be on the 5th and for the purpose of influencing this convention and to show to the Country the great number of Mr Calhoun's[5] friends[,] they have resolved to hold the meeting in the Park on the 4th[,] a day previous to the Syracuse Convention. Is it possible that you can send the address here in time for the meeting which will be Monday afternoon 6 o'clock? For it is a matter of great importence [*sic*] as you are fully aware that this being the first demonstration of this Character that it should be one which will tell the country through[,] as we have all reason to hope it will[,] in numbers as doubtless it will by the character of the address which will come from your able and powerfully impressive pen.

Where there has been a reballoting on account of the irregularity of procedure or a tie Mr Calhoun's has on the whole come of[f] conqueror! It adds much[,] very much[,] to give one confidence in the strength of his friends to be aware that this was all done without *any* preconcerted action on their part–it was spontaneous–while on the other hand all the party machinery and caucusing were in the hands of Vanburen's[6] friends who are not remarkabel [*sic*] for their tender consciences in party tactics.

Not expecting John home before next Saturday[,] he being now in the country[,] and not knowing precisely how or what he wrote to you[,] you will be able with this remark to account of my addressing you on this subject in his stead and what ever misapprehension I may have fallen under as regards the contents of his letter.

Will you be so kind as to inform us immediately whether you will have the address on here in time? For I suppose they will have to make other preparation in its stead if it does not come in time. Can you let us know by the first returning mail?

Remember me to your Wife[7] and to your Son Orestes[8] and Family.

Yours with deep Respect and Love

Isaac.

P.S. Will you give the enclosed to Mr Green[9] to send on its value in your addresses when published? I wish them for to distribute and to be read by your friends.

I[saac]

*Brownson, *BEL*, pp. 335–36.

1. John Hecker (1812–1874), prominent Episcopalian businessman and philanthropist, political activist and politician; a devotee of education and author of *The Scientific Basis of Education* (New York, 1866).

2. Dated 20 August 1843; see Appendix: Letter 2.

3. The City Hall Park in New York City.

4. The New York Democrats conducted a state convention at Syracuse to elect delegates for the upcoming Democratic National Convention to be held in Baltimore (May 1844).

5. John Caldwell Calhoun (1782–1850) of South Carolina; became congressman 1811, U.S. vice-president 1824, U.S. senator 1832; sought the presidency in 1821 and again in 1843–44.

6. Martin Van Buren (1782–1862), Democrat, eighth U.S. president 1836–40, resought the Democratic presidential nomination for 1844.

7. Sally Healy Brownson (1804–1872) of Elbridge, N.Y.; married Brownson on 19 June 1827.

8. Orestes Augustus Brownson (1828–1892), Brownson's oldest son, Catholic convert 1845; eventually a schoolteacher, author, and editor of a chess magazine.

9. Benjamin H. Greene, Boston bookseller and publisher of Brownson's *Boston Quarterly Review* 1838–42.

6

BROWNSON TO HECKER • 2 SEPTEMBER 1843

Boston Sept 2, 1843

Dear Friend,

I regret that it will not be in my power to furnish the Address. I did not get my article[1] off for the D[emocratic] R[eview][2] till yesterday afternoon, and I am worn out. It would have given me great pleasure to have furnished it, had it been in my power, but it is not.

I have concluded the Essays on Government.[3] I hope that you and your brothers will like them.

The Oration[4] is out, and I will see that yours are sent on Monday. I have taken great pains with it, and in a literary point of view, I think it as good as anything I have sent out.

Make my respects to Rev. Mr. Haight,[5] and thank him in my name for his pamphlet. Tell him, not to believe the report that I have gone, or am going over to the Roman Catholics. I stop before I get to Rome.

Remember me kindly to your [e]xcellent Mother,[6] and to your brother John's Wife,[7] as well as to your brothers John and George.[8] I hope to see you all the coming winter, but cannot promise myself certainly that pleasure.

Calhoun is gaining ground with us every day. I do not despair of him yet. Rouse up your folks, and have a meeting that will tell. Let the lamp be hung again.

Van, Van
  Is a used up man.[9]

I am [e]xpecting to go back to the Hospital,[10] though I have not yet received my appointment. I have not yet returned to preaching.[11]

I am glad that you are at home. I believe upon the whole you will find it better for you. These Communities after all are humbugs. We must rehabilitate the Church, and work under its direction. Brisbane[12] has been here lecturing, and has produced no sensation. Fourierism will not take with us, and Brisbane will not recommend it.

We are all well, and remember you with cordial affection.

Yours truly

O. A. Brownson

Isaac Hecker
New York.

1. "Origin and Ground of Government," *The Democratic Review,* XIII (October 1843), 353–77.

2. *The United States Magazine and Democratic Review,* popularly known as *The Democratic Review,* founded at New York in 1838 by John L. O'Sullivan to formulate Democratic opinion and taste in literature, the arts, and politics.

3. "Origin and Ground of Government," *The Democratic Review,* XIII (August 1843), 129–47; (September 1843), 241–62; and (October 1843), 353–77.

4. Most probably Brownson's Oration on "The Scholar's Mission," delivered at Dartmouth College on 26 July 1843.

5. Benjamin Isaac Haight (1807–1889), Episcopalian priest, rector of All Saints Church in New York, professor of pastoral theology at the General Theological Seminary 1841–55.

6. Susan Caroline Friend (1796–1876), married to John Hecker (senior) (1782–1860). Both were German-born.

7. Catherine Gorham, married to Hecker's brother John in 1838.

8. George Valentine Hecker (1818–1888), Hecker's older brother and closest friend, Catholic convert 1845; businessman and active lay Catholic, financial benefactor of many of Hecker's endeavors.

9. A campaign slogan directed against Martin Van Buren.

10. Through the political influence of the noted historian and Democrat George Bancroft, Brownson acquired the stewardship of the Chelsea Marine Hospital near Boston from 1838–41, but he lost this position when the Whigs assumed political power in 1841.

11. Brownson quit preaching in 1839 but resumed again from April 1842 through a good portion of 1843.

12. Albert Brisbane (1809–1890), leading Fourierist in America, lecturer and author, co-editor of the Fourierist journal *The Phalanx* 1843–45.

7

HECKER TO BROWNSON • 6 SEPTEMBER 1843*

New York Sept 6, '43[1]

Dear Friend

You will perceive by the paper sent with this letter that a committee of three were appointed by the Calhoun mass meeting in the Park[,] one of which was my brother John[,] to draft an address to the people of the U.S. to set forth the grounds of preference for John C Calhoun the Democratic candidate for the Presidency. This was done with the private understanding that you would with pleasure furnish such an address if circumstances would permit—the time set for it you will see by the proceedings is indefinite. Have we presumed to[o] much? If not please do let us know what time you will have this address ready.

This meeting that was held was in every respect all that his friends could have wished, in its numbers, respectability, and enthusiasm; and it is now the purpose of his friends to follow it up by a proper plan of organization.

Mr. Brady [,][2] one of our most talented speakers and one who has always struck me as destined to make an impress upon his country ['s] history [,] quoted your remarks[3] upon Mr Calhoun's rare study of the theory and principles of our government[4] as coming from one of the greatest men in our country.

I feel too often that I am not within two hours ride of your presence when my heart and head is full to overflowing but I feel an inexpressible gratitude and an unfathonable [*sic*] thank fullness for your kindness towards me and the great benefit of your influence–may my conduct be accordingly.

I whent [*sic*] to see Wm Channing on Sunday [;] he asked with great interest about you and your circumstances. He is still in the protestant epoch of sectarianism or Individualism. He is catholic in heart, protestant in head. If once he gets his head, heart, and hands, in unison, in harmony, what beauty–what music would come forth.

Dr Vethake[5] has called to see me twice since I have been home, and I have been to see him, he is very poor, his sensibility is very delicate, and is a profound Swedenborgean.[6] This latter is my interpretation of his present crisis for so I consider it for his organization being now so extremely sensitive he thinks [,] feels [,] hears and sees more than his constitution will permit. He is one who I commune with deeper, and more, than any one I have met with since my return. The Dr is much altered. I have seen Edward Palmer[7] 3 or 4 times. His formula is to act in society and this best you can. He has ceased to act against it. I love him very much.

The Family remember you with lively affection.

Remember me to your kind Wife.

Yours Sincerely

Isaac

PS Will you please answer this as soon as convenient. My health is good. My diet is unleavened bread and fruits.

Your addresses[8] I have just rec'd. I have glanced through one what will the Tammany Democracy say? What of Sullivan's Note?[9] Reviving of the B[oston] Q[uarterly] R[eview].[10] I hope so. So did Wm Channing.

*Brownson, *BEL*, pp. 336–38.

1. On the envelope of this letter, Brownson is addressed for the first time as Rev. O. A. Brownson, Chelsea, Mass.

2. Possibly James Topham Brady (1815–1869), New York lawyer and politician.

3. "Constitutional Government," *BosQR*, V (January 1842), 27–59; "Popular Government," *The Democratic Review*, XII (May 1843), 535–36.

4. *Speeches of John C. Calhoun, delivered in the Congress of the United States, from 1811 to the present time* (New York, 1843).

5. John W. Vethake, M.D., New York (Brooklyn) physician and author.

6. Emanuel Swedenborg (1688–1772), Swedish physical scientist, turned spiritualist theologian and biblical commentator.

7. Edward Palmer, radical Transcendentalist from New Jersey, a member of the Newness Group, published a pamphlet (1840) advocating total rejection of money and private property.

8. The Essays on Government (see Letter 6, n. 3), very critical of the popular understanding of democracy as majority rule or popular sovereignty.

9. John Louis O'Sullivan (1813–1895), editor of *The Democratic Review* 1841–46, wherein he wrote a Note critical of Brownson's Essays on Government; see *The Democratic Review*, XIII (September 1843), 262.

10. Brownson had terminated his *Boston Quarterly Review* in 1842 to merge with and to write monthly for O'Sullivan's *Democratic Review.*

8

BROWNSON TO HECKER • 11 SEPTEMBER 1843

Boston Sept 11, 1843

Dear Isaac,

Say to your brother, that I will send on the draft of an Address in the course of 8 or 10 days. The Van Buren folks are cutting their own throats. We shall make a move here responsive to yours in a few days. Mr. C[alhoun]'s friends must bestir themselves. Say to our friends in New-York, not to be discouraged. We will beat the little magician yet, and seat the Statesman in the presidential chair. The Spectator[1] at Washington will be a daily paper soon.

In going for Mr. C. have it understood that we go for the one term principle. Mr. C. himself consents to this. Who drew up your resolutions? They are able, though perhaps a little too heavy, for popular effect, yet I am delighted with them. They take the right ground.

My own movements are yet undetermined. We are all well. My respects and remembrances to all the family. God bless you all.

Yours truly

O. A. Brownson.

1. *The Spectator*, a weekly paper designated by the Calhoun Central Committee in Washington, D.C., as his official campaign organ in early 1843; it became a daily on 28 November 1843.

9

HECKER TO BROWNSON • 14 SEPTEMBER 1843*

New York Sept 14. '43

Dear Friend

The friends of J. C. Calhoun intend to start a paper[1] in this city for Mr. C. as a candidate for the presidency, and are now making arrangements for such a purpose. They have the assurance of $5,000 to commence it with, and are now desirous of securing an able editor. You having expressed a willingness to occupy such a place, some time ago, we thought perhaps you might be willing to accept the present opportunity, which is now offered to you by those who have this matter in hand.

If you are willing to accept this offer what conditions are necessary to your acceptance of it? If you are willing to accept it with certain necessary conditions such conditions of acceptance we will present to them and let you know the result as soon as possible. If they cannot fully comply we will inform you what they can do.

Would it not be more commanding and better suited to your tasks if you should receive the Hospital appointment to start the B[oston] Q[uarterly] R[eview]? Much as I would desire your coming on here, still I would regret much more the loss of your pen in that higher sphere which the Review would be the channel of, and the newspaper not. Still this may present advantages to you that I am not aware of. The paper I believe would take and the men are responsible men.

There will be a mass meeting of all the Districts on which occasion it is their intention to present the address from your pen.[2]

Alcott and Lane[3] have been here 5 days; they started for home yesterday morning. They occupied their time in visiting different individuals and holding conversations. They held three while they were here, one at Wm Channing's place and there was present Channing, Margaret Fuller,[4] Vethake, and Alcott, and Lane. How they took, I know not, for if they are the "newness" to a Boston transcendental audience what must they be to a New York one? They made our place their home while they were here.

I have read your address and I feel it is precisely what we want—what we ought to have had before and what we should practice now. All that have read it, like it, and I intend to leave one for Park Godwin[5] who inquired of me particularly what you are doing &c.

We are all well.

My Mother[,] Sister[6] and Br[o]th[e]rs wish me to remember them to you while I remain Yours

Truly in deep affection

Isaac

P.S. Wm Channing's paper the Present[7] will be out in a few days. It will be monthly.

*Brownson, *BEL*, pp. 340–41.

1. The *New York Gazette*, which first appeared after mid-November 1843 under the direction of Thomas P. Kettel.

2. This address was not written; see Letter 10.

3. Charles Lane (1800–1870), English periodical editor, social reformer, co-founder with Alcott of the Fruitlands project.

4. Margaret Fuller (1810–1850), Transcendentalist, editor of *The Dial*, contributor to the *New York Tribune* 1844–46.

5. Parke Godwin (1816–1904), author and founder of the socialist journal *The Pathfinder* in 1843, leading Fourierist and editor of *The Harbinger* (of Brook Farm's Fourierist phase 1844–47), associated with the *New York Evening Post* 1836–81.

6. Elizabeth Hecker (1816–1845), married to Henry Rose, died on 1 August 1845 shortly after Hecker left for Europe.

7. *The Present*, published at New York from September 1843 through April 1844; attempted to foster Christian unity and social reform through Fourierism.

10

BROWNSON TO HECKER • 18 SEPTEMBER 1843*

Chelsea Sept. 18, 1843

Dear Isaac,

The Address I have not prepared. I went as a delegate to Worcester [Mass.] last Tuesday, and did not get home till Thursday. And when I returned I found the committee had sent forth [an] address, the one sent them I presume by Mr. Maxcy.[1] So I concluded not to prepare one. Moreover I have been sick all the week, and in my present state of suspense, am utterly incapable of any intellectual effort. With regard to the Editorship, I need not say that it would please me, for I should delight in being at the head of a daily paper in your city, devoted to the support of Mr. Calhoun. So much I can say. As to terms, the persons who have the management of the business, must decide themselves what they will do, and make me an offer on such terms as seem to them good; if the terms meet my wishes I will accept; if not, I shall say so at once. I of course can state no conditions; they must come from the party soliciting my services. Let them state,

1. What they will [e]xpect me to do,
2. What compensation they will assure me.

One condition only I mention, namely, that [I] will have nothing to do with the pecuniary affairs of a paper; my business shall be solely editorial, with no responsibility but editorial responsibility.

Remember me to all the family.

Yours truly

O. A. Brownson.

*Holden, *EY*, p. 183 (with omissions); Ryan, *OAB*, pp. 225–26 (with omissions).

1. Virgil Maxcy (1785–1844), Maryland lawyer and politician, correspondent with and supporter of Calhoun, became American chargé d' affaires in Belgium 1831.

11

BROWNSON TO HECKER • 3 OCTOBER 1843

Chelsea Oct 3, 1843.

Dear Isaac,

I have been [e]xpecting to hear before this from our Calhoun friends in the city of New-York. But I pray you to stop all proceedings on my behalf, if any are making. I have altered my plans, and do not wish to become the Editor of the paper. I fear that I should not be the choice of all concerned, and, moreover, I wish to resume the Quarterly.[1]

I am preparing the first number of the new series, which I intend to have out by the first of the year. This I know will be good news to you. I am only waiting to hear from O'Sullivan,[2] in order to begin to print. I shall come out boldly for the Church on the principles you and I have so often discussed, and independent of, but not in opposition to, existing organizations. I shall throw myself on Providence, and labor for the new organism, and seek to rally all the forces I can around the great central Idea of fraternity & Christian Communion.

Also I wish to ask you and your brothers, what prospect there is of succeeding in the course of Lectures in your city the coming winter, so [=say] of three or four? I am straining myself on the Review and Lecturing for support, and am resolved to commence propagandist. I must stay at home & write, go abroad and make proselytes, & get subscribers. As I intend lecturing the coming winter in Philadelphia & Baltimore, I should like to give a short course in your city on the dangers and wants of the Times, in relation to both Church and State.[3]

Remember me affectionately to all the family and believe me,

very truly & sincerely yours

O. A. Brownson.

P.S. We are all well. Orestes goes to sea, about the middle of this month. I have got him a good voyage to Calcutta, with a captain[4] who I think is a worthy man.

1. The *BosQR* was resumed as *Brownson's Quarterly Review* in January 1844; in all it comprised twenty-four volumes and ran from 1844 to 1864, then from 1873 to 1875.

Since *BrQR* changed series and volume numbers so often, we have chosen to omit volume numbers, giving the month and year, followed by the original pagination of the articles in *BrQR*.

2. O'Sullivan terminated Brownson's relationship with *The Democratic Review* in a letter dated 9 October 1843 (BP, UNDA).

3. Brownson did not give his proposed lectures in New York City; see Letters 15 and 17.

4. A certain Captain Austin of the *Dover*.

12

HECKER TO BROWNSON • 16 OCTOBER 1843*

N.Y. Oct 16. '43

Dear Friend

Your letter came just in time to prevent me from writing at that time the case as it then stood, which was not very hopeful, not having collected all the means that were expected, and they now have finally agreed to start the paper without an exclusive editor, but under the supervision of one of the many contributors, that one is now McCracken[1] who wrote the address.

The materials for publication have been provided, and it is expected to be out next week.

It is not in my power to express to you the very great pleasure it gave me to hear from you that the Review is to be recommenced with that purpose you mentioned. I regret that I had grown somewhat lukewarm, superficially so, to the importance of the religious revolution which is now in the process of growing. It was my apparent silence on the Church, affected perhaps, by the influence of the society in which I have moved. Still it was necessary to have this susceptibility of their influence to be able to understand, and appreciate, their movement, and spirit, not having a priori perceived any vital sin in the men or measures; for susceptibility may lead to vice as well as virtue, in binding myself to it I have gained in the period I was from N.Y. a very fruitful experience. Underlying, and of infinite more importance, seems to me the Church movement than these personal, social, and political reforms, it being the soul centre of all life, and reform, and as men and women become conscious of their own deep wants, and those of Humanity, so will they labor in and out of season for the realization of that Catholic Church foreshadowed in the past, lost sight of by Luther, and his coadjutors in his movement, reseen in our day by the inspired men active in a counter movement, tho much more than merely a counter movement. If you arrange matters as you desire and start the Review it will give me much, as well as my brothers [,] pleasure to aid in any way in our power.

Should you not have the opportunity offered to you which you would prefer to a course of lectures delivered without any other connection, we will consider it a labour of love to arrange matters to suit your other engagements, and the public. There is no room to doubt that the announcement of your name would collect a very large audience and especially with the subjects you propose. Let us know in time when you would desire to stop here and deliver your lectures, in season, if necessary for us to prepare for them. I have understood, not being there, that last sabbath morning Wm Channing in speaking of your three last published articles[2] on Government which he pronounced as calculated to excite a very great interest, he took occasion to speak of you as a man, which he did in the very highest terms, and with great warmth, and eloquence. I regret much that I was not there. Greeley[3] has noticed your address[4] and promised a renotice of it. Godwin and others I have supplied with it. Mackenzie has started a newspaper in opposition to the renomination of Martin [Van Buren], perhaps he has sent you a copy, if not I will see that it is done.

Orestes is then going, may it be a trial which will increase his strength and virtue.

Remember me to your Wife who I am sensible of deep indebtedness to, for her goodness.

Believe me to be

Yours truly And ever gratefull [*sic*].

Isaac

Our mill[5] is quite prosperous.

*Brownson, *BEL*, pp. 504–6 (with omissions).

1. J. L. H. McCracken of New York, a Calhoun supporter nominated for the presidency (after Calhoun's withdrawal) by New York Democrates of the Sixth Congressional District on 8 February 1844.

2. See Letter 6, n. 3.

3. Horace Greeley (1811–1872), Fourierist, journalist and lecturer, founder and editor of the *New York Tribune* 1841.

4. Brownson's address on "The Scholar's Mission" was noticed with a promise of further treatment in the *New York Tribune*, 10 October 1843, p. 2; his address was not renoticed but defended from an attack in the *Tribune*, 13 October 1843, p. 2.

5. The Croton Flour Mill, owned and operated by George and John Hecker.

13

BROWNSON TO HECKER • 8 NOVEMBER 1843

Chelsea Nov. 8, 1843

You will see, my dear Isaac, when you receive the first number of the Review,[1] that I have taken up, and answered, as well as I could, the very questions laboring in your mind. I wrote some two weeks since an article on the Church as an Agent of Reform,[2] which I am afraid I shall not have room for in the first number, in which I show beyond the possibility of cavil, that no work of reform can be carried on with any prospects of success, till we have recovered the unity and catholicity of the Church as an outward visible institution. In it I show that no theory, however true it may be, if born as pure theory, can ever embody itself in a practical institution. It must be born in union with its institution, as the child, if living, is born the union of soul & body. It is as impossible for men to embody spirit, as it is for them to animate a body in which the spirit is not.

You will see the proof of this in Platonism, which though substantially the same truth as the Christian, yet could do nothing, for it was a theory, a speculation. In Christianity we find the same truth, but in a body. Plato is a philosopher, Jesus an Institutor. Fourierism may be theoretically true, but it is a theory, a spirit without a body, and therefore remains, and will remain dead, unless taken up and quickened by the Church. Man can Institute nothing greater than himself; therefore, man can never, of himself, as mere man, found anything which will raise the age above what he himself really is. No *man* can be a reformer.

I look at Channing's movement[3] in New-York. His theory of Christian union is beautiful, nay true; but he will fail. For to succeed he must Institute a New Church, and to do that he must be a New Christ, and even greater than Christ. He starts outside of the Church, and says, "go to none[,] let us all be one Church." The principle of union, he says, is love, nothing more true. Therefore, if you love, you will all be one, nothing again more true. But, the precise difficult[y] is men do not love, and it is *because* they do not love that they are alienated, and divided. Now with no power but what these divided and alienated men already have, is love to be quickened in them? So far from seeking Christian love as the basis of the union of the Church, we must seek the unity of the Church as the condition of creating Christian love. These Unitarians are [e]xceedingly superstitious. They worship the means. They take it for granted always that the Church is the end, that you must be good in order to come into the Church, instead of coming into the Church as the condition of being good. They do not believe in the *Mediator.*

I hope you will find that you can associate yourself with Mr. Haight's congregation. I cannot myself go with any of the fragments. My mission and destiny is fixed; but I believe, in the present state of the Christian world, no denomination should be more acceptable to the soul yearning after union & catholicity, than the Episcopal. If I was in it I would not go out of it; but being as I am I cannot go into it. But you young men, it seems to me, might find a home and a sphere of action in it. I say to all my friends who consult me on this question, join the Episcopal Church, if you can with a good conscience. The movement in that Church interests me much, and I am with it in spirit. Go as far towards accepting the Church, as your principles will let you. The time is not far distant when the union of all the fragments will be effected, and then it will not be asked to *which* fragment you were previously united.

The [flour] Barrels I presume are at the depot. I shall inquire to-morrow. In the meantime, accept my thanks for the kindness in remembering me, and for the valuable gift itself, which in my present condition is no trifling affair.

We are all well. My wife is quite smart again, with her little boy, Edward,[4] three weeks old Monday last. She always remembers you with affection.

I think I shall give the lectures. Say, four, in the early part of January. I intend to spend the whole of the month of January in lecturing in your city, Philadelphia and Baltimore. I am to be in Baltimore[5] the last Wednesday in December.

Remember [me] to your Mother, to your Brother John & his wife, and to George. I recall always with pleasure and gratitude the many delightful hours I have spent in your family.

Yours truly,

O. A. Brownson

1. *BrQR*, January 1844.
2. "No Church, No Reform," *BrQR*, April 1844, pp. 175–94.
3. William H. Channing's Christian Union was organized in April 1843 under the creed of Humanity, Wisdom, and Holiness; it viewed Jesus Christ as a Savior from sin and an annointed messenger from God, stressed the divinity of humankind over sectarian and individualistic concerns, and saw 'the true priesthood' as "the innumerable company of earnest, upright, loving souls."
4. Edward Patrick Brownson (1843–1864), Brownson's second youngest son, born 16 October; he died in a Civil War battle at Reams' Station, Va., as a young captain in the Union Army of the Potomac.
5. On 19 October 1843 Brownson received an invitation to lecture from the (Lord) Calvert Institute of Baltimore.

14

HECKER TO BROWNSON • 14 DECEMBER 1843*

Dec. 14, 43[1]

The necessity for a medium through which the spirit can act, that man as man can be no reformer, and that the Church is the only institution which has for its object the bettering of men's *souls* by giving to them a diviner love; (all other institutions make only the pretension of giving freedom for the activity of that which we are) are clear and important truths to me [;] to whom I am indebted for these truths it would be unnecessary for me to say to you.

The distinction, you draw between Plato and Christ is an important fact. But I will not say that Pathagoras [,] Socrates [,] Plato are to me as miraculous men as Jesus was but for my life it is impossible for me to keep him out from the same Category. I can no more account how the past could produce such men as they were than how it could produce Jesus, nevertheless the dogma of the miraculous birth [,] the incarnation I should be very lost to give up under my present state of mind. What rules the birth of men is and perhaps always will remain a mystery. I cannot see how the sinful children of Adam could give birth to such a divine being as Jesus Christ and I confess to a degree how they could give birth to many other great men called providential. I would not reason God out of the Universe [,] no [,] I feel He is ever present but I know of no solid argument which makes these facts plain [,] comprehensible; and I must most likely fall back upon authority leaving them to the domain of faith. The question has arisen in my mind dear friend about the immortality of Christ or in other words what relation does he bear to the present Church? where is he? are the Sacraments the medium through which He imparts his life to those who duly receive them? Or did he once for all give at the time he was upon the earth all that was to be given and that and no more is transmitted to this age through the Church and to us through the Sacraments? Or are they both combined? I shall have the pleasure soon I hope of seeing you in person when these and many other thoughts will be readily responded to.

I have read over your letter again and find that you are to be in Baltimore the last wednesday in December and that you prefer giving your lectures here in the forepart of January. This will [,] if you stop here before you go on to Baltimore which I suppose you will, give us the opportunity of preparing the proper arrangements for them while you are at Baltimore, if you think otherwise let us know, and we will arrange matters sooner. The two courses of lectures that are now being delivered [,] the Mercantile & Lyceum,[2] are the poorest that have ever been offered to the Public. The Mercantile commenced in the Tabernacle but had to go back into their room they were so poorly attended.

Therefore I think we may reasonably expect a good attendance at yours; altho the present rage appears to be for music still the taste for good lectures is not abated.

I hope you will be here over one Sunday so as to give the individuals who attend Channing's discourses an opportunity of hearing you. I mean you an opportunity of telling them some wholesome truths.

Did you read an article editorial in the Commercial[3] about a fortnight since on your late articles in the D[emocratic] Review?[4]

That you will kind friend give us the pleasure of receiving you when you visit this City if not [an] other place offers to you which you prefer we sincerely wish.

I shall always remember you with inexpressible gratitude and your kind wife. My past seems to me like a dream and so it is but a day dream. The deeper we drink of life the more mysterious it seems.

The Episcopal Church is well but I cannot join a Church which asks no more of me *practically* than what I am. I asked Height[5] his views of individual social and political [matters]. Alas that I had not asked the latter.

Yours Truly

Isaac

*Brownson, *BEL*, pp. 506–8.

1. Since this letter lacks a salutation, its opening paragraph(s) may be missing.

2. The *New York Daily Tribune*, 12 December 1843, advertised the "Fourth Lecture of the Course" being conducted by the Mercantile Library Association, "Selections of English Poetry, with Comments," to be delivered that evening by the Rev. S. H. Cox, D.D., at Clinton Hall.

The New York Lyceum lecture nearest the date of this letter was "Life and Times of Charles Ist, King of England," given on 15 December 1843 by Rev. Leonard Bacon, D.D.

3. An unsigned editorial entitled "O. A. Brownson & the Democracy" appeared in the *New York Commercial Advertiser*, XLVI (5 December 1843), 2.

4. Brownson's three Essays on Government; see Letter 6, n. 3.

5. Benjamin Isaac Haight, whose name Hecker spelled 'Height.'

15

HECKER TO BROWNSON • 21 JANUARY 1844*

Mon. Jan 21. '44 N.Y.

Dear Friend

We have anticipated your presence or a letter from you ever since the [*sic*] you spoke of coming on here and we could not imagine what could have delayed your coming except you were unwell or your family. Is it either of these or some other cause be so kind as to inform us when you have the leisure.

Horace Greely asked in the Tribune[1] of last Saturday if we were not to have O. A. Brownson on here to lecture before the season closes? Are we? Your views of progress of reform seem to have an effect upon all those who consider them. Wm Channing spoke of them in his discourse last Sunday morning in a way that it seemed to me as if they had had an influence upon him. If they only could be more widely dissemminated [*sic*]? The present views and movements for reform around us seem to me to be very defective and partial, so necessarily from the nature of their origin. Protestantism is reëxhibiting to the world as well as it knows how the need of the institutions and orders already existing in the Catholic Church. The different institutions in the Catholic Church are the organized wants of men under the Christian dispensation and it seems to me they will respond to the wants of the race so long as it is under the Christian dispensation. Doubtless the growth of the Race will require new orders &c. We do not find the demand for new institutions &c. in Catholic countries nor among Catholics, is this to be attributed to their want of vitality? Or our disorder? It some times seems to me that this constant demand for Reform has become a habit. If we would have divine Families[,] Associations and Communities let us go about making them in quietness in meekness as speedily as possible. Do like St Bernhard.[2] The attempt of Wm Penn[3] seems to me to have been as imposing as it promised success for the establishing a new order of society[,] alas and what is its fruits?! No man has a right to demand of Society more than he is himself. Those I have met who have read your Review have read it with great interest. Is it not necessary to many to understand the force and importance of your present arguments and views to have read your Essays on the Church in the Christian World?[4] How different is the view of Leroux[,][5] of Berkley[6] than the one published in Blackwood[7] in '41[,] two years ago if I am right! Is your Review as well supported as you expected?

The members of our family are all well.

Have you heard from Orestes?

Remember me to your kind Wife and believe me to be

Yours Truly with love and deep gratitude

Isaac

*Brownson, *BEL*, pp. 508–10.

1. The *New York Tribune* of 20 January 1844 stated: "Orestes A. Brownson ought also to be heard before the season closes. Shall he not be?" All

indications are that Brownson did not give his intended lectures in New York City; see Letters 11 and 13.

2. St. Bernard of Clairvaux (1090–1153), French Cistercian, ascetical writer, monastic reformer and theologian, a doctor of the Church.

3. William Penn (1644–1718), English Quaker, proprietor of the colony of Pennsylvania and founder of the city of Philadelphia.

4. A series of eight articles entitled "The Mission of Jesus," which appeared weekly in *The Christian World* from 7 January 1843 through 25 February 1843; see also the issues of 1, 8, 15 April 1843.

5. Pierre Leroux (1797–1871), French philosopher and democratic socialist, whose doctrine of communion Brownson adapted for his own purposes.

6. Bishop George Berkeley (1685–1753), British idealist philosopher.

7. (William) *Blackwood's Edinburgh Magazine;* see "The Crisis of Modern Speculation," ibid., L (October 1841), 527–36, and "Berkeley and Idealism," *BrQR*, January 1844, pp. 29–55.

16

HECKER TO BROWNSON • [9 MARCH 1844]*

[Undated][1]

Dear Friend

I feel and perceive the need of advice and counsel in the present event of my life, this being so leads me to you for, there is no one who I look up to with so much confidence and in whose judgment I put so much trust in as in yours.

When I left New England my supposition was that the opportunity was opened to me at home to do all that I saw men around me doing[,] therefore I left and came here to effect what seemed then to me probable and possible to effect there.

I have lived and labored up to the present moment to realize in life, in bussiness [*sic*] the spirit which animates me and tho having ameliorated some certain outward conditions I now perceive the impractibility of my going farther in this direction and am now at a stand still with an irresistible energy laid upon me to do, to live. A new step seems inevitable. Since I have seen the impossibility of doing more in the direction in which I supposed my life purpose might be accomplished[,] my interest has been gradually decreasing and my energy in that direction constantly failing and my attention has been drawn in another way. My sense of duty made me feel the responsibility of devoting an equal amount of energy with my brothers in the labor of our bussiness[,] to do this and to study for the intention of a different end at the same time was impossible. At present I find myself in this predicament with my body here and my soul and heart somewhere else. Almost useless to others and benefitting my self very little. The step I contemplate of taking is to devote my whole energies and time for the purpose of becoming a laborer in the cause of the Church. So far as I can interpret my purpose of being and my life reveals itself it seems to flow in that direction and I am now ready to embark *not with out I confess great timidity*, upon the tide which shall carry me to that end. The question with me now is what are the wisest and most prudent means for me to adopt? Two answers present themselves which I submit to your judgment. The first is to go through the necessary preparations to enter college and to enter one when prepared. To this answer I will submit to you a few objections which appear to have some weight with me.

I would have to devote myself for a great length of time *exclusively* to the accomplishment of the classical languages. This I would have no objection to if I were younger, but now I have. Again there are many books through which it is required for every student [to] wade, which in my circumstances to me it does not seem necessary. And other standard books tho good do not seem to me the *best.*

The second method and the best in my judgment is this to put myself under the direction of some well qualified person probably a clergyman who would direct and hear all my studies, and as to the classical languages they might be a part but not the necessary step before any others might be taken.

My object would be to put myself under the direction of a man whose capacities and learning should be such as to materially benefit me as a person.

This is the idea I have much of it of course will be modified and changed in a practical arrangement of this character.

So far as I have a positive end in view[,] I have laid it before your observation and with it the means which seem to me in my case the best to accomplish the aim in view.

Your counsel as a Friend, as a spiritual Parent to me, I with deep gratitude for what you have already done for me, with love and reverence for you as a man, I affectionately ask your wise counsel.

Be not backward in speaking to me: your frankest and plainest thoughts, whatever your sense of duty may lead you to say, be assured, will excite in me a greater love and deeper gratitude for your true kindness for me. You know my position. I have *brothers* but no Parent in this sense and to you dear friend I am led to look for one. Will you be one to me? I trust you will find me to pay respect and reverence for all your counsels and bear a love to you as a true son.

You need not hesitate in giving your opinions for my br[o]th[e]rs' sakes. They are willing, br[o]th[e]r John is interested, that what every course I feel called to adopt to help and encourage me onwards. I have spoken to them and opened my mind to them and as my intentions have become plainer they are satisfied and ready to aid if necessary my attempts. On this point all is harmony.

It is hard for one to make a true estimate of himself, he either under or over rates himself; now if you think I have not the capacity to be of use in this cause which I am about devoting myself to[,] be perfectly candid to me and tell me so in plain English. The self denial[,] the singleness of aim[,] the devotion of time to this one object and many more difficulties which will have to be encountered are not hid from my vision nor do they daunt my courage.

We each have our object in life and if we find ourselves mis-placed we must put ourselves in the right place if place is necessary to it.

Francis[2] tells me your Review goes well. Your article in the next on Kant[3] I expect a great treat from it. *Metaphysics* & Philosophy seem to be out of fashion. Channing is drawn farther & farther into the Fourier Movement. Without religion as the basis and that presupposes the Church [it] seems to me there is no hope for these movements. Our Family are all in good health. Bussiness with us is quite good.

I suppose you have heard Georgianna Bruce[4] is staying here with us on a visit. The Fourier movement of B[rook] F[arm] drove her away but I think she will find herself there again very soon.

Remember me to your Wife.

Truly yours,

Isaac

*Brownson, *BEL*, pp. 510–13.

1. This undated letter bears the postmark 9 March, New York; its subject matter places it within the year 1844.

2. Possibly Convers Francis (1795–1863), Unitarian pastor, charter member of the Symposium or Transcendental Club 1836, professor at the Harvard Divinity School 1842.

3. "History of Philosophy," *BrQR*, April 1844, pp. 137–74, reviewing the seventh edition of Kant's *Critique of Pure Reason* (1828).

4. Georgiana Bruce Kirby (b. 1818), English-born, member of the Brook Farm community, author of *Years of Experience* (New York, 1887).

17

BROWNSON TO HECKER • 11 MARCH 1844

Mt. Bellingham March 11, 1844

My dear Friend,

I thank you for the respect and confidence you show me, in asking my advice. I want before giving it, information on one point. Have you united with the Church, Episcop[al], or Catholic? If not, do you contemplate uniting? If so, with which?

My own feelings and convictions, in spite of my struggles to the contrary carry me to the Catholic Church, and I foresee plainly, that I must sooner or later become a member of it. There is no help for it. I seek however to maintain my present position for the present. You will infer from this that I cannot advice [*sic*] you to become a minister save as a member of the Church. It is idle to attempt a separate and independent movement.

If you have united with the Episcopal Church, or propose to do so, or with the Catholic Church, in either case, I say frankly, that I should rejoice to see you devoting yourself to the ministry. I believe it your vocation. I have believed so ever since I have known you, and on this point my own judgment is made up, and I have no hesitancy in saying, devote yourself heart and soul to the ministry.

I will say more. My convictions are everyday becoming stronger that nothing but the Church can save us, & it is only through it that we can work effectually for our age and country. I grow every day more and more of a Church man. If you were here, I could tell you much, and convince you of the paramount importance of the Church, and that all movements attempted without it or in opposition to it, though from the best of motives end in disaster and disgrace. We must have our standpoint outside of the world, in God, if we would move the world. Come and see me, and we will talk this over. A journey here, and a visit will do you good.

With regard to your specific questions, I am not altogether of your opinion. I am myself forced now after forty to resume and perfect my classical studies. I am plunged head and ears in Greek. Great questions are coming up, and we must be thoroughly prepared. I however, would not recommend precisely a collegiate course. You should master the Greek and Latin; they are indispensable to you. The German and French you already have. Pursue in some school, or with a private tutor, the studies necessary to introduce you into a theological seminary, and then go through a regular course of theological studies. It will take time, but count no time spent in preparation lost. One year's labor after thorough preparation is worth a dozen before. I feel in my own case all the evils of having entered the ministry without thorough preparation. The proper age for entering upon the duties of the priesthood among the Jews was thirty, and in the Middle Ages no one could become a doctor in theology before thirty six. One of the most famous of the Doctors of the Middle Ages, Raymond Lully,[1] the Illuminated Doctor, was forty before he commenced his studies. You will get through with your preparatory studies by the time you are thirty or thirty two, which is surely enough, full young enough to enter upon the practical discharge of the responsible duties of a Christian minister.

I want you to become a Christian priest, but I want you should prepare yourself thoroughly for the work. You must discipline your zeal and energy to the work of preparation. You will find your advantage in it. I think, however, that you might so manage as to make four years amply sufficient for the studies preliminary to your theological course.

Still your own plan is the shortest, is not without its advantages, and would answer in your case no doubt very well. Perhaps, all things considered, it is the best for you, though I own I should prefer the other.

I had hoped to visit New-York, but I have been out of health nearly all winter, and have been obliged to work with all my might. I have scarcely had time to be civil to my friends, and this must be my apology for not having answered your several favors. Thank you for Bishop Hughes's[2] Lectures,[3] though I received copies of them direct from the Bishop himself. I esteem them very highly.

My Review has thus far done very well. I have obtained already nearly six hundred subscribers. The next number[4] will be out next week. I think you will like it better than the first. I have thrown all my strength and wisdom and honesty into it.

We are all well now, and, though poor neither discouraged nor discontented. My wife sends her kind remembrances. Remember me affectionately to all the family. I owe you all more obligations than I can ever discharge. But God bless you all. Let me see you, if not hear from you soon, and the blessing of God on your resolution.

Yours truly

O. A. Brownson

1. Raymond Lull (c. 1232–1316), Majorcan scholastic philosopher, mystic and ascetical writer, lay missionary to the Moslems.

2. John Joseph Hughes (1797–1864), Irish-born preacher, apologist, and leading Catholic churchman, became bishop coadjutor of New York 1838, bishop 1842, and first archbishop 1850.

3. "The Importance of a Christian Basis for the Science of Political Economy, and Its Application to the Affairs of Life" (17–18 January 1844), and "The Mixture of Civil and Ecclesiastical Power in the Middle Ages" (14 December 1843). Both lectures were published in 1844 and reviewed in *BrQR*, April 1844, pp. 278–80.

4. *BrQR*, April 1844.

18

HECKER TO BROWNSON • 15 MARCH 1844*

N. Y. March 15, '/44

My nearest Friend

Your letter came to hand last evening and I take the earliest opportunity this morning to answer it.

It is impossible for me to express how much encouragement, hope and firmness of purpose your letter gave to my convictions and to what extent your advice harmonizes & suits my wants.

First of all I will briefly relate to you what I have been doing since I wrote you last and this will at the same time answer the questions which you put to me concerning my union with the Church.

Some few months ago there was published in the N.Y. Churchman[1] a letter addressed to a Sincere Enquirer.[2] This letter met my warmest [,] deepest sympathies & seemed to accord with that philosophy of the Church which I have been taught by you. If I can get a copy of it I will send it with this letter. So the Author of this letter who I found to be through Rev B. F. Height, the Rev Wm A. Norris[3] of Carlisle, Penn—to him I have addressed a letter the purport of which I shall recite to you.

After giving an apology for my addressing him without any previous acquaintance and expressing my sympathy with the views in his letter I gave him a brief statement of the views I hold in relation to the Church and its office. I said, That all outward reforms presuppose an inward regeneration of the heart as their cause and foundation and no institution but the Church has the power to effect this nor has this aim [in] view. Therefore I would yield myself up wholly to the Church as the only means of Redeeming the Race from the innumerable evils under which we now suffer. I said, Having mixed in the Social and Political movements of our time more than most young men who are led to enter the Christian Ministry at the same time feeling and perceiving [the] spiritual view to be the highest [,] I would always have in view the embodying these higher and diviner ideas in all our spheres of activity that I would never forget that the Kingdom of Heaven is to be established upon Earth that I would never loose [*sic*] sight of bringing down the Heavenly Jerusalem on this Planet. I said, At present I am not a member of any branch of the Catholic Church but whatever branch I may be led to unite myself to [,] it would be as a Catholic to labor for the reunion and catholicity of the Church as the prerequisite to all other movements which have for their object the advancement of Humanity. I told him my views and sympathies were with the movement of the oxford divines[4] and in a greater degree with that portion of them who exhibited a greater friendliness and love toward the other branches of the

Catholic Church and that I had no sympathy with protestantism considered as placing the individual judgment above or equal to the voice of the Universal Church, and I considered this had been as fatal to real progress as its philosophy is unsound. I concluded with stating the object of my letter which was whether he would be willing to become a Tutor to me &c. The purport of the practical part of the letter was this that if he had any willingness to accede to such a relation it would give me great pleasure to have a personal interview with him. Rev Mr Height sent a letter with mine to Rev Mr Norris.

Most probably I will call to see Bishop Hughes to see what facilities the Catholic Church affords for me. I am a Catholic, and believe that the Roman Church has preserved the true Catholic faith so far as Her General Counsels [*sic*] are concerned.

It is not in my contemplation to join either the Roman or Anglican Church until I have made some considerable progress in my studies. One of these two *will be my choice* and it depends much upon the result in the mean time of the oxford movement in the Anglican Church whether there even will be room for me to choose.

Your statement of your present necessity of directing your attention to the Greek language and your advice to me to prepare myself at first, in the Greek and Latin will stimulate me to make this an object in my study of the first importance. I will not decide upon any plan until I see you personally, which I hope to do soon, or receive from you your advice upon whatever scheme may seem best for me.

I shall never consider any amount of time lost in the preparation if it really helps me to the aim in view. I will keep you informed from time to time what progress I make in this purpose.

Dear Friend you perfectly un-man me when you speak of gratitude to us. How much are we indebted to you for!! 'Tis I who should speak what have you not been to me! And where would I have been if it had not been that your home had not been offered so kindly to me? Alas God knows. Brother John having some bussiness [*sic*] with Bishop Onderdonk,[5] in conversing on different topics your name happened to be mentioned. The Bishop spoke of your views freely and said he read your Review with great interest, he expressed his belief that time would bring you into the fold of the Church.

There is some talk of Channing's[6] giving up his efforts here and going on to Brook Farm this spring. Last sunday morning the text of his sermon was[:] first seek the Kingdom of Heaven and then all things will be added there with. His sermon was first seek all outward things and the Kingdom of Heaven will come. Fourierism.

Very truly your son in spirit & love,

Isaac.

That your Review has been so *far* successful is very good news to us.

Have you dear friend any place or person in view that you would recommend [to] me? However I shall write you soon or see you.

*Brownson, *BEL*, pp. 514–17.

1. *The* (New York) *Churchman*, Episcopalian newspaper begun in 1830, descended from *The Churchman's Magazine* (1804), supported the Oxford and the High Church movements.

2. "A Letter to a Sincere Inquirer," *The Churchman*, XIII (18 November 1843), 145.

3. William Herbert Norris (1814?–1880), Episcopalian priest, rector of St. John's Church, Carlisle, Pa. 1842–51.

4. Anglican churchmen and leaders of the British Oxford Movement, such as John Henry Newman, Edward B. Pusey, and John Keble.

5. Benjamin Tredwell Onderdonk (1791–1861), became Episcopalian bishop of New York 1830, professor at the General Theological Seminary.

6. William Henry Channing.

19

HECKER TO BROWNSON • 28 MARCH 1844*

New York March 28, /44

Dear Friend

I have been waiting patiently since I last wrote to you for an answer to the letter I wrote to Mr Norris and yesterday I received a very frank & interesting letter from him. You will perceive in what he says there is no opening there with him for me. He says that he has only been three years in the Holy orders and that his meagre attainments have been made he hardly knows how, and that his theological library might be carried in his arms. How can I, he says direct you in a course of Theological study when I have my self persued [*sic*] none deserving that name save what I should now flee from as this pestilential breath of antichrist. Of Books he says[,] I know very little. So far as I have mastered the Catholic faith I have done it since I was in orders & in the midst of peculiarly harrassing parochial labors. My great guides have been the Creeds, the Liturgy of our Church and the New Testament—as illustrating these I have read Newman's Parochial sermons[1] & within the last year past Hooker's celebrated 5th Book.[2] He says though he has read little he has thought much. He then states how he proce[e]ded. In speaking of the Athanasian Creed[3] which seemed aimed especially at Nestorianism.[4] I wished then to discover the great evil of Nestorianism of which people now a days seem to be marvellously indifferent. It asserted our Lord's Godhead; might not that be sufficient to save it from an Anethema [*sic*]? The Church had not thought so. What next? It affirmed a human personality—nor this did not seem to interfere with Lutheranism nor any phase of Lutheranism. It did not seem especially to disturb what has passed for High Church doctrine; and yet the error did oppose some truth *necessary to the integrity of the faith.* It asserted that the Man Christ Jesus was one of Adam's species, whereas nothing is more distinctly asserted in scripture than that instead of being one of Adam's kind He is Himself *another Adam*, the beginning of a new creation, the fountain head of a New Humanity which is predestined to be immortal, incorrupt, pure & perfect, as Himself is, nay absolutely like Him in Body & in Soul. Here then I arrived at the foundation of the sacramental system &c. What think you dear friend of that letter I sent to you of his? And what think you of the above? He tells me he wrote a letter to the Churchman [,] in reply to some strictures made upon the one he published by a Catholic paper [,] [5] which the Editor[6] has not published which he desires me to get and read. He kindly invites me to come and see him after Easter and says, It does not seem that I can do anything but talk to you. I may thus give you some right principles which may safely guide you, & he recommends me to enter the general theological seminary.[7] I called to see Bishop Hughes last week.

The requisites for a candidate for Holy Orders in the R[oman] C[atholic] Church, are first a two years previous membership of the Church, and a recommendation and certificate of fitness of character, ability, &c, from his Priest. This is all very proper and necessary to the well being of the order and discipline of the Catholic Church and so far it commands my judgment, but dear friend, I am not prepared, in other words I cannot join this Church without willfulness, and it is impossible for me to do this, at the present time, tho probably I may eventually be led to take this path. In the meantime I would be employing my time for such a probable event and the way in which I think best for me to do this is to study the Greek & Latin languages as you have advised. Now the only question before my mind is *where* can I best do this? Here at home there is something to be said in favor but I think there is more that can be said against it. There is every temptation to keep me from instead of inducing me to study [,] hence I have thought it best to look for some better place [,] one more conducive to the object in view. Where is this to be found? This is the question which I wish to submit to you for your advice. Much depends upon my industry but not a little depends on the person who shall be selected as a teacher. But one place is now before my mind and that is in Concord under George Bradford.[8] He has got a small school there which occupies him about 3 hours a day and I have understood from other persons that he is desirous to teach the languages when unoccupied with his school.

The advantages that this presents to me are these. He will take an interest in learning me the languages in the shortest time but *none the less thorough.* Instead of mere[ly] hearing me recite certain lessons he will be personally interested in giving all possible knowledge which he possesses which will speed and give me a sound knowledge of the languages. Then I shall not be confined to an hour or an half hour or any definite time of recitation but the object will be to receive as much as possible, not necessarily limited to time but to capacity. And last but not least in my mind is that I shall not be *so* very *far* from the invaluable *influence* of *your mind*; this last will be to me a means of gaining more in one moment than in days of indefatigable toil. I am not unconscious nor blind to the transcendental atmosphere which Concord is famous for but dear friend with you as my friend and with the experience—life & philosophy which I have I trust I shall be impregnable to all such influences especially as I have not been unacquainted with them heretofore. However I leave this all to your better judgment and decision. My object is to seek the best conditions for the purpose I now have in view and that is to study the dead languages in order to prepare myself for a regular theological training. All other conditions and advantages I feel bound to sacrifice to this however I might desire other advantages. I will repeat the question [:] to whom & where shall I go that I may in the *best* and speediest manner receive that instruction which is needful for me? I have scarcely left room to speak of your Review which we rec'd yesterday. The first art. that I read was No Church &c.[9] You have brought the question between the Fourierists and yourself to an issue which must call them out before the public in a way not altogether pleasant to them. It has seemed to me for some time back it wanted one who had the ability to bring them to the point you have done to bring their well meant theories to an end in the public mind. Mr Channing[10] will probably be supported here another year. To-day I shall be able to read your first article.[11] I am engaged in reading Kant's Theory of religion within the bounds of pure reason.[12] It is pure Rationalism with a curious mixture of belief in a sort of catholic faith in the universality &c. of the Church.

My action will be delayed until I rec'd an answer to this. I am very sorry that I am a source of so much trouble to you and hope to be worthy of your regard.

Deiner [*sic*] Sohn

Isaac

*Brownson, *BEL*, pp. 517–21 (dated 25 March 1844).

1. John Henry Newman (1801–1890), leading Tractarian of the Oxford Movement in England, Anglican priest who entered the Catholic Church in 1845, ordained a priest of the Oratory 1848, prominent author and

theologian, became a cardinal 1879; *Parochial and Plain Sermons,* preached from 1825–43.

2. Richard Hooker (c. 1554–1600), prominent Anglican divine; *Treatise on the Laws of Ecclesiastical Polity,* eight books (1594–1662): book V was published in 1597.

3. A creed professing the orthodox belief in the Trinity against Arianism; though its origin, date, and authorship is not certain, it was attributed to St. Athanasius (c. 293–373) because Arians called Western Catholics "Athanasians."

4. The heresy, condemned by the Third Ecumenical Council at Ephesus in 431, that in Jesus there were two distinct persons or beings instead of two natures (divine and human) in one divine person.

5. *The Catholic Herald,* the weekly paper of the Diocese of Philadelphia, begun in 1833.

6. The Rev. Samuel Seabury, D.D., Episcopalian clergyman.

7. The General Theological Seminary of the Protestant Episcopal Church in America, located in New York City, established by an act of the Episcopalian General Convention 1817.

8. George Partridge Bradford (1807–1890), Harvard Divinity School graduate 1828, professor of belles lettres at Brook Farm, left it and founded a school at Concord, Mass.

9. "No Church, No Reform," *BrQR,* April 1844, pp. 175–94.

10. William Henry Channing.

11. "History of Philosophy," *BrQR,* April 1844, pp. 137–74.

12. *Religion Within the Limits of Reason Alone* (1793).

20

HECKER TO BROWNSON • 6 APRIL 1844*

N.Y. April 6, 44

Dearest Friend

Chrls Dana[1] offers an opportunity of my sending to you a few words which I will write as I must in some haste. The Fourier Convention[2] I have attended its two days deliberations which doubtless have been the same in substance except a smaller audience and less enthusiasm than the one held lately in Boston.[3] Those who did not assume it as the basis of their remarks laid it down as their fundamental basis that the evil in the world is not the result of inward individual depravity but the result of the outward arrangement of things—this was affirmed from Ripley[4] downwards. The doctrine of unity and diversity of action in the industrial world as held out by these men[,] what is it but Catholicity in the industrial world? So it strikes me and I am not a little astonished to see the effects these views have had upon them.

It has rid them of their transcendentalism[,] of their protestantism and most of their pernicious results. It seems to me I have greater hopes of Mr Ripley than I ever had. He is now laboring on the results which the Catholic Church of Christ is destined to realize in time[,] not on the cause which only can do this. Not that I believe in the innumerable speculations of Fourier or that these men in their present movement will effect much by their plans tho I do firmly believe it will be the means of opening their eyes to those Catholic principles developed in the history of the Church. I am daily more and more firmly convinced of the opinion you expressed in your letter that only in the Church can we possibly benefit the age in the highest degree. Ripley has spoken once or twice with an earnestness and enthusiasm very great. This is his apprenticeship for the priesthood. Those who have tried to succeed in reform out of the Church and have failed know the value of its aid and its life[;] those who have been in the church physically speaking leave it just at the time they should feel most indebted to it and remain to realize in it its life. These never seem to me nearly ready to enter society and the Church as true and efficient members.

It would have been to me a moment of great pleasure to have met you before now to have your advice upon the subject of the plans in view of my education but certain difficulties have prevented me. I have made no further efforts since I last wrote you except to write Mr Bradford to know of him if he had the time and disposition to teach me the languages if I should come to Concord but of my coming I made no assurance. I have thought it very probable that you might conceive of a plan which would be preferable to the one I submitted to you. When you have the leisure will you let me know how this is.

The questions between the Anglican & R.C. Church have mostly occupied my attention of late and the impressions that I have been left are that the conduct of the Anglican clergy in the time of the separation is to be severely condemned and that the conduct of the Pope is not alltogether [*sic*] reconci[la]ble with real Christian Catholic principles. I don't know but that the *court* of Rome has claimed a power insuportable [*sic*] on the true grounds of the Church. Is he more than an executive head of the counsels [*sic*] the constitution of the Church? The organization of the Church[,] has it not been very incomplete[,] indefinite? And has not this been the chief cause of so many schisms in its body? Has not the Anglican Church preserved the true catholic faith? If the Anglicans have sinned in separating themselves from the Roman See are not the Roman Catholics extremely blameable in some of their practices? The former error is vital and not to be too much feared[,] still it is not a heresy in faith is it? But these questions I would trouble you with if you will bear them when I shall see you.

I will send the report of the doings of the Convention in the Herald[5] as for its correctness you know how correct the papers generally report. For Ripan read Ryckmany.[6] For Hecker *read Hempel.*[7]

My faith in Christ, my interest in the Church, my hope in it as the means of Redeeming mankind, my willingness to leave all for the field of the Church, increases upon me daily, deepens continually.

Your dear Son in the love of Christ

Isaac

I have broken open this letter since I have found that Chrls is not going home to-day. The Convt adjourned sine die this afternoon. To-night they are to have a dinner in commemoration of the birth of Fourier.

I feel within me a life which these plans & schemes, tho I sympathize ever so much with the individuals, do not move or in any way touch.

Your article on Philosophy[8] I have read and how much it has interested and enlightened you can scarcely conceive unless you were acquainted with what I have been reading. The Areopagite Dionysius[,][9] Johannes Scotus Erigena[,][10] Bernhard[,][11] Hugo[12] & Rvad[13] von St Viktor[,] Meister Eckart[14] &c. of the Scholastics & Mystics so called. Of this alone I would have written to you a letter but I send this so as to let you know it was not me who spoke at the convention and the time does not permit me to write another.

I.

*Brownson, *BEL,* pp. 524–27 (postscript omitted; postmark recorded as New York, 6 July).

1. Charles Anderson Dana (1819–1897), Harvard graduate, taught Greek and German at Brook Farm, Fourierist, became editor of the *New York Sun.*

2. The National Convention of Associationists (Fourierists) convened at Clinton Hall, New York, on 4 April 1844.

3. During the last week of December 1843 and the first week of January 1844.

4. George Ripley (1802–1880), onetime Unitarian minister, newspaper editor, social reformer and founder of Brook Farm, Fourierist, literary editor of the *New York Tribune.* Ripley was elected president of the Fourierist convention (n. 2 above), Dana (n. 1 above) its vice-president.

5. The *New York Herald* covered the Fourierist convention on the front page of its 5, 6, 7 April 1844 issues, and on 9 April 1844, pp. 1–2.

6. Lewis W. Ryckman of New York, Fourierist author, elected to the business committee at the convention.

7. Charles J. Hempel of New York, chosen to co-edit the Fourierist journal *The Phalanx* at the convention.

8. "History of Philosophy," *BrQR*, April 1844, pp. 137–74.

9. Dionysius the Pseudo-Areopagite (c. A.D. 500), presumably a Syrian monk, mystical writer and theologian.

10. John Scotus Erigena (c. 815–77), Irish theologian and philosopher, translated into Latin the works of Dionysius (n. 9 above), including *The Celestial Hierarchy* and *Mystical Theology*.

11. St. Bernard of Clairvaux.

12. Hugo (Hugh) of St. Victor (1096–1141), Saxon mystic, pioneer scholastic theologian, educator and author, a member of the Augustinian Canons of St. Victor in Paris.

13. Richard of St. Victor (d. c. 1173), Scottish mystic and systematizer of mystical theology; together with Hugh (n. 12 above) he mediated the mysticism of Dionysius (n. 9 above) into the mainstream of Western spirituality.

14. Meister Johannes Eckhart (c. 1260–c. 1327), German Dominican mystic, preacher, and author.

21

HECKER TO BROWNSON • [9 APRIL] 1844*

Tuesday 7, /44[1]

Since I last wrote to you I have spoken to Mr Ripley touching the social movements now in progress and have seen Dr Seabury.[2] The information which I received from them I have thought might not be uninteresting to you.

In my last I spoke of the religious aspect the associative movement has assumed of late especially with some of the interested individuals and was aggreeably [*sic*] confirmed in this by the conversation I had yesterday afternoon with our friend. He gave me to understand that his religious views had been considerably modified since I had last seen him and though I perceived he has not the Catholic understanding of the Church still the time is not far distant it seems to me when his eyes will be opened and he be *prepared* to embrace it. One point he has gained and that is he now sees the place for *A* Church and the necessity of ministers. They seem to be intent about exhibiting life not caring about the means of receiving it. Tho they[,] that is[,] the best & wisest of them recognize Christ as the life and light of men[,] they do not perceive the mediatorial office of the visible Church. It astonishes me repeatedly to hear from the best speakers such sound fundamental catholic views on some points mixed up with the most contradictory and irreconcilable statements. I have never heard from any one man's lips such hetereogeneous and opposite views with out any unity or harmony in principle or arrangement as I have and do constantly hear from the lips of Mr Channing[3] in his preaching. One moment it is catholic[,] the next ultra protestant[,] then human depravity[,] then the integràl harmony of the passions[,] then the immediate communion with God[,] again the opposite and so through all modern theories and philosophies without any reconciliation or unity in result.

Dr Seabury is one of the most social & familiar men that I have ever met. He said to me that he had read your last Review[4] all through with great delight but says he I am a little afraid of Brownson[,] he looks to[o] strong towards Rome. Now I am not said he opposed to Rome in any essential point of faith nor do I seek to build up the Anglican Church to which I am attached as the Catholic but the assumptions of power assumed by the Pope of Rome the oath of allegiance of all the Bishops to the pope and his infallibility and many practices which have grown up under her system I do not like. She presents said he many attractive features more so than our Church. I admit said he our ceremonies & discipline are not so grand & have been neglected &c but said he we cannot accept the Church of Rome as she now is and I am afraid that the influence of Brownson upon the Roman Church is such as to make her cling to her exclusiveness and her practices which are not catholic. We accept all the catholic councils but says he since the great separation of the Grecian Church there could not be a catholic council. He even said that he had no objection of accepting the council of Trent[5] but the interpretation given to it by the Church of Rome the Anglican Church might in some minor points differ from it. He is perfectly willing and desires that there should be called an oecumenical council of those branches of the Church which have preserved the Catholic faith and restore the visible unity of the Church. His views struck me as extremely liberal[,] broad and without much sectional feeling.

To-morrow morning it is my intention to go & see Mr Norris & probably spend a few days with him and when I return if I shall not receive any news from you which will alter my purpose I should like to come to Boston to see you.

You will find in the Regenerator[6] an address by Mr Smolineker.[7] He is a man of remarkable learning and of curious genius. Like many other good intentioned men the Church is to him only the vices of its members. He says he has the spirit of Christ and is sent by him as the messenger of Peace and all those that do not aid him in the great enterprise he excommunicates.[8]

In the bond of Christ

Isaac

Remember me to your kind wife.

This is election day, the Native Americans have made a serious inroad upon both parties.[9] We may loose [*sic*] the city. It is probable.

*Brownson, *BEL*, pp. 527–29. Microfilm, roll two (calendared 7 April 1844).

1. Though the month was not written, this letter was postmarked Boston, 12 April. April 9 is the correct date since the 7th was a Sunday, not a Tuesday, and the 9th was the date of the New York City mayoral election mentioned in this letter (see n. 9 below).

2. Samuel Seabury, D.D. (1801–1872), Episcopalian priest and editor of *The Churchman,* became bishop 1853 and a professor at the General Theological Seminary 1862.

3. William Henry Channing.

4. *BrQR,* April 1844.

5. The Council of Trent (1545–1563), held to counteract the Protestant Reformation and to restate Catholic theology vis-à-vis the Reformers.

6. *The Regenerator, A free paper for the promotion of universal inquiry and progressive improvement;* published at New York, begun on 1 January 1844.

7. "Address of Andrew Bernardus Smolnikar, founder and agent of the Peace-Union, prepared for the general convention of the Friends of Association, assembled in New York the 4th, 5th, and 6th of April, on Thursday, Friday and Saturday, before Easterday, 1844." *The Regenerator,* I (8 April 1844), 58–59.

Andrew Bernardus Smolnikar (b. 1795), a native of Illyria, entered the Benedictines 1825, professor of biblical studies at the Lyceum of Clagenfurt 1827–37; after 1837 he came to Limestone, Warren County, Pa. to set up a "Peace-Union" providing land for poor men, including "coloreds."

8. In his address (n. 7 above), Smolnikar relates how he saw a morning star on 7 February 1835 while writing a treatise on the "congeniality of all languages in the world;" he took this to be a foreboding of the regeneration of nations, which meant "the abolishment of Popery and all other sects from the Church of Christ." Hence he "excommunicated" several people at the Fourierist convention, including the Catholic bishop of Boston (Benedict J. Fenwick, S.J.).

9. James Harper (1795–1869), eventually a noted publisher, was handily elected mayor of New York as an Independent who supported the Native Americans against foreign immigrants, especially the Irish.

22

BROWNSON TO HECKER • [c. 12 APRIL 1844]*

[*Undated*][1]

My dear Friend,

I should have written you sooner, but have been very unwell, very busy, and very negligent.

I like your plan of going to study with Bradford, and can think of nothing better at least for the summer. I have much I would say, but in the hope of immediately seeing you, I will merely add that I am as always

Truly yours

O. A. Brownson

I want to see that Scotus Erigena you have been reading. My remembrances to the family. Let us see you as soon as you can.

*Microfilm, roll nine (calendared [10 April (?) 1844]).

1. This undated letter apparently responded to Hecker's of 6 April 1844 (Letter 20), which mentioned Hecker's reading of Erigena, and possibly also to that of 9 April (Letter 21). The dating depends on the time it took for Hecker's letter(s) to reach Brownson and for Brownson's reply.

23

HECKER TO BROWNSON • [c. 16 MAY 1844]*

[*Undated*][1]

Dearest Friend

You will forgive me for not informing you of my life here sooner than I have. It was not that I had no desire to do so but I have ever waited, and waited, for a change which would give me more freedom in so doing.

My communion with the invisible seems to be to me much more than the study, in which I am partly engaged, and often draws me very often from my study, would you advise me to act willfully against this life, this tendency? Whether willful activity would in the end overcome this union which now seems to be so intimate, and real, and almost uninterruptedly [,] would be determined by such an effort. What inward trials and struggles which my Soul has endured of late have wholly arisen from *my* efforts for *self* control; in the struggle with that, what ever it may be named, which in the end has ever subdued me; would you recommend me to renew this effort in this case which seems to present itself to me now? Let me humbly confess I have not the heart to do it, the struggle would be much more interior than ever it has been, and the consequences I fear and shudder from. There seems to be but one path for me to tred and this is the one of humble submission and trust in God. It may be very true in the eyes of many that I am foolish (not that I feel or think you are of this number) and am neglecting a good opportunity of gaining what would be of great value to me at some future period of life, how can I help this? I see no future distinct before me, and am without any proposed object. But by this I do not mean to say that I am not conscious that there is a purpose in my being, tho I cannot say what it is, where it is, or what good or benefit it may be to others. Here I am, and so it is with me, and if all my friends should loose [*sic*] their sympathy for me tho this I would regret yet I feel prepared to stand alone in the pitiless storm of the world, let it flash and thunder about me as it may.

There is not much reason to hope that this will pass of[f] without some effects; if my past experience is any judge for me, and it does seem no sooner am I settled and at peace for a moment than a hand should be laid upon me and a voice saying go, this is not for you, go and suffer your cup has not been half drunk. What avails my pleadings, prayers, and supplications I am driven, and no one can help me, their arms are all to[o] short because they are of flesh.

Do not think that I am left alone without society and comfort, of these I do not lack, tho they be not of this world, they are the nearer, and sweeter for it. Whether after a short period I shall be enabled to continue my studies as I have intended here, or whether some other plan or way may be made clear before me, now I cannot speak a word about. However I do not feel that any sudden movement will take place regarding my location. To my friends at home I would not reveal a word of this, for they at best could but sympathize, and not understand; but of either of these I do not feel a conscious need of, but at best they are as well of[f] and better in not knowing anything concerning my interior life.

I thought before I came here that I should be interested in Xt. history, especially of the Church, and the languages, and such like studies, but such is not the case, all my life is within, and as it were in constant conversation and communion within an unseen world; and all attempts at study are fruitless. To make effort against this would be to throw me on the bed less than three days, notwithstanding the desire I have to learn the languages. You see my position, and my only course is to be quiet and wait peacefully until a change of some kind takes place.

Let me add a short note to this which was written three weeks ago. Since this was written you will be able to detect the course in which the stream of my life is flowing, and if you have the opportunity, and the will to give me a few words of counsel you feel assured that they will not be wasted by me.

After having heard Collins[2] and Abby Folsom[3] I was more impressed with the profoundness of your article on comeouterism[4] than when you read it to me and then I was much pleased with it. Collins truly said that the Church (Churches he said) is based on the principle that it is the medium of a life a power not granted to all men and this he flatly denied, and Abby the truest of all the abolationists [*sic*] denied the right of thrusting any mediums between her, such as organizations, presidents, committees, &c and her activity. So we have the doctrine of mediatorial means denied transcendentally and emperically [*sic*] and with the goading of these two sections on each side of the abolation [*sic*] party the true and religious portion will soon be brought to their senses. There is no half way house between the Church and atheism, that Germany has clearly demonstrated. And as France[,] England and our own country have followed to a very great extent the philosophy of Germany so will they be forced into the same consequences. The lines are now in the two latter countries fast being drawn so that the contest must end in the Church on one side and atheism and heathenism on the other. The first will soon give way to a new generation, and the latter disappear like morning mists before the approaching sun when the Church presents Her united front with Her full divine power before the decaying superstitions of the past.

In the Churchman of last week[5] a correspondent takes bold grounds as to the doctrine that the Church is a corporate body. I trust your article[6] will give them some hard nuts to crack on this subject. It comes just in the right time. *Bishop* Hughes what is the matter with him to get in a newspaper controversy.[7]

Truly yours

Isaac

*Holden, *EY*, pp. 216–17 (with omissions).

1. The account in this letter of Hecker's difficulty in studying situates the timing of its composition within the Concord period of May–June 1844. When he finally determined to send it, he continued: "Let me add a short note to this which was written three weeks ago." Then in his diary entry for 5 June 1844, Hecker stated: "Yesterday I sent off to O.A.B. two letters, one of which was written some weeks ago but which I did not send on account of its subjectivity; the other was written yesterday" (HP, APF). This evidence justifies Holden's proximate dating as [16 May 1844], *EY*, pp. 217–18, n. 25.

2. John Anderson Collins (1810–1879), abolitionist and social reformer, founder of the Skaneateles Community in central New York 1843.

3. Abigail Folsom (1792?–1867), radical author, active in the abolition movement in New England, a regular participant in abolition meetings and

conventions, associated with Abigail Kelley Foster (1810–1887), abolitionist and woman's rights lecturer.

4. "Come-Outerism: Or the Radical Tendencies of the Day," *BrQR*, July 1844, pp. 367–86.

5. "Individual Christianity–Its Practical Effects," *The Churchman* XIV (1 June 1844), 49.

6. "Church Unity and Social Amelioration," *BrQR*, July 1844, pp. 310–28.

7. A controversy generated in the *New York Herald*, 22–24 May 1844, by the publication of Bishop Hughes's pastoral letter on "The Philadelphia Riots and Their Causes" (17 May 1844). Hughes complained to Mayor Harper of New York City about an alleged attempt on his life stemming from the riots and charged the *Herald's* proprietor, James Gordon Bennett (1795–1872), with nativist or anti-Irish sentiment.

24

HECKER TO BROWNSON • 4 [JUNE] 1844*

Concord April 4, /44[1]

Dear Friend

On wednesday afternoon I returned to this retired and quiet spot now called my home.[2] Before I went I called at Mr Green's two or three times to see you but found you not.

My attractions were so strong towards home no inducement seemed great enough to retain me any longer in Boston.

Here my time is occupied in reading a little, studying less, and thinking and contemplating the remainder part of the time, which is the most. My study is to me now what my labour was to me a year ago, then no motives, and I felt not a few, which *should* have led me to labour did not, and now[*?*], with all the desire I have to learn the languages, and the certain knowledge I have of their great advantage, do not bear upon me with sufficient force to direct and confine my attention to them. The union, I feel conscious, with spirit, is a source of so much more life in every direction that all other sources seems to me lifeless, and dry compared with this. I deplore deeply that I cannot continue the studies for which I came here with that energy and application which they require, and my hope was that this would be possible without interrupting this other willess [*sic*] life, but such seems not to be the case, and what else can one do than accept things as they are with as good a grace as possible? This willess life is making silent irresistable progress within me, and when I speculate about the end to which it may probably lead me, sometimes there seems reason to hope and smile, and at other times equal reason to weep and sigh.

All that which tends to more perfectly unite me to this spiritual life, interests, quickens, and fills me with energy of intellect, and sentiment, and otherwise all seems dead.

If I make the attempt to force myself to study it is as if my whole mind vanished, and all is blank & void before me, thought, memory, and feeling is gone, and I stand alone like one without soul or heart and empty body void of any sense.

I have just looked for the letter[3] which I wrote some time ago, but which I did not send, but will now enclose it in this that you may see and judge and give such advice, if you so feel inclined, as you may deem suitable.

I ask no more questions, nor attempt by reason to foreknow the future, but am simply resigned to give all up to the invisible guide who alone is the true guider to right issues. Man rules his destiny only by perfect submission to God; or by perfect cooperation with His will.

At present there is no objective purpose before me at which I aim, not that my love for man is less, or that my earnestness is the least abated; this is not so, never have I felt the love I now feel, never have I been conscious of living such an earnest deep effectual life as I am now conscious of living. My very existence seems to be one perpetual act. And every day is filled with life, love, and wisdom. 'Tis true this is not the ordinary way in which young men prepare themselves for benefitting man, and I may be labouring under a self delusion; if this be delusion, it never has so well counterfeited the truth, and I trust some friendly hand will strip it of its garb, for I trust I am not so far gone as not to recognize it when it stands before me in its naked colours.

That a certain amount of intellectual culture and information are necessary and essential to certain public offices to which many true young men devote themselves to no one with their eyes open can bring into question. This I have been fully conscious of and this has placed me in my present position. My object was to acquire this needy information, so that if in the end I should be directed to any place that would require this, I would not be unprepared; and I have very partially laid before your mind the attempt.

With the consciousness of the responsibleness of this deeper life, in memory, and in presence of its fruits to me, I cannot say that I would have it otherwise than what it is, and my hope is that ere long I may be enabled to devote more time to study than it is possible for me now to do.

There seems to me two points of view from which most men start in life. One sees an object before him which he has the aspiration to secure, and to this end he sacrifices all that is in his way that he may secure it. The other is the perfect submission to the will of God and His purposes without the persuit [*sic*] of an outward end. The first may be successful in the worldly sense, but the latter if true must receive the approbation of God.

Let me not talk any farther on this matter to you dear friend whose wisdom in these matters is so great, and whose time I feel unworthy to engage with my private life, or what I have to say. My sense of nothingness increases upon me, and I trust Abraham's hand will not be staid as of old. What soul delight it would be to offer up this life for the sake of man with heaven in view, or if not worthy of this privelege [*sic*] of one still-greater—to be forsaken by all, Man, Heaven, Angels, God, All. It is the nobleman that God calls to great to impossible deeds. I love you my dear friend with a very deep love, and never think of you without an inexpressible grattitude [*sic*].

Yours truly

Isaac

*Brownson, *BEL,* pp. 521–24 (dated 4 April 1844); Holden, *EY,* pp. 221–22 (with omissions). Microfilm, roll two (calendared 4 April 1844).

1. This letter was inscribed with the date 4 April 1844, but it should have been dated 4 June 1844. Its postmark of 4 June, Concord, Mass., identifies it as the second letter ("written yesterday") that is mentioned in Hecker's 5 June 1844 diary listing (See Letter 23, n. 1).

2. After a visit to Brook Farm, Hecker returned on May 29 to the Main Street home of Henry David Thoreau and his mother in Concord, where Hecker had arranged for room and board.

3. See Letter 23.

25

BROWNSON TO HECKER • 6 JUNE 1844*

Mt. Bellingham June 6th, 1844.

My dear Isaac,

I thank you for your letter, and the frankness with which you speak of your present interior state. You ask for my advice, but I hardly know what advice to give. There is much in your present state to approve, also much which is dangerous. The dreamy luxury of indulging one's thoughts, and ranging at ease through the whole spirit-world is so captivating, and when frequently indulged in acquires such power over us, they [=*that*] we cease to be free men. The power to control your thoughts and feelings, and to fix them on what object you choose is of the last necessity, as it is the highest aim of spiritual culture. Be careful that you do not mistake a mental habit into which you have fallen for the guidance of the All-Wise. Is it not the very sacrifice you are appointed to make to overcome this spiritual luxury, and to become able to do that which is disagreeable? Where is the sacrifice in following what the natural tendencies and fixed habits of our mind dispose us to? What victory have you acquired, what power to conquer in the struggle for sanctity do you possess, when you cannot so far control your thoughts and feelings as to be able to apply yourself to studies which you feel are necessary? Here is your warfare. You have not won the victory till you have become as able to drudge at Latin or Greek, as to give up worldly wealth, pleasures, honors, or distinctions.

But, my dear Isaac, you cannot gain this victory alone, nor by mere private meditation, and prayer. You can obtain it only through the grace of God, and the grace of God only through its appointed channels. You are wrong, you do not begin right. Do you really believe the Gospel? Do you really believe the Holy Catholic Church? If so, you must put yourself under the direction of the Church. I have commenced my preparations for uniting myself with the Catholic Church. I do not as yet belong to the family of Christ. I feel it. I can be an alien no longer, and without the Church I know by my own past [e]xperience that I cannot attain to purity and sanctity of life. I need the counsels, the aids, the chastisements and the consolations of the Church. It is the appointed medium of salvation, and how can we hope for any good [e]xcept through it? Our first business is to submit to it, that we may receive a maternal blessing. Then we may start fair.

You doubtless feel a repugnance to joining the Church. But we ought not to be ashamed of Christ, and the Church opens a sphere for you, and you[,] especially you[,] are not to dream your life away. Your devotion must be regulated, and directed by the discipline of the Church. You know that there is a large German Catholic population in our country, especially in Wisconsin. The Bishop[1] of that Territory is a German. Now, here is your work to serve this German population, and you can do it, without feeling yourself among foreigners. Here is the cross you are to take up. Your cross is to resist this tendency to mysticism, to sentimental luxury which is really enfeebling your soul, and preventing [you] from attaining to true spiritual blessedness.

I think you better give up Greek, but command yourself sufficiently to master the Latin, that you need, and cannot do without. Get the Latin, and with that and the English, French, and German which you already know, you can get along very well. But don't be discouraged.

I want you to come & see our good bishop.[2] He is an [e]xcellent man, learned, polite, easy, affable, affectionate and [e]xceedingly warm hearted. I spent two hours with him immediately after parting with you in Washington Street, and a couple of hours yesterday. I like him very much.

I have made up my mind, and I shall enter the Church if she will receive me. There is no use in resisting. You cannot be an Anglican, you must be a

Catholic, or a mystic. If you enter the Church at all, it must be the Catholic. There is nothing else. So let me beg you, my dear Isaac, to begin by owning the Church and receiving her blessing.

My health is very good, the family are all well; I hope you are well. Let me hear from you often. Forgive me, if I have said anything harsh or unkind in this letter, for all is meant in kindness, and be assured of my sincere and earnest affection.

Yours truly,

O. A. Brownson

*Holden, *YP,* pp. 90–91; *EY,* pp. 223–24. Elliott, *LFH,* pp. 145–47.

1. John Martin Henni (1805–1881), Swiss-born priest, known as "the apostle of the Germans," became first bishop of Milwaukee 1843.

2. Benedict Joseph Fenwick, S.J. (1782–1846), one of the first Jesuits ordained in the U.S. 1808, president of Georgetown College 1817–18 and 1822–25, second bishop of Boston 1825, founder of the College of the Holy Cross 1843.

26

HECKER TO BROWNSON • [24 JUNE 1844]*

[*Undated*][1]

Dear Friend

On thursday morning I left Worcester for NY and this is the reason why I did not write to you from Worcester having gone from there sooner than I had anticipated. I returned to Boston befor [*sic*] I came on here and stop'd at Mr Green's in hope of seeing you but did not and my time was too short for me to go to Chelsea.

The College[2] is very finely situated on Patchogue Hill[3] which commands a very extensive and pleasant scenery. The Professors[4] or Scholastics as they term them you are aware are Jesuits and they seem well prepared to fulfill their proper offices.

There are there now 25 Scholars & students whose range of studies are from the simplest to the most profound. They adapt themselves to the simplest branches of education. No scholar is taken under 8 years of age. Of the twenty five there are I think no more than 5 or 8 young men, the rest average from the ages of 8 to 12 & 14.

They get up in the morning about 5 o'clock[,] hear mass which takes them a half hour, then study one hour before taking breakfast. After breakfast they go to the chapel inside of the college to say prayers and then they are given an hour or a half[,] I do not recollect which[,] for recreation, after their time for recreation has elapsed they are called to their recitations. Before and after each meal excepting when Mass is said which is said every morning previous to breakfast they all go to the chapel to say prayers and also previous to their retiring to bed in the evening 8 o'clock. After dinner they have an hour and a half more for amusement[,] then they are called in the study room for they all study in one room quite large each having a desk and there is one who they call a prefect who sits by a desk as in our public schools to oversee them.

Their diet is what you would call a very generous one. The boys seemed very happy and full of spirits and no restraint is put upon their innocent freedom. The place as it now is is better adapted to such as they now have there boys, and I feel quite assured if your Wife should make them a visit and see the order[,] cleanliness and the spirit of the place that she would be pleased with the College.

There are no women there for obvious reasons[,] protestant slander would be ready on any pretext to injure them & cast suspicion & vile abuse upon them.

The proffessors [*sic*] that I had the pleasure to speak to were well educated in the circle of Catholic Education which seems to be the Scriptural and historic grounds of their Church[,] as for its philosophic basis they seem to me profoundly ignorant and so long as the conversation was kept within their circle they were at home, otherwise they behaved as strangers. Their method is a very short one in settling difficult points[,] Scripture & the Church, not appreciating any other method however important and profound it may be to the welfare and success of the Church in her present position in the World. These men have done well to keep & preserve the Church but a new generation must take their place if Catholicism is to be reestablished in the World. I feel so in their presence that if it was to them that I was to be united I should shrink but it is not to them but the Church. These men *seem to me* are wanting that vital consciousness of divine eternal life and high spiritual aspirations which have animated so many of the children of the true Church. I had to ask them repeatedly if that was the ground on which they based a true christian life[,] the lowest and the least that the Church demands of us. Understand me I believe these very men have private virtues which if I knew would command my deepest respect and reverence for their individual characters but I wish they did not take so much snuff and that even in the midst of that holy awful sacred Sacrafice [*sic*] the Mass. Oh my dear friend there must be something deeper[,] more eternal and invisible than what we see with the outward or sense[5] that can attract a Soul to the Church as she now is in this country.

Tomorrow I am going to see Rev Mr McClusky.[6] I have delayed it that nothing might interfere with the duties that may be required of me when I commence. To my friends I have not spoken a word respecting my union with the Church. The life that leads me to the Church is deeper than all thought and expression and if I attempt to give a reason or to explain why I am led to the Church afterwards I always feel that it never reaches the reason and I feel its inadequacy. Let men say as they may it is only by grace that we come to the knowledge of the truth as it [is] in Jesus. You will be so kind as to excuse the hurry of this. I have an opportunity of sending this with a friend and after having seen Rev Mr McC[loskey] I will write to you again.

Very truly yours in the deepest love

Isaac

*Brownson, *BEL*, pp. 532–35 (not dated but postmarked Boston, 30 June). Microfilm, roll two (calendared 30 June 1844).

1. Holden dates this letter 24 June 1844 (*YP*, p. 422, n. 45), because Hecker wrote therein: "Tomorrow I am going to see Rev Mr McClusky." This meeting took place on 25 June 1844 in New York.

2. The College of the Holy Cross, the Jesuit college at Worcester, Mass., founded in 1843 by Benedict Fenwick; its first president was Thomas Francis Mulledy, S.J. (1794–1860), superior of the Maryland Province 1838, twice president of Georgetown College 1829–37, 1845–48.

3. Pakachoag Hill (Hill of Pleasant Springs); also known as Mount St. James.

4. Although the precise list of faculty members is not available, there is evidence that the following priests, scholastics, and laymen taught there at this time: Rev. Thomas Mulledy, S.J.; Rev. Joseph Balfe, S.J. (d. 1881); Rev. George Fenwick, S.J., the bishop's brother (d. 1857); Rev. James Power, S.J., (d. 1866); Mr. Robert Boone, S.J. (d. 1849); Mr. John McGuigan, S.J. (d. 1859); Mr. James Hutton or Fitton[?]; Mr. James A. McGuigan (d. 1876); and Mr. Joseph O'Callaghan (d. 1869).

5. Hecker probably meant to say "with the outward senses."

6. John McCloskey (1810–1885), Hecker's spiritual advisor, co-adjutor to Bishop Hughes of New York 1844; became bishop of Albany, N.Y., 1847, archbishop of New York 1864, named first American cardinal 1875.

27

HECKER TO BROWNSON • 15 JULY 1844*

New York July 15. 1844

Dear Friend

Shortly after I wrote to you a fortnight ago I went to see Bishop McClosky. The Bishop pleased me personally more than any Catholic I have met. He is a man of wide information mild and affectionate in his intercourse, one in whose company I hope to be much benefitted. He spoke of you with profound respect and said he read your Review with great interest and pleasure. I have rec'd from him some books to read one of which I think worth while mentioning to you. Its title is Considerations on the Eucharist by Abbe P. Gerbert.[1] Translated from the French. He is a profound writer and the book is well written. Bishop Fenwick has it no doubt in his library.

This morning I went again to see the Bishop he has been ever since I first saw him at Troy [N.Y.] where he went to consecrate a new church. In eight or ten days I expect to receive conditional baptism.[2]

I went to see Rev Mr Height last week. He took up the objections I have made to the Anglican Church. This historical ones we did not enter upon for we had spoken of them heretofore, and as for those touching their delapidated state of affairs their neglect of discipline and want of &c. faith in their Church of certain admmited [*sic*] Catholic doctrines &. &c. this he did not dispute. He loaned me two books and we parted friendly.

Wm Channing I have met since my return. Few words that drop't from his mouth in conversation will give you an idea where he now stands. He said if the institutions of the middle ages had been perpetuated and perfected they would satisfy all his hopes and aspirations. He did not think it necessary to recusitate [*sic*] them and did not know of anything which would answer as a substitute for them. He looks for a *Something* to come to answer his heart and does not think the Catholic Church is the thing. And said the movements of the day needed a more spiritual life to succede [*sic*] to any great extent. This much dear friend exoterically.

My time since I have been here has been partially engaged in the bussiness [*sic*] tho my heart is far from it as ever. I look to my union with the C. Church as my first step and this as the condition of knowing the next. Further than this I do not ask. Conditions for a contemplative life for a certain length of time under the discipline of the Church is what my heart demands, but this I am prepared to sacrifice if I can. All that I ask is conditions for the realization[,] the expression of the life which I feel an imperative call upon me to live. I do not ask these of others believing that all true life will create its own conditions. At present I do not see what I can do and be useful, but this does not trouble me, feeling assured that obedience to heaven will more than give me what my hopes dare dream. I am in the path, obedience[,] fortitude[,] faith and courage will secure the rest.

That the inspiration of Christianity is the cause of modern civilization and improvement I have no doubt, and believe the Church the center from which flows all progress in art[,] science and industry, and the best method for to labour for the good of the Race is in the cause and advancement of the reign of the Church. That Christianity has been the highest source of inspiration to inborn capacity of genius is evidently proven by their higher devotion to the expression of its life in all the variety of genius. Until we perceive heaven we cannot feel the loss we have sustained in our fall.

Will you be so kind dear friend as to put those books in a wrapper and mark them for Chrls Dana and have them left to Miss Peabody's[3] before the 1st of September, which I loaned from Mr Parker.[4] He is I believe to be home then and Chrls wished me to return them to him by that time.

The family are all well.

Sincerely Yours

Isaac

*Brownson, *BEL*, pp. 535–37.

1. Olympe-Philippe Gerbet (1798–1864), French bishop, theologian, and philosopher, disciple of Lamennais, pioneer of social Catholicism in France; *Considerations on the Dogma of the Eucharist* (London, 1840), was translated from the French original entitled *Considérations sur le dogme générateur de la piété chrétienne* (Paris, 1829).

2. In the case of an adult convert to the Roman Catholic Church who was previously baptized in another Christian denomination but where there remains uncertainty whether the sacrament had been administered validly, baptism is conferred conditionally rather than absolutely. Conditional baptism is given privately with holy water and without the usual ceremonies.

3. Elizabeth Palmer Peabody (1804–1894), Transcendentalist, prominent educator, bookseller and author of *Record of a School* (1835–36).

4. Theodore Parker (1810–1860), radical Unitarian preacher and intellectual, pastor at West Roxbury, Mass.; author and social reformer, leader in the anti-slavery crusade.

28

HECKER TO BROWNSON • [2 AUGUST 1844]*

[*Undated*] [1]

Dear Friend

This morning I go to the Cathedral to receive the Sacrament of baptism; tomorrow to confession; after that receive confirmation.[2] It is a rule of the Church to defer the baptism of adults for a short time that the intentions of those who solicit baptism may be better ascertained.

The life surrounding me here is not such as engages my attention any length of time. The object for which it is planned is not mine. And as for the mere physical subsistance this labor and waste of time is not necessary. We never shall labor for better physical circumstances. The conditions for progress in spiritual life are in inverse ratio to those for physical indulgence. In the worst physical conditions, we have enough, and often more than enough to over-come even the temptations they present. We feel best when freest of external conditions. Jesus had power to lay down and take up his temporal life at pleasure.

Men know not what man is until they are one with Jesus. The conditions for receiving spiritual life are not consistent with the gratification of the physical wants as man's nature now is. Until his nature is restored to its primeval innocence its likings are not all lawful.

I have an idea of a project which I think would be more than one way beneficial to me. It is to make a penetential [*sic*] journey to Europe, even as far as Rome. To work my passage over the sea and to work[,] walk and beg whatever distance I may go. A better penance I cannot think of. It is better much better than being a recluse either here or in a cloister.

Do you think so? This project is only in thought[,] in imagination. I have my eye upon one person who can live on bread and water and sleep upon the earth, who can walk his share; if he should consent to go I might go. It is Henry Thoreau[3] I mean. We see not why pilgrimages may not be made now as well as they were in the Ages of Faith. If this thought becomes more serious with me I shall inform you, if so.

Mornings I engage myself as far as possible in the bussiness [*sic*]. Afternoons I have chiefly to employ as I wish.

I find difficulties sufficient in the circumstances I am now in but the way in which I would meet them is not the way others would, and as we are three and not one, I would not disturb any arrangements, preferring them to be as they are. The world is wide on purpose to give freedom.

Probably I shall take up my studies if I remain, and can do so. We are willing to undertake any discipline which shall bring about this end if desireable [*sic*].

My time has been chiefly employed in reading books concerning the sacraments[,] disciplines and ceremonies of the Church.

Our feelings increase with the knowledge of the Catholic Church. (We feel an inward constraint to use the plural pronoun, we [know] not why.)

Digby[4] the author of Mores Catholici[5] became a catholic in preparing himself to refute Milner's[6] end of controversy.[7] He was one of the finest and most pious scholars of Cambridge and was chosen for that purpose.

Your blessing upon me dear friend I must now leave to go and receive baptism

Isaac

*Brownson, *BEL*, pp. 537–39 (H. F. Brownson wrote of this letter: "No date, postmark illegible").

1. Dated 2 August 1844 in view of Hecker's baptism day mentioned in the letter; it was also postmarked 2 August, New York.

2. Hecker was baptized by Bishop McCloskey at old St. Patrick's Cathedral; the following day (3 August 1844) he confessed his sins, and on 18 May 1845 he was confirmed by McCloskey, taking the confirmation name of Thomas in honor of St. Thomas Aquinas.

3. Henry David Thoreau (1817–1862), Transcendentalist, naturalist, and social critic, author of *Walden* (1854).

4. Kenelm Henry Digby (1797–1880), English author, Catholic convert 1823.

5. *Mores Catholici, or The Ages of Faith*, eleven volumes (1831–40), three volumes (London, 1845–47); written to illustrate how the eight beatitudes (Mt. 5:3–12) were exemplified in the Middle Ages.

6. John Milner, D.D. (1752–1826), dominant English Catholic apologist, named vicar apostolic of the Midland District 1803, leader in the movement for Catholic emancipation in the British Isles.

7. *The End of Religious Controversy, In a Friendly Correspondence Between a Religious Society of Protestants And a Catholic Divine, In Three Parts* (London, 1818).

29

HECKER TO BROWNSON • [17 AUGUST 1844]*

[*Undated*][1]

Dear Friend

One or two events of little interest since I last wrote to you impel me to write to you again. But it is more in the thought that I am writing to you than else makes me do it. My present mental and moral position is one that costs me much anxious thought and often painful feeling. My activity seems all to be inward. We can neither be excited to external activity nor are we incited to it. This is not me, we know it, but know no remedy. We say will the period of our activity ever come. We ask not in what, if it even were in the bussiness [*sic*] around me. It seems the easiest act we now could do is ceasing to be at all. We seem to have stopped progress in all external life and all our life is within another sphere. Had we the choice of something we should have the power to do, but we are without any choice or special determination. Our Spiritual discernment seems to increase but not our power to do. We fear to wait, by waiting this may increase. We are neither enlivened by hope or darkened by despair. We are here is all we can say, and we would say anything else but this. To be patient in this would to some augur indifference, and it is painful to be so, in itself, seeing as we do the world all busy and active around us.

Choose! We would rather say with a smile strike. We have but few weak ties that bind us here. Our present life as it is we hold not dear. We are inexpressible [*sic*] grateful for the gift of a body through which we commune and receive so much joy [,] knowledge and love [,] they are debarred of who are devoid of a gift of this character. Therefore we would preserve it pure as when it first was given. But we do not feel called upon to sacrifice the man for his dress. Christianity is the love [,] the light and life of man but it does not change his elementary character. Our life may be changed but the destiny of humanity is immoveable [*sic*]. Is it not? In one sense we look upon Christianity as a free inestimable gift of God to man; Man is not bestowed to it. Man's primitive nature must be gloriously great if Christ the Son of God alone could ransom it. The progress of man toward God under the influence of Christianity is like the ascension of a released spirit towards heaven. Every breath awakens new & purer being into life. We feel ever an imperceptible influence in attending the mysteries of the Church. The mysteries of the Church are the mediums of the mystic life. A church without mysteries is without a Soul, a congregation of corpses. The facts we wished to state you were these. Dr Vethake[2] called here yesterday and he has undergone a change as desireable [*sic*] as it is unexpected. He has got as far as Puseyism[3] and says he is making all efforts to keep himself from catholicism but is sensible [;] he is going rapidly towards that point. All his troubles he says have ceased at once. I never saw him so happy [,] healthy and in good spirits. Six months will make him wholly a catholic.

In speaking with Bishop McClosky who I often go to see. He told me a day dream as he called it which he had indulged respecting yourself. It was just such a dream which you have related to me of establishing an American

Catholic Review. He had it all mapped out in his mind and had a fine historical Catholic scholar who says it [is] his delight to handle historical subjects as your co-editor[,] Spaulding[,][4] the Reviewer of Doubigny[,][5] and you as the head editor of the Review. I wish you would see McClosky. You would like his acquaintance better than either of the Bishops you know in your vicinity or Bishop H[ughes] here. He spoke with great confidence of success of such a project and of the necessity of a Review of this character on this side of the atlantic. He has a *very high* estimation of your ability.

Shall we hear from you in reply to the articles in the Churchman[6] and Phalanx[7] *before your* next number of your Review? If you have a few leisure moments will you write a few lines to me of *advice* and information. The project is going to Europe seems rather to increase as yet I have not heard from H[enry] T[horeau].

Truly

Isaac

I open this letter for joy hearing that you have approached the Sacrament of Confession. Oh dear friend what unimagined peace[,] happiness & love it is our privilege to enjoy! The Bishop told me this dear news he having hear [*sic*] it from one of the clergy who is here from Boston. I was admitted to the holy Eucharist to partake of the communion last Sunday morning. Shall I not hear from you father[,] brother and friend soon?

What will be the character of your next No?[8]

*Brownson, *BEL*, pp. 543–45.

1. This undated letter was postmarked 17 August, New York; its contents definitely place it within the year 1844.

This is the last letter that Hecker addressed to Brownson as Rev. O. A. Brownson. After this date, his letters are addressed to O. A. Brownson, *Esq.*, until the mid-1850s when OAB is called *Dr.*

2. John W. Vethake, M.D.

3. Edward Bouverie Pusey (1800–1882), Anglican priest, Regius Professor of Hebrew and Canon of Christ Church at Oxford; a leading Tractarian of the English Oxford Movement, which stressed the doctrines and sacraments of the Holy Catholic (not Roman) Church as well as apostolic succession.

4. Martin John Spalding (1810–1872), church historian and apologist, became bishop of Louisville 1850 and archbishop of Baltimore 1864; his book entitled *D'Aubigne's "History of the Great Reformation in Germany and Switzerland," Reviewed* (Baltimore, 1844) evolved into his two-volume *History of the Protestant Reformation* . . . (New York, Louisville, 1860).

5. Jean Henri Merle D'Aubigne (1794–1872), Swiss Calvinist ecclesiastical historian, preacher, founder of the College of Geneva. His volume *History of*

the Great Reformation of the Sixteenth Century in Germany, Switzerland . . . was reviewed by Spalding (see n. 4 above).

6. "Ultra-tenderness Toward Weaker Brethren," *The Churchman*, XIV (3 August 1844), 85–86.

7. *The Phalanx: Organ of the Doctrine of Association*, I, nos. 14 and 15; these issues responded to Brownson's article "Church Unity and Social Amelioration," *BrQR*, July 1844, pp. 310–28.

8. *BrQR*, October 1844.

30

HECKER TO BROWNSON • 5 SEPTEMBER 1844*

New York Sept. 5. /44

Dear Friend.

I have received a note from Charles Dana concerning those books[1] of Theo Parker's which I left with you. He says he expects Mr Parker home soon and he desires to return them to his library before he returns. Will you be so kind as to have them left at Miss Peabody's directed to Charles as soon as you can make it convenient for you to do so.

Yesterday I called on Bishop McClosky, through the travelling of the Priests to an fro from your region he seems to pick up a little news concerning you now and then. I heard from him that you had written a reply to Dr Seabury.[2] Bishop McC[loskey] and H[ughes] take a great interest in you. B. McC. said that B. Hughes thought of writing to you whether you would come on to N.Y. and start a Catholic Review. There is no question Bishop H. is the most able Bishop we have, and that a Review started here in NY with his patronage would have much greater advantages than at any other place in the union. You would find the heads of the Church more to your mind in N.Y. than in Boston it seems to me. And more able and with greater enthusiasm to second your plans. I don't hesitate to say that they look to your union with the C Church as an era in Catholic America. They feel much stronger, and are disposed to break the silence which the Church has suffered herself to keep. If you are disposed to restart your Quarterly under different auspices I think it would be well for you to see the Bishops of this diocese prior to this undertaking. I think it is very probable that B. Hughes will write to you soon by what B. M.C said to me. It would not be prudent I suppose to speak to any one until it comes in an official form which I have but little doubt that it will.

Do you see a catholic paper called the Tablet[3] printed in London? If not you should. It is edited by Mr Lucas[4] the author of that letter Whittier[5] gave you to read. I have pored over his paper with more delight and deep interest than any thing I have seen for a length of time. He grapples with the greatest questions like a master. No lack of courage in him. You must get this paper. It is mostly filled from his own pen and it contains all the European catholic intelligence in Religion[,] Art[,] Politics &c &c. He is a host. Strange that the Church should be indebted at the present day for her greatest writers in the English language at least to converts from protestantism. I have been reading one vol. of Mores Catholici[6] english edition[;] it is a great luxury to read such books as these.

My project of going to Europe has so far failed. Henry Thoreau is not disposed to go and under present circumstances I am not inclined to go on such a tour alone. This has thrown me back on the languages which may be of much more permanent good to me than the monk tour.

Dr Vethake is travelling on fast. All [?] I could say I look as usual[,] I speak as usual[,] I philosophize as usual[,] but how changed is all within. *Is* it true that

"Reaching above our nature does not good;
We must sink back into flesh & blood."

We feel an interior dryness and misty void but not moved from the permanent centre. Those days are not forever gone.

An opportunity[7] of going to Boston by the way of Providence to-day presents itself on account of the Dorr mass meeting[8] that almost irresistibly forces me to go.

Very Truly

Isaac

You will not forget those books.

*Brownson, *BEL*, pp. 546–48.

1. Eberhard's (?) *Mystical* was one of the books borrowed from Parker's library.

2. Samuel Seabury was editor of *The Churchman,* but was not the "Catholic Churchman" who authored the article critiqued by Brownson (see Letter 29, n.6).

3. *The Tablet,* a Catholic weekly founded in London in 1840.

4. Frederick Lucas (1812–1855), English-born Catholic convert from Quakerism 1839, founded *The* (London) *Tablet* (n. 3 above), became an Irish nationalist after moving to Dublin.

5. Possibly John Greenleaf Whittier (1807–1892), American poet and abolitionist.

6. Reviewed in *BrQR*, July 1844, pp. 412–13.

7. For a visit to George William Curtis (1824–1892) and his brother James Burrill Curtis, friends from Brook Farm; G. W. Curtis became an author and orator, associate editor of *Putnam's Monthly*, and editor of *Harper's Monthly Magazine* 1863.

8. Thomas Wilson Dorr (1804–1854), Rhode Island politician and reformer who agitated for the extension of the suffrage in Rhode Island and the abolition of its old English charter; when Dorr was jailed for leading skirmishes against the governor's troops in September 1844, mass meetings were held in his honor.

31

BROWNSON TO HECKER • 24 SEPTEMBER 1844

Boston Sept. 24, 1844.

Dear Isaac,

You will begin to think that I have grown forgetful or negligent. I am guilty of negligence but not of forgetfulness. But I have some [e]xcuse in the many occupations & troubles I have had. I rejoice to know that you have gone into the Church, and before this I presume have been admitted to [the] blessed Eucharist. The tone of your last letter encouraged me much, and has led me to hope that you are beginning to find yourself equal to your position whatever it may be. I am glad that you have abandoned the pilgrimage. Everything in its time and place. Even self-denial may become a luxury, and defeat itself. But you have a spiritual advisor more competent to direct you than I am. I hope you will find it consistent with your convictions of duty, to resume your studies, and prepare for the ministry. We have so great a demand for priests, that any young man who has any vocation that way owes it to his countrymen to become one.

I have made slow progress, though a few of the preliminary steps have been taken, and I am in the hands of my confessor, and follow his directions. I hope the time will soon come when I may feel that I am in the Church. I have no hope in myself, for I am all unworthy, but God's grace is infinite, and I cannot despair.

I am glad that you like the New York Bishop. I like ours not less. I love Bishop Fenwick as a father. He [is the] best man I ever knew. He comes the nearest to being a saint, and no man can do more for his diocese than he is doing. I am strongly attached also to Bishop Fitzpatric.[1] He is my confessor. He is a man of powerful intellect, and devoted to his office. Nothing would be to me more painful than to separate from them.

I do not like the project of a Catholic Review, at New-York. Such a

Review would necessarily be confined almost [e]xclusively in its circulation to the Catholic population. It is better to let mine go on as it is. If the Catholics will support it, it will live, and go among Protestants also. We are here decidedly on this opinion, and I presume, your own Bishops are also.

I wish you to tell Bishop M'Closkey from me, not to think my joining the Church is matter of thanksgiving or hope beyond the simple fact that it may be the means of saving my soul. I bring nothing with me but my sins, and a desire to obey it, and be saved. I do not think it will have much influence in [e]xtending the Catholic faith. I have myself no such [e]xpectations. I go into the Church because I need it, not because it needs me. Whether I am permitted the blessed privilege of laboring for it, depends on the merciful Providence of God, and whether I do not bring a scandal on it, depends on the same promise. All I can say is that I am nothing, but such as I am I am the Church's, and if it can use me I shall be thankful, if it cannot, it is no matter. Let all be done to the glory of God, and no man boast of his gifts, or be flattered for them. Tell me no more of the kind things which may be said of me. I am proud and vain enough, and have hard work enough to acquire the humility that becomes me.

I have met with very good success with my Review thus far. I have not many back nos. on hand. I finish in my next number my critique of Kant.[2] I reply to the Phalanx,[3] and I think demonstrate conclusively that Fourierism is repugnant to Christianity. I reply also to The Churchman in an Article, headed, The Anglican Church Schismatic.[4] Our friends here to whom I have read it, regard it as unanswerable. I am however afraid that Dr. Seabury will not meet it fairly. I have also two political articles[5] which may interest you. They are necessary to keep up the circulation of the Review.

William[6] & Henry[7] have gone to the College at Worcester. John[8] will go to sea this fall. We are all in tolerable health. My wife remembers you affectionately. Remember [me] to your brothers, and especially to your mother. Persevere, my dear Isaac, in the way you have begun, and may God bless you.

I was at Brook Farm last Sunday, & prepared a discourse to them. Two or three will become Catholics.[9] Mr. Ripley, I fear[,] is worse than an infidel. The atmosphere of the place is horrible. Have no faith in such associations. They will be only gatherings of all that is vile, to fester and breed corruption. Let me hear from you as soon and as often as convenient. You will get the Review the last of this week. I should be happy to see you.

Truly yours

O. A. Brownson

1. John Bernard Fitzpatrick (1812–1866), studied at Séminaire de St. Sulpice in Paris, became Fenwick's co-adjutor and then, in 1846, his successor as bishop of Boston; served as Brownson's instructor in the Catholic faith and censor for *BrQR* until 1854.

2. "Kant's Critic [*sic*] of Pure Reason," *BrQR,* October 1844, pp. 417–49.

3. "Fourierism Repugnant to Christianity," ibid., pp. 450–87.

4. "The Anglican Church Schismatic," ibid., pp. 487–514.

5. "The Protective Policy," ibid., pp. 514–32, and "The Suffrage Party in Rhode Island," ibid., pp. 532–44.

6. William Ignatius Brownson (1834–1864), Brownson's third oldest son (originally named after William Ellery Channing); he was killed in an accident near Virginia City in the Nevada Territory.

7. Henry Francis Brownson (1835–1913), Brownson's fourth son, author, lawyer, and major in the U.S. Army, his father's biographer and editor of his *Works*, twenty volumes (Detroit, 1882–87); he married Josephine Van Dyke at Detroit on 8 January 1868.

8. John Healy Brownson (1829–1858), Brownson's second oldest son; he married Anna Isabella Rogers at Brighton, Mass., on 26 August 1856, died in an accident at St. Paul, Minn.

9. In time Sophia Dana Ripley, George Ripley's first wife, and her niece Sarah F. Stearns did enter the Roman Catholic Church; Miss Stearns also became a nun. There have been unverified reports that other Brook Farmers embraced Catholicism, including William J. Davis, Buckley Hastings, George C. Leach, Charles King Newcomb, and Arthur Sumner.

32

HECKER TO BROWNSON • 29 [OCTOBER] 1844*

N.Y. 29 /44[1]

Dear Friend

The desire of informing you that I was actually engaged in doing something has been *the cause* that has prevented me from acknowledging your last letter to me sooner. After my union with the Church was fully completed I asked myself what now is my next step? What can I do? The idea of a pilgramage [*sic*] siezed me with much force and had I succeeded in getting a comrade in all probability I should not now be here. I did not, and the project is delayed probably to die forever at least in that form. What next was there for me to do? I had already tried to reenter the persuit [*sic*] of my brothers before the the idea of going to Europe occurred to me but it was a vain and useless attempt as the same thing heretofore has proven. It was to me what the atmosphere of the air is to the fish. Idleness is a mortal sin. To remain in the position I was seemed to argue that it was more the nature of a weakness than a virtue of character. What to do? To throw myself immediately in these conditions of becoming a servant of the Church is you are aware quite a different thing from that of any other ministry. I was not and am now not fully prepared to do this tho probably may be. I may magnify the difficulties from a sense I have of my own unworthiness and the greatness of the objects before me. It is true that decision is one half but decision to remain firmly fixed must be based upon a permanent basis and my present state of mind is not altogether of this character. Submitting myself to this power which has guided me thus far I came to the determination of recommencing the study of the languages, and the encouragement of your letter dear friend added much strength to the resolution. Providence in the course of events may open the path I am to tred more clearly and at all events, in any case, these studies cannot prove disadvantageous. We confess we act from presentiment which speaks to us in a voice tho not audible yet absolute. We feel no self in our study, and we trust in God that we are as far from the idea of self culture as heaven is from hades. Study, pure mental study, we can conceive is to be not one of selfishness but which to the devout soul may cost much denial and sacrifice of self-happiness. It is now better than a week that I have been studying in this City under a well qualified teacher,[2] and the difficulty that obstructed my progress in this way at the latter part of my being in Concord, and which I feared would here, so far I am extremely happy to say has not seriously interfered with me, and I hope will not. All that I do is done with the consent and advice of my Spiritual Director.[3]

You would be happy to see me. Dare I not say how much happier I should be to see you? Have I not incomparable reasons for saying so? Oh how much it adds to friendship to know that your friends behold and enjoy in common the same glorious mysteries and great blessings in Christ. A faint conception of the mystery and glory of Christ's Church overpowers all mundane expression. Like Dante the great Christian Poet who seemed so wrapt up in beatific vision as to be scarce able to speak audibly. Oh what a cadence there is from the Divine Comedy to that of Paradise Lost to that of Faust. Are these not historical pictures?

Thanks for your last Review.[4]

Our family is all well.

Remember me to Mrs O A B and forgive me for not writing to you earlier.

Your most unworthy friend

Isaac

*Brownson, *BEL*, pp. 548–50 (month not given).

1. Though the month was not written, this letter was postmarked 30 October, New York.

2. Rev. John J. Owens, principal of the Cornelius Institute in New York, founded in 1840 in memory of the Christian minister Elias Cornelius for the purpose of offering a free academic education to prospective Christian ministers. Hecker enrolled on 17 October 1844.

3. Bishop John McCloskey.

4. *BrQR*, October 1844.

33

HECKER TO BROWNSON • [26] NOVEMBER 1844*

Nov. 27. /44 N.Y.[1]

Dear Friend

My time being so completely occupied with my studies has prevented me from writing to you as soon after my last as I have desired to do. Oh that I could come to you. From the disharmony of the views of the society with which I am surrounded, with those I hold, my communion is in consequence much restricted. All my beliefs, hopes, and aspirations, find so few responses in other hearts that I feel most free when most alone from these. My faith is like a tender plant growing between rocks. The life which would ascend and burst forth in flowers is now buried beneath the soil in bulbuous [*sic*] roots for want of genial atmosphere. It is winter now with me, the spring and summer time will come when the sap husbanded shall rise and the tree put forth its leaves, blossoms, and its fruit. We have no word of complaint to utter. Were all so deeply at peace and invisibly happy. We feel free from but not indifferent to the demands of the external world.

What a work the Catholic Christian sees and has before him! How wide are the aims of protestants, of protestant education, p— society, p— government from those of catholic christianity! Can it be, can it be, that so many have been led so far far astray we ask ourself. How sadly has piety, the love of the arts, and society degenerated under the influence of protestantism! When I contemplate the holiness[,] the beauty[,] the piety[,] the sweetness of the Catholic faith my heart is filled with ineffable joy, while the only redeeming feature in protestantism is that it has preserved a few traces from that which it has fallen. He cannot be a catholic who sees not in society as it is his work to do.

I feel deeply interested in the success of your Review. Will you be sustained. Has Seabury rec'd it? He has not noticed its reception nor your article. Your articles I read and reread on metaphysics.[2] I am not satisfied until I imagine I have seized all your meaning. The views put forth in the last no.[3] of the inseparability of the mind into faculties seemed to me very important. Speaking of Reviews, the N[orth] A[merican] Review the last no. had quite a liberal article[4] on Ignatius Loyola.[5] The writer comes to the sage conclusion that the only way to do away with Catholicism is by living a deeper life than the Catholics. Amen we say but it must be first got.

Dr Vethake was here this morning and opened to me the designs of his to attempt to get the office of the Surveyor of this Port if Mr Calhoun is retained in the next administration. I think it is rather whether Mr C. will stay. The Dr is well qualified to fill the office and will be backed by good names for the office. He wished me to ask of you whether you would give him your aid on the condition of J. C. Calhoun's remaining? The other side is hostile to the Dr. Dr's suitableness for the office I think there can be no question. Brother John promises to procure some important names. What may be your pleasure I know not, but that I should be sorry to be the medium of anything displeasing to you. This I do feel and know.

In my studies my progress is not to be complained of, all my time and attention are bent to them. I told you that I had commenced to take lessons on the piano at the *same* time that I commenced the other studies. This is quite a recreation for me.

I cannot, dare not, hope to see you before next summer when I shall have liberty by vacation to do so. I have nothing to love here but ideal objects. My confessor I love—but Oh how many meanings that word love is made to bear.

Believe me to be yours always undeservedly,

Isaac

Remember me to your Wife. Our family is well.

*Brownson, *BEL*, pp. 550–52 (dated 27 November 1844). Microfilm, roll two (calendared 27 November 1844).

1. Though the date 27 November 1844 was written, this letter was postmarked 26 November, a day earlier.

2. On Kant's philosophy in *BrQR*, April 1844, pp. 137–74; July 1844, pp. 281–309; October 1844, pp. 417–49.

3. "Kant's Critic of Pure Reason," *BrQR*, October 1844, pp. 417–49.

4. "The Founder of the Jesuits," *The North American Review*, LIX

(October 1844), 412–34; based on *Des Jesuits* by MM. Michelet et Quinet (Paris, 1843).

5. Ignatius de Loyola (1491–1556), Spanish founder of the Jesuits or the Society of Jesus 1534.

34

HECKER TO BROWNSON • 14 JANUARY 1845

NY Jan. 14 1845

My dear Friend

If I did not feel that I communed with you otherwise than through this medium I could not restrain myself from communicating to you oftener. I know that I do or that there is a rare coincidence of development.

I see and feel one thing before me and that is the cause of Jesus, aside from this nothing but trouble, defeat, and death. The ways of the world grow farther from me. All that is contrary to the spirit of Jesus must be sacrificed if we would realize the glory of our true nature. I feel deeply for those who are seeking the things of this world in order to obtain the happiness of being. Their prayer should be for defeat. They are those who are wasting the things of God upon harlots. The only field for action is in, with, and for, the Church of Christ. I count all that labor worse than lost which is performed with other than the love of Jesus. It is all to be repented of and to be made good by pennance [*sic*]. Oh what a gain it would be to grow up in our childhood in Jesus' arms. I see no other foundation where on a man can build either for the salvation of the Soul [,] the good of society [,] the prosperity of Nations than the Church of Jesus and this I feel must be boldly spoken in the face of such an age as this. We dare not be bold with Jesus. That self denial that was primitively taught should be renewed. We fear almost at times that the world has been permitted to creep to[o] far in the Church. We see enough in Christ to call forth the blood of a thousand martyrs in the face of this age. Has the glory of martyrdom departed from the Church of Jesus. Never should this be said in a world as wicked as this. Christ is ever inviting us to leap from the precipice of faith that He may receive us in the arms of his love and carry us to heaven. Do we not see the poor but rich in Christ scarce[ly] permitted to adore and [k]neel at a distance at the sacred mysteries while those rich in the things of this world occupy the place of the babes in Christ. Is the Church the Church? Oh God forbid that I ever should doubt this. We cannot cry peace with the world as it is. Submission to the Church means not peace with the things of this world where ever they may be found. I am not ashamed of Christ but ah I cannot say this of all that is done in his name. Oh that He would strengthen me. When we are with the poor we are with Jesus. When we depend on faith we embrace Jesus. If we are not of this world wherein do we walk differently from its children. It is the fear of the world that makes the heads of the Church adapt its precepts and obligations to the weak consciences and propensities of men. Oh for the Church, the Church, the Church. My heart burns to realize the Catholic Church. Shall the children of heresies do more for the Souls of men and desire to ameliorate the conditions of the poorer classes than those of the true faith. How is this [,] are we to take pattern after them. I have no eyes for our virtures but for our faults and the virtues of the enemies of our faith.

I trust you love me. I am happy to feel that you do.

I make respectable progress in my studies. Your last Review[1] I have read as yet but 3 articles. The article[2] by Mr Clerkenwell is one which when I read Anna Carmody [*?*] [3] about 4 months ago gave me strong hopes of seeing. Your, I beg pardon Mr Clerkenwell's article, was father no doubt to my thought.

I have been reading Tasso's[4] Jerusalem Delivered.[5] It is all song, springing from a warm catholic heart of love. I have now a Vol. of St. Augustine's Sermons Oxford Edition[6] before me lately pub. Two of his sermons I have read. They are full of wisdom and rich with the catholic faith. I wish I could place them in your hands. St Augustine was one of the greatest of men. I look forward with joy when I shall be able to read and receive from the fullness of life of the Fathers.

Mention my name in remembrance to the Misses Sturges.[7]

Your wife thinks of me I hope.

Unworthily yours in Jesus

Isaac

1. *BrQR*, January 1845.

2. S. A. C. P. Clerkenwell, "Edward Morton," *BrQR*, January 1845, pp. 98–129.

3. It is uncertain whether Anna Carmody [*?*] refers to a person or to a book.

4. Torquato Tasso (1544–1595), Italian poet.

5. *Jerusalem Delivered*, epic poem finished in 1575 and published in 1580, dealing with a love story set during the Crusades and the attempt to liberate Jerusalem.

6. *A Library of the Fathers of the Catholic Church*, XVI: (St. Augustine) *Sermons on Selected Lessons of the New Testament* (Oxford, 1844–45).

7. Caroline Sturgis Tappan (1818–1888) and her sister Ellen Sturgis Hooper (1812–1848), poets and Transcendentalists, both known to Hecker from Brook Farm.

35

HECKER TO BROWNSON • [15 JANUARY 1845]*

[*Undated*][1]

The letter inside of this dear friend I wrote to you yesterday. If I had the time I would not send it to you but write another. I have not and you will not misunderstand what I have said in this. It is not all true that in some things I feel too sensibly. I am inclined to lean more upon providence than what men call prudence.

Is it not true that we are to lean more upon the Catholic life than on councils &c not that they are contradictory to themselves or the life of the Church. No, but because they are no more than an expression of that [which] we possess and which would not have been spoken unless for heresies.

Isaac

*Microfilm, roll two (calendared [23 January 1845]).

1. Rather than treating it as a fragment or as a sheet from a missing letter, this brief note is taken to be the cover letter for Letter 34. Based on internal and external evidence, it can be dated 15 January 1845. It seems most likely that the preceding letter (which has no postmark) was enclosed with this one, whose envelope was addressed to O. A. Brownson, Esquire, Chelsea, and was postmarked 23 January, Boston, indicating that it was posted by someone who carried it there, since Hecker was in New York during this period.

The complaints found in the letter of 14 January 1845 about the place allotted the poor people at Holy Mass coincide with an entry recorded in Hecker's diary for 20 January 1845, wherein he registered his abhorrence for the system of renting pews in Catholic churches. He also stated that he voiced his objections about this practice to Bishop McCloskey "last Wednesday" (15 January); the bishop's sympathetic response may have led Hecker to reconsider his letter of the day before. In the diary entry, Hecker continued: "I wrote a letter to O. A. B. in which I gave vent to my feelings on this subject [pew rent]. And said there was, temporally speaking, much to be done and undone in the Church as it now is" (HP, APF).

36

HECKER TO BROWNSON • [c. 8 MAY 1845]*

New York New York Thursday [*Undated*][1]

Dear Friend

Since I last wrote to you Dr Vethake has called to see me. He said that he his whole family had determined to be united to the Catholic Church. His eldest daughter had resolved to do so whether he did or no. He is not yet in, but it is seldom that one that has made up his mind so far, having passed through what the Dr has, that recedes from his determination. Brother George will be confirmed on Trinity Sunday with me at the same time.[2]

I see by the Public papers that you are to deliver an oration at Baltimore some time in July. If this be so, you will I suppose pass through this city, and probably stay a few days with us, and then I shall have the opportunity of seeing you without going to Boston.

The German Priest[3] that was mentioned in my last belongs to the order of Redemptorists[4] of St Alphonsus[5] of which there is a small missionary body from this Society from Austria in our city devoted to the German population. I have visited them quite frequently since then and have spent some good hours with one of their body. It happens just in my present state of mind concerning the choice of a vocation that this meeting with this one has been quite providential to me. He loaned me a book[6] of St. Alphonsus written on purpose for one who is about making choice of a vocation in the religious life. The Priest himself has been much help to me. However books and men are books and men, and it requires as much right judgment to discriminate in their advice what strictly is applicable to one as it does in them to give right advice. This is the position in which I know [*sic*] feel myself in, unable to choose and a perfect willingness to obey. I will knock–seek–pray–ask for God has promised to give a response to all these.

Does the Church in your diocese celebrate this month as the Month of Mary? If so you know more than I can tell you about this beautiful impressive ceremony.

Question. Can all that is worthy among the Greeks, Hindoos, and Romans be accounted for satisfactorily by the doctrine of primitive revelation and the amount of primitive virtue not lost by the Fall? When I look at some of their attainments in arts, in morals, and even in right dogmas in religion I am astonished and ask myself the question I have put. Do you know of any work or writer that throws any light on this subject? This very question? I think that I shall find much when if ever I am able to read the primitive Fathers who had to battle with Heathenism and overthrew it on this point. Will this not be so? I want to see a generous appreciation of the Heathen world such only as a catholic can give, for the Dogmas of the Catholic Church are the only answer[s] that have answered the problem of this World at least, and the destiny of men, without denying what is, and what has been, and affirming what is not, nor never has been.

My time is as it was wholly devoted to study. It is late in life for me to commence but in the end it may be all for the best. Some times I now think I can see it so.

This afternoon I purchased a copy of Cicero to commence in on Monday next. I have not got far in Caesar, not much more than half of the 1st book, but this change is made in order to give a better arrangement to the Classics. My decision will necessarily take me from this City. This is not the best place for me to be in the world.

Sincerely

Isaac

*Brownson, *BEL,* pp. 530–32 (dated May 1844). Microfilm, roll two (calendared 21 May 1844).

1. Even though this undated letter was stamped 21 May with the seal of the Baltimore & Ohio Railroad, it was more likely written about Thursday, 8 May 1845. This date is determined by two events specified in the letter, namely, the fact that Hecker was confirmed on 18 May 1845 and that he first met the Redemptorists on 14 April 1845.

2. Both George and Isaac Hecker received the sacrament of confirmation from Bishop McCloskey on Trinity Sunday, 18 May 1845, with George taking the middle name of Valentine, and Isaac that of Thomas.

3. Gabriel Rumpler (1814–1856), German-born, popular preacher and pastor of Most Holy Redeemer Church, also rector of the Redemptorist House on Third Street on the Lower East Side of Manhattan.

4. The Congregation of the Most Holy Redeemer (C.SS.R.) was founded by St. Alphonsus (n. 5 below) in 1732 at Scala, Italy, for the purpose of preaching the Gospel to the poor and to abandoned sinners. In 1832 the Congregation came to the United States to minister to the German-speaking Catholics in the Diocese of Cincinnati; then in 1842 Bishop Hughes invited these missionaries to work among the German Catholic immigrants of New York. The Redemptorists in this country were under the jurisdiction of the Belgian province until 1850, when America became a separate province, headquartered in Baltimore, under the direction of Father Bernard Hafkenscheid.

5. Alphonsus Maria Ligouri (1696–1787), Italian founder of the Redemptorists, ascetical writer and moral theologian, a doctor of the Church.

6. Either *Instructions and Considerations on the Religious State* or *The True Spouse of Jesus Christ.*

37

BROWNSON TO HECKER • 25 JUNE 1845

June 25, 1845

My dear Isaac,

I am unpardonable for not having answered your kind letters before. I heartily rejoice at the conversion of your brother George. As to your resolution to become a religious I am not surprised at it, and have no doubt that you have a religious vocation. It is difficult to advise another in regard to the order to be selected. I prefer the Jesuits, but they are not rigid enough to satisfy you. Your disposition I should think, would lead you to the Carthusians, but could you not content yourself with the Dominicans? If you could would you need go farther than Philadelphia? The Redemptorists or Priests of the Mission, though they have not I believe a strictly monastic rule, offer some attractions I should think to you, as they are in this country mainly Germans. Bishop Fitzpatrick recommends the Dominicans. I take it for granted that your intention is to become one of the regular clergy instead of one of the saecular [*sic*] clergy, because your services as a priest are much needed in this country, where we have so few priests.

So our Dr. Vethake is on his way. God grant he may enter. The Dr will be happy as a Catholic. He will find what truth his mind and his heart need. How is brother John? Is he wavering?

My Review[1] is printed and I suppose [you] will get one in a day or two. I hope you will like it. We regard it as a strong number. It is all from my own pen. The first article will interest you, as it is the first of three[2] intended to be a thorough discussion of Transcendentalism in its fundamental principles, and I think you will find some difficult questions disposed of not unsatisfactorily. After you have read it be so good as to give me your opinion of it. I will value your opinion because you are well acquainted with the subject.

And how do you like on trial Catholicity? I grow more and more Catholic, and less and less of a Protestant. My great trouble, after the regulation of my own spiritual life, is that the mass of our Catholics are not Catholics. *Inter nos,* I do not like in general our Irish population. They have no clear understanding of their religion, and though they can fight for it, they do not seem able in general to die for it, and our *Irish* priests are either bent upon making money, or else they are Irishmen before they are Catholics. There are however some noble [e]xceptions to this remark. But we want American priests as fast as we can get them. I have three boys at college. John thinks of becoming a priest. May God grant him a vocation, and also William and Henry.

We have not many recent converts, but a large number on the stacks. One young man[3] from one of our old families, well-known and loved, has gone to California, and promises to become a sincere and devout Catholic. His life and conversation are quite edifying. Some four or five women I trust will soon make their abjuration. There is a good deal of stir amongst our Protestant population, and I trust in God something will come of it. But of all these matters I will speak when I see you.

I trust to be in New-York on Monday night. I shall come in the Long Island train, & be in in the afternoon. Shall be happy to meet you at the Depot. If I do not, I shall come directly to your house. I shall stop overnight, for I have some business in the city on Tuesday.

My kindest regards to your Mother, your brothers, and to your brother's wife.

Believe me truly your friend & brother

O. A Brownson.

1. *BrQR*, July 1845.

2. "Transcendentalism, Or Latest Form of Infidelity," *BrQR*, July 1845, pp. 273–323; October 1845, pp. 409–42; "Transcendentalism. – Concluded," October 1846, pp. 409–39.

3. Joseph Coolidge Shaw (d. 1849), of a prominent Boston family; Catholic convert and ordained priest 1845, entered the Jesuits 1849.

38

HECKER TO BROWNSON • [23 JULY 1845]*

[*Undated*][1]

Do not put yourself to any trouble in answering what I now say. It will be time enough when I shall feel more certain of acting as I have suggested. It is possible to be sure of my acting sooner than I imagine. I shall enquire more about the matter. My confessor will be home in a week or so.[2] You know if I should think of joining such an order as the Redemptorists if it were found that I might be useful in this country they would send me here. The only reason or at least the only one that influences me most is that I feel the need of being under stronger catholic influences than are, so far as my experience goes, in this country. I only suggest the R[edemptorists] not that I have spoken with them about the matter or are decided in my own mind. I would be consumed by God. And the speediest means to this end is what I eagerly seek for. I do not find here the room to loose [*sic*] my life. I feel the need of being met. If I am deluded then I need something to be laid upon me to show up my delusion. Who will take me in hands? I want some one to kill me stone dead, or make me cry out enough, enough. If this desire is wrong I must be commanded to resist it. If I need restraint, it must be laid upon me. The Church is all. I feel the worst in it, and I do not wish to be so, therefore I cry for her help. I want her to crush me, so that she may be all in me, which she now is not. There is no use of compromise. There can be no looking back. I want a discipline that sinks deeper than what I have yet experienced. I have too much liberty. This liberty abridges my freedom. Too long have we been fed on pap until we have all become whinning [*sic*] rogues. But you see more than I can say and understand me too better I hope. It is evident where we are. Some centuries ago this would not have been said but been done. Our heads are much larger than our hearts. We say a good deal & live a little at best. But you see how the tide runs.

Have you seen Faber's,[3] the Anglican minister, Sir Lancelot?[4] I suppose not. There are some things in it that are quite bold and tell home. But these Anglican creatures are still John Bulls. But however this book will help on the right movement. He sees and points out the promised land[5] and like many other of his kind are willing to die this side of it. One is tempted to say they don't see it. In part they don't. And yet they see as those who see and do not. He speakes [*sic*] of the Anglican Church as the "separated church" and the Catholic Church as the "offended." Of Luther he says in speaking of "the inane self praise" "& self complacence vile" that corroding lies in the A[ngli-can] Church. "Engendered of that dark and atheist creed which an apostate monk three ages back begot through his lust-blinded intellect." "Seek recon-cilement with the offended Church," "minding that hour when Christendom arose and shook thee from her as a leprous thing." There are spots in the book that will pay a catholic heart for reading. Yet withal he submits his conscience to this leprous thing. Probably he knows & is aware that this poor creature is dead dumb [,] not having the organs of speech.

I will either write or come to you soon.

Very Truly

Isaac

*Brownson, *BEL*, pp. 539–41 (year not given). Microfilm, roll two (calendared 23 July 1844).

1. This undated letter was postmarked 23 July. Its contents place it within the year 1845, i.e., Hecker's deliberating about a religious vocation, and Hecker's confessor Bishop McCloskey leaving for a two month visitation of the Diocese of New York in early June 1845 and returning toward the end of July 1845.

2. Bishop McCloskey was about to conclude a visitation of the Diocese of New York (see n. 1 above).

3. Frederick William Faber (1814–1863), Catholic convert from the Oxford Movement 1845, ordained priest 1847, founded the London Oratory 1849, noted hymnologist and ultramontanist.

4. *Sir Lancelot*, an 11,000 line poem published in 1844; just as Lancelot suddenly found himself excommunicated from the Church, so did Faber (n. 3 above) find himself "excommunicated" from the Church of England for suggesting that Nature could substitute for the Church as an avenue for spiritual life and expression.

5. The following erasure occurs here: "tho he is to[o] big a . . . to enter it himself or more probably as he hints at himself. . . ."

39

HECKER TO BROWNSON • 24 JULY 1845

N.Y. July 24, 1845[1]

Dear Friend.

Your long stay from N.Y. worried me somewhat. But now it is all right. It may be that I will come to see you in a week or so. I have a strong desire to come. "Inter nos" I will tell you why I do not come immediately. The new establishment of my brothers has absorbed all their capital, and not to seem unmindfull of their interests I stay at home. I may come the expense is little. Some pleasant morning I may go on foot for New England.

Old and forgotten sins come up afresh to my memory, and recent actions that I thought not sinfull seem now to me full of sin. Verily I am a mine of sin without bottom. Oh what a work have we. How much courage, truthfullness, & humility, do we need for it. Freedom a word how different do we understand from the protestants. To us it means the annihilation of our own wills, to them it is the following of theirs. They seek what we strive to avoid. They fight for that which we fight against. If we have the hardest battle surely we have the sweetest reward. That we have a hard and difficult contest we need no assurance from others. That it is a cross to any one's self is true. That it is difficult, exceedingly so, for one always to distinguish rightly between his own will and the will of God is a matter of common experience. And the farther we go in this matter, the greater is the difficulty. I would not move a finger, nor draw a breath, nor speak, nor eat, nor drink, nor sleep, nor wake, says one, unless moved or commanded by God so to do. Oh who has this assurrance [*sic*] and how shall we obtain it? If we reckon how much in one day which we do interiorly & exteriorly that which we are neither commanded nor called to do, not to say how much more we do contrary both to the commands & inspirations of God. Surely it is enough for to cover us with confusion all our days.

The good moments of our life will not number sufficient to make a rosary at our death by which we can say our prayers. It is impossible as the experience of the Church has shown, and as the example of our Saviour teaches us, to overcome the Enemy of Souls except by long fastings and much time given to solitude. Solitude which the worldling fears & the Christian loves. And that too for the same reason namely the sight of one's self. Our enemy so often as he is defeated so often does he renew the contest. When I consider no saint however holy has been freed from being tempted I shudder at the thought how open & vulnerable must we be to the shafts of Satan. Surely unless it were for the prayers of the sainted & the watchfullness of those who guard us we should fall ten times, a hundred times ten, where we now fall once. But how will I rejoice when I shall be freed from my own self direction to which I am now necessarily so much involved. It will go hard, and often my will will murmur, but there can be no cure without a pain. I will not be alone. Freed from myself and in the hands of a God commissioned man. I feel as if I could not stay a moment where I am. Ah how much have I lost by lingering. But even being here where I am gives me no little joy. Do you think I could get that kind of direction here that would free me from my own will entirely, entirely? The idea of going to Europe in order to get that discipline which I need still remains with some force with me. There is there that far separation physically speaking from the world, that distant solitude, that severer discipline and spirit, which daily I feel more and more the need of, and which I fear is here not. I may be mistaken in my estimation of what is here, and respecting myself, and it may be most prudent for me to enter the seminary at Fordham,[2] but still these thoughts are deepest & uttermost in my mind, and I know I throw them out to you. I am fully convinced of this[:] I can be only so far useful as I am subject to Christ, and I would be therefore nothing of myself. What think you of my going to Europe? There I shall breathe a catholic atmosphere, and walk upon earth consecrated with the footsteps of Saints. There too I shall be freed from all other relations than those which tend to aid me on in the work. I shall be decapitated at once instead of wasting a life of long lingering pain. If anything useful to others can be made of me why I may be sent back here to you again. If not, not.

[*Unsigned*]

1. This letter was enclosed in the ensuing letter (Letter 40) of 25 July 1845.

2. St. John's College (later Fordham University), founded in 1841 by Bishop Hughes as the diocesan college and seminary, with Rev. (later Bishop) John McCloskey as its first president.

40

HECKER TO BROWNSON • 25 JULY 1845

July 25, 1845

Since I wrote the enclosed letter I have seen Padre Rumpler Superior of the Redemptorists and enquired more particularly about their order, and this morning I went to see Bishop Hughes in order to know more about the College at Fordham, and receive his advice. His advice to me is to go to St Sulspice [*sic*] at Paris.[1] There is all that I need—discipline, example, learning. Fordham will not be the place for me. It will require sometime before all things will be fully regulated in this country. But what objections have I towards St Sulspice? Two: the first is that I fear it will not go far enough for me. But in this matter truly I am not even a novice. It may go too far and I be rejected. But I stake frankly to you the suspicions in my mind. I have been delaying too long already. But to the second—the expense. This I am not fully aware what it will be. Rev J. R. Bailey[2] at the College was educated at St Sulspice and the Bishop advised me to see him for further information. But any expense is an objection with me. With the Redemptorists all that my expenses can be is my voyage out & if I should return my expenses back. The first objection I am disposed to give up with advice from my spiritual director. The second may disappear after knowing definitely what they may be at St Sulspice, and on having a talk with my brothers. Thus you see where I now stand. The other orders of the Church the Jesuits & the Dominicans &c. I know of only in so much as I have read & heard others speak of them. If I decide in favor of Paris, it will give me a good opportunity of becoming personally acquainted with most of them if not all. Considering this matter once more all over again, I have come to this conclusion, that it is quite certain that I shall leave this country, and very probable I shall go to St Sulspice.

Now dear friend something deeper touches me. This education for something my humility shrinks from. First for the reason of my manifest inferiority, and second for the fear of the temptations that I shall be subject to. If we have a vocation the grace of God is undoubtedly sufficient to support us. This is good but, and ah but. However I will try the mildest form of discipline first tho I am inclined to receive the severer.

You will forgive me for taxing you so much as to read what I have written to you. You have told me to write to you and for this I am very grateful. As soon as I shall come to any more determinate conclusions you will be the first thought in my mind. You need not put yourself to any trouble of replying to what I say unless you see I am going one side, or need some of your experience, and sometimes a little of encouragement. Rev. J R Bailey will not be at home before a week, so that I shall not be able to see him before then. It may be that in the mean time I shall see you at your home. I hope so. I desire very much to see Bishop Fitzpatrick. Bishop Hughes sends two young men on the 1st of September to St Sulspice, and if I go I shall be ready then at least.

Very Truly

Isaac.

1. Séminaire de St. Sulpice, established in 1642 at Paris (later moved to Issy) by Jean Jacques Olier (1608–1657), founder of the Priests of St. Sulpice (Sulpicians).

2. James Roosevelt Bayley (1814–1877), Episcopalian priest who converted to Catholicism 1842, ordained Catholic priest 1844, held administrative posts at St. John's College, became first bishop of Newark, N.J., 1853 and archbishop of Baltimore 1872.

41

HECKER TO BROWNSON • 29 JULY [1845]*

Tues–19–July[1]

Dear Friend

When I last wrote to you I had then so far decided in favor of St Sulspice [*sic*]. Now if nothing interferes with me I expect to go on this friday[2] with Mr MacMaster[3] & Mr Walworth[4] to join the Redemptorists. The reason for this is simply that I have given up all idea of becoming one of the secular clergy. If I should receive from you any reasons that are convincingly in favor of any other order I should consider my step. You spoke to me of the Dominicans, and that Bishop Fitzpatrick tho't well of them, and as their aim is not much unlike that of the Redemptorists, if there were any grounds why they should be preferred to the Society of St Liguori I would not hesitate in giving myself up to them. You know my noviciate will give me the opportunity of choice. Tho the Redemptorists do not present to me the external attractions such as a residence at Paris or Rome would[,] yet these are not the objects which should influence my decision. I saw Bishop Hughes this morning and he approves my choice.

I shall feel freer now being freed from all monetary relations with the world. I go with out a regret of leaving this continent or all that it contains. If ever I should be sent back to it as I may be[,] it would be my joy to be spent in its true enlightenment & progress. But the Catholic lives but for one object be he in China or at the opposite hemisphere. I do not expect to stay over next friday or saturday at the farthest. The provincial general[5] goes on the 16teenth of August. If I should remain to go with him then I probably would make you a visit. But this is not at all probable. Will you then write to me immediately and send me the watch. O[h] how I should be pleased to receive from Bishop Fitzpatrick his blessing before I go. He will give it to me tho I be not visibly present. Mr MacMaster is a very fine and talented man. He is a convert from the Puseyites. A correspondent of Newman[,][6] Oakely[7] &c&. Walworth is the son of the Chancellor[8] of our city. An earnest & serious young man. We will be good companions for each other. Walworth is too a convert. They both sacrifice much this world much more than I for the love of Christ.

My mother and John feel very bad about my going. Brother George not so much. George is alone. You will be his friend and give him what you know he needs in encouragement. When I am away will you give my mother a few kind words. My going may do much good in the family. I shall write to you again before I go. I must close to get this in this afternoon's mail.

Very Truly

Isaac

*Brownson, *BEL*, pp. 541–43 (year not given).

1. Though the year of this letter was not written, its contents, especially the reference to Hecker's departure for the Redemptorist novitiate, surely place it within 1845.

2. Friday, 1 August 1845, when Hecker sailed for St. Trond, Belgium, to enter the novitiate.

3. James Alphonsus McMaster (1820–1866), influenced by the Oxford Movement as an American Episcopalian, Catholic convert 1845, lay apologist, became editor of the *New York Freeman's Journal and Catholic Register* 1846.

4. Clarence Augustus Walworth (1820–1900), noted missionary preacher and author, involved in the American Oxford Movement at General Theological Seminary, Catholic convert 1845, ordained a Redemptorist priest 1848, became a pastor in Troy, N.Y., 1858, entered Paulists 1861, rejoined Albany Diocese 1865.

5. Frederick de Held, C.SS.R. (1799–1881), Belgian provincial superior on visitation in the U.S. at Baltimore.

6. John Henry Newman.

7. Frederick Oakeley (1802–1880), British Catholic convert from Anglicanism 1845, ordained priest 1845, became Canon of Westminster 1852.

8. Reuben Hyde Walworth (1788–1867), jurist, politician, last chancellor of New York State 1828–48.

42

BROWNSON TO HECKER • [31 JULY 1845]*

[*Undated*] [1]
Thursday.

Dear Isaac,

I did not receive yours in time to reply yesterday. I will send your Watch on by Express, if I can; but I hardly know how to do so with safety. I am sorry I did not have it for you, or rather that I took it [at] all. But I will return [it] if on going to the city I can find any safe way of doing so.

I think you have made a good decision under the circumstances as the best I think in your power. I hope however you will wait till the Father Provincial returns. I shall regret your absence from the country, but I shall feel [more] anxious about you than I have done. I suppose I may speak freely to you. You have a very lively and active imagination, more so than you are aware, which joined to a quick sensibility and a warm heart and ardent temperament, [e]xposes you to many dangers, against which you are not likely to be on your guard. Your danger is on the side of Mysticism. You are liable to receive the truth under a form too subjective, and to mingle too much of sensibility with the objective forms of faith. Here is your danger, and how you are to be on your guard. Here is the rock on which many a great saint has been wrecked. I mention this, not because I have many fears, but because I see where your tendency is.

The Church is objective. It proposes truths to be believed, and acts to be performed. It concerns almost [e]xclusively the reason and the will. It demands a clear understanding & an obedient and reverent will. You may even in your desire to obey be after all following your own will and judgment, instead of renouncing them. But remember, my dear Isaac, that it matters little what our outward circumstances are, our great business is to do what God commands us *now* and where we are. Many of the notions I threw out on the doctrine of Communion [2] I look upon now as false & even hurtful. It is best for us to take the Church in the old way, without studying to find a philosophical basis for what it teaches. We want a logical basis rather than a philosophical basis. The notion of Communion I formerly advanced and which wrought such a revolution in us both, served its purpose, but, if [e]xtended very far it is dangerous and heretical. Even Dr. Moehler[3] carries it too far. Distrust all modern writers, even if Catholic. Protestant notions have affected even the ablest of our authors, & especially among the Germans.

But you will be in hands every way competent to guide you, and I alas, am making no progress. I advance backwards. I am solitary, and were it not worldly circumstances compel[ling] me to labor I fear I should sink into nothing. Do not [e]xpect any thing from me. I feel that my race is nearly run, and the goal I fear is not near. God has been good to me, has been liberal in his gifts and graces, but I have abused them all, and my name may yet become a scandal. You must not forget to pray for me. I would save my soul, but I tremble lest I become a castaway.

I shall not forget George. I am sure he will do well, and whatever I can do to encourage him or comfort your mother, I shall most assuredly do. I hope I shall see you yet before you leave. If I do not, be assured that I shall remember you with many pleasant & grateful recollections, and shall never forget to pray for your spiritual prosperity. I am sure Bishop Fitzpatrick would send you his blessing but I cannot see [him] before mailing this. Yet take the blessing of God with you. You go to devote yourself in his service. You leave all for him. A blessed privilege, for if you persevere you know an infinite award awaits you. Good bye, my dear Isaac, & God bless you, preserve you, guard you, and at last receive you to the heritage of the saints. If we meet not again here, may we meet in heaven.

Yours truly,

Brownson.

*Microfilm, roll nine (calendared [31 July 1845?]).

1. This undated letter was postmarked 31 July, though the year was illegible; but the letter was obviously written in view of Hecker's imminent departure for Europe on 1 August 1845. Hence the letter was written on the Thursday immediately following Hecker's (Letter 41) of Tuesday, 29 July [1845].

2. Pierre Leroux's doctrine that the "I" lives by communion with the "Not-Me," with that which is not ourselves; more specifically we commune with nature through property, with other persons through the family and the state, and (in Brownson's adaptation) with God through the Church.

3. Johann Adam Möhler (1796–1838), German Catholic priest, theologian, and professor at the University of Tübingen, author of *Die Einheit in der Kirche* (1825) and *Symbolik* (1832).

43

HECKER TO BROWNSON • 18 SEPTEMBER 1845

St Trond Sept. 18/45

Dear Friend.

By the time that you will receive this letter I shall have made a spiritual retreat, and have received, so I trust, the habit of a novice of the order of the Redemptorists. This places me under the Rules of the Novitiate for one year. Should it become evident at the end of the year that my vocation is to be a missionary Priest then it will be my duty to take the vows of the order, and if this should not be the case then whatever may be my vocation it will be pointed out to me by my Director.[1] The conditions here are perfect, and all that can hinder me from gaining the end for which God gave me being is a non compliance on my part. The spirit of the Church with such conditions must produce a true catholic life. And this is so. All our wants both spiritual and physical are watched & provided for with a love that exceeds the parental affection. To any other than a catholic mind this would be an enigma, but we carry the solution of it ever in our hearts. The twenty four hours of the day are regulated with such wisdom that there cannot be either uneasiness or dissipation without a violation of the Rules. Our walks and the hours of conversation are sanctified by obedience. I must smile when I think that these frequently fall upon new beginners and such as have been accustomed to follow their own wills as long as I have as some what of the character of a penance. To go to walk when you would remain at home retired, to converse with cheerfullness when you would remain silent, to eat when you would fast, and such like duties, often cost more than what may be looked upon by some as the severest penances. Indeed a full compliance with all the rules demanded an offering up of the whole will to God.

There are between 30 & 40 novices in this house and about 8 postulants who will receive the habit at the same time with us americans. Their ages are from 18 to 30. The younger novices have finished the study of humanities and some of the oldest have in part finished their theological studies. French is the language that is spoken here, tho all are understood and are spoken by a few. But the novices are required to be able to speak the French before they are received. We americans are studying it with all diligence.

Father Bernard[2] told me that he saw you in Boston just before his departure. He said that you promised to send him your Review. This will save you the trouble of sending it to me, as it would not be read here by any, nor by me, until I shall go to the place where you intend sending it. But if you have the opportunity of writing to me, I should esteem it a great favor if you would give me an index and table of its contents.

It is no[w] positively certain that Mr Newman is about leaving the Protestant Church of England. This may be no news to you. He is at present occupied in writing a book[3] upon the grounds why he takes this step. This a person[4] told me who is intimate with him and saw him a week or two ago. He was then occupied in writing this work. There is but little doubt, if any, that all of any importance of that party will follow his steps.

The address for a letter to reach me should be written thus. R. F. F. Redemptorists, a [*torn*] St Trond, Belgium. With my name super-scribed. I hope it will not be long before I shall see one thus addressed from your hand.

You will have the kindness after that you have read this sheet and the one enclosed to put them in a wrapper and direct them to my relatives in New York.

Remember me to Mrs Brownson.

Your humble friend

Isaac

O A Brownson Esq.

1. Rev. Leopold Ottman, C.SS.R., Hecker's novicemaster at St. Trond, Belgium.

2. Bernard Hafkenscheid, C.SS.R. (1807–1865), prominent Dutch preacher and missionary, became first U.S. Redemptorist provincial superior 1850.

3. *Essay on the Development of Christian Doctrine*, written before but published after John Henry Newman's conversion to Catholicism 1845.

4. Most probably James A. McMaster, who went to Littlemore, England, to see Newman and John Dobree Dalgairns (1818–1876), another convert to Catholicism from the Oxford Movement 1845 and later a priest of the London Oratory.

44

HECKER TO BROWNSON • 13 SEPTEMBER 1846*

Sept 13 /46

Dear Friend.

Having the opportunity I take the pleasure to send you these psalmes of

St Bonaventura,[1] knowing they would gratify your devotion towards the Blessed Virgin Mary, who is worthy of all honor and all that one can do is too little.

In two weeks I commence the Retreat of fifteen days before taking the vows. I am altogether unworthy of this blessed grace, and I hope you will aid me in rendering gratitude to our Lord and the Blessed Virgin for this unmerited favor.

I shall feel ever indebted to you my dear friend and Mrs Brownson for the great kindness you have shown towards me.

I hope to write you a letter after having taken the vows.

Until then I remain your brother in the faith of our blessed Lord and friend, who implores your prayers.

Remember me to my friends

Isaac

O. A. Brownson Esq

St. Trond

*Microfilm, roll two (part omitted).

1. St. Bonaventure (Giovanni di Fidanza, 1221–1274), Italian Franciscan philosopher and theologian, named cardinal 1273, doctor of the Church.

45

HECKER TO BROWNSON • [1 NOVEMBER 1846]*

Oct. 1, 1845[1]

My very dear friend

It was my intention to have written to you on the day of my taking the [profe]ssed vows[2] but being unable to make the time I had to wait for another opportunity.

You are aware that my life for some years past has been an enigma to others and a mystery to myself. This mystery to a certain extent no longer exists, and I feel it to be a duty to communicate to you, to whom I feel bound by many real and intimate ties, the little knowledge that I have by the grace of God upon this subject. It is well known to you my friend that there are recognized in the Church two ways in which the grace of God leads the Soul to that perfection for which He created it. The one is called passive and the other active; these have given birth to the orders contemplative and the orders active, and from which have sprung the Theology mystic and the Theology scholastic as they are termed. Neither one of these ways are entirely separated from the other, still the predominancy of one is sometimes so great as to fully warrant this distinction. There are those Souls who have been plunged suddenly into the state passive tho they are very rare. In the one grace is acquired by the means of the activity of the faculties of the Soul, in the other it is as it were infused immediately into the Soul. The one is governed by its intelligence & reflection &c, the other by the simple instinct of grace. But you are sufficiently acquainted with this distinction and it is the last, the way passive, that I wish to explicate a little to you. God does not put the soul in the way passive until he has gained at the bottom of the will its full consent, and is sure of its fidelity, morally sure. God when it is his design to unite the soul to himself in this way commences by infusing into it his infinite love, the object of which is to detach the soul from the irregular pleasures of the senses, the inordinate social attachments, and the desire of the riches, honors, and vanities of the world. Hence the chief occupation of the soul is to suffer, suffer the cruel operation of this divine love. This love of course must be stronger and greater than these passions otherwise the soul could not nor would not detach itself from one to unite itself to another. But this love is obscure, confuse[d], & almost unperceptible to the soul, hence it is not so much the pain of being separated from its former pleasures that causes its trouble as the fact of being lead & driven by whom? Where? & How? It knows not. If it could but see the hand of God which is laid upon it, if it knew what was required of it, it would not complain, but if it k[new*?*] this h[and*?*] [*torn*] of exercise [*torn*] confidence and heroic abandonment that God exacts from it. It is this that made St John of the Cross[3] call it the "night obscure of the Soul," and St Catharine of Genoa[4] viewing it from the other side terms it "the separation of the soul from the body." The temptations besides to which the Soul is delivered at this time & the interior struggles are indescribable, & are in proportion to its fidelity & courage, & the perfection God has destined it for. This denial of all gratification of the senses, this separation from those who are the nearest & dearest to our heart, this abandonment of all that can excite our ambition is the work of God *Sole*, it is a purgatory in this world, but it is only the first degree. But what else is there for it to do after it has conquered the dominion of its lower appetites & its earthly desires? Much more than it has done. It has only fought & conquered its domestic enemies, itself is still to be vanquished. This is a war which demands a great font[*?*] of generosity & heroism. The second night is to the first as the midnight is to the evening. God augments & throws a purer & more subtel [*sic*] love into the soul at this moment in order to despoil the soul of the willful use of its faculties. This love penetrates to the centre of the will, the Soul, and purges it from all that is destructible and improper. It is as if the Soul was bound down upon a rack by an invisible cruel & unrelenting force[;] it is unable to express its agonies, to move, or to receive any consolation from either God or man. The self will must be torn up from its roots. "The seperation [*sic*] of the spirit from the Soul" is the expression that St Catherine of Genoa uses for to describe the result of this stage. This second night is terrible, the Soul seems as it were held over the horrible abyss of hell by an invisible power, abandoned by God, a prey, and a subject of mockery to the demons. God seems to reject its prayers before it can utter them. All within the soul is thick darkness and without there is no reality, nothing firm, permanent, eternal. It is deprived of the use of its faculties, it can neither think, feel, or act. O great God how wonderful is the work of Thy infinite Love. The soul is made to feel to its centre its feebleness & entire dependence upon God even for the most ordinary function of its existance [*sic*]. But to be brief after the soul has been despoiled of all that is unpleasing in the sight of God, God takes up His habitation in the Soul. Already has commenced the dawn, the aurora has appeared, the full day of which is the clear vision & happiness of the blessed in the other world. This third epoch that of union of the spirit with God, will with will, of a loveful & simple regard of God & his infinite perfections, which is called contemplation, is the beginning of the recompense of its fidelity, courage & generosity. The Soul ceases to chant the lamentations of Job & Jeremiah and begins to sing the Song of Songs. It has found him whom it has sought. "My beloved," it says, "is all mine & I am all his". The effects and different degrees of this union or transformation in God are according to the different degrees of purgation that the soul has passed. You will perceive my dear friend that these three stages correspond to the purgative, illuminative, and unitive of the way ordinary or active, which is true in reality, but the way passive is much shorter tho covered with many dangers and difficulties that the other is not. To support the soul while passing through these terrible pains & agonies of purgatory, without any exterior or human aid as this is impossible, to arrive at a perfect union with God, God at different stages gives to it such consolations, gifts, and moments of light as the case demands. Hence its danger of its mistaking the gifts of God for God, of being too deceived by the arch deceiver, and these favors becoming the cause of its loss. What is much to be deplored is that these are so few in our day, especially those who have the care of Souls in the Church, who have made this branch of theology a subject of their study.

But not to detain you any longer on this matter, I would refer you my dear friend to the works of St John of the Cross which are contained in three duodecimo vols. and are complete on this subject, and most estimated. The "Dialogues" of St C. of Genoa, and her treatise on "Purgatory" will pay you well to read them.

Thus my dear friend I have attempted to give you a brief statement by which you can form some idea of the past conduct of your friend. It will explain to you many facts which must have been as inexplicable to you as they were to myself. Deo gratias. I have left Egypt, passed the Desert, and am now in Israel, the land flowing with milk & honey.

I have said nothing of my having taken the vows. But what can I say? I have taken them and am free. Free, I have never understood that word until now. Render thanks and gratitude to God for my freedom for I know not how. Aid me for the grace is to[o] great & grand for my heart.

My dear friend if you send your Review it does not reach here. Perhaps it is on account of the direction you give it. We have only the three numbers that Rev Pere Bernhard brought with him. The address you have in my last note to you. R.R.P.P. Redemptoristes, Wittem, Province de Limbourg, Hollande. I will request my friends in N. York to send me the back nos. the first opportunity they have.

Remember me to my friends & your family

Yr brother in Christ,

Isaac.

Wittem

O. A. Brownson.

*Microfilm, roll two (calendared 1 October 1845).

1. Though this 1 October 1845 date was written in the letter, it is clearly mistaken. Hecker made his vows on 15 October 1846, and this letter was sent from Wittem, Holland, sixteen days later (see Hecker's letter to his mother of 15 October 1846 in Holden, *EY*, pp. 242–44).

2. The professed vows are the evangelical counsels of poverty, chastity, and obedience.

3. St. John of the Cross (1542–1591), Spanish mystic, monastic reformer, author of *Dark Night of the Soul* (c. 1587).

4. St. Catherine of Genoa (1447–1510), Italian mystic, devoted to works of charity, author of *A Treatise on Purgatory* and *Dialogues.*

PART TWO

1851–1864

This middle section of the correspondence extends from the time of Isaac T. Hecker's return from Europe to the Civil War period. During the six years that Hecker was abroad for priestly formation, Dr. Brownson had become the foremost champion of the Catholic Church in the United States. Besides his vigorous advocacy of the harmony between democracy and Catholicism, the controversial editor expressed himself on numerous public issues, such as Native-Americanism, Irish immigration, and the temporal power of the papacy. His theological writings, however, continued in the traditional Counter-Reformation pattern of historical apologetics.

Letters from Father Hecker predominate in this period, and many of them touch on his important missionary labors. Doubtless, these extensive tours made it difficult for Brownson to write to him. Hecker was part of a group of Redemptorist revivalist preachers who gave parish missions to English-language congregations throughout the land. The notable success of these undertakings sustained his confidence in the convert apostolate in the U.S. His bold vision of a Catholic America was undergirded by a non-Scholastic philosophical apologetic that stressed the positive features of Catholicism.

Coming to share Hecker's progressive perspective, Brownson moved his periodical to New York in 1855. In unison they endeavored to promote the Catholic cause by introducing fresh approaches to their Protestant countrymen as well as suggesting new measures for a revitalization of faith among their co-religionists. Later the attempt by Isaac Hecker and his companions to establish an American mission house brought about his expulsion from the Redemptorists but resulted in the foundation of the Paulist Fathers in 1858. Then the burden of family tragedy and ecclesiastical polemics effected a conservative shift in Orestes Brownson's outlook, which coincided with the discontinuance, in 1864, of his *Quarterly Review*.

46

HECKER TO BROWNSON • 22 MARCH 1851*

Jesus, Mary, Joseph
St Alphonsus!

Sat. 22 March. /51

My dearest friend,

It is with the greatest pleasure that I announce to you my arrival at N.Y. after a boisterous passage of 52 days via France.[1]

It would be a great gratification to me to speak with you. I hope some arrangements will be made in such a way that I shall have the opportunity of visiting you at your Residence. Perhaps you will be coming on here shortly? If this should be the case, or if you should likely be from home within a short period, will you do me the favour to inform me as early as you can make it convenient?

Will you have the goodness to present my humble respects to your Rt. Rev. Bishop?[2] I beg on my kness [*sic*] his fartherly [*sic*] blessing.

Remember me kindly & affectionately to Mrs Brownson your dear Wife & to all your children, and such friends as you may chance to meet.

You can easily imagine why I cannot say anything except my arrival & my desire to see & speak with you for if I began to speak what I have to say I fear I never should end & if that, I should find I had said nothing.

The experience you have acquired since I have been abroad, & what I have gained, would not only be gratifying, but I feel convinced eminently useful for us both to communicate to each other.

Yours affectionately & truly

I. Th. Hecker C.SS.R.
German Catholic Church[3]
Third Street Near Avenue A.

To O. A. Brownson Esq.

*Brownson, *BML*, pp. 271–72.

1. Hecker sailed from Le Havre, France, on 27 January 1851 and arrived in New York on 20 March 1851.

2. Bishop John B. Fitzpatrick of Boston.

3. The Church of the Most Holy Redeemer, a Redemptorist parish founded in New York City in 1844.

47

BROWNSON TO HECKER • 28 MARCH 1851

Boston. March 28, 1851.

Rev. I. Th. Hecker,

My very dear Friend, you cannot imagine what pleasure it gives me to learn [of] your arrival in New York. Your letter would have been sooner answered, but owing to my negligence in going to the city. I want to see you much, very much. You have much to tell me that is needful that I should know, and I beg you to come & see me. Tell your superiors from me, that your visit to me will be more than an act of charity to me personally, & that it is highly necessary, not merely as a matter of pleasure to us two, that we should meet, and tell them that I earnestly beg to have you come & spend a few days with me. I am sure they will permit you to do so, in furtherance of the work in which I as well as you are engaged, and I have a special reason for wishing to see you now. I would willingly visit you at New York, or anywhere in the United States, this side [of] the Rocky Mountains, but there is no place so appropriate as my own house. You will find me, not in the house in which I lived when you *last* visited me, but in the house where you paid me your *first* visit. I am more indebted to you for having become a Catholic than to any other man under heaven, and while you supposed I was leading you to the Church, it was you who led me there. I owe you a debt of gratitude I can never repay.

I could write a long letter, but I cannot begin to write what I would say. We must meet, come, if possible, and as soon as possible. If you cannot, let me know, and I will go & see you.

My wife is delighted to hear of your return. She has been sick all winter, and is not well even yet, but to see you will do her great good. She is a good Catholic, and like me owes much of her conversion to you. My children are nearly all [away] from home. I expect one[1] soon home today, one concerning whom I have much anxiety, and whom I wish you to lecture. He has faith, but he has not behaved well, though he has done nothing very bad. Orestes is married[2]—John is in his second year of theology,[3] and Frank is thro' his novitiate, and now a scholastic[4] with the Jesuits.

Remember me, I beg you, in your prayers, and do come & see me.

Yours truly

O. A. Brownson.

1. Most probably William Ignatius Brownson.

2. Orestes A. Brownson (Jr.) married Pauline Capett on 21 June 1849 at at Evansville, Ga.; she died in 1855, and subsequently he married Margaret Baker on 18 March 1856 at Sweet Springs, Va.

3. The second of four projected years of theological study for the Catholic priesthood.

4. Henry Francis Brownson was engaged in philosophical studies following a two-year novitiate with the Jesuits.

48

HECKER TO BROWNSON • [c. 13 APRIL 1851]*

Jesus, Mary, Joseph, Alphonsus!

[*Undated*] [1]

My Dearest friend,

It is with no little regret that I must inform you of the impossibility of my being able to come to see you even after the Mission we are now engaged in here at St Joseph's.[2] Rev. f[ather] Provincial[3] had already given me the permission to visit you for several days as soon as the Mission should be closed, but since he has rec'd an invitation of the Rt Rev Bishop of Pennsylvania[4] to give several missions in his Diocese both English & German and having accepted them, I shall be obliged to be in Pittsburg the friday following Easter Sunday—the day on which the Mission here closes. Once having entered on our labours I do not know when I shall be free to visit you, but as soon as the opportunity offers, I have the permission to embrace it.

Our Mission here at St Joseph's is successful beyond our anticipations—beside us four American fathers[5] who are chiefly occupied in preaching, giving instructions, catechizing etc, there are seven other fathers[6] who speak english engaged in hearing confessions. The work that seems ready for us here in the U.S. is very great, & already other applications from different pastors of congregations in this city to have missions in their churches have been made. Our church is crowded not only in the evening but even in the morning at the 6 o'clock instruction. I trust that our labours will be a great means in the hands of D[ivine] Providence of infusing a new zeal among the faithful in this country & leading them to a more catholic & devout life which cannot help reacting on the world & making our holy religion felt as it is, & the Holy Church exercise that influence on public taste, mind & character which she must, if our country is to be one of the holy conquests of her divine faith.

My sincere love to Mrs Brownson & your children. Should you come this way I should be most happy to see you. I cannot ask you to come for that would be too much. *Perhaps* in June I shall have the time to make you a visit. Till I see you believe me yrs in the sacred hearts of Jesus & Mary,

I Th Hecker CSR.

Pray for me as I do for you.

St Joseph's Church. 6th Avenue.

*Microfilm, roll three (calendared [1851]).

1. The mission at St. Joseph's (n. 2 below) mentioned in this letter was held from 6 April to 20 April 1851. Since Hecker implies that it is in process, this letter is dated c. 13 April 1851.

2. An Irish parish located on Sixth Street in lower Manhattan; the mission here lasted from 6 April to 20 April 1851.

3. Bernard Hafkenscheid, C.SS.R., superior of the Redemptorists in America 1850–53.

4. Michael O'Connor (1810–1872), Irish-born, ordained priest 1833, became first bishop of Pittsburgh 1843, entered the Society of Jesus 1860.

5. Fathers Hecker, Clarence A. Walworth, Augustine F. Hewit (see Letter 56, n. 4), and John B. Duffy (1826–1874), Irish-born, Redemptorist missionary priest.

6. The group included Fathers Alexander Czvitkovicz (1806–1883), John Hespelin (1821–1899), Christian Kauder (b. 1817, dispensed from vows 1852), Francis Krutil (b. 1815, returned to Europe 1859), Robert Kleineidam (1818–1883), and Adolph Kittel (d. 1852).

49

HECKER TO BROWNSON • 15 MAY 1851*

Jesus, Mary, Joseph, St Alphonsus!

Loretto May 15. 1851.

My dear friend,

I cannot help giving you some account of our labours since our arrival & the good Almighty God pleases to work through us poor instruments, knowing your interest in our labours & the pleasure you will take in hearing of the fruits of them.

You have heard of the Mission at St Joseph's.[1] 8 & 10 fathers were engaged in it. The mission lasted a fortnight; 6000 confessions were heard

& communions given. The effect of the ceremony of the renewal of the Baptismal vows was touching & wonderful. The people suddenly burst into tears, & for a time the preacher could not make his voice heard for the noise of their sobbing. The consolation of the congregation after mission was beyond all expression; & the good pastor[2] of St Joseph desired nothing so much as to engage us to repeat yearly our Missions which of course we couldn't. Tho it is a rule of ours to make a renewal after a certain lapse of time.

3 days after our Mission in N.Y. we were on our way to our Mission in this place at Loretto;[3] a village situated in a valley on the top of the Alleghanies [*sic*]. Its site is picturesque & beautiful. It was founded by Prince Gallitzin.[4] The prince spent his fortune & his life which was one of great austerity & apostolic, in building up this place. The population of the township is about 2,300, all catholic excepting 3 families. The people nearly all americans by birth. You can from this easily imagine what a fine field we had to work in, when we began the Mission. Our greatest difficulty was in the beginning in getting people to attend the exercises—both in the morning at 7, & the evening at 5. The first few days everything dragged heavily. But at length the people became aroused, & from that moment the Mission went on better & better until its close. Those who lived at a great distance took lodgings in the village near by & remained till the Mission ended. The disposition of the people was such as to excite our astonishment. The conversions among the hardest & most abandoned sinners were remarkable. You can judge from the fact that every person in the parish made the Mission, except two, a father a freemason & his son. Between 16 & 1700 hundred confessions were heard & communions given. 10 protestants were converted, & we left only two protestants in the village, a man & his wife, the daughter of a protestant parson. Some time[s] the scenes were such as to excite laughter. One old sinner had come determined not to be moved. He heard a sermon of one of the fathers, & on coming out he was heard to say scratching his head; "That preacher beats the devil." And so it was for the converted. Another famous dare devil sort of a fellow, the very thought of whom in connection with the confessional or any other act of piety was the most ludicrous of all incongruities, was caught, & afterwards was the foremost in our procession carrying the battle axe. Our B[lessed] Lady too did not fail to show her powerful intercession. One poor woman came with fear of her husband killing her when she returned. He was a drunken wretch. She was told to go to & pray to our B. Mother & Queen of heaven & behold her husband met her on her way returning & fell on his kness [*sic*] & begged her pardon, & came & did his duties! But I must describe to you in a few words the closing ceremony the plantation of the Cross. We all assembled in the Church on Sunday afternoon at 3½ to recite the Rosary. The procession then was formed outside of the Church. First came the processional cross with the boys; then the men carrying a large cross 41 feet long entwined with garlands of flowers born by 60 of them; on each side of the

cross was a file of soldiers with a band of music; then came 20 or 30 Franciscan brothers of the 3rd order[5] with their cowls; then the clergy; after them the missioners in their habit, followed by the Sisters of Mercy, & then by the girls & women. The number of the procession was about 4000. We marched through the village to the site of the cross with music, & there we blessed & erected the cross in a most conspicuous place. The farewell sermon was preached at the foot of the Cross & the Papal Benediction given. The soldiers fired a salute as the finale. It was a novel scene for america, a famous [*?*] one for our holy religion, & one which never will be forgotten by those who witnessed it. The Cross overlooks the whole village & when you look that way you will always see some one or more saying their 5 paters & aves to gain the indulgence of 10,000 years which is attached to the Missionary Cross.

Sunday next we begin a Mission[6] in Holidaysburg [Pa.] about 40 or [*?*] miles from here. After that I don't know where we shall be sent, as the Cathedral of Pittsburg[7] is burnt down, for we were to give a Mission there. But if I have leisure, I hope to be able to get to see you.

Remember me affectionately to your wife & family. I beg earnestly your & their prayers. I do not forget you in mine.

And believe me yours sincerely & affectionately in the sacred hearts of Jesus & Mary

A poor servant in XP.

I Th Hecker, CSSR

To. O. A Brownson Esq.

*Brownson, *BML*, pp. 273–76.

1. See Letter 48, n. 2.
2. Rev. Michael McCarron (1803–1867), pastor of St. Joseph's.
3. St. Michael's Church at Loretto, Pa., from 27 April to 11 May 1851.
4. Prince Demetrius Augustine Gallitzin (1770–1840), Dutch-born son of a Russian prince, first priest ordained in the U.S. 1795, missionized western Pennsylvania.
5. Comprised of lay persons who do not take formal religious vows but follow certain patterns of Franciscan spirituality; Franciscan priests (O.F.M.) comprise the first order, and nuns (the Poor Clares) the second.
6. St. Mary's Church, 18–28 May 1851, Hollidaysburg, Pa.
7. St. Paul's Cathedral; a mission was eventually given there 14–28 October 1855.

50

HECKER TO BROWNSON • 27 JUNE 1851

Jesus, Mary, Joseph, St Alphonsus!

June 27. 1851.

My dear friend,

The death of one of our fathers[1] since my return has kept me from fulfilling my promises so soon as I had wished. However in the meantime I have found a copy of Görres[2] in a german book store at a very reasonable price $6 which I will send by the parcel delivery with this note & a discipline.[3] You will have to wait for the cilices[4] till I get time to make them myself, for the brothers here don't know how to make them. Rev. f[ather] Müller[5] will write to the Politische Blätter[6] for you if you wish it. But as we are unacquainted with the conditions which are usual in such exchanges if you will state them, he will send them to the Editors. It is a Journal perhaps of 10 years standing. If the exchange is to be made from the present date you must tell us.

The Journal Historique[7]—Rev. f. Provincial is well acquainted with the Editor & perhaps other fathers in the U.S. Till I see one of these I cannot give you exact information about it. I think the House at Baltimore takes it as well as the other.

If you could get the Politische Blätter from its commencement it would be a valuable addition to your library, for it contains the best articles ever written in germany & on german & other affairs. This those who are capable of judging such matters all say. If you [*torn*] wish to write yourself send your letter on here & Rev. f. Müller will direct it to one of [*torn*] head men there & add a note which will ensure its success.

I send you at the same time a copy of the "Cottage Conversations"[8] a little work I brought with me from England. It is written by a convert[,] a lady—Mrs Wood.[9] Would you take the pains to look it over closely & give a notice of it. *And give your opinion whether it would not be well to republish it here in the U.S.* When I read it it made a good impression upon me & appeared to meet the difficulties of a certain class of readers. I am not personally acquainted with the authors, but I think it would be well to republish it here. Can you give a notice of it in your next Review.

Donnegan[10] the Bookseller was here yesterday morning to see about publishing the "Glories of Mary"[11] of St Alphonsus. The Dublin copy is garbled, bad english & full of mistakes. Is there any one whom you are acquainted with capable of translating from the Italian[,] if fairly remunerated? I have dropped a note to Mrs Ripley[12] to know whether she can &

is willing to do it. The Dublin edition has too a long introduction to refute objections brought against St Alphonsus in his Glories of Mary, & a number of foot notes to the same effect–in my opinion it would be well in the next edition to dispense altogether with these. Do you think so? An introduction of a few pages might be made which would answer all that is needed.

I have tho't over the subject we spoke of, & I am sure that if you could make a Retreat under Rev. f. Neuman[13] the Rector at Baltimore for 8 or 10 days, you would find in him the kind of director your soul needs & this after all is what makes the good effects of a retreat lasting. Begin well under a good director & with a good will you cannot help but advance & persevere. In my judgment you had better waite [*sic*] till fall & then make a Retreat under F. N[eumann] unless you can find some one in whom you can place equal confidence.

Remember me to your kind & pious wife & all friends. Yours truly in the love of the most sacred hearts of Jesus & Mary,

I Th Hecker C.SS.R.

1. Adolph Kittel, C.SS.R., of Most Holy Redeemer Church in New York City, who died 22 June 1851.
2. *Die Christliche Mystik* (Regensburg and Landshut, 1836) by Johann Joseph von Görres (1776–1848), German lay theologian, political philosopher, romantic mystic.
3. A discipline is an instrument of penance, such as a small whip or scourge, used for self-inflicted mortification.
4. Hair shirts for penitential purposes.
5. Joseph Müller, C.SS.R. (1809–1876), Redemptorist rector at New York City.
6. *Historisch-Positische Blätter fur das Katholische Deutschland,* published at Munich, begun in 1838.
7. *Journal Historique et Littéraire,* founded in 1834 at Liege, Belgium.
8. *Cottage Conversations,* volume II (London, 1849).
9. Probably Ellen Wood (1814–1887), English Catholic convert and author.
10. Edward Dunigan of Dunigan & Brother, New York Catholic publishers and booksellers.
11. *The Glories of Mary,* two volumes, translated by a Catholic clergyman (Dublin, n.d.). Dunigan & Brother brought out the first American edition, translated from the Italian by Sophia Ripley (n. 12 below) in 1852.
12. Sophia Willard Dana Ripley (1803–1861), Transcendentalist, skilled linguist, married George Ripley in 1827, taught belles lettres at Brook Farm, Catholic convert 1847.
13. John Nepomucene Neumann, C.SS.R. (1811–1860), Bohemian-born missionary, ordained priest 1836, first Redemptorist professed in U.S. 1842, bishop of Philadelphia 1852, canonized as the third American saint on 19 June 1977.

51

HECKER TO BROWNSON • 29 JULY 1851

Live Jesus, Mary, Joseph, St Alphonsus!

July 29, 1851.

My dear friend,

Did you receive Gorres's Mystic[1] etc which I sent to yr address 123 Washington St soon after my return from Boston? I have been expecting you on here with yr sons for some weeks, when are you coming? I leave the city the coming friday for New Jersey to take care of a small English Mission[2] there, & return the following tuesday.

Often my mind is seized with the idea of a future development of our holy faith in this country. Our people are capable of great enthusiasm, & if once this is turned into the right channel, it must & will produce effects worthy of our faith & our spiritual Mother the Church. Our people *are young*, & not like europeans, & were they filled with a lively faith, new ages of faith would spring up on this contenent [*sic*].

But catholic enthusiasm which is super-natural, full of piety, & humble to the entire forgetfulness of self. The precise contrary from protestants— can only be gained by an ascetic & thorough religious training. It must be got before it can be given. And those who lead must get it first.

The catholic young men of our country have no catholic religious ideal future. We are so scattered that we seem not to be body & have no common life. Our young men therefore [,] as a matter of course, fall into those unholy persuits [*sic*], or plung into politicks [*sic*], or if they dream of an ideal life it is pagan,—like all protestants. We as catholics have a future; we alone have an ideal, by this I mean, a beautiful & glorious future. Our young men need to be told this, inspired with it, & shown the means to attain it. We are a young people, a vast immeasurable field is before us, and have no overpowering monuments of the past to check our fresh enthusiasm, or to dishearten us in our youthful attempts. Let it then be known that we have a future, and have faith, hope & love it [,] & our young men will not if they are shown the way, be wanting in devoting themselves to it.

Remember me to your pious wife & to her prayers & in yours & believe me your humble servant in the sacred hearts of Jesus & Mary

I. Th. Hecker, C.SS.R.

O. A. Brownson Esq
N.Y.

1. *Die Christliche Mystik.*
2. Either at St. Joseph's Church, Macopin, or St. Mary's Church, Rahway, N.J.

52

HECKER TO BROWNSON • 5 SEPTEMBER 1851

Jesus, Mary, Joseph, Alphonsus!

Sep. 5. 1851

My dear friend,

Your two sons John & Henry left here on tuesday morning for Europe.[1] On saturday we visited the ArchBishop[2] & sunday he took dinner with us at our convent. So far as my duties permitted I endeavored to make their stay here agreeable. I shall not forget them in the Holy Sacrifice, & hope they will have a pleasant voyage, & return after their term of studies well-trained & holy priests.

It gratified me to hear from your sons, that you had determined to make a retreat in the fall at Baltimore. Perhaps you can fix your time of retreat in such a way as to be in N.Y. during one of our Missions which we are about Sep. The 2nd will be in the Cathedral[4] beginning on the 3d Sunday in October & ending on the 2nd of Nov. The feast of All Saints. The one at St Peter's closes on the 2nd Sunday of October. Perhaps you will be able to come so as to be present at the close of the one in the Cathedral.

The few words we had together on Spiritual things will[,] I trust, encourage you to persevere in your meditations. So long as one remains in the presence of God during the time of meditation, it matters little how he passess [*sic*] his time. He may not be aware of doing any thing at all, autant mieux. St. Antony[5] says that the best prayer is when one does not know that he prays. Follow your attrait in prayer; no one ever advanced in spiritual life contre son attrait. The best prayer for each one is that in which he succeeds best; from which one draws the most profit, it matters not what sort of prayer it may be called. Let us not be afraid of big names; if God gives us the grace of contemplation even in the beginning, as he does to some Souls, let us not through a false fear reject it, but correspond to his goodness by a generous confidence. If he leaves us in dryness & darkness let us endeavor to be equally willing to suffer; but never give up the exercise of meditation.

Until we have a higher tone of catholic life in our country we shall do nothing. We shall make some progress in material things, & perhaps in numbers, but in the end we shall do little for the greater glory of God, the good of Souls or for our country. We can do no good without enthusiasm. Religious enthusiasm is the activity of the passions supernaturalized.

And this is brought about by a thorough discipline—an ascetic life. If our words have lost their power it is because there is no power in us to put into them. The Catholic faith alone is capable of giving to a people a true permanent & burning enthusiasm frought [*sic*] with the greatest of deeds. But to enkindle this in others we must be possessed of it first ourselves. But without it, we shall do nothing of great importance. As Thomas a Kempis[6] says: Nisi homo sit in spiritu elevatus, et ali omnibus creaturis liberatus, ac Deo totus unitus, quid quid scit, quid-quid etiam habet, non est magni ponderis. L[iber] iii. C[apitulum] 31.[7]

Somehow or other I did not receive the letter you wrote me some time ago. Your sons told me that you had rec'd Görres. About two thirds of the 1st Vol. is taken up with an essay on the significance of the sign of the Cross. This is very obscure, & not an essential part of the work, & not necessary to be read to understand what follows, this the author in some place says himself. I would advise you to pass it over, & begin towards the end of the 1st Vol, where he begins properly the history of C. Mysticism.

Do not forget to notice the Cottage Conversations in your next Review,[8] & give your opinion whether it is worth republication here.

Begging your prayers & hoping you & your family are in good health I remain your humble servant in the sacred hearts of Jesus & Mary.

I. Th Hecker CSSR.

N.Y. 153 Third Street

P.S. John your son paid me for Görres.

1. In September 1851, Henry and John Brownson departed for the Seminaire de St. Sulpice, Paris; their brother William I. Brownson was at a seminary in Quebec. None of Brownson's sons were ordained priests.
2. John Hughes of New York.
3. New York City's oldest Catholic church, from 28 September to 12 October 1851.
4. Old St. Patrick's Cathedral on Mott Street, from 19 October to 3 November 1851.
5. St. Anthony of the Desert, also called Anthony the Abbot (b. c. 250), desert hermit, monastic founder, father of the cenobitic life.
6. Thomas à Kempis (c. 1380–1471), German-born Augustinian canon, spiritual writer, probable author of *The Imitation of Christ* (c. 1418).
7. "Unless a man be elevated in the spirit, and also detached from all creatures, and totally united to God, whatever he knows, also whatever he possesses, is of little consequence" (*The Imitation of Christ,* book III, chapter 31).
8. *BrQR,* April 1852, p. 283.

53

HECKER TO BROWNSON • 27 OCTOBER 1851

J.M.J.A.

Oct. 27. 1851.

My dear friend,

Your sons told me that you intended to make a retreat at Baltimore. I wish you could make it convenient to come on here before our mission[1] closes next Sunday. The fathers would be highly gratified to see you & I would wish you to be present at the concluding exercises.

Get here by thursday if you can.

Yours truly in the sacred hearts of Jesus & Mary

I Th Hecker CSSR.

Mon.

1. The mission at old St. Patrick's Cathedral, which closed on 3 November 1851.

54

HECKER TO BROWNSON • [c. 6 NOVEMBER 1851]

Jesus Mary Joseph Alphonsus!

[*Undated*][1]

My dear friend,

I accompanied to-day the Vicar General of Indiana[2] a german priest to the steamer for Europe. Acquainted as he is with some of the head men of the court of the young Emperor of Austria[3] & wishing to bring before his notice your articles on Hungarian affairs[4] & the one on Webster's Reply,[5] I obtained for the V[icar] G[eneral] the 4 last copies of yr Review from our own Library by promising Rev f[ather] Rector[6] that you would willingly replace them.

The V.G. was a constant reader of yr R[eview] & took a deep interest in it. He intends translating passages from it on his voyage to have them in readiness when he reaches the court. He will have an audience with the young Emperor.

I have rec'd to-day Ida Countess Hahn-Hahn's: "Von Babylon nach Jerusalem" and "Aus Jerusalem."[7] Two small volumes relating to her conversion, replete with stirring thoughts & great ideas. They would give matter for a most interesting article in your Review, but as you know I cannot send them as I have thanks be to God & our Lady—nothing.

Monday I go to "Erie" [Pa.] to give with other Fathers a mission.[8] Our mission [*torn*] the Cathedral[9] [*torn*] great success.

Have you heard from your sons?

Hoping you & yr family are in good health believe me your [*sic*] truly in the s[acred] hearts of Jesus & Mary.

I Th Hecker CSSR

*Microfilm, roll three (calendared [Nov. 1851]).

1, Dated c. 6 November 1851 on the basis of the ending of the New York mission and the start of Hecker's upcoming mission at Erie, Pa., 17–28 November 1851.

2. Rev. Joseph Kundek (1810–1857), Croatian-born vicar general of the diocese of Vincennes, Ind. who traveled to Austria in 1851.

3. Franz Joseph I (1830–1916), emperor of Austria 1848–1916.

4. "The Hungarian Rebellion," *BrQR*, January 1851, pp. 29–67; April 1851, pp. 164–97; "The Hungarian Nation," *BrQR*, October 1851, pp. 492–526.

5. "Webster's Answer to Hülsemann," *BrQR*, April 1851, pp. 198–230. The Webster referred to here was Daniel Webster (1782–1852), at this time secretary of state under President Millard Fillmore.

6. Joseph Müller, C.SS.R.

7. Ida Marie Louise Hahn-Hahn (1805–1880), German countess, Catholic convert 1850, novelist and author of *Von Babylon nach Jerusalem* (Mainz, 1851) and *Aus Jerusalem* (Mainz, 1851).

8. St. Patrick's Church, Erie, Pa., 17–28 November 1851.

9. Old St. Patrick's Cathedral in New York City (see Letter 52, n. 4).

55

HECKER TO BROWNSON • [6 JANUARY] 1852

J.M.J.A!

Epiphany 1852.[1]

Dear friend,

I wish to remind you of a request I made of you some months ago. I gave a german priest[2] 3 nos. of your Review containing the 2 articles on Hungary &

the one on Webster's letter, as he wished to bring yr Review to the notice of some of the principal austrian statesmen. F[ather] Rector[3] wishes to have ours bound, & if you don't send me these I shall not presume so soon again to act in yr favour.

Are you acquainted with Abbé Rohrbacker's universelle history of R.C. Church.[4] You will find him ultra montaine [*sic*] enough. It is in 25 or 6 Vols. Pub. at Paris. The Belgium Ed. is very cheap. It is now going through a 2nd Ed. with corrections from the author who was formerly a disciple of Lamnenais.[5] A year or more ago I read in yr Review a commendation of Lingard's history.[6] It could not have been from yr pen. I am glad to find it rightly appreciated in your art no. 1 in the last Review.[7] I cannot help expressing my delight in the tone of your last no.

I have returned but a few days from some missions in the western part of Pennsylvania.[8] At the one at Crossingville [Pa.] we planted near the Church a large & beautiful cross. It was 30 feet high & 18 inches square. After it was planted & the sermon given, we gave 3 cheers in honour of the holy Cross. And such loud & hearty cheers never before came from men's throats. The backwoodsmen & Yankee farmers understood this language, & it gained their hearts for us. I look forward with some anxiety for the time when D. Providence will open the way for us in the eastern states. In a few weeks we go again on Mission [at] Saratoga,[9] Troy,[10] Buffalo,[11] Detroit.[12]

My brother John is mixed up in the Kossuth humbug.[13] The poor man knows not what he is about. His wife would become a catholic if it were not for his most violent opposition.

Remember me to yr pious wife & family, & believe me yours sincerely in the sacred hearts of Jesus & Mary.

I Th Hecker CSSR.

P.S. Don't forget yr Retreat.

1. The feast of the Epiphany is celebrated on 6 January.

2. Rev. Joseph Kundek; see Letter 54, n. 2.

3. Joseph Müller, C.SS.R.

4. *L'Histoire universelle de l'Eglise catholique,* twenty-eight volumes (Paris, 1842–49), by René François Rohrbacher (1789–1856), French Catholic priest and church historian, seminary professor at Nancy, France 1835–49.

5. Félicité Robert de Lamennais or La Mennais (1789–1856), French priest, ultramontane apologist, pioneer of Catholic liberalism, founder of the journal *L'Avenir* 1830, broke with the Catholic Church 1837.

6. *History of England, from the first invasion by the Romans to the accession of William and Mary in 1688*, eight volumes (London, 1819–30 by

John Lingard (1771–1851), English priest and Catholic church historian. The fifth edition, revised and enlarged (London, 1849), was reviewed by Brownson in *BrQR*, July 1851, p. 415.

7. *BrQR*, January 1852, pp. 134–35.

8. At St. Patrick's Church, Erie, Pa., 17–28 November; St. Philip's Church in Cussewago (near Crossingville), 1–9 December; and St. Vincent's Church, Youngstown, Ohio, 10–20 December 1851.

9. St. Peter's Church, Saratoga, N.Y., c. 6–18 January 1852.

10. St. Peter's Church, Troy, N.Y., c. 25 January–8 February 1852.

11. Though Hecker wrote Buffalo, he probably meant Albany, N.Y., where a mission was given at St. Joseph's Church from 15 February to c. 1 March 1852. At this time John McCloskey was bishop of Albany.

12. Sts. Peter and Paul Cathedral, c. 8–c. 22 March 1852.

13. Lajos (Louis) Kossuth (1802–1894), Hungarian revolutionist and orator, leader of the 1848 Magyar uprising which was crushed by the Austrian empire. Invited to the U.S. by Congress and President Millard Fillmore, the defeated hero was enthusiastically greeted as he toured this country 1851–52.

56

HECKER TO BROWNSON • 2 JUNE 1852

Jesus Mary Joseph Alphonsus!

June 2nd 1852.

My dear friend,

I am gratified to hear that you will give a Lecture[1] in this city on tuesday next. I have just returned from the city of Phila. where we have given two missions,[2] on wednesday next I shall have to leave N.Y. for Cahoas where we intend to open a mission[3] on Thurs, Corpus Christi. I hope to see you before I leave. Tell me therefore when you will be on here & where you will stay in the city.

Give me this information as soon as you can, so that I can inform my fellow missionaries F[athers] Walworth & Hewit[4] to stop here on their way to Cahoas as they are very desirous to see you.[5]

My sincere affection to the members of your family & believe me your most humble servant in the sacred hearts of Jesus [&] Mary.

I Th Hecker C.S.R.

N.Y.

1. A lecture entitled "Protestantism Incompatible With Liberty," delivered on 8 June 1852 at the Broadway Tabernacle under the auspices of the Catholic Institute of New York.

2. At St. John's Church, 2–16 May 1852, and the Church of the Assumption, 19–31 May; both churches were located in Philadelphia.

3. At St. Bernard's Church, Cohoes, N.Y., 10–20 June 1852.

4. Augustine Francis Hewit (né Nathaniel Augustus Hewitt) (1820–1897), missionary, educator, theologian; left the Congregational Church for the Episcopal Church 1843, Catholic convert 1846, ordained priest 1847, entered Redemptorists 1850, an original Paulist 1858, managing editor of *The Catholic World* 1866, second superior general of the Paulist Fathers 1889.

5. Hewit and Walworth first met Brownson in May 1852 in New York City.

57

BROWNSON TO HECKER • [c. 5 JUNE 1852]

Philadelphia Saturday [*Undated*][1]

My address will be on Tuesday. I shall be in New York on Thursday. I should like to meet you in Baltimore. You can come on Monday.

Quite well, have done something, but am in great haste.

Yours truly

O. A. B.

1. This undated letter is difficult to date exactly. It may have been written on Saturday, 5 June 1852, in response to Hecker's of 2 June 1852 (Letter 56), which mentioned Brownson's scheduled lecture in New York City on Tuesday, 8 June 1852. Brownson frequently lectured on the Philadelphia, Baltimore, New York circuit both before and after his conversion to Catholicism in 1844.

58

HECKER TO BROWNSON • [16 JULY 1852]

J.M.J.A.

Feast of O[ur] L[ady] of Mt Carmel.[1]

My dear Friend,

I send you by the express to-day the two vols of Countess Ida Hahn Hahn.

There must be something that stings in them for they are prohibited to be read in Russia, Prussia, Bavaria & Wurtemberg. She is a *papist*; I think they should be translated, at least the 2nd. Vol "Aus Jerusalem." Their price is $1.80 cts.

I ordered on my return Mr Dunnigan to send you the lives of St Leonard[2] & Pere Segneri.[3]

Father Provincial[4] writes me that he can get from your agent at Baltimore all the nos. of your Review from 1845 to 52, except the Jan. no. of 45, and the Jan. April. & July nos. of 1846. Can you furnish these? Or would it be any advantage to you to furnish him with the whole set?

Do him the favour to answer. His address is. St Alphonsus Church, Baltimore, Md.

I come back on the books of the Countess—in my opinion their circulation among us, particularly among our old friends would do some good; she is a brilliant writer, & her thoughts have a freshness about them which make her writings attractive to all. Her reputation as a writer previous to her becoming Catholic, & the prestege [*sic*] of being prohibited books would ensure them a large circulation. Would it not be a good work for your son John? It would make him brush up his german & be perhaps not a bad debut for him before the public.

By the way I will venture to put with the others her Marienlieder.[5] That will make your bill $2.50 cts. If you give a notice of them, tell whether you will get them translated, for perhaps I may get it done if you do not.

My best respect & love to yr family.

Yours affectionately in the sacred hearts of Jesus & Mary

I. Th Hecker C.SS.R.

N.Y.

Can you not send us those 3 Reviews with the articles on hungary?

1. The feast of Our Lady of Mount Carmel is celebrated on 16 July; the year is 1852 in view of the mention of Countess Ida Hahn-Hahn (see Letter 54, n. 7) and Brownson's articles on Hungary (see Letter 54, n. 4) and the reference to the year 1852 in the body of the letter.

2. Leonard of Port Maurice (1676–1751), Italian mission preacher, advocate of such popular devotions as that to the Sacred Heart of Jesus.

3. Paolo Segneri, S.J. (1624–1694), Italian preacher, missionary, and ascetical writer.

4. Bernard Hafkenscheid, C.SS.R.

5. *Unserer lieben Frau* (1851).

59

HECKER TO BROWNSON • 20 NOVEMBER 1852

J.M.J.A!

Nov 20. 1852.

My Very dear Friend

The solemn consecration of our Church[1] here in N.Y. takes place on Sunday the 28 inst. It would be gratifying to F. Provincial[2] & each one of our community to have you present, and it being the first occassion [*sic*] of your witnessing this ceremony, it would be no less interesting to you.

The consecration begins in the morning at 6½ by the Archbishop[3] of the Diocese. High Mass at 10. Sermon in English by Bishop.[4] We hope to prevail on the Bishop of Boston[5] to sing the High Mass. Vespers at 5 p.m. Sermon by Bishop Neuman.[6]

Endeavour to come by all means, perhaps you will bring your Lady and daughter[7] with [you]. Afford us the pleasure to see you in our midst.

Remember me to your Family & believe me yours affectionately in the sacred hearts of Jesus & Mary

I Th Hecker C.SS.R.

Dr. O. A. Brownson.

1. The Church of the Most Holy Redeemer on East Third Street, formally consecrated on 28 November 1852.
2. Bernard Hafkenscheid, C.SS.R.
3. John Hughes, archbishop of New York.
4. John McCloskey, bishop of Albany, N.Y.
5. John B. Fitzpatrick; Bishop John N. Neumann, C.SS.R., actually celebrated the Mass.
6. John N. Neumann, C.SS.R., of Philadelphia.
7. Sarah Nicolena (Maria) Brownson (1839–1876), novelist, biographer, journalist; Brownson's only daughter, married William J. Tenney 1873.

60

HECKER TO BROWNSON • 6 MAY 1853

J.M.J.A!

May 6. 1853

My dearest Friend,

I had engaged yesterday a berth in the Steamer Asia for Rev. F[ather]

Bernard [,] our Provincial, the steamer leaves on the 28 Inst. He will do any commissions you may have for Europe with pleasure.

Rev. Mr. Kundigs[1] the Vicar Gen. of Milwaukie [*sic*] has returned from Europe—the gentleman to whom I gave 3 nos. of yr Review containing articles on Hungary. He presented them to the Young Emperor, & spoke with the Cardinal[2] at Vienna & the Prime Minister[3] upon the same subject: e.g. the character of yr Review. I should feel much obliged to you if you would supply our set with these 3 nos.

Affectionately yours in the S. hearts of Jesus & Mary

I Th Hecker CSSR

1. Here Hecker intends to name Joseph Kundek, the vicar general of Vincennes (see Letter 54, n. 2) and not Martin Kundig (1805–1879), Swiss-born, vicar general of Milwaukee 1849–79.

2. Probably Vincent Milde, archbishop of Vienna 1832–53, who was succeeded by Archbishop Joseph Rauscher in 1853.

3. Prince Felix zu Schwarzenberg (1800–1852), Austrian prime minister 1848–52, under Emperor Franz Josef.

61

HECKER TO BROWNSON • 30 MAY 1853

J.M.J.A!

May 30th, 1853

My dearest Friend,

As every thing that touches yr Review in England must interest you, I send you a note[1] which I have just rec'd from a friend[2] who was once an anglican minister; seeing that there is nothing private in it & regards matters of which you are the judge.

At the same time I will enclose the little Book on the Scapulars which I promised.

I am at home again for a time in order to recruit in spiritual & physical strength to begin our next mission campaign next fall.

Hoping that you are in good health & yr family,

I remain affectionately yours in the S. hearts of Jesus & Mary

I Th Hecker CSSR

1. Richard Simpson (n. 2 below) to Hecker, 4 April 1853 (BP, UNDA); see also Brownson, *BML*, pp. 395–96.

2. Richard Simpson (1820–1876), English Catholic convert 1846, liberal Catholic, author and editor of *The Rambler* 1848–62 and its sequel *The Home and Foreign Review* 1862–64.

62

HECKER TO BROWNSON • 19 JULY 1853

July 19. 1853

Dear Dr.

I have a note from Donohue[1] in which he says: "Should Dr Brownson write to me in relation to his forthcoming book,[2] I will deal with him to the very best advantage."

Dear Dr strike while the iron is hot.

faithfully yours,

I Th Hecker,

O A Brownson LL.D.[3]

1. Patrick Donahoe (1811–1901) of Boston, Catholic journalist and publisher, founder of the *Boston Pilot* 1836.

2. *The Spirit-Rapper: An Autobiography* (Boston, 1854), a polemical novel directed against spiritualism.

3. In 1846, Norwich University, Northfield, Vt., conferred the doctor of laws degree on Brownson; Fordham University (then called St. John's College) did likewise in July 1850.

63

HECKER TO BROWNSON • 14 SEPTEMBER 1854

J.M.J.A!

Sep 14. 1854.

My dear Friend,

Mrs Ripley tells me that you intend coming by this way as soon as cold weather sets in. It is cold now, shall I expect you soon? I am anxious to see you when you do come and wish you could inform me when that will be, for we soon commence our campaign of fall missions. The principal reason why I should like to see you at present is to get your counsel & direction in the matter which now engages me.

Mrs R. I trust gave you some idea of what I am about.[1] I would attempt to give you an idea of it, but I find it impossible to do so in a letter. My object in view is to bring minds similarly constituted as my own to similar convictions & results, by the same process as I passed through. The leading idea is to expose the wants of the heart and demand their proper objects, rather than a logical defense of the Church. My 1st Question is–Has man a destiny? 2d What is it? Which is God's own destiny–to know him, love him & do his will here. 3d. Dignity of man. 4. Every man has a special destiny. 5. Many are called to live a life above the common life. 6 Proof[:] Ancient[–] Pythagorens, Essennians, Therapeutics. 7 Modern–Brook Farm, Fruitlands, Valley of the Cross.[2] 8 Christ the Model of the Divine Life. 9 Idea[3] of a church to answer man's wants. 10 Application of this idea to protestantism. 11 Catholic Church.

One of the leading ideas is the religious life. If I am not deceived the manner in which the different points will be treated will be a little new. I take an occasion to break a lance with Emerson[,][4] Channing,[5] etc whenever I meet them. There will be no want of boldness & aspiration in it.

Another leading idea is that the Church must meet & satisfy all the wants of man's heart or religious nature–and I say that the affections of the heart when pure, are no less unerring guides to truth, than the logic of the intellect.

I have penned down roughly nearly the whole. Those here to whom I have communicated my thoughts encourage me to go on. I must see you. Tell me when you intend to come this way.

Besides this I am full of things I should like to communicate to you personally–& talk about.

My best respects to Mrs Brownson & to the members of your family.

Most affectionately yours in the s.
hearts of Jesus & Mary.

I. Th Hecker CSSR

1. Hecker was preparing his first book *Questions of the Soul* (New York: D. Appleton, 1855).

2. A reference to the Brotherhood of the Holy Cross, a monastic community founded at Valle Crucis, N.C., in 1845 by Levi S. Ives then Episcopal bishop of North Carolina. Dr. Ives was influenced by the Oxford Movement.

3. The word 'institution' was crossed out here.

4. Ralph Waldo Emerson (1803–1882), former Unitarian minister, foremost New England Transcendentalist, lecturer, poet and essayist, author of *Nature* (1836).

5. William Ellery Channing (1780–1842), eloquent preacher, author and social critic whose religious liberalism promoted the Unitarian movement in the U.S.

64

HECKER TO BROWNSON • 23 SEPTEMBER 1854

J.M.J.A!

Sep 23, 1854.

My dear friend

About ten days ago I wrote a note to you wishing to know whether you were coming to N.Y. soon, & when, as I am very desirous to get your advice about the subject upon which I am writing.

If it is not probable that I can see you in N.Y. some time this fall, I will ask for permission to go to see you at your house. It would be difficult for me to get this permission at present, as our missions are now about to commence. Very likely we shall give our first mission in the Diocese of Newark on the 1st Sunday in October.[1] However this winter our missions[2] will be at no great distance from the city of N.Y. Hence if you come, & I know the time, I can always get to the city to meet you.

My best respects to your family & believe me yours faithfully in the s. hearts of Jesus & Mary

I. Th. Hecker. CSSR.

Do me the favour to give me an answer.

1. A mission held later in Patterson, N.J., from 29 October to 9 November 1854.

2. Missions were held at the Church of Our Lady of the Mountain near Emmitsburg, Md., 19–26 November 1854; St. Peter's Church, Baltimore, 3–13 December 1854; St. Patrick's Cathedral, Newark, N.J., 31 December 1854 to 14 January 1855; St. Mary's Church, Charlestown, Mass., 28 January–11 February 1855; and St. Patrick's Church, Utica, N.Y., 21 February–4 March 1855.

65

HECKER TO BROWNSON • [1 OCTOBER 1854]

J.M.J.A!

[*Undated*] [1]

My dear Friend,

I had a very good time with the Bishop as you can easily imagine.

I have understood that something will be done in the Synod[2] concerning Catholic Journals & News papers. I know that our ArchBishop has the intention of writing something on this matter.[3] The thought struck me that on this account & for other reasons you would still like to make your visit to N.Y.

The enclosed is to defray yr expenses. If you do not wish to come then do with it what you please.

My brother George would be happy to have you stay with him while here. His residence no[.] 23 Rutgers Place.

If at any time my service will be of any use to you or I can do anything for you in any shape, you have only to command them and feel no obligation to me & I shall be happy.

Affectionately yours in Jesus and Mary.

Remember me to your family.

I Th Hecker CSSR

1. This undated letter has 1 October 1845 written on its cover, but Hecker was not a Redemptorist in 1845; the year 1854 is meant since the synod referred to in this letter (see nn. 2, 3 below) was convened in 1854.

2. The First Provincial Council of New York opened on 1 October 1854 (First Solemn Session) and closed on 8 October 1854 (Third Solemn Session).

3. No decree was issued concerning Catholic journals or newspapers at this council. However, in the Pastoral Letter of 8 October 1854, emanating from the council, Catholic journals formed a subject engaging the attention of the Archbishop, John Hughes, and the bishops of New York; see *The Pastoral Letter of the Archbishop and Bishops of the Province of New York, in Provincial Council Assembled, to the Clergy and Laity of their charge* (New York: Edward Dunigan and Brother, 1854).

66

HECKER TO BROWNSON • 29 OCTOBER [1854]

J.M.J.A!

Oct. 29.[1]

My dear Friend,

Do give in yr next Review a notice of "Thoreau's Life in the woods".[2] He places himself fairly before the public and is a fair object of criticism. I have not read all his book through, and I don't think any one will except as a feat. I read enough in it to see that under his seeming truthfulness & frankness he conceals an immense amount of pride, pretention & infidelity.

This tendency to solitude & asceticism means something, and there is a certain degree of truthfulness & even bravery in his attempts to find out what this something is; but his results are increased pride, pretention & infidelity, instead of humility, simplicity, & piety.

He makes a great ado about the cheapness of his house, and gives us a list of his articles of diet as something to be looked at & admired; but why a house at all? Why this long list of luxuries? The Hermit Fathers[3] did without all these. They dwelt in holes & caves & lived on roots & water.

Thoreau lives a couple of years in the midst of [the Walden forest]— with the help of his friends, and lo he sets to crowing to wake up his neighbours. The Hermit Fathers lived 60 [to] 100 years & upwards in perfect solitude & silence & when discovered plunge deeper into the desert, and die as they lived in solitude & silence. The poor man Thoreau does not know what cheap stuff his heroism is made of. He wants waking up.

He brags of not having committed himself in not having purchased a farm, he forgets that he takes a deed for his book in the shape of a copy right.

His recontre [*sic*] with the Catholic Canadian[4] shows according to his own account to every other mind except his own, that of the two, the Canadian was the truer, braver, & greater man. You can give him a good notice, for he was a young friend of yours. What has all his efforts & struggling done for him? What would these efforts not do inside & under the divine influences of the H[oly] Church. The time is coming when our young, earnest, and enterprising American youth will find that it is the Church of God they seek—and they will find in her bosom the sphere for their activity & the true objects of their search & aspirations.

Your visit to N.Y. is still talked of. Mr Ripley & Bancroft[5] were perfectly delighted. R[ipley] was enchanted with his visit to you at my brother's. McMaster[6] takes another tone. I hope we shall be able to keep him at least for a time in the same. Have you seen R['s] criticism of Comte's Positive Philosophy[7] in the Tribune of last week?[8] I think. It is most masterly. If it comes in your way say a good thing about it. B[ancroft] delivers his Lecture[9] in Nov. Mr Fairbanks[10] from Boston suggested to get him to deliver it in Boston. This would be capital. B. will publish it after the delivery of it in N.Y. Perhaps he could delay its publication to deliver it in Boston. Fairbanks is a member of a commercial institution & will try to get it to invite him. This lecture would I think make a stir among the unitarians. He will hit it, hard hits. B. has courage. I am told that he reads the essays of Donoso Cortes[11] that I lent him, with the greatest interest.

I put into the hands of Appleton[12] to-day or to-morrow the first 12 chapters of my book. Including "The Model Man" & "The Model Life"[,] two chapters which I have written since I saw you. I think I have been successful in doing what I intended [with] these two chapters which I considered the most difficult task from the begginning [*sic*]. Only one thing remains to be determined & that is the titlle [*sic*]. The nearest I can come to it at present is "The Soul; its wants; & the answers of the 19th Century". Or the one of George. "The Day-dawn to the Soul in darkness". *Which?* If any new or better titlle suggests itself to you do me the favour to communicate it to me. I hope to see it published in 2 months or 3 at the latest. It will be carefully corrected before it is put into the printers hands by Mr Ripley.

F[ather] Hewit has written to me about "The Spirit Rapper[;]"[13] he read it with great interest. F. Walworth is occupied with it & expresses the same interest.

I am now engaged here at Patterson on a Mission. If at any time you have a word for me, it will reach me by addressing your note to the house in N.Y.

George will take steps concerning the lectures you spoke of to him.

My best respects to your family.

faithfully and affectionately yours in the
s. hearts of Jesus & Mary

I. Th. Hecker CSSR

I pray more earnestly for you & also for Mc[Master] for I think you are called to head a great movement in America.

1. Though the year was not written, it was 1854 since Hecker's mission at Patterson, N.J., mentioned in this letter, was held from 29 October to 9 November 1854.

2. *Walden, or Life in the Woods* (Boston, 1854). Brownson did not notice *Walden* in *BrQR*.

3. The Hermit or Desert Fathers of early Christianity, such as St. Anthony of the Desert.

4. Described early in chapter 6 of *Walden*.

5. George Bancroft (1800–1891), Harvard graduate 1817, educator, prominent American historian and lecturer, Democratic politician and U.S. Minister to Prussia 1867–73.

6. James A. McMaster, editor and proprietor of the *New York Freeman's Journal and Catholic Register*.

7. Auguste Comte (1798–1857), French positivist philosopher and social critic, author of *Catéchisme positiviste* (1852).

8. "Comte's Positive Philosophy," the *New York Tribune*, 28 October 1854, p. 6.

9. "The Necessity, the Reality, and the Promise of the Progress of the Human Race," delivered before the New York Historical Society on 20 November 1854.

10. Charles Bullard Fairbanks, Jr. (1827–1859), Catholic convert 1852, novelist and journalist (with the *Boston Pilot*), associated with Donahoe's publishing firm of Boston.

11. Juan Francisco María de la Salud Donoso Cortés (1809–1853), Spanish statesman, historian, and author of *Ensayo sobre el Catolicismo, el Liberalismo, y el Socialismo* (Madrid, 1851).

12. D. Appleton & Company, founded in 1838 by Daniel Appleton (1785–1849), a merchant turned publisher, together with his son William Henry Appleton (1814–1899), who expanded the publishing firm and continued it through his son William Worthen Appleton (1845–1924).

13. *The Spirit-Rapper* (1854), Brownson's recently published novel, noticed in his own *BrQR*, October 1854, p. 531.

67

HECKER TO BROWNSON • 2 DECEMBER [1854]*

J.M.J.A.

Dec. 2, /53[1]

My dear friend,

I am anxious to put you au current [*sic*] concerning Bancroft's Lecture.[2] Mrs Ripley writes me that "there was something very solemn & sublime in his announcement[3] of his belief in the H[oly] & B[lessed] Trinity, at that time. It seemed as if he felt he had it to do, before he lived another day, & had made a clean breast of it. May Heaven bless him for the act, though it was made with the lisping accents of a child's first prayer. Mr B[ancroft] & Mrs B[ancroft] are quite desirous to hear what the catholics say to it, but I suppose they will have to wait for the Jan. No. of the Quarterly.[4] . . .

Mr Ripley is trying to convince himself & others that Mr B. did not mean quite all that he said, but he finds this rather difficult & I think will come out a wiser man from the effort. He is anxiously awaiting Mr Brownson's Dictum."

It seems to me that the only thing new & true at the same time is Mr B['s] profession of faith in the B. Trinity. This is what has made the stir. This no doubt was the uppermost tho't in B's mind, & he seems to have dragged it by the hair into his Lecture. However that is not our affair.

Mr. B. no doubt is in a crisis of his religious faith. He gets sympathy no where. The idea that has got possession of his mind if developed must open to him the C. Church. It is this point that makes his Lecture interesting to us catholics. What you will say therefore in your Review will have no small influence upon Mr B. & his wife as well as Mr Ripley.

Mr[*?*] Ripley has taken the care of putting my book through the press. Appleton is to be the publisher. It is published at my brother George's expense. I have put into the hands of Mr R. the 1st 10 chap. & requested him to have it pub. as soon as it can be done & done well. Appleton said to me it could be published in one month. Mr R. suggested for its title, "The destiny of the Soul, or An Answer to the Question of the Age." I think I will let it go with that.

If we do not break down in our arrangements we hope to be in your neighborhood about the latter part of Jan. for the Mission at Charlestown.[5] Shall you be at home. We begin a Mission here tomorrow at St Peter's.[6] We closed one last Sunday & a retreat for the students at Mt. St. Mary.[7] You have a good friend in Dr Caffrey.[8] So also in Mr. Miles[9] who was there, & with whom I formed an acquaintance. The evening before we left the students after having given us several hearty cheers; I gave with them 3 cheers for "our country" 3 more for "its conversion" & 3 for our "B. Lady". You should have heard them—they were hearty cheers.

Affectionately yours in the s. hearts of Jesus & Mary my love to your family,

I Th Hecker CSSR

Baltimore.

*Microfilm, roll three (calendared 2 December 1853).

1. This letter was wrongly dated 1853; the year 1854 is definitely meant since the mission at St. Peter's (n. 6 below) began on 3 December 1854 and the retreat at Mount St. Mary's (n. 7 below) was conducted in November 1854.

2. See Letter 66, n. 9.

3. See the published text of Bancroft's lecture on the Progress of the Human Race (20 November 1854) in his *Literary and Historical Miscellanies* (New York, 1855), pp. 502–4, especially 504.

4. See *BrQR*, January 1855, pp. 135–37, noticing Bancroft's *History of the United States* . . . , VI (Boston, 1854).

5. St. Mary's Church, Charlestown, Mass., 28 January–11 February 1855.

6. St. Peter's Church, Baltimore, 3–13 December 1854.

7. Mount St. Mary's College and Seminary, founded in 1808 near Emmitsburg, Md., by John Dubois (1764–1842), French-born Sulpician who became third bishop of New York.

8. John Henry McCaffrey (1806–1881), educator and catechist, ordained priest 1838, president of Mount St. Mary's College and Seminary 1838–72.

9. George Henry Miles (1824–1871), novelist and playwright, Catholic convert 1836, professor of English at Mount St. Mary's College.

68

HECKER TO BROWNSON • [c. 12 MARCH 1855]*

[*Undated*] [1]

J.M.J.A!

My dear Friend,

You no doubt rec'd my book on your return or soon after. There have been several notices of it in the secular & protestant press.[2] Some of them quite amusing[,] other[s] quite fair. On the whole the book is likely to have a wide circulation.

I mailed a Tribune of last Friday for you with Mr Ripley's notice.[3] I am sorry to say that he has not understood the book, and that his demon has got a little the mastery of him. There is no antagonism between the inner testimony of the soul & an external infallible authority. And no attempt is made to show in the book that there is. On the contrary it is the inner testimony of the soul that is made the ground work & basis of the book, and made to show the necessity of an external infallible authority–in a word the C. Church. Besides it is ungenerous not to say ungentlemanly in him to say that it will find an echo among other hearts those "*that cherish a stronger passion for the illusion of fancy than for the intuitions of truth.*" His notice is calculated to circulate the book, and he thinks, so I am informed, that his notice is a very favorable one. Of course I don't mind it farther than it shows not a catholic tone of mind in him.

I will get a Churchman with a notice[4] of its Editor[,] of whom John[5] seems to have held his elbows while writing it, and send it to you. It will amuse you.

I spoke to the Appletons to delay it for the Catholic press, whether he has done so, I cannot say.

There are a few mistakes in the first edition of 1000 copies[;] in the next which will go to press in a few days, these will be corrected, among others, that of your name. Ripley when he first saw it, laughed, & said who will dare say after this that Brownson is not O.K.?

I am little curious to read your notice,[6] & hope you will favour me with a copy of it, as soon as you can do so conveniently.

Yours affectionately in the sacred hearts of Jesus & Mary.

I Th Hecker CSSR.

*Microfilm, roll four (calendared [1855? Feb.]).

1. Dated c. 12 March 1855 since it was written shortly after the reviews of Hecker's *Questions of the Soul* appeared in *The Churchman* (n. 4 below) and the *New York Tribune* (n. 3 below).

2. Among those in the secular press were, the *Boston Transcript* and the *Boston Atlas*; in the religious press, the *New York Observer*, the *Philadelphia Presbyterian*, and the *New York Evangelist.*

3. The *New York Tribune*, 9 March 1855, p. 6.

4. *The Churchman*, XIV (8 March 1855), 14.

5. Hecker's brother John was the proprietor of *The Churchman*, an Episcopalian journal, at this time.

6. "Questions of the Soul," *BrQR*, April 1855, pp. 209–26.

69

HECKER TO BROWNSON • 27 MARCH 1855

March 27, 1855

J.M.J.A!

My Dear friend,

A couple of days ago I rec'd a note[1] from Mr Bancroft the contents of which no doubt, will be interesting to you. He says:

"How shall I enough thank you for choosing me as one of the first to whom you communicate your deeply interesting volume? It is a beautiful daguerrotype [*sic*] of a gentle, affectionate, & spotless soul. I took it with me on my travels and have read it in the great solitudes, all of it once, and much of it twice. There is, as I believe you do not need the assurrance [*sic*], very much in the volume to which I cordially assent. I agree with you with regard to Goethe and his school, except that I do not call Goethe a transcendentalist; he is rather a pantheistic conservative. There are some parts where my heart is in accord with the spirit that dictated them, and when I yet do not agree with the statements. Truth is I think to be discerned by the aid of that light which lighteth every man; I have not learned to lull myself to rest in the easy cradle of authority.

["] Your volume is clear and simple in style, (& clearness and simplicity are in writing the highest graces), rich in illustration; all the dwellers in Parnassus seem to bring their willing offerings to your writing table. I look upon your work as one of the signs of the times, that men are beginning to look inward, and desire with a loftier earnestness to solve the great problems of existence. I hope when I return to town I shall have the pleasure of seeing you often, and old as I am, I shall be delighted to learn from one so sincere as you—

very truly ["] etc.

In a note to Mrs Ripley in which the above was enclosed he says on the same subject,

"Pray find some way by which you can get the enclosed note to Father Hecker or rather Brother Hecker. I have read his book with delight. He seems to call together all the poets of all time and make them join in his chant to the glory of God and the perfection of the church. With the first I agree heartily; but everything in which man plays a part is imperfect, even the church on earth. Do you remember that I in my incredulity rather smiled at the power of the good St Rose of Lima[2] over the gnats, beetles, and musquitos [*sic*] when you first showed it to me and yet the chapter on the church & nature interested me most of all. I think I see now that the idea of the superiority of spirit to matter lies at the bottom of the catholic notion of the miracles and in the general statement it is a true one. But what charmed me most was the picture of the B[lessed] Henry Suso,[3] standing in the midst of the Universe, and beating time for the song of all created things."

My Brother Geo. brought to me the other day your notice. For I am at present engaged on a mission at Manhattanville[4] and staying at Mr Donnelly's,[5] who remembers your visit here last summer with pleasure.

You cannot imagine how much I was interested in your analysis of the true elements of the American character. There is no doubt that if we hope for the conversion of our country we must aim at the conversion of the class of minds you describe. What you say of myself modesty forbids me to say that I believe even one half, on the other hand, you have given to me such a lesson of practical humility that you have only excited envy in my breast.

It seems to me from what I have already seen & heard this book has made the call for another[6] necessary, and that to meet the same class of persons. To show the adaptation of the Church to these wants or requirements of the Intellect. Ripley, Bancroft and several others do not deny the adaptation of the Church to the wants of the heart but refuse to yield on the score of the intellect. These men need to be shown that the first demand of the Church is that man should follow the guide of Reason; that faith, authority, etc are demanded by reason to its full growth & perfection. This would give an occassion [*sic*] to show the beautiful logical unity in the mysteries & dogmas of the Church, and how great a respect & reverence the Church shows to man's reason in demanding his faith & obedience. *We* know that it is *only* the Church that pays the respect & that true deference to reason which this divine gift to man ought to have. We should have to show how reason was made to know the truth. How the Church supposes this. Exemplify it by her different treatment of infants & adults. And that the supposition she acts upon, that Truth has been revealed, is in harmony with the attributes of God & the dictates of reason etc. *To show how the dogmas of the Church answer in a way, to the demands of the intellect, as the sacraments do to the wants of the heart.* Having made this class of mind interested, they will become now willing listeners to *"The Claims of Reason."*

Of course I do not intend to make an attempt at this, but merely throw out these hints as they arise in my mind.

Yours affectionately & sincerely in the s. hearts of

Jesus & Mary

I Th Hecker CSSR

Manhattanville

1. George Bancroft to Isaac Hecker, 14 March 1855 (APF), forwarded by Sophia Ripley.

2. St. Rose of Lima (1568–1617), Peruvian mystic, Domincan nun, first canonized saint of the New World 1671.

3. Blessed Henry Suso (c. 1295–1365), German Dominican ascetic, spiritual writer, a disciple of Meister Eckhart.

4. At the Church of the Annunciation (of the Blessed Virgin Mary), Manhattanville, N.Y., 18 March–1 April 1855.

5. Rev. Arthur J. Donnelly (1820–1890), Irish-born, first pastor of Annunciation parish 1854, named vicar general of the Archdiocese of New York 1888.

6. Eventually Hecker's book *Aspirations of Nature* (New York: James B. Kirker, 1857).

HECKER TO BROWNSON • 7 APRIL 1855

April 7, 1855.

J.M.J.A!

My dear friend,

Since my last note to you I have read nearly all of your last Review.[1] You cannot imagine with what interest and pleasure I read it. It seems to me that you have given a different general tone to the whole Review, and that by this, greater interest and sympathy will be excited in its readers there can be no doubt.

Your article[2] on F[ather] Chastel[3] has tended to open the thought in my mind which I communicated to you in my note[4] at Manhattanville. If I made the attempt to write another book it would be on the Theme I spoke of "how the dogmas, & mysteries of the C. faith in a manner answers the requirements of Reason as the sacraments do the wants of the heart." I should endeavour first to show the excellence, dignity & rights of Reason. Here I should give to Reason its true value, & have the opportunity to talk a la American. 2nd the beatitude of Reason. This presents the place to speak of truth, of true liberty, and true happiness. 3 *Duties of Reason.* The obligation to seek the Truth, to obey it when found, & to follow it at all hazards & sacrifices. These 3 Chap. would answer as a sort of premise & give tone to the character of the whole contents of the book. 4 *Wants of Reason.* Its insufficiency to guide man to his true destiny. 5. *Necessity of Revelation.* 6. *Divine Authority.* To interpret Revelation. 7. *Miracles,* as a mark of d[ivine] authority. Now I come to the answers *1st of Philosophers. 2nd of Protestantism.* Here I would attempt to show that the first step of protestantism was the repudiation of Reason etc. 3d *The Church*. The deference it shows to Reason. How she possesses all that Reason demands. Revelation. D. Authority. Miracles. Finally *"Catholic Worship.* The basis of C[atholic] worship [is] the principle of all life. In her bosom the whole man–Reason, heart, senses, all is turned to the worship of its creator.

Such is the plan as it now presents itself to my mind. How does it strike you? Should *I* undertake it? If so, would you have it modified? You would do me a great favour to pen me a line or two in answer to these questions.

You will find a remarkable preface to the "Heroines of Charity"[5] pub. by Burns, written by Audrey De Vere.[6] They are so much like your own in the art. on "Liberalism &c."[7] that you can but be struck with the similarity–almost in expression. They recall also to my mind tho'ts which for several years have occupied my mind & taken a deep hold of my heart. The evil of the prot. heresy has become finally social. This has given rise to Socialism. Will the present order in the C. Church answer all the wants & meet the special demands of modern society. The author of this preface, appears to think so. I would be glad to think so too. But somehow or other I have the conviction that we need a body in the Church for this special purpose. An order that would have for its object the special charge of dispensing the eleemosanary [*sic*] aid of society & of individuals to the needy & miserable. To do this as its work of devotion. I must acknowledge that this tho't came to my mind several years ago while I was making my studies, & in such a way as to make a deep impression on it. Socialism is right in wishing to better the arrangements of society & to aid the downtrodden & needy, but this can be done without all society being converted to Socialism. Socialism has a special work to do. These are mere suggestions which come to my mind, and do not take them to mean any more.

Monday I shall be on my way to Kentucky.[8] Any note from you between the 15teenth & 23d of this month would reach me if addressed to the care of "Rev. Mr Butler,[9] Lexington, Ky."

Daily my confidence in creases that Providence has destined me to do an important work for our country. Let us strive to be more faithful to his grace & inspirations, and he will grant us the petitions of our hearts.

Believe me yours sincerely & affectionately in the s. hearts of Jesus & Mary.

I Th Hecker CSSR

N.Y.

P.S. I send you a copy of the 2nd edition of the "Ques. of the Soul," with fewer mistakes.

1. *BrQR*, April 1855, pp. 209–26.
2. "What Human Reason Can Do," *BrQR*, April 1855, pp. 227–45.
3. Marie-Ange Chastel, S.J. (1804–1861), French theologian, defended reason as an apologetic tool against the supernaturalism of the Traditionalists; *De la valeur de la raison humaine* (Paris, 1854), reviewed by Brownson (n. 2 above).
4. See Letter 69.
5. *Heroines of Charity; containing the Sisters of Vincennes, Jeanne Biscot, Mdle. Le Gras, Madame de Miramion, Mrs. Seton, the Little Sisters of the Poor, etc., etc.,* with a preface by Aubrey De Vere, esq. (London, 1854).
6. Thomas Hunt Aubrey De Vere (1814–1892), Irish poet, literary critic, essayist.

7. "Liberalism and Socialism," *BrQR*, April 1855, pp. 183–202.

8. For missions at Lexington, 15–25 April 1855, and at Frankfort, 29 April–3 May 1855.

9. Rev. Thomas Butler (1803–1869), vicar general of the Diocese of Covington, Ky.

71

HECKER TO BROWNSON • 16 APRIL [1855]*

J.M.J.A!

April. 16[1]

My Dear Friend,

On thursday last I left Pittsburg with Bishop O'Connor[2] for Cincinnati. On the way we talked on several topics. Among others when we arrived at Cincinnati was that of Development.[3] You know that B[ishop] O'C[onnor] was at Rome at the declaration[4] of the dogma of the I[mmaculate] Concep[tion] of our B[lessed] Lady. He told me that at the assembly of the Bishops he made some objection to certain words or statements in the Bull as it was read to them on account of its seeming to countenance that view of development which he considered false. This drew out Perroné,[5] who made a speech of a half hour's length defining what he considered the true & false doctrine on this point. Bishop O'C. took notes of P[errone's] speech & has them at home. Some of the Italian prelates wondered what B. C. was driving at, when Dr Grant[6] of Southwark rose and said some words about Dr Newman,[7] & they saw then. The words in the Bull were changed.

Bishop O'Con. says that there is a capital statement of the true doctrine of development in the Bull, but as we could not find the document, he was not able to point it out. The Latin Bull & not its translation must be read to find it. He said also that Perrone held precisely the same doctrine as he did on this point. And B. O'Con. expressed his satisfaction of your course in regard to that controversy. He also told me that he thought of sending you a note on this subject, but I think he feels too sore about his recent discussion with you, to do it, tho I urged him to write. The last No.[8] of your Review he considered as one of your best.

But there is another reason for my writing this note. It is this. The irish prelates & priests have become mighty tender on the point of Nationality. Your dose on Native Americanism[9] has operated on them, & operated powerfully, and especially in the west. They feel sore, and let me add also weak from its effects. You gave an additional dose in another form in your article on the Question of the Soul.[10] Perhaps if you knew that the first dose had not ceased operating you would not have administered another so soon. The truth is, I fear, that there may before long, come a collision on this point in our Church. The American element is in creasing steadily in numerical strength, and will in due time predominate; and at the pesent moment on account of the state of the public mind has great moral weight, and this in itself, must excite unpleasant feelings on the other side. Is it not the better part of wisdom at the present moment, for us to abide our time, & say no more than we can help? I think what you have said is doing its work, and will effectuate it, and perhaps without further effort. I would not have you to modify a word that you have written, but my wish has been to give you a hint of the state of feeling existing on this subject, having the opportunity of seeing pretty extensively the prelates & priests of the Church, and all sides.

It was generally rumoured that you would make an onslaught on Chandler in this No.,[11] & nothing of the kind being found in it, gave general satisfaction.

You cannot imagine with what delight I have heard different persons speak of the gratification they found in your last No., detecting something they knew not what in its tone that pleased them. I feel quite assured that you have adopted the right course, and caught the right spirit to accomplish a vast deal of good to our people in the Church as well as out.

I enclose also a sort of a programme of another book[12] if you think well of it. Let me have a line from you if it meets with your approval.

Yours affectionatelly [*sic*] in the
s. hearts of Jesus & Mary,

I Th Hecker CSSR

address. Very Rev T Butler
Lexington, Ky.

*Brownson, *BML*, pp. 561–63 (year not given).

1. Though the year was not written, the contents of this letter certainly place it within the year 1855.

2. Michael O'Connor, Bishop of Pittsburgh.

3. The debate over the development of Christian doctrine; the proclamation of the dogma of the Immaculate Conception (n. 4 below) was interpreted by both parties to the controversy as supporting their position.

4. Declared by Pope Pius IX in the Bull *Ineffabilis Deus* on 8 December 1854.

5. Giovanni Perrone, S.J. (1794–1876), Italian Jesuit, became professor at the Collegio Romano 1824, influential theologian at the First Vatican Council 1869–70, leading papal theologian of his time.

6. Bishop Thomas Grant (1816–1870), became rector of the English College in Rome 1844, bishop of Southwark England 1851.

7. John Henry Newman's *Essay on the Development of Christian Doctrine* (1845) set off the development controversy; for Brownson's critique of Newman's ideas, see "The Development Theory," *BrQR*, July 1846, pp. 342–68, and "Newman's Theory of Christian Doctrine," *BrQR*, January 1847, pp. 39–86.

8. *BrQR*, April 1855.

9. "Native Americanism," *BrQR*, July 1854, pp. 328–54. See also "The Know-Nothings," *BrQR*, October 1854, pp. 447–87 and January 1855, pp. 114–35; and "Romanism in America," *BrQR*, April 1855, pp. 145–83.

10. *BrQR*, April 1855, pp. 209–27.

11. Joseph Ripley Chandler (1792–1880), Catholic convert 1849, journalist, U.S. congressman from Pennsylvania. In a congressional speech on 11 January 1855, Chandler critiqued Brownson's doctrine of the indirect temporal power of the pope; for Brownson's reply, see his "Temporal Power of the Pope," *BrQR*, October 1855, pp. 417–45.

12. *Aspirations of Nature* (1857).

72

BROWNSON TO HECKER • [c. 1 JUNE 1855]*

[*Undated*][1]

Rev. & very dear Father,

I should very much like to have Dr. Ives[2] review the late work of Dr. Kenrick,[3] and if he will prepare me an article for my October No.[,] I shall be very much obliged to him, and will, if in my power, make him some compensation for it. I shall want it during the first half of August.

With regard to the other matters you speak of I think as you do. The simple truth is our old controversialists have their method, and they will look with distrust on our new method, & fancy it full of danger. Very few of them have any suspicion that times have changed and that old errors are to be refuted under new forms & from a different stand-point, yet I do not despair.

Our great difficulty in getting our religion fairly presented to the American mind is the real dislike of the American people and character felt by a large portion of our bishops & clergy, and their settled conviction that nothing can be done for their conversion. They are not missionaries, but have the characteristics of an old national clergy, but of a nation not ours. There is the great difficulty. We cannot appeal to our own countrymen, and use those forms of expression necessary to render ourselves intelligible to them without seeming to them to attack either the Irish clergy or the Irish people. But God in his good Providence will enable us to surmount in due time this obstacle. The Irish people, the laity, are far less unamerican than their clergy, and if permitted to follow their own sympathies will very soon be prepared to second us. They are a noble people when not misled.

My Review for July[4] is nearly all prepared. It has some variety, but nothing very striking, [e]xcept another article on Gratry,[5] and an article from Montalembert,[6] translated from the Revue des Deux Mondes.[7] I hope to give you a good number in October.

I beg you to give yourself full freedom in your new book. What we want is free, fresh, and spirited writings. I like the plan of your book much. You will find a hint or two in my second article on the Abbé Gratry written before I went south, which may be in your line. I am more and more convinced of the necessity of presenting the positive side of Catholicity, and of doing it in a way to meet the actual wants of our countrymen. The point I am laboring now is to show that the deplorable state of some Catholic countries now and at other times is owing to the State and not to the Church. It is mainly the political [and] social aspects of the case I am concerned with just now.

Pray remember [me] kindly to your mother & brothers, and respectfully to all the good fathers, and believe me most truly & sincerely

Yours in Christ

O. A. Brownson

Rev. I. T. Hecker S.S.R.

*Microfilm, roll nine (calendared [June?]).

1. Dated c. 1 June 1855 since the July 1855 issue of *BrQR* is about to appear (see n. 5 below); normally *BrQR* appeared after the middle of the month preceding the publication date, i.e., *BrQR* for July 1855 appeared after mid-June.

2. Levi Silliman Ives, D.D. (1797–1867), became Episcopal bishop of North Carolina 1831, Catholic convert 1852, founder of the New York Catholic Protectory 1863, author.

3. *Vindication of the Catholic Church* (Baltimore, 1855) by Francis Patrick Kenrick (1796–1863), Irish-born, learned theologian and author of seminary textbooks, became bishop of Philadelphia 1830 and archbishop of Baltimore 1850.

4. *BrQR*, July 1855.

5. Auguste Josephe Alphonse Gratry (1805–1872), French priest of the Oratory, theologian and philosopher, became professor of moral theology at

the Sorbonne 1863; author of *De la Connaisance de Dieu* (Paris, 1853) reviewed by Brownson, "Gratry on the Knowledge of God," *BrQR,* July 1855, pp. 281–300; see also *BrQR* January 1855, pp. 1–21.

6. Charles Forbes René de Montalembert (1810–1870), French author and historian, politician and leader of liberal Catholics in France.

7. This article "L'Empire Romain Après la Paix de L'Eglise," *Revue Des Deux Mondes,* IX, n.s. (January 1855), 177–90, in translation appeared as "Rome After the Peace," *BrQR,* July 1855, pp. 300–322.

73

HECKER TO BROWNSON • 7 AUGUST 1855

Aug 7, 1855.

[*Fragment*][1]

But he had only glimpses. He speaks of certain men who are able to understand those outside of the Church & at the same time her own doctrine; "from the role of interpreter they will become reconciliators." The value of his articles seems to me to lie in these glimpses.

You do not know how much I expect from your labours. My convictions are my prayers, & my prayers are my convictions. No day passes that I do not remember your nominatum in the Holy Sacrifice of the Mass.

We both have a double work to do. To labour to bring up the catholic body to catholic truth intellectually & morally, & to open the way to the American people to see the same truth in all its beauty.

Your last No.[2] excited my interest especially the first[3] & last[4] article. The conclusion of the last was well deserved. The American people will never believe, or be convinced, that we love our country, so long as we do not show genuine patriotic feeling for its interest & destiny. And they are right.

Believe me

Yours sincerely and affectionately in
the S. hearts of Jesus & Mary

I. Th. Hecker CSSR

N.Y.

My kindest remembrance to your Wife & family.

1. Only this fragment of the letter exists.
2. *BrQR,* July 1855.
3. "Gratry on the Knowledge of God," ibid., pp. 281–300. Gratry stressed

the primacy of the heart and the emotions over the intellect in religion as well as an innate sense of the infinite.

4. "A Know-Nothing Legislature," ibid., pp. 354–410.

74

HECKER TO BROWNSON • 23 AUGUST 1855*

Aug. 23, 1855.[1]

J.M.J.A!

My dear friend,

For a long time I have entertained the desire to unite in some way those who are awake to the interests of the Church at the present moment in our Country. Last week I succeeded in getting together at McMaster's home, Dr. Mannahan,[2] Capt. Monroe[3] & Cavanagh.[4] The Capt. is a capital man, relative of old president Monroe. His articles in the Freeman[5] are signed "M." Cavanagh is also a writer of the F[reeman's]. He has a vigorous pen.

There was a perfect agreement in our views. We came to the conclusion to labour in propagating them in the Freeman with earnestness. We meet again in a fortnight. Come of this what may, my efforts will be in this direction.

There is another subject on which Dr Mannahan & I have spoken—Your coming on to N.Y. You will remember on my visit last summer you suggested this. At that time it did not seem to me best. But my views are changed. If you have still a notion to change your place of residence to N.Y. I should like to know it. For if so, my intention is to do all in power to prepare the way for it.

I look for the next No.[6] of yr Review with great hopes & interest.

The third Edition of the Ques. of the Soul is in press.

Affectionately yours
in the s. hearts of Jesus & Mary,

I Th Hecker C.[SS.] R.

N.Y.

*Microfilm, roll three (calendared 23 August 1853).

1. The year could be read as 1853, but 1855 is the correct year, especially since the third edition of Hecker's *Questions of the Soul* (1855), mentioned in the letter, could not have appeared in 1853.

2. Rev. Ambrose Manahan, D.D. (1814?–1867), graduate of the College of the Propaganda in Rome, but fought the "Europeanizing" of American Catholics and seminaries; author of *The Triumph of the Church* (New York, 1859).

3. James Monroe, grandnephew of fifth U.S. President James Monroe; Catholic convert, U.S. Army colonel killed in the Civil War at Harper's Ferry 1861.

4. Most likely Hecker is referring to Captain John Kavanagh, who was associated with the *Freeman's Journal* as writer and business manager.

5. The *New York Freeman's Journal and Catholic Register,* a weekly newspaper founded in 1840 and transformed by Bishop Hughes into the New York diocesan organ in 1842, edited by Rev. James R. Bayley. With the financial backing of George V. Hecker, in July 1848 James A. McMaster became its sole proprietor and editor.

6. *BrQR,* October 1855.

75

BROWNSON TO HECKER • 29 AUGUST 1855

Boston 29 Aug '55

Rev. & dear Father,

My own opinion is that it would [be] far better for me and for my Review if I were once established in New York. There are many reasons why I should like to remove to your city,[1] and I have only one reason against doing so,—that is, the [e]xpense of moving and getting established in a new home. I do not know whether it would need cost me more to live in New York than here, whence settled, but I think it would not.

I think I should be with you more in the midst of friends, and could [e]xert far more personal influence than here. I have more and warmer friends in New-York than in Boston, and I could leave all here except the bishop[2] without much regret. This diocese is becoming more and more Irish. I think I could now get along with His Grace the Archbishop[3] without any serious difficulty, and I think I could better breast the storm still raging and likely to rage for sometime against me in New York under his patronage than here. So upon the whole, if my way can be prepared, I really do wish to remove to your city. I am not certain but my future success depends on it. I shall be very grateful to you and such of my friends in New York as may aid in preparing my way.

I am very glad to hear of the move you have been making. This bringing together men of similar views with regard to the action desirable upon our non-Catholic countrymen is very important, & something will come of it.

I have been sorry not to receive Dr. Ives' articl[e][4] in season for my next number. It will be too late now for October, if it makes more than 25 pages. He must, however, let me have it for January.

My Oct. No. I think will please you. The first arti[cle] is on "The Tem. Pow. of the Pope,"[5] designed to show that if the American people ever become converted to Christianity at all it will [convert] to it under the ultramontane form, as the only form congenial to their stern republican character. The second, is a review of Hume's work,[6] with a glance at Reid,[7] Kant, Sir William Hamilton,[8] Cousin,[9] Rosmini,[10] Schelling,[11] Hegel, the Traditionalists,[12] the Thomists, and Gioberti[13] on the judgment of causality. The third, is on The Know-Nothing Platform.[14] The fourth, a very favorable Review of Pere Ventura's Discources on the Catholic Reason & the Philosophic Reason.[15] I think Mr. McMaster will like all these articles, especially the 1st & 4th. The other articles will be a Review of Wordsworth,[16] giving the basis of Aesthetics, & a brief article on Russia and the Allies,[17] with the usual literary notices, all by myself, and all written and published without any submission to the Bishop.[18] So I alone am responsible.

I have taken the preliminary step to a reconciliation between Dr. Huntington[19] & myself, and at his request I shall try & make a friend of J. G. Shea[20] of your city. The Bishop here is as warm a friend as ever, & is, I hear, getting the administration of his diocese into a proper shape. But for myself I have here now none but him to sympathize with me, no literary or cultivated friends or associates, for Mr. Roddan[21] fritters himself away.

I hope you get on well with your new book.[22] Your first book[23] is working well, and producing perhaps a greater effect than was anticipated.

With a thousand thanks for your warm affections & disinterested services for me, I pray you to believe me.

Your most devoted friend in Jesus & Mary,

O. A. Brownson

Rev. Isaac T. Hecker.

1. Brownson did move his family to New York City after he completed the October 1855 issue of *BrQR*.

2. John B. Fitzpatrick, bishop of Boston.

3. John J. Hughes, archbishop of New York.

4. Ives's review of Kenrick's *Vindication of the Catholic Church* (1855) appeared in *BrQR*, January 1856, pp. 26–62.

5. *BrQR*, October 1855, pp. 417–45.

6. "Hume's Philosophical Works," ibid., pp. 445–73.

7. Thomas Reid (1710–1796), founder of the Scottish common-sense school of philosophy.

8. William Hamilton (1788–1856), Scottish philosopher and logician, editor of Reid's *Works.*

9. Victor Cousin (1792–1867), French eclectic philosopher, mediated Hegelianism into French philosophy; his doctrines (especially that of the Absolute or spontaneous Reason) influenced Brownson from 1836–44.

10. Antonio Rosmini-Serbati (1797–1855), Italian priest, philosopher dealing with the idea of being, intellectual perception, and the origin of ideas; founder of the Institute of Charity (Rosminians).

11. Friedrich Wilhelm Joseph von Schelling (1775–1854), German idealist philosopher.

12. Fideists or supernaturalists who held that the divine revelation given to humankind in Adam was necessary in order to know with certitude not only supernatural truths but also truths of the moral and metaphysical orders, such as the immortality of the soul.

13. Vincenzo Gioberti (1801–1852), Italian philosopher and patriot, Catholic priest, ontologist and political liberal; he influenced Brownson's philosophical theology of God in his post-conversion period.

14. "The Know-Nothing Platform" *BrQR,* October 1855, pp. 473–99. The Know-Nothings, a nativist society active in the 1850s, originally known as the Order of the Star-Spangled Banner.

15. "Ventura on Philosophy and Catholicity," *BrQR,* October 1855, pp. 499–525. Gioacchino Ventura Di Raulica (1792–1861), Italian priest and philosopher, became the master general of the Theatines 1830, a liberal nationalist during the European revolutions of 1848, lived at Paris after his exile from the Papal States 1851, author of *La Raison philosophique et la raison catholique* (Paris, 1851–53).

16. "Wordsworth's Poetical Works,"*BrQR,* October 1855, pp. 525–38.

17. Apparently this piece was not included in the October 1855 issue of *BrQR.*

18. Brownson had previously submitted his articles in *BrQR* to Bishop John B. Fitzpatrick of Boston for ecclesiastical approval.

19. Jedediah Vincent Huntington (1815–1862), Episcopalian priest, Catholic convert 1848, editor of the Catholic monthly *Metropolitan Magazine.*

The disagreement between Brownson and Huntington stemmed from Brownson's review of the latter's novel *Alban; or the History of a Young Puritan* (see *BrQR,* January 1853, p. 135) and Huntington's remarks on Brownson's doctrine of the indirect temporal power of the Pope (*BrQR,* July 1854, pp. 187–218) in the *Metropolitan*; see Brownson to Huntington, 23 August and 25 August 1855, in reply to Huntington's to Brownson, 19 August 1855 (BP, UNDA).

20. John Dawson Gilmary Shea (1824–1892), author, prominent historian of American Catholicism, founder of the U.S. Catholic Historical Society 1884.

Brownson's clash with Shea began with his criticism of Shea's essay on American Catholic literature; see *BrQR,* January 1855, p. 142. Furthermore, Shea had translated from the French Henri De Courcy's book *The Catholic Church in the United States* and had assisted in its preparation; when Brownson severely criticized De Courcy's book in his *BrQR* (see Letter 82, n. 3), Shea took it as a personal attack on him.

21. John T. Roddan (1819–1858), Rome-educated Catholic priest of the diocese of Boston; author, editor of the *Boston Pilot* 1848–58.

22. *Aspirations of Nature* (1857).

23. *Questions of the Soul* (1855).

76

HECKER TO BROWNSON • 1 SEPTEMBER 1855

J.M.J.A!

Sat. Sep. 1, 1855

My Dear Friend,

Dr Mannahan & Cummings[1] called on me last week, & Dr M[anahan] this evening to talk about your coming on to N.Y. I told Dr. M. your answer.

The question now is when can you come? Can you come before Winter sets in if a suitable house can be got?

If so, what is the rent per year for a house that will suit you, that you are willing to pay? And how large a house will you require?

We have thought that a house at Manhattanville would be pleasant, both as regards the location & the society. Several families of our best catholics reside there. Dr M. is in the neighborhood, & you can get to the city in less than an hour by Rail-Road or omnibus.

Your friends here intend to pay the first year's rent of your house. The ArchBishop will be spoken to as soon as it is certain of your coming.

Considering that the first year's rent will be paid for you, would it not be best to seize the present occassion [*sic*] even tho you have rented your present house until next spring?

Please favour me with an immediate answer as I shall *probably* leave the city for a Mission[2] on friday, & should like to see this matter arranged before my leaving.

Surely every catholic & american especially at the present moment, who can hold a pen in his hand & write, ought to direct it against our common enemy. We must be friends. But as regards Shea,[3] it is well to be on good terms, but he does not seem to me to be a man of large sympathy nor of profound judgment. Conciliate but don't expect a large return.

It would take me at least three hours to say all that I have to say on matters which mutually interest us, but the bell has rung for me to be in bed so I must stop.

I have not seen Dr Ives since the reception of your Note.

Yours aff[ectionately] in the s. hearts of Jesus & Mary

I Th Hecker CSSR

1. Jeremiah Williams Cummings, D.D. (1814–1866), lecturer and hymnodist, graduate of the Urban College of the Propaganda in Rome, first pastor of St. Stephen's parish in New York City 1848, contributor to *BrQR*, arranged Brownson's lectures in New York City.

2. At Canandagua, N.Y., in the Diocese of Buffalo, 9–17 September 1855.

3. See Letter 75, n. 20.

77

HECKER TO BROWNSON • 1 OCTOBER 1855

J.M.J.A!

Oct. 1. 1855.

My dear friend,

This afternoon I called on the ArchBishop.[1] In the course of conversation he mentioned that he had heard that it was your desire to come to N.Y. I told him, it was with his approbation. He replied that he "would be quite pleased at your coming, and that if I wrote to you I should tell you so." These were his words.

As regards a house not much progress has been made. I have just returned from a Mission, and my brother Geo. has been unwell. Yet inquiries have been made. My intention was to go myself to-day, but it storms violently.

You will find it difficult to procure a suitable place near the city, rents are so high. Dr Mannahan has been searching in Yorkville & told me last week that there is a house quite near him which he thought you would be pleased with, having modern improvements, renting for the moderate sum of $350.

I think on the whole the most satisfactory & expeditious way to settle the whole affair would be for you to come on here & see what houses are to let & make your own choice. Now that the ArchBishop's consent is given. I will, if it clears up to-morrow, go and see what I can find to let. So that when you come you will have only your choice to make.

Drop me a line & inform me if you do not come immediately yourself, what you think is best.

Dr Doane[2] the convert has been stopping at our Convent several days to prepare to receive the sacraments. He left on friday last. He is a fine, noble young man. He goes to St Sulpice to study for the priesthood.

Yours affectionately in the sacred hearts of
Jesus & Mary,

I. Th Hecker.

In eight days I shall leave the city for a Mission at Pittsburg.[3] Is the *Oct.* No. out?

My Brother Geo & wife[4] would be pleased for you to stay with them.

1. John J. Hughes of New York.

2. George Hobart Doane (1830–1905), Catholic convert 1855, ordained priest 1857, became chancellor of the Diocese of Newark, N.J.

3. At St. Paul's Cathedral, 14–28 October 1855.

4. Josephine Mary Wentworth, married to George V. Hecker in 1849.

78

HECKER TO BROWNSON • 12 APRIL 1856*

J.M.J.A!

April. 12. /56.

My Dear Friend

It delights me to know that you will deliver the Lecture[1] on the subject you mentioned. Let me remind you of what you know, that if your second Lecture tells as well as the first,[2] the future is yours. You can talk to the American people mind to mind, heart to heart. I have no doubt that you will give that care to your preparation which your present position before the American public demands. You stand before our people as an American & the champion of Catholicity. The reconciliation which has taken place in your own heart between these is to take place also in the nation. Never before had you such a task. The nation's destiny & the interests of God's Church are at stake.

Let recollection, prayer, communion, our Lady enter into your preparation.

F[ather] Hewit & I have just closed a Mission at Norfolk.[3] We really concluded it on Sund. evening. The three first evenings of this week F. Hewit gave a lecture on each evening. There was quite a curiosity to hear one from me. Tho I had but a little time for preparation on Thurs. evening I gave one "On the Popular Objections Against Catholicity." It brought a large audience. F. Walworth was present. He was delighted, & declares it was the best Lecture he has heard in the U.S. Every one seemed equally pleased.

I broke new ground, put Prot. on the defense, & appealed to human nature for support. The effect of the Lecture I considered would indicate whether D. Providence intended me to labour in this way or not. If others are judges there is no room for a doubt. The success far surpassed all my hopes.

We had 4 or 5 converts at each place. A large number for the first time were instigated to investigate the Claims of the Church.

We are here now at Richmond. The good Bishop[4] looks on the dark side of affairs. Yesterday evening we opened batteries against each other. To-day he talks more encouragingly.

We open our Mission[5] here to-morrow Sund. 13. of April. Two weeks from now I hope to be again at N.Y.

Your last no.[6] I have seen, but have not had the time to read yet.

By the way, on the course of Lecture of next fall which you may give, when you come southward, consider yourself engaged for Norfolk.

Yours affectionately in the s. hearts of Jesus & Mary,

I Th Hecker CSSR

My health is very good.

*Brownson, *BLL*, pp. 62–63 (with omissions).

1. A lecture on "The Church and the Republic; Or, The Church Necessary to the Republic, and the Republic Compatible With the Church."

2. Brownson gave two lectures on "The Church and the Republic" at the Broadway Tabernacle in New York City, the first in February, the second in April 1856. The first lecture was extempore and reported in the *New York Times,* the second in the *Freeman's Journal.* The substance of both lectures was adapted into an article "The Church and the Republic . . . ," *BrQR,* July 1856, pp. 273–307.

3. At St. Patrick's Church, 30 March–6 April 1856.

4. John McGill (1809–1872), became third bishop of Richmond 1850.

5. At Sacred Heart Cathedral, Richmond, 13–23 April 1856.

6. *BrQR*, April 1856.

79

HECKER TO BROWNSON • 31 JANUARY 1857

J.M.J.A!

Jan. 31, 1857

My Dear Friend

The enclosed check of 50 dollars is a little present for you from a friend of yours at the South. The giver forbade me to mention his name, & as he made me his agent to you, I assumed an agency on your part, & expressed your hearty thanks & kindest acknowledgments.

My stay at the South has been most gratifying & full of interest, and gives me additional encouragement in laboring for the conversion of our fellow countrymen. There is much I have in store which will interest you personally. If I am not mistaken F[ather] Hewit wrote to his Brother[1] about the Edgefield converts,[2] & I told him to tell the Dr. to show the letter to you. If your labors had but this effect you should feel new hopes, and labor with new zeal in the cause of our good Saviour and that of Souls. Is not Edgefield an indication of a bright future for catholicity among our people? We must not abate in faith, in hope, in charity & in our prayers, for the conversion of this great country to the cause of God's holy Church.

On thursday of this week I came with F. Hewit from St Augustine[3] to this place. My stay was delayed for two weeks after the close of the Mission, on account of a species of neumonia [*sic*] contracted here.[4] Probably I will stop here for one week, & then if I can get leave, go on to Charleston to be there at the close of a Mission[5] now being given by my fellow missionaries. And the week following[,] if my health permits, return home. F. Hewit left yesterday to assist at the Mission of Charleston.

Kind remembrance to friends, & believe me ever sincerely

Yours in Jesus & Mary

I. Th. Hecker CSSR

Savannah.

1. Henry Stewart Hewit (1825–1873), became M.D. 1847, Catholic convert 1855, U.S. Army surgeon with the rank of colonel; also Brownson's personal physician.

2. From a mission at Edgefield, S.C., a place which was notorious at this time for its lawlessness and anti-Catholic hostility.

3. A mission at the Church of St. Augustine, St. Augustine, Fla., 4–11 January 1857.

4. Hecker went to Cuba to recover from this attack of pneumonia and stayed from 10 March to 22 May 1857. This was probably a factor in the lack of correspondence during those months.

5. At the Cathedral of St. John, Charleston, S.C., 25 January–7 February 1857.

80

BROWNSON TO HECKER • 5 AUGUST 1857

New York. Aug. 5, 1857[1]

Rev. & dear Father,

I learn with much pleasure that you propose to start to-day for Rome with a view of making arrangements with your superiors for establishing in this city an English house of your Congregation, or perhaps I should rather say an American House. From all I can see and learn of your Congregation, it is still in its first fervor, animated by a true Missionary spirit, and better prepared to engage in the work of converting this country to the Catholic Church than any other body of Religious I am acquainted with.

Hitherto no direct efforts have been [made] by the clergy, secular or regular, for the conversion of our non-Catholic countrymen, for they have had as much and more than they could do to attend to the wants of the Catholic population already here, and because it has appeared to most our foreign born and educated clergy almost useless to dream of any general conversion of the American people. The Church here has hitherto been & is even now to a great [e]xtent the Church of a foreign colony, with a foreign or quasi-foreign clergy, with slender acquaintance with the real American character and less sympathy with it. But it seems to me that the time has come when it is possible to commence a change in this state of things and to initiate measures for bringing this great and powerful nation into the Church of God. The task of conversion will certainly prove laborious and difficult, for here the Church has and can have no extrinsic aid, & can advance only as she convinces the reason, & wins the hearts of individuals.

The dispositions of the American people are much less unfavorable, however, to the Church than is generally supposed, and owing to the breaking up of Protestantism, and the wild, fanatical, & offensive course of its ministers on a great variety of subjects, their attention is turned to the study of Catholicity as it never has been before, and if approached now in a proper manner, with earnestness and charity, in their language and tone, by a clergy free from those foreign habits and manners which repel their confidence, and who sympathise with their free & independent spirit, I cannot [but] believe that a rich harvest of souls will be reaped.

There are many wrong notions entertained abroad & by a portion even of our own clergy with regard to the American people. They are supposed to be at heart, when not in conduct, a nation of rebels and filibusters, whom hardly the grace of God can render loyal and obedient. You and [I] know, Rev. Father that this is not so. Blind obedience, and unreasoning loyalty, certainly is not [to] be expect[ed] from [them]. They cannot be governed as slaves or as machines, but they are at heart a loyal people, only they will be loyal to law[,] not to persons, to principles, not to men, and will invariably, instinctively distinguish between the office and the incumbent, and bow to the officer, not to the man. They retain and will retain even in the most perfect obedience a certain independence of feeling & manner in [the] presence of authority which belongs to men brought up in freedom, & which men who are accustomed to more supple and servile forms mistake for the spirit of pride and disobedience. But it is not so. No people are really more submissive or easily governed than Americans, only you must give them a reason, and govern them as free men.

My own belief has been that it would be necessary for the conversion of the country that a congregation should spring up of native origin & growth; but I am not certain that the Congregation founded by St. Alphonsus will answer every purpose.[2] The Fathers who I understand are to be associated with you in your new House, in case your Mission is successful, are men of the country, well acquainted with the American people, and fair representatives of the American mind, and if permitted to work as they must work, if they are to have influence on their non-Catholic countrymen, they will everywhere be bestowed with respect, and after a little while, with God's grace, by crowds eager to catch their words, and learn to know & obey the truth. The experiment, at any rate, is worthy trying, and it strikes me that now is a most favorable conjunction for trying it. There need be no fear of the *rebellious* Americans. No people are more ready to submit to legitimate authority, and none will be more submissive than they when converted to the authority of the Holy See, or more devoted to the successor of St. Peter. The [e]xceptions will be among foreigners resident here, or half Americanized foreigners, who never learned submission to law as such.

I need not say that I hope your Mission will be favorably received, and meet the issue I know you so ardently desire. My good wishes, & my prayers will go with you, and may you succeed, and return to us in renewed health & renovated spirits, bringing back with you from the Eternal City, assurances that our poor countrymen are not forgotten or despised by those who have the power to aid them.

With the sincerest respect, I have the honor to be,

Your most obedient servant in X[Christ][3]

O. A. Brownson.

Rev. I. T. Hecker, C.SS.R.

1. Holden (*YP*, pp. 244, 469 n. 56) considers this letter to have been a testimonial letter from Brownson on behalf of Hecker's journey to Rome to establish an English-speaking house of Redemptorists. Hecker left for Rome on 5 August 1857.

2. The Redemptorists in America ministered primarily to the immigrant German Catholic population and spoke German in their houses.

3. Hereinafter the closing 'X' will be understood to mean 'Christ'.

81

HECKER TO BROWNSON • 1 SEPTEMBER 1857*

Rome Sep 1, 1857

My Dear Friend,

Almost every word of your letter was a prediction. And what has not proved so, may yet become so.

I was condemned & dismissed without a hearing. I demanded a full hearing & was led to believe that it would be granted, but the contrary was decided & my vows relaxed & I dismissed from the Congregation. But I am fully convinced that had a full hearing been granted it would not have helped me or our affair in the least. These good men from their education politically & religiously are led with bona fide intentions to misconstrue our motives, misinterpret our language, & misunderstand our actions. It is well the crisis has come. Why wait & see the interest of God & our country suffer?

On the whole, & after prayer & reflection, the course persued [*sic*] I think was the best one. The results will have to show.

I shall not act hastily, but endeavor to be well prepared, & be as sure as one can be of the safety & success of every step.

Your notice of my new book,[1] if you will be so kind as to give one in your October number, may be of the greatest service, & the highest importance to me here, in getting a hearing in high, & the highest quarters. You might insinuate something to this effect if you judge prudent. But [do] not mention a word of my present relations to the Congregation in either in your Review or to any person in private. These are not yet settled—power has been exerted—but it is yet to be seen whether it was rightly exerted.

If you give my book a notice, please send me a half dozen copies as soon as printed of your Review. If the proof sheets could be sent, a copy of them earlier, it might serve me greatly. A stone shall not be left unturned to accomplish what we believe to be the cause of God, & of His Holy Church, in our own dear country.

My resolution is to act with deliberation, advice, and with much prayer & determination. With the copies of the Oct. number, send two of the one with the first article on Questions of the Soul.[2]

Now that my hands are free, I shall act more largely, and shall endeavor to have translated into Italian & published in a pamphlet form, or some other way[,] your article "Mission of America".[3] If you yourself could write an introduction leaving aside what regards Dr Spalding[4] personally, it would ar[ri]ve in time. For it only takes two weeks for the mails, and no doubt I shall have to remain here some time; perhaps a long time to [do] my work thoroughly; but thoroughly it shall be done, God & our B. Lady assisting me.

I shall see the book publisher,[5] with whom I am already acquainted, tomorrow, about the translation & publication of "Mission of America". If you have any suggestion on this, or any other points, regarding these matters, do write, & speedily.

Allow me to suggest that if you notice my book, to mention the dissolution of Prot[estantism] in the shape of Calvinism—the Beechers[6]—etc, & their endeavors to get at Catholic Truth, tho they are not aware of it. Make mention that now is the time to prepare the way for the conversion of the American people.

This article may also be published along with the other. If this letter comes late, & you find it necessary to delay some days the publication of your Review to accomplish this, I beg of you do it. Now is the time to strike the blow. For God's sake & the love of our country & its free institutions do not let it pass.

Upon you under Divine Providence depends the success of the great cause we have at heart.

George[7] will see to any expense this undertaking may cost you.

I shall write & inform you of my movements—but we must by all means keep them quiet, work hard, & pray.

Oh if God grants me to be the means of having our country understood here at Rome, & aid me in preparing the way for its conversion all that I have suffered these few days past will be as nothing—

My address is—

"Giuseppe Spithöven. Piazza di Spagna."

Pray for me and believe me ever faithfully yours in the love of Jesus & Mary

I. Th. Hecker

O. A. Brownson

*Brownson, *BLL*, pp. 112–14.

1. Hecker's second book, *Aspirations of Nature* (published in September 1857), was reviewed by Brownson in *BrQR*, October 1857, pp. 459-503.

2. *BrQR*, April 1855, pp. 209–26.

3. "The Mission of America," *BrQR*, October 1856, pp. 409–43.

4. Martin J. Spalding's *Miscellanea* (Louisville, 1855) was used by Brownson as the starting point for "The Mission of America" (see n. 3 above).

5. Giuseppe Spithöven, Roman bookseller and publisher.

6. Hecker refers to Catharine Esther Beecher (1800–1878), educator and social reformer, author of *Common Sense Applied to the Gospels* (1857); Edward Beecher (1803–1895), Congregational clergyman, author of *The Conflict of Ages* (1853); and Harriet Beecher Stowe (1811–1896), novelist and author of *Uncle Tom's Cabin; or, Life among the Lowly* (1851–52), According to Hecker, the writings of the Beecher family, whose patriarch was the prominent "New School" Presbyterian minister Lyman Beecher (1775–1863), demonstrated the inability of those who rejected Calvinism to find a satisfactory religion outside of Catholicism.

7. Hecker's brother George, who financed most of his projects.

82

BROWNSON TO HECKER • 29 SEPTEMBER 1857

New York. Sept. 29, 1857

Rev. & dear Father,

I am neither surprised nor disheartened by the information conveyed in yours of the 4th inst. On Saturday your brother George and I communicated it to Fathers Walworth, Hewit, & Deshon.[1] They received it as you wish. They will do all they can to save the usefulness of the Congregation.

Permit me to say, with all respect, the General[2] has committed a mistake, and if he does not recede the interests of the Congregation are sacrificed, and its usefulness in this country[,] save to a portion of the German immigration[,] is gone. If he persists, not an American will enter its ranks, its House of Studies cannot be kept up, & its Novitiate will fail, for the want of subjects. Of this no reasonable man who knows the existing facts can doubt. If I could have any influence with the General, I would on my knees beg him as he values the interests of the Congregation in the United States to wander from his course, and restore the American Fathers to his confidence, and to grant them their very moderate request.

A glorious course opened to the Congregation, and it had the opportunity of being the instrument in the hands of God of recovering this great country to the Church. This opportunity it is now casting away, and thus providing that it is not worthy of the signal honor it might have won. I regret it for the sake of the Congregation, I regret it for the sake of my country. But almighty God will provide some other instrument, and leave the Congregation to expire in its own narrowness and imbecility.

It is singular that the General should suppose foreigners who really know nothing of the American people, though living as to their bodies in the country, more trustworthy in their statements than men born and bred in their country. This distrust of American Catholics is very unwise as well as ungenerous. The only men in the country who really understand the American people thoroughly are the converts, & the American Fathers of the Congregation are of all others [the ones] on whom the General can with the most safety rely for information concerning them. I know no man who better understands the American people than yourself, or whose judgment in all that concerns them may be more safely followed. If the General would render his Congregation useful to this country, tell him from me, an old gray bearded man, to listen to your advice, for I know you well, and know well my own country. His rejection of your Mission, and punishment of the Fathers who favored it will be regarded him as an insult to our country & an undeserved reproach upon the faith & loyalty of every American born Catholic. It will prove the ruin of the Congregation here, for I can assure the General that its prosperity as well as popularity in the country it has owed in no small degree under God to the American Fathers, selected for the most part from the very elite of American society.

Your good people at Rome seem to have a totally erroneous idea of us Americans. They seem to read us thro' the spectacles of that narrowed minded, blundering Frenchman Henri de Courci.[3] There is not a more loyal people on earth than the American, or more ready to obey the law; but they of course cannot be made submissive to the arbitrary will of any man. They will obey cheerfully and scrupulously the law, or the man who governs in the name of the law or as the vicar of our Lord, but they will not obey arbitrary power, & never can be made to submit to a centralized despotism, whether exerted in the name of religion or politics. They must be governed as free men, not as slaves, as men endowed with reason and free will, not as machines. Whoever would exert a favorable influence on them must prove to them that the Church leaves them their autonomy.

The things cited abroad which cast so much discredit upon us are[,] you and I both know, to a great [e]xtent the work of Europeans and of Europeans not infrequently born in the bosom of the Church, who have migrated hither, and who never understand liberty in the American sense. The licentiousness of the country we owe in great part to the rebels, revolutionists, & apostates that Europe annually casts upon our shores. Let the responsibility rest where it belongs. For much has been made of the Know Nothing movement at home and abroad. And I am sorry to find that it has had a serious effect on the minds of many Catholics here who ought to have seen in it nothing more than one of those devices of the enemy which are sure to turn to his own disgrace. A few acts of violence have [been] committed, but nothing here has occured like what is constantly occurring in countries governed by nominally Catholic princes, nothing a thousandth part so alarming as the late Appel d' Aubus[4] in the case of the Bishop of Moulins in France. There is no Catholic country in the world where the laws are so favorable to Catholicity as with us, even in the matter of Church property. The difficulties on the subject we experience grow out of the neglect on the part of our Catholic authorities to study and take advantage of them. We might with perfect ease, without any sacrifice of anything the Church holds essential[,] have the whole force of the law in our favor. The Church here stands legally on a par with the most favored sect and is freer than any where else on earth. Yet these silly Know Nothing movements have created a distrust in many minds of republican institutions, and the influence of the clergy in France is felt by our own bishops & clergy.

There is the great difficulty. France not Rome governs the Catholic mind in this country, and while French Catholics remain Imperial, the great body of Catholics in this country, at least of those who are in authority[,] will be openly or secretly anti republican in their tendencies. American born Catholics are generally republican, attached from feeling & conviction as well as from policy to their country and her institutions, alike opposed to despotism and to radicalism. Hence they are distrusted by the European party amongst us, who feel every action and reaction in the Catholic populations of the Old World.

The question to be decided at Rome is whether we who love our country and wish her to be converted to the Church without being brought under the political system of Europe, are to be sustained, or are to be discouraged, and only those protected or countenanced who insist that Catholicity and Europeanism shall stand or fall on our soil together! Can our people become Catholics without ceasing to be Americans, or without becoming foreigners in this our native land, won from the wilderness by their labor, & defended by their arms?

You and I, my reverend Father, have maintained that our institutions[,] our civilization in a word, are perfectly compatible with Catholicity, and we have labored to prove it. We have contended that nothing is needed by our people to be thoroughly a Catholic people but their conversion to the Catholic faith, that our institutions are good, and are as well fitted to Catholics as to non-Catholics, indeed far better. Are we to be in this sustained or are we to be censured at Rome? This is the question. If the Vicar of Christ says we are wrong, he may rely on our submission without a murmur. But I do not believe he will ever say that.

My review[5] of your book is long, elaborate, and not unfriendly. It had been in print several weeks before your letter arrived. The *animus* of the review is not unkind, but I have aimed to write it as an impartial critic, and on two or three points, which are mere matters of opinion I have ventured to differ from you, and on other points to guard your statements from being misapprehended. My article has been written, as you will see, with the intention of refuting the unfounded suspicion that there is formed amongst us an American party or an American clique. I have disclaimed everything of the sort, so far as my knowledge [e]xtends. I have disclaimed everything of the kind for myself and for you, and all my friends among the laity, as you know I could with strict truth and justice. You know we none of us want a native party, or entertain any other than true fraternal feelings towards our Catholic brethren of European birth. If you are suspected at Rome of wishing to build up an American party, or seeking to draw a line between Catholics of one nationality & Catholics of another, every one who knows you can bear witness to its gross injustice. I have borne witness in my article to your singular and most commendable freedom from every thing of the kind.

I have aimed to show that there is no American clique, and to allay the suspicions to the contrary entertained as you and I both know in certain quarters, as also the suspicions of our intention to raise up a lay party through the press against the hierarchy. I say some things of the conversion of the country. On this point I confess I am less sanguine of *immediate* success than you are. I am devoted as heartily, in my sphere, to the work as you are, and am as confident of its ultimate success, but I think, as you know, the difficulty of the work as greater than you consider it. greater on the part of non-Catholics, and greater on the part of Catholics. The conversion of the country I regard as a great and difficult work. We have serious obstacles in the present dispositions of our non-Catholic countrymen, perhaps even more serious obstacles in the present disposition of our Catholic body. The mass of our Catholics think only of enjoying their religion for themselves, and lack every thing like a Missionary spirit. They migrated hither from the lowest classes in Europe not from religious motives, but from hope of gain. Not a few are opposed to making efforts to convert the country, because in their view conversion would increase the power of the American element and diminish that of the European. Hence there is not so hearty a response on the part of Catholics to our appeals as we could wish. Our appeal is construed by many to mean placing the government of the Church here in the hands of native born Americans, the refusal henceforth to have any but native born bishops or priests.

I have in my article managed this feeling as well as I could, and declared against saying too much about converting the country, or making it a hobby. We cannot go far ahead of the body with which we must act, and I do not think that at this moment the Catholic body, especially those whose perogative it is to govern are prepared to sustain any measures having for their direct object the conversion of our non-Catholic countrymen. This will enable you to understand certain expressions you will find in my article. There is nothing in the article, if rightly understood that can embarrass you at Rome. What I write to you now I write with the same pen with which I wrote my article, and I assure [you] that I have the fullest confidence in your plan, and in the wisdom, prudence, and good sense of your self and the Fathers associated with you. You are none of your young enthusiasts, but full grown men, who ought to be trusted as men who know what they are about. You[,] all of you[,] know your religion, have been trained to a religious life, are men of large experience, and wide observation, and you all know well your countrymen. If they will not trust you at Rome, they must refuse to trust any American and treat us all as unworthy of the slighest confidence.

I have no time to write a preface to *The Mission of America.*[6] I doubt the wisdom of publishing it at Rome. They will misunderstand it, and I am afraid that it will harm rather than benefit your cause. Though of that you must judge for yourself. I presume I have no *status* at Rome, and that they have already been deeply prejudiced against me, with one or two [e]xceptions. You know the influences[7] which have been and are at work against me.

My own affairs are gloomy enough owing to the commercial collapse and money pressures; but I put my trust in Providence. I can but starve at worst, and perhaps my friends will prevent that. I think it doubtful whether I shall be able to keep up my Review. I have been out of health, and am more profoundly discouraged than ever before in my life. Well, if I fail, it will prove Providence had no more work for me to do.

If you publish the *Mission,* put such an Introduction to it as you judge proper. The article was inspired by you, & you stand its godfather.

My family are all well, except myself, and I am well enough in body. Write me when you can, and believe that, if there is anything so feeble and uninfluential a man as I can do to serve your cause I shall always be happy to do it. Forgive the length of this letter, which I have not had time to shorten, and believe me more truly than ever

Your friend in X

O. A. Brownson

Rev. I. T. Hecker

1. George Deshon (1823–1903), West Point graduate and professor, Episcopalian convert to Catholic Church 1850, ordained Redemptorist priest 1855, one of the original Paulists 1858, elected third superior general of the Paulists 1897.

2. Most Rev. Nicholas Mauron, C.SS.R. (1818–1893), French Redemptorist provincial superior, elected first rector major or superior general of the Transalpine Redemptorists 1855.

3. Henry De Courcy (1820–1861), French historian, foreign correspondent for the French paper *L'Univers;* author of *The Catholic Church in the United States* (1856), which Brownson severely criticized in *BrQR*, October 1856, pp. 514–24.

In the Introduction to the second edition of De Courcy's book, John Gilmary Shea (see Letter 75, n. 20) indicated that there would be no reconciliation between him and Brownson for the latter's slighting of De Courcy and consequently himself; Shea had translated De Courcy's book.

4. "Appeal as from an Abuse," or recourse by an injured party to civil or secular justice regarding the conduct of a churchperson or an act of an ecclesiastical authority.

5. "Aspirations of Nature," *BrQR*, October 1857, pp. 459–503.

6. *BrQR*, October 1856, pp. 409–44.

7. Chiefly opposition from certain American bishops because of his *BrQR* writings on Nativism, the Irish question, the indirect temporal power of the pope, and the school question (whether Catholic children should attend public schools or the newly emerging parochial schools).

82 Draft

BROWNSON TO HECKER • [29 SEPTEMBER 1857]*

[*Undated*][1]

No American Catholic who cares for the interests of religion will acquiesce in his [the General's] course. Every American Catholic, when once he learns what has been done, will feel himself and his nation most grossly insulted, and will feel that to be a Catholic he must submit to a centralized despotism. Let your dismissal remain, and let him inflict a degrading punishment on the American Fathers who have agreed with you, it will be the heaviest blow to religion in this country that can easily be given. It will ruin the Congregation. It will cause the very evil your General so much dreads; the division of Catholics here according to their nationality. Americans will scrupulously obey the law in letter and spirit, but no power on earth can make them submit to the imposition of the arbitrary will of any man. It is well that this trait of American character should be known.

My review of your book had been some weeks printed before your letter reached me, and it was too late to make any alteration or addition. I have reviewed your book neither as a friend nor as an enemy, but as an impartial critic, mainly with a view to refuting the unfounded suspicion that there is an 'American' Catholic party or clique formed or forming against us. You know perfectly well that there is not and never has been any such clique or party, and I have taken pains to disclaim for myself and friends everything of the sort, and to state, if any thing of the sort does exist, I am ignorant of it, and neither you nor your book are in the least implicated in it. You know that we have neither of us ever favored any movement American in any other sense than for the conversion of our countrymen and the prosperity of our religion in the United States. Undoubtedly we see that foreigners mistake our national character and misinterpret us, but we have always been submissive to authority in whose hands soever lodged, and anxious to keep the body one without its having an American side or a foreign side.

For my part, I assure you that I have full confidence in the wisdom of your project, and though I certainly am less ardent in my hopes of *immediate* success in converting my countrymen than you are, yet I am as thoroughly devoted, in my humble sphere, as any man can be, and as strong in my hopes of ultimate success as you are. I had looked to your Congregation as the great instrument in the hands of God of effecting the conversion of the country. If your plea is heard, if your councils are listened to and followed, I shall continue to look to it; if not, I shall look elsewhere, and, trust that Almighty God will raise up some other congregation to whom he will give the honor and glory of adding this great nation to the inheritance of the successor of Peter. Whatever you may read in my Review, be assured of my full confidence in your mission, and in you and the Fathers who have approved it. Do not be discouraged. They are just at Rome, and they will give you a hearing. The Vicar of Christ is there, and He will protect you. I am sure your motives were good. I am sure the end you proposed was laudable, and I cannot believe it possible for you to fail. I enclose a brief introduction to the Mission of America. Believe me with sincere affection & confidence more truly yours than ever,

O. A. Brownson.

Rev. I. T. Hecker.

*BP, UNDA (dated [1857]); Brownson, *BLL*, pp. 114–16 (with omissions).

1. This undated incomplete draft of Brownson's letter of 29 September

1857 (Letter 82), differs significantly from the actual letter sent. Henry F. Brownson (*BLL*, pp. 114–16) assumed that this fragment was the entire letter.

83

HECKER TO BROWNSON • 24 OCTOBER 1857*

Rome Oct. 24, 1857.

My Dear Friend,

Your welcome letter & also yr. notice of "Asp[irations] of Nat[ure]" arrived here on the 19 inst. At this moment, having just returned from a pilgrimage to the tomb[1] of St Alphonsus, my hands are full of affairs, otherwise I would equal yr. interesting & affectionate letter in its agreeable length.

The article on "As. [of] Nat.", I have read again & again, & surely it is a source of great regret that men who have the same noble & let me say, divine work at heart, should find so many differences between them. This seems to be the usual accompaniment of all really good undertakings. It is however most unfortunate that these were put in print & made public at this juncture. The article will increase the unfounded suspicions of the General here & the Provincial[2] in the U.S. & I fear that the latter will use it with terrible affect against the American Fathers.[3] What you say to exculpate me, however sufficient, & true, will not be regarded by minds filled with suspicions. Parts of your letter which touches [*sic*] on these points, I will have translated to counteract this influence of the article if [it] be used in that way. My trust is in God, who often turns the greatest difficulties into means of success. With God & our B. Lady I can weather any storm.

On becoming better acquainted with the state of mind here & the position of things, I found that it would be more prudent to write an article or two[4] for the Civilta Catolica[5] than to translate the "Mission of America." It was all important that the matter should be published in the C[iviltà] Cat[tolica] and a translation would not find acceptance, indeed it was looked upon as a singular thing that my articles were accepted. There are two, one is translated by one of its editors[6] & will appear in the no. of the 3d Sat. of November, the other the 1st. Sat. of Decemb. As soon as I can get a copy of the proof sheets you shall have them. My purpose is to show by different movements in the social, religious, and political world in the U.S. D. Providence has been preparing our people for conversion to the c. faith. The views of the Asp. of Nat. are motive in these. There is not a word in these articles that can give the slightest offense to *any one* or *anywhere.*

They are calculated to aid the general cause, my own particular affairs are not hinted at.

In regard to my affairs I cannot tell you how they stand. Everyday the[y] involve higher & more general interests. I do not see a step ahead, all I know is that I find myself in the hands of D. Providence *completely,* and am ready to follow its lead in any direction.

Your affairs distress me–in every sacrifice I pray particularly for you. Courage, a change for the better is not far distant. God is with us. Thanks for yr. letter–write soon again.

Ever truly & most sincerely your friend & servant
in the service of Jesus & Mary

I. T. Hecker.

Kind remembrance to Dr Hewit[7] & friends.

*Brownson, *BLL*, pp. 121–23.

1. Located at Nocera, Italy.

2. Rev. George Ruland, C.SS.R. (1817–1885), Bavarian-born, entered Redemptorists as a priest 1846, became vice-rector of the American Redemptorists 1852, provincial superior 1854.

3. Namely, Fathers Walworth, Hewit, Deshon, and Francis Aloysius Baker (1820–1865), Episcopalian priest, Catholic convert 1853, ordained Redemptorist priest 1856, mission preacher and original Paulist 1858.

4. "Riflessioni sopra il presente e l'avvenire del Cattolicismo negli Stati Uniti d'America," in *Civiltà Cattolica*, VIII, (21 November 1857), pp. 385–402, and 5 December 1857, pp. 513–29.

5. *Civiltà Cattolica*, Jesuit periodical founded at Rome in April 1850; though not the official voice of the Holy See, it was considered as the Vatican's semi-official voice.

6. Joseph Brunengo, S.J., Italian refugee, early professor at the College of the Holy Cross (Worcester, Mass.), author, assistant editor of *Civiltà Cattolica.*

7. Dr. Henry S. Hewit.

83 Draft

HECKER TO BROWNSON • 24 OCTOBER 1857*

Rome, Oct 24, 1857.[1]

My Dear Friend

Your welcome & affectionate letter arrived here on the 19th inst.; and the notice of "Aspirations, etc." My hands are full, as I have just returned from a visit to Nocera, the place where the remains of St. Alphonsus are kept, otherwise I would equal your interesting letter in its length. But I must be brief, having so much to write & arrange.

It is certainly a cause of regret that men who have the same noble & divine cause, as it is, to heart, should find so many differences between them. This, however, seems to be the usual accompaniment of all good undertakings. Judging according to human sagacity, it seems an unfortunate moment for them to be put in print and at this juncture, yet I trust in D. Providence who knows how to change the greatest difficulties into means of success. No one appreciates your motives, and is more ready to understand your remarks in the spirit in which they were written than I am. But I fear that the Provincial will use some expressions in your article to confirm the baseless suspicions entertained by the General against the American fathers. I shall have part of the contents of your letter translated into French which touches on this subject, to counteract the use which he might make of them, in case he does. All these things are in the hands of the good God, and my trust in Him, and the protection of our Dear Lady, will enable me to weather any storm.

On becoming better acquainted with the state of mind here, and the dispositions of important personages, I found that it would be too hazardous to translate the article "Mission of America". Besides, as a translation, I could not get it inserted in the Civitta Catollica [*sic*], and this is altogether necessary, it being a journal of extensive influence having in Rome about 900 subscribers. With the approbation of Card[inal] Barnabo[2] & Mons[ignore] Bedini,[3] I have written two articles for that journal on "the present & the future prospects of the Catholic faith in the U.S. of North America".[4] The first article will be inserted in the No. of the 3d Saturday of November, and the second in the No. of the first Sat of December. My purpose is to show that Divine Providence has by singular events prepared the American people for conversion to the Catholic faith. I endeavor to show by the transcendental movement, the Beecher movement, the memorial papers,[5] the Know-Nothing movement, and that of Abolishonism [*sic*], & by the character of American institutions, that all these things are by the Providence of God so many ways of leading our people to the Catholic truth, provided we do our duty. There is not a word in both articles that can give the slightest offence to anyone, *anywhere*. My own personal affairs, of course, are not even hinted at, but the articles are calculated to aid the general cause. One of the editors who finishes today the translation of the first, expresses his gratification of it. Do not let this come out, for if any suspicions were excited, it might even yet defeat their publication. I will send you the proof sheets as early as possible.

As regards my own affairs, I cannot tell you how they stand, they are so complicated, & involve every day other interests. I am in the hands of God, & He alone knows where this will end. Be assured I shall do nothing against His most Holy Will, & shall follow faithfully Card. Barnabo.

I feel distressed at your state of affairs. In every Mass I pray for you particularly; were I home, I might do more.

Thanks for your kind letter and believe me ever yours sincerely & faithfully in the service of Jesus & Mary,

I. T. Hecker.

Do let me hear soon again from you—and let nothing separate us. My articles will help to explain the views taken with As[pirations] of Nat[ure].

Best respects to Dr. Hewit.

Dr. Brownson

*HP, APF (omitted from microfilm).

1. This draft of Hecker's letter of 24 October 1857 (Letter 83), though similar, contains important elaborations not found in the letter actually sent.

2. Alessandro Barnabò (1801–1874), Italian churchman, secretary, then prefect, of the Sacred Congregation for the Propagation of the Faith, supervised the English missions, named cardinal 1856.

3. Gaetano Bedini (1806–1864), Italian churchman, papal nuncio to Brazil 1853, secretary of the Congregation for the Propagation of the Faith, named cardinal 1861. As the representative of Pius IX, Archbishop Bedini's tour of the U.S., June 1853–February 1854, sparked nativist riots.

4. See Letter 83, n. 4.

5. A reference to the so-called Muhlenberg Memorial, named after its first signer, William Augustus Muhlenberg (1796–1877), presented by a group of Episcopalian clergymen to the Episcopal General Convention in New York City on 18 October 1853; the Memorial questioned the adequacy of the Episcopal Church in its present state to do God's work "in this land and in this age."

84

HECKER TO BROWNSON • 27 NOVEMBER 1857*

Rome Nov 27, 1857.

My Dear Friend.

The two articles from the Civil[tà] Cat[tolica] which I sent a copy of to you two weeks ago, seem to have given complete satisfaction to those who have read them here. They give a clearer insight into the state of things & the minds of the Am. people, so I am told, than anything that has hitherto been published in Italy. Tho regarded as American to the core, no one objects to a word, but the knowing ones say, that if an Italian had written them, he would have been brought up before the Holy Office[1] without delay! I am aware that I have presented the fair side of our country, this was done by design, to attract attention, and interest the rulers of the Ch[urch] in behalf our our country. The reverse side & in the darkest colors, has too long occupied the minds of men this side of the Atlantic. Intentionally therefore, I left out obstacles in the way of the conversion of our countrymen, & but slightly hinted at the means to be adopted to accomplish this. Card[inal] Barnabo insists upon my writing more, and this will give me the opportunity to take up the *difficulties*, & show *how* they are to be managed & overcome. In this connection I will show the origin, nature & bearing of Mormonism,[2] spiritualism etc which are little understood here; and it will give me also the opportunity of coming closer to the object of my journey to Rome.

My articles were printed before your notice of the Aspirations reached here. We have touched in common several points, and if I am not mistaken, these articles will justify your exculpation of my wishing to pervert things in a wrong direction, or to make any movement a hobby. You will rejoice in seeing the views which we hold in common brought out here in Rome, passing the apostolical censure, and meeting with general approbation.

On p. 24 from the word "Diciamo" to the end of that paragraph, these words were not mine but attached as a note by the editors to the quotation from the aBp.[3] They were in a different shape & fearing it might be construed as a covert attack, I changed them, & embodied them in the articles as they now stand. The only reason for them was that they *feared* my meaning might be perverted by the radicals: & for the same reason the note on p. 26 was put. As this motive does not exist in the U.S., there is no reason for not leaving them out, if the articles get in print.

I saw Padre Curci[4] the other day and he told me that they were so crowded with matter that he would not be able to publish my new articles[5] before two or three months. The Card. told me that was no consequence, I must write them & have them published then. This will give me plenty of time to prepare them and if you have any advice or suggestions to make, they will be in time & render me a great service.

Since writing the above I have met several who have read the first art. in the Civil. Cat.[,] among others Card. Reissach.[6] It seems to have opened the eyes & given its readers to understand the great object for which I came to Rome; excited their sympathy for the cause, & for me, & given me a quasi status here in Rome. My coming here will I trust, prove in the end the work of D. Providence; it will have served as a means to give a better idea to persons in authority of the american people, and also to engage their interest, & excite their sympathy in their behalf. And tho I do not know the way in which it will be brought about, still my confidence increases that the special end of my journey will also be gained.

Most sincerely & devotedly yours in the service
of Jesus & Mary

I. Th. Hecker.

O. A. Brownson

*Brownson, *BLL*, pp. 123–25.

1. The Holy Office, a congregation of the Roman Curia, established by Pope Paul III in 1542 to combat heresy and to safeguard and defend the faith and moral teachings of the Catholic Church; in 1965 it was renamed the Congregation for the Doctrine of the Faith.

2. In the winter of 1843–44 Hecker had met in New York the Mormon apostle Parley Parker Pratt (1807–1857).

3. Archbishop John Hughes of New York, whom Hecker quotes as follows: "I regard the Constitution of the United States a monument of wisdom —an instrument of liberty and right, unequalled, unrivalled, in the annals of the human race" (from Hughes's lecture, "The Mixture of Civil and Ecclesiastical Power in the Middle Ages," 14 December 1843).

4. Carlo Maria Curci, S.J. (1810–1891), Neapolitan, author and theologian, co-founder and editor of *Civiltà Cattolica* 1850; expelled from the Jesuits 1877 (his political activity and favoring of a United Italy had angered the Pope) but reinstated before his death.

5. These proposed articles were never written.

6. Karl August von Reisach (1800–1869), became archbishop of Munich 1846, named cardinal 1855, served on many Roman congregations with special interest in German affairs.

85

HECKER TO BROWNSON • 19 FEBRUARY 1860

New Britain. Conn. Feb. 19, 1860

My Dear Friend.

You will remember very likely, of my placing in your hands Dr E[dward] Beecher's "Conflict of Ages" and I think also Catherine E. Beecher's "Common

Sense applied to Religion."[1] Miss C[atharine] has just publ. another book by the same publishers the Harpers,[2] entitled "An appeal to the People,"[3] which I have just read. These vols. treat of the same subject, original sin, and they would it seem to me, give you subject matter for an interesting, opportune, & profitable article for your next number.[4]

Miss C. confounds the Jansenistic interpretation with the true interpretation of St Augustine, consequently confounds the Catholic doctrine of original sin with that of Calvin. She is strangely ignorant for one who writes in theology, ignorant of what the Catholic Ch. teaches, and seeing no escape from Calvinism except in Pelagianism she embraces it in preferrence [*sic*]. In my opinion it would be of great utility to her, & those who hold like views, to bring out the Cath. doctrines, & show how they beautifully reconcile the natural & supernatural; & [at] the same time escaping both extremes. To this class of minds it seems to me, we have the task to show that it is not necessary to repudiate nature to be a Xtian, on the contrary, Xtianity supposes nature, & esteems it at its real & true value.

Miss C. complains that her book by every effort she could make private & public has not been noticed by the Religious press or theologians. I am quite convinced, fully convinced, that an article from your pen on this subject would attract the attention of a large class of persons, and do more to open their eyes to the truth of the catholic doctrines than any thing else that has been done for years. I surely think that it is worth while to embrace this opportunity of reaching a class of minds which if I am not mistaken, is not small in numbers and influence.

I would send you the copy I have, but it is borrowed—Sadlier[5] could obtain for you a copy from the Harpers.

F[ather] Hewit & I opened a mission[6] here yesterday, which will last probably eight days.

He sends you his kind remembrance.

yours faithfully in XP

I. T. Hecker

P.S. I have read the above to F. Hewit & he agrees with it.

1. See Letter 81, n. 6.

2. Originally the publishing firm of J. & J. Harper of New York City, founded in 1817 by James Harper (1795–1867) and his brother John (1797–1875); in 1833 the firm became Harper & Brothers with the addition of two other brothers, Joseph Wesley (1801–1870) and Fletcher (1806–1877).

3. *Appeal to the People in behalf of Their Rights as Authorized Interpreters of the Bible* (New York, 1860).

4. Brownson did not follow Hecker's suggestion at this point; see, however, "St. Augustine and Calvinism," *BrQR*, July 1863, pp. 289–312.

5. The Catholic publishing firm of D. & J. Sadlier, founded in New York City in 1836 by Denis Sadlier (1817–1885) and his brother James (d. 1869), both Irish-born who emigrated in 1830. James Sadlier expanded in the firm in Montreal in the 1840s and returned to New York in 1860.

6. At St. Mary's Church, New Britain, Conn., 18–28 February 1860.

86

HECKER TO BROWNSON • 16 MAY 1862

New York May 16, 1862

My Dear Friend,

I have just received a note[1] from Simpson containing some lines which refer to a matter perhaps of some importance to you.

He says: "Is Brownson going on with his Review? If not, do just give me a line by return post, that we may offer him terms in our new Quarterly.[2] I think if his own organ is no more, and he cannot be heard otherwise in Europe, he will not object to write for us. Will you sound him on this point. You may hint that the question of Dollars & cents is not absolutely ignored. The pay is 5£ a sheet of 16 pp.

["] I must tell you our plan. The Review is divided into four portions. 1 Editorial articles, for which as wholes & in details the Editors are responsible. From this department we shall banish things calculated to give great offense to the catholic body, or to any considerable section of it.

["] 2nd. Communicated articles (including excommunicated also.) for which the Editors are not responsible, except so far as they, by publishing them, declare them to be fit for consideration. There is an arena for fair fighting, & if Brownson writes a passionate defense of the Northern Democracy, we shall put him here, & get Jef. Davis[3] to answer him in the next number.

["] 3. Short Reviews & notices of current literature, English and European. If you could manage to get us a man who would do the American for us, not at great length, & not noticing any books but those of mark, & not including the South,—why then we should be much obliged to you.

["] 4. Notices of current events. Our great principle is truth & free discussion! Our motto *sen vetus est verum diligo, sive novum.*[4] This more important than any one particular opinion—the right of all opinions to have their rights.

["] Then we are anti-revolutionary, anti-democratic. We stick up for rights in opposition to interests; & hold that the Roman government has no right to be oppressive and tyrannous for the interests of the Church. Many other things we also hold, which will be fully disclosed to you in our first number.[5]

["] Now this is to be a very short letter, because I want an immediate answer about Brownson."

If you wish to answer this proposal directly, address your letter

R. Simpson. Esq.
4 Victoria Road
Clapham Common
London.
G. B.

Please give it your earliest attention, and in writing to me address: *Station E.* I have been told that you are not in good health, which gives me pain. Don't get sick when you are most needed.

Yours faithfully

I. T. Hecker.

1. Richard Simpson to Hecker, 1 May 1862 (HP, APF).
2. As the successor to *The Rambler, The Home & Foreign Review* (1862–64) was a lay-controlled, liberal Catholic quarterly edited in London by Simpson and the historian Sir John Emerich Edward Dalberg (later Lord) Acton (1834–1902).
3. Jefferson Davis (1808–1899), American statesman and president of the Confederacy 1861–65.
4. "I love truth, whether it be old or new."
5. *The Home & Foreign Review* (n. 2 above) first appeared in July 1862.

87

HECKER TO BROWNSON • 25 DECEMBER 1862

Dec 25, 1862

Dear Dr.

I hardly think that you need to be introduced to my most esteemed friend Dr Gouley,[1] for you know him. I have thought that a note to Stanton[2] from you in favor of Dr Gouley would be of great service to him. The Dr. has such testimonials from high authorities of the profession that there can be no doubt of his fitness. As a man & as a Catholic I cannot say enough in his favor. He is in every respect one of the right stamp.

Any favor to him I would regard as done to myself.

faithfully yours,

I T Hecker

1. Dr. John A. Gouley, an assistant consulting surgeon of the Lincoln Hospital in Washington, D.C., wanted Brownson to write the U.S. secretary of war (n. 2 below) for promotion to the rank of medical inspector in the U.S. Army.

2. Edwin McMasters Stanton (1814–1869), lawyer, became U.S. attorney general 1860, secretary of war 1862.

88

HECKER TO BROWNSON • 4 DECEMBER 1863

N.Y. Dec 4. 1863

My Dear Friend,

Friday last we returned from our labours in the West. All of us are gratified with our visit as you promised we would be.

In the ArchBishop of St. Louis[1] we have found a friend, also in the Bishop of Chicago.[2]

The character of the priests which we met, was above the average elsewhere. The trip west has been valuable in experience for each one of us.

I send you an early copy of the new Vol. of Sermons[3]—in sheets, with the hope that you will yet find time and room in your Review to mention its publication among your book Notices.[4]

Come and make us a visit as early as you can—I have much that I would like to speak with you about.

faithfully yours

I T Hecker

1. Peter Richard Kenrick (1806–1896), Irish-born, author, brother of Francis P. Kenrick; became co-adjutor bishop of St. Louis 1841, its first archbishop 1847.

2. James Duggan (1825–1899), Irish-born, became bishop of Chicago 1859.

3. *Sermons Preached at the Church of St. Paul the Apostle, New York, During the Year 1863* (New York, 1864); Hecker gave Brownson an early copy in sheets.

4. *BrQR*, January 1864, p. 125.

89

HECKER TO BROWNSON • 11 JANUARY 1864

January 11th. 1864

Dear Dr.

I have Appletons' decision which is in favor of publication. He offers to publish the Volume,[1] and give ten percent on the retail price, after the cost of the manufacturing is paid.

If Sarah accepts the offer, there are some suggestions made by the Appletons, and one or two of my own, in the interest of the book, that I would make to her whenever she would call on me. I shall be free on any day except saturday afternoon, and to find me home it would be advisable for Sarah to drop me a line when she intends to come.

I have heard that Sarah has written a story for the new Monthly[2] at Chicago. Sadlier told me that his wife[3] was highly pleased with it. I should like to see it.

My kindest regards to Mrs Brownson [,] Henry & Sarah.

Yours faithfully,

I. T. Hecker.

1. *At Anchor: a story of the American Civil War* (New York, 1865); although this novel was published anonymously—"by an American"—it was the work of Sarah Brownson (see Letter 59, n. 7).

2. *The Monthly* (January-December 1865), established at the University of St. Mary's of the Lake (later Mundelein Seminary) near Chicago by Rev. Dr. John McMullen (1832–1883), Irish-born president of St. Mary's and first bishop of Davenport, Iowa; the magazine's first editor was Professor Peter John Foote (1840–1888).

3. Mary Anne Madden Sadlier (1820–1903), Irish-born, editor and prominent Catholic novelist; married publisher James Sadlier 1846.

90

HECKER TO BROWNSON • 27 JANUARY 1864

Jan 27, 1864.

My Dear Friend,

I did not hear of your late illness until you had recovered. Had I known of it in time, I would have visited you without delay. May God spare your life and your pen multos annos, and give you health and grace to assist carrying our country through its present crisis[1] not only safely but to its improvement.

Healy[2] the artist from Chicago will be in this city on Saturday and dine with us on Sunday and also Lafarge[3]—can you not make us a visit and stay with us over Sunday? I promised Healy your presence, and he looks forward to meeting you with great pleasure.

I am interested in the new programme[4] of your Review, and in its support; and shall be glad to hear from you what are your prospects.

Kindest regards to your wife & family.

faithfully yours,

I T Hecker.

Please give me a line if you cannot be here.

1. The Civil War; Brownson had prepared a National Series of *BrQR* (see n. 4 below).

2. George Peter Alexander Healy (1813–1894), Catholic historical and portrait painter. Both Brownson and Hecker sat for Healy portraits.

3. John LaFarge (1835–1910), prominent American Catholic artist, author, and lecturer.

4. "Our New Programme. Introduction to the National Series," *BrQR*, January 1864, pp. 1–12.

PART THREE

1865-1872

This third section of the Brownson-Hecker correspondence consists primarily of their frequent exchanges regarding the conduct of *The Catholic World,* the monthly magazine begun by Hecker and his associates in 1865. Dr. Brownson was a prolific contributor to this periodical, and his articles dealt with many salient issues of the postbellum period including modern science, the women's movement, and the school question. As with his other initiatives, Hecker viewed this enterprise as a means of fostering the Paulists' conversion apostolate.

A crucial juncture in the alliance of these correspondents was reached in 1868, culminating in a series of theological disputes. The division between the two friends also involved Father Augustine F. Hewit, who was the censor for *The Catholic World.* Their disagreement centered on speculative questions like the interpretation of original sin, ontologism, and the Church's role in modern civilization. Missionary strategies and the meaning of political developments in Europe formed another field of argument. Significant documents in this section strikingly demonstrate the distance between Brownson and Hecker over the topic of church-state relations.

After Orestes Brownson withdrew from *The Catholic World* in 1872, his correspondence with Isaac Hecker came to an end. Although a warm personal bond endured, their poor health and intellectual divergence brought about the termination of their professional relationship. Not only do these closing letters uncover the lives and personalities of these two remarkable religious leaders, they likewise testify to the amazing vitality and diversity within American Catholicism during the nineteenth century.

91

HECKER TO BROWNSON • 26 JANUARY 1865*

Jan. 26, 1865.

Dear Dr.

The Appletons retain the right to publish, but not the copy right of the book;[1] and if the book sells sufficiently to pay for the expense of its publication, the 10 per cent dates back to the beginning. The plates are theirs.

I send you two pamphlets by Frothingham.[2] Both useful in the intended Review. I am told that in the Unitarian paper[3] of last week, Frothingham was said to be the author of the 1st. art[icle][4] in the Ex[aminer]. This may be well for you to know—in connection with his authorship of "*The New Religion of Nature.*" You will see on p. 3. first column that he has trotted me out again. What a satanic imagination must have suggested the last sentence of this paragraph.

In the Review of Hedge[5] you will find a defense of this "New Religion;" and I think there can be no doubt that Hedge is that leader spoken of as having returned to supernaturalism.[6]

The Armitages[*?*][7] are furious against F[rothingham] for his attack in the Examiner. I have written to Boston, and will know in a day or two whether Fields[8] will publish the pamphlet.[9]

The title might be—"A Review of Xtian Examiner on Catholicity and the New Religion of Nature." I shall get the Unitarian paper, & make due of the authorship of the art[icle]. In the meantime if necessary, you can assume it.

The terms of the Appletons were so much better than I had supposed that I gave him Sarah's address & told them to go on.

The earlier you can give the Review the more satisfactory.

faithfully yours,

I. T. Hecker

*Brownson, *BLL*, pp. 447–48 (dated as 25 January, with omissions).

1. Sarah Brownson's *At Anchor; a story of the American Civil War* (see Letter 89, n. 1).

2. Octavius Brooks Frothingham (1822–1895), Unitarian pastor and author, social critic, radical humanist, and religious naturalist who advocated the free and scientific discussion of religion.

One of Frothingham's pamphlets, mentioned in this letter, was undoubtedly *The New Religion of Nature*; the other possibly was his discourse *The Unisons of the Liberal Faith* (New York, 1865) or two discourses entitled *Childhood and Manhood of the Spirit in Jesus, and New Year's Gifts of the Spirit* (New York, 1865). Brownson was preparing a reply to Frothingham.

3. *The Liberal Christian,* published in New York City, edited by Henry W. Bellows.

4. "The Order of St. Paul the Apostle, and the New Catholic Church," *The Christian Examiner,* LXXVIII (January 1865), 1–26.

5. Frederic Henry Hedge (1805–1890), Unitarian pastor, expositor of German literature, original member of the Transcendental Club 1836.

6. See F. H. Hedge, "Anti-supernaturalism in the pulpit," *The Christian Examiner,* LXXVII (September 1864), 145–59.

7. Possibly a reference to Thomas Armitage (1819–1896), British-born author and Baptist preacher; became pastor of the Fifth Ave. Baptist Church in New York City 1859.

8. The firm of Ticknor & Fields in Boston, publishers, booksellers, and importers; the firm included as partners James Thomas Fields (1817–1881) and William Davis Ticknor (1810–1864).

9. *Catholicity and Naturalism,* a pamphlet in answer to Frothingham and published anonymously by Patrick Donahoe of Boston (see *Works,* VIII [1865], 339–59); this piece was Brownson's first publication following the cessation of *BrQR* in 1864.

92

HECKER TO BROWNSON • 17 MARCH 1865

New York March 17, 1865

Dear Dr.

The Reply[1] gives entire satisfaction. The ArchBishop[2] expressed himself the other day to me, as being highly delighted with both spirit and substance of the Reply.

I keep occupied with the annuity,[3] and am doing my best to bring matters to a definite settlement. These two days past I have made enquiries at different companies about it. I should feel an increased satisfaction in having the annuity continued to Mrs Brownson in case she should survive you. *Please tell me her age,* that I may learn what would be the additional sum to secure her in this case, the annuity.

"The Catholic World"[4] meets with singular sympathy and encouragement from prelates, priests, and laity. It will be out in a week.

I have not had time to find out when "at Anchor" [*?*] [5] will appear. I look for it with great interest.

If you do not come to the city this week, please drop me a note in answer to the annuity matter and help [*?*].

Your[s] faithfully

I. T. Hecker

1. *Catholicity and Naturalism,* Brownson's reply to Frothingham; see Letter 91, n. 9.
2. John McCloskey, who became archbishop of New York in 1864.
3. An annuity purchased from Manhattan Life of New York, chiefly financed by George Hecker, guaranteeing Brownson a thousand dollars a year for life; the arrangements were concluded in August 1865 and the annuity was presented to Brownson on behalf of his friends by Rev. Jeremiah W. Cummings in September 1865.
4. *The Catholic World: A Monthly Eclectic Magazine of General Literature and Science* (henceforth *CW*), founded by Hecker and the Paulists in April 1865. In January 1972 it became the *New Catholic World.*
5. Sarah Brownson's novel *At Anchor* (see Letter 89, n. 1).

93

BROWNSON TO HECKER • 28 APRIL 1866

April 28, 1866.

My dear Father Hecker,

I sent last Monday the article on the use and abuse of reading,[1] with a notice of Herbert Spencer's Biology[2] to Kehoe,[3] with a request that they should be placed in your hands at the earliest possible moment, and that you should make all the alterations you saw proper.

I did not make so much use of the French article[4] as I proposed. I found it difficult to do so, but I preserved its spirit, and wrote such an article as I thought would best serve the end I understood you to have in view. I hope it met your approbation. Spencer's book is a humbug, but very instructive in its way. I had no idea but on reading it of the absurdities into which our modern savans [*sic*] are running. It will be necessary soon to write a new Hermias[5] against them. They are Leucippus, Democritus, Molagoras,[6] & Epicurus over again.

I have read Father Hewit's first chapter on the Problems of the Age.[7] His general aim is the same as mine in the work I am writing, but our methods are so different that we can hardly interfere with one another. The philosophy that underlies each work is substantially the same, but he must pardon if I say that I fear that he understands Gioberti in the sense in which he is generally understood, and is in danger of classing himself with the Ontologists of Louvain,[8] and defending or seeming to defend the doctrine that we have immediate intuition of God, which is not true. We do not in this life know God or even that he is[,] intuitively. We have immediate, direct intuition of Ens, or Ens as idea, under the ideas of the necessary, the universal, the immutable, the eternal, the perfect, the true, the good, the fair. What philosophers call necessary or absolute ideas are affirmed or affirm themselves to us in immediate intuition, but that the Ens so affirmed is God, or that these ideas are God, that the ideal is really God is not affirmed in intuition, & hence St. Thomas denies that Deum esse sit per se notum,[9] or that God is self-evident quoad nos. The identification of Ens or the ideal with God is the work of reflection, of demonstration, and hence again St. Thomas maintains that Deum esse sit est demonstrabile.[10] In my Review[11] I have frequently [e]xplained the matter by saying that we have ideal intuition of that which is God, but not that it is God. Gioberti does not give as the Ideal formula, Deus Creator, nor Deus creat [e]xistentias, but *Ens* creat existentias, L'Ente crea l'essestenze,[12] for though the Ens is identically God, we do not know that it is intuitively, but subsequently by reflection.

So again the Ideal formula as a formula is not intuition, but that only which the formula asserts. What is asserted by the formula is intuition, but the formula itself is not; it is the last and highest achievement of philosophy, and though when obtained [it is] rationally certain and the basis of all logic, especially of all scientific induction, it never could have been obtained without revelation, infused along with language into the first man, and preserved or transmitted in the infallible language of the Church. Language is the necessary medium of reflection as well as of instruction. Language became corrupted with the Gentiles and they lost the ideal formula, as it is corrupted with Protestants, who have lost the formula, Verbum incarnatus creat ecclesiam.[13]

I do not suppose I am saying anything here that F[ather] H[ewit] does not know far better than I or that he does not as fully accept as I do, but I fear that he has been less careful than he might be to conform his technology to it, and thus escape in appearance as well as in reality the error of the Louvain Ontologists, and the cavils of the Thomists.

Be so good as to tell me if my article is acceptable, and believe me

Very truly & sincerely
Your obliged Friend

O A Brownson

Very Rev. I T. Hecker.
Paulist Convent.

Elizabeth

1. "The Use and the Abuse of Reading," *CW*, III (July 1866), 463–73.

2. *Principles of Biology*, vol. I (London, 1864) by Herbert Spencer (1820–1893), British philosopher of evolutionary theory.

3. Lawrence Kehoe (1832–1890), Irish-born publisher and editor, publisher and business manager of the *CW* and the Catholic Publication Society.

4. Pierre Toulemont, S.J. (1826–1889), "Appel aux consciences chrétiennes contre les abus et les dangers de la lecture," *Etudes Religieuses, Historiques et Littéraires*, VIII.

5. *The Shepherd of Hermas*, a second-century Christian document by an unknown author, written in defense of divine revelation and urging personal repentance from sin.

6. Brownson probably meant Anaxagoras (c. 500–428 B.C.) of the Greek atomist tradition; Brownson likened Spencer's positivism to the materialism of Democritus (c. 460–370 B.C.), Leucippus (5th century B.C.), and Epicurus (341–270 B.C.).

7. "The Problems of the Age," *CW*, III (May 1866), 145–50.

8. A group of ontologist professors at the University of Louvain, chiefly Gérard-Casimir Ubaghs (1800–1875) and Nicolas-Joseph Laforêt (1832–1878), and including Julien-Jacques (Bernard) Van Loo (1818–1885), Pierre Claessens (1817–1886), and Arnold Tits (1807–1851).

9. "God's existence is self-evident"; *Summa Theologica*, book I, question 2, article 1.

10. "God's existence is demonstrable" by reason; *Summa Theologica*, I, q. 2, art. 2.

11. See *BrQR*, January 1850, pp. 1–39; April 1852, pp. 141–64; October 1855, pp. 445–73; January 1859, pp. 58–90; and October 1861, pp. 462–91.

12. "Being creates existences"; see Vincenzo Gioberti, *Introduzione allo studio della filosofia* (1840), I, iii and II, i.

13. "The Incarnate Word creates the Church," or the Second Person of the Blessed Trinity, as incarnate in Jesus Christ, creates the Church.

94

HECKER TO BROWNSON • 1 AUGUST 1866

NY. Aug 1, 1866

Dear Dr.

Will you favour the C. World with an article from your pen anytime within 3 weeks or a month. Earlier the better, and on any subject you please, except philosophy as F[ather] Hewit will have an article[1] on that subject in the number.

I am not well or I would call on you.

faithfully yours

I T Hecker

1. "Problems of the Age," *CW*, IV (October 1866), 1–14.

95

BROWNSON TO HECKER • 15 AUGUST 1866

Aug. 15, 1866

Very Rev. & Dear Father,

In consequence of the answer of Fr. Hewit, I have delayed my article, and it will not be ready until sometime next week. It is on the *Independence of the Church,*[1] and is suggested by the present state of affairs in Europe. I trust I am steering clear of both rocks and quicksands, and am conservative enough to satisfy the Archbishop.[2] My main thesis is that the Church is one & Catholic, & therefore independent of man, and the accidents or vicissitudes of time and space. I think it will meet your approbation; however it will be submitted to your judgment to be accepted or rejected, or manipulated at your pleasure. I am not well, my wife is not well, & my son Henry is very ill, and so I could not venture to leave home this week, even if my article were ready.

Yours most truly

O. A. Brownson

V Rev. I T. Hecker

Elizabeth

1. "The Independence of the Church," *CW*, IV (October 1866), 51–64.
2. John McCloskey, archbishop of New York.

96

BROWNSON TO HECKER • 14 JANUARY 1867

Eliz. Jan. 14, 1867.

Dear Father Hecker,

I send you an elaborate article on *Church & State.*[1] It is a pendant to the article on *The Church and Monarchy.*[2] I do not think that I have run against a snag, or step on anybodies [*sic*] corns. I think the view taken is yours, and that in the article I am coöperating heartily with your purposes. But of all this you must judge for yourself. I am with you heart & soul, & if I run athwart any of your plans, it is unconsciously. I have no pet theories or crotchets of my own to further.

I hoped to send the article sooner, but I had so much else to do that I could not, & it took me so much time to prepare it that I could not. I have engaged to furnish–inter nos–four columns a week for the Tablet,[3] which with two articles a month for the Ave Maria,[4] keeps me pretty busy. The articles in the Tablet you must not [e]xpect to see as I write. They are altered by dear Molly,[5] as she sees proper.

My health is good, but I am confined at home, by my feet. I hope to be able soon to get me some shoes made to fit my feet & then I hope to get out again. I want to see you very, very much. I hope you are well, and that you get time to eat. I wish you all the good wishes of the season, & beg you to present the Fathers & the Levites[6] the compliments of the season from me, and to believe [me] yours sincerely, reverently, & affectionately,

O A. Brownson

Very Rev. I. T. Hecker.

1. "Church and State," *CW*, V (April 1867), 1–14.

2. "The Church and Monarchy," *CW*, IV (February 1867), 627–39.

3. *The Tablet*, a New York weekly newspaper acquired by the Sadliers in 1857 (formerly *The American Celt* 1850–57), edited by Thomas D'Arcy McGee (1825–1868); *The Tablet*'s first editor was Bernard Doran Killian.

4. *The Ave Maria*, a Catholic weekly magazine published at the University of Notre Dame, founded in May 1865 by Rev. Edward Frederick Sorin, C.S.C. (1814–1893), French-born founder and first president of Notre Dame 1842; *The Ave Maria*'s first editor was Rev. Neal Henry Gillespie, C.S.C. (1831–1874).

5. Mary Anne Madden Sadlier, of Sadliers publishers.

6. A term referring to Paulist seminarians.

97

HECKER TO BROWNSON • 14 APRIL 1867

April 14, 1867

Dear Dr

You will receive with this note a volume entitled the Papacy.[1] Only your pen[2] can do it justice. With it I send the french copy,[3] and I have been told that the translation has been subjected to alterations; but have had no time to examine it.

Cleve Coxe[4] has given an introduction—please pay your respects to that *gentleman.*

Your article on The Union of Church and State[5] has given unqualified satisfaction to all parties. The one on Cousin goes in the June number.

I have secured a house for "The Catholic Pub. Society"[7]—& open it on the 1st of May—126 Nassau St.

Chabrol[8] desired me to express his regrets to you in not having the time to pay his respects to you before leaving.

The work I have on hand gives me no leisure or I should have been at Elizabeth to see you. I wish you would get those shoes to fit your feet and give us a visit.

Kindest Regards to your wife.

faithfully yours,

I. T. Hecker.

1. Abbé François René (Vladimir) Guettée, D.D. (1816–1892); *The Papacy: Its Historic Origins and Primitive Relations With the Eastern Churches* (New York, 1867).

2. "Guettée's Papacy Schismatic," *CW*, V (July 1867), 463–79; (August 1867), 577–93.

3. *La Papauté schismatique: ou Rome dans ses rapports avec l'Eglise orientale* (Paris, 1863).

4. Arthur Cleveland Coxe (1818–1896), Episcopalian priest and author, became bishop of western New York 1865.

5. *CW*, V (April 1867), 1–14.

6. "Victor Cousin and His Philosophy," *CW*, V (June 1867), 333–47.

7. The Catholic Publication Society (hereafter CPS), founded by Hecker and the Paulists to publish and distribute inexpensive Catholic pamphlets and books, ranked first among nineteenth-century American Catholic publishers in output; it later became the Columbus Press 1890, then the Paulist Press 1913.

8. Count Guillaume de Chabrol (1840–1921), French liberal Catholic, associated with Montalembert; writer for *Le Correspondant*; toured U.S. and met Brownson and Hecker 1866–67; deputy to French Assembly 1871; arranged for the publication of the French translation of Elliott's biography of Hecker: *La Vie du Père Hecker* (Paris, 1897).

98

BROWNSON TO HECKER • 9 DECEMBER 1867

Eliz– NJ. Dec. 9, 1867.

Very Rev. & dear Father,

Fr. Henry O.S.B.[,] [1] pastor of the German church in this city[,] requests me to write you that he proposes visiting you, if possible someday this week. He is building a new school house, with chapel & house for the Benedictine sisters, and finds himself as so many others do short of money. He proposes to visit you to get you to help to reach the rich Catholics of New York. I have told him that you wanted all the money you could get to carry out your own plans, and I doubted the utility of the application. If however you can help him or put him in a way of helping himself, I shall feel under great obligations to you, for I think he is doing here amongst the Germans an excellent work.

I am writing an article for the Feb. No. on the infallibility of the Church,[2] which I hope to send in a week. Did the article on Nature and Grace[3] prove to be what you wanted? Is the one on the Duke of Argyle's[4] Reign of Law[5] accepted? Judge Tenny[6] brought me the Mühlbach books[7] from the Appletons, & I wrote a notice[8] of them. If you do not like it I will return the books. At any rate I will notice no more [e]xcept at your request. I am to lecture in Boston on the 20th. My health is good, and I hope yours is the same. My respectful regards to all the Fathers.

Very truly & respectfully yours,

O. A. Brownson.

Very Rev. I T Hecker. Superior Paulist Community.

1. Peter Henry Lemke (1796–1882), German-born Benedictine priest, Catholic convert 1824, pastor of St. Michael's Church in Elizabeth, N.J., 1860–70; laid groundwork for two Benedictine parishes and a motherhouse for Benedictine sisters.

2. "The Infallibility of the Church," *CW*, VI (March 1868), 788–803.

3. "Nature and Grace," *CW*, VI (January 1868), 509–27.

4. George Douglas Campbell (1823–1900), eighth duke of Argyll; Scottish scientist, theologian, statesman and member of the British House of Commons; author of *The Reign of Law* (London, 1867).

5. "The Reign of Law," *CW*, VI (February 1868), 595–606.

6. William Jewett Tenney ("Judge Tenney") (1811–1883), lawyer, journalist and editor, Catholic convert c. 1840; married Brownson's daughter Sarah Maria on 26 November 1873 at Elizabeth, N.J.

7. L. Mühlbach (pseudonym), Frau Klara Mundt (Müller) (1814–1873), author of three historical romances translated from the German: *Frederick the Great and His Court, Berlin and Sans-Souci,* and *Joseph II and His Court* (all New York, 1867).

8. *CW*, V (May 1867), 285–87.

99

HECKER TO BROWNSON • 17 DECEMBER 1867

NY. Dec 17, 1867

My Dear Dr.

Your articles are all received, to be published, and perfectly satisfactory. The one on Argyle [*sic*] was crowded out of this number. It will go in the next.

Did Kehoe write to you about an art. on the Monks of the West[1] by Montalembert? He told me that you had rec'd them from him—Montalembert.

Suppose you come and stay a day, or overnight with us before you go to Boston? Have a talk on the subject—and aliis. If you cannot stay over night before going, do so on your return.

I lectured in Boston and had a good time—a large audience and not altogether displeased with my lecture. Subject "Luther and the Reformation."

Father Henry I shall be pleased to see, but as for helping him to obtain money, that is altogether out of the question. I am overwhelmed in that direction from all parts of the country.

faithfully yours,

I. Th. Hecker

1. *The Monks of the West, From St. Benedict to St. Bernard,* seven volumes, authorized translation (Edinburgh and London: W. Blackwood and Sons, 1861–79); the seven-volume French original was entitled *Les moines d'Occident depuis saint Benoît jusqu'à saint Bernard* (Paris, 1860–77).

100

HECKER TO BROWNSON • 8 JANUARY 1868

NY. Jan 8, 1868.

Dear Dr,

I have only this moment obtained a copy of the Church Review. It has an art. on "Orestes A. Brownson as a philosopher."[1] apropos to your art. on Cousin.[2] I send you the Review.

There will be no philosophical article for the April number unless you write one[3] in answer to the Church Review—which I would be glad if you did. Have you done anything towards the Monks of the West? Father Chocarne,[4] Dominican—author of Lacordaire's[5] Inner life—now in Kentucky, writes to me, and offers to take up the subject.[6] If you are inclined to do it, only say so, and I shall be pleased.

This whole week I have been ill with gastritis and headaches—an offset to your gout—and probably from a common cause. I have been unable to do anything—even to go down town—or put pen to paper. Yesterday was my first better day.

I hope that your illness has operated as beneficially towards me as mine has towards you, making me appreciate better your virtues and deepening the attachment I have always felt for you.

faithfully yours,

I. T. Hecker

1. "Orestes A. Brownson as a Philosopher," *The American Quarterly Church Review and Ecclesiastical Register,* XIX (January 1868), 532–47.

2. *CW,* V (June 1867), 333–47.

3. "The Church Review and Victor Cousin," *CW,* VII (April 1868), 95–113.

4. Bernard Chocarne (1826–1895), French Dominican spiritual writer; author of *Le Rev. Père H.-D. Lacordaire de l'Orde des frères prêcheurs; sa vie, intime et religieuse* (Paris, 1865); translated as *The Inner Life of the Very Rev. Père Lacordaire, of the Order of Preachers* (New York: CPS, 1867).

5. Jean-Baptiste Henri Lacordaire (1802–1861), ordained priest 1827, onetime disciple of Lamennais, became Dominican 1839, renowned preacher and Catholic liberal leader.

6. Chocarne's review of the first five volumes of Montalembert's *Monks of the West* appeared in the *CW,* VII (April 1868), 1–10.

101

HECKER TO BROWNSON • 22 JANUARY 1868

NY. Jan 22, 1868

Dear Dr.

Are you recovering? I grieve to hear that you are ill.

Shall we have an article from your pen for the March number of the C. World?

F[ather] Young[1] has just returned from Albany where he gave a Lecture for the poor of F. Walworth's congregation.[2] F. W[alworth] is in good health & hard at work in building a new Church.

F. Y[oung] says that [he] heard your articles spoken of several times with great satisfaction. The Feb. number of the C.W. is very readable.

The comedy of Convocation[3] has quite a sale. Kehoe must send you a copy—if he has not.

Kind Remembrances to your wife and family.

faithfully yours

I T Hecker

1. Alfred Young (1831–1900), Catholic convert 1850, ordained priest 1856, became Paulist 1861; renowned preacher and liturgist.

2. Clarence A. Walworth left the Paulists in 1865 to become pastor of St. Mary's Church, Albany, N.Y., a position he held until 1900.

3. *The Comedy of Convocation in the English Church, in Two Scenes,* edited by "Archdeacon Chasuble," reprinted by Hecker's CPS (New York, 1868).

102

BROWNSON TO HECKER • 24 JANUARY 1868

You need not read the whole letter at one sitting. *OAB*

Eliz–NJ. Jan 24, 1868.

Very Rev. & Dear Father

I send herewith an article on The Church and her Attributes.[1] It is not so complete, nor so well written as I could wish. And I can hardly flatter myself that you will like it. I think, however, that I have avoided any direct conflict with Father Hewit, and indeed the article is really only a development of his assertion, "The Church, then, is the human race in the highest sense."[2]

Since I saw you I have for the first time read what Father H[ewit] says in the Problems of the Ages on original sin, and the Church.[3] What he says of the Church I accept as I understand it. What he says of original sin seems to me to need modification. I speak nothing of the point where you and I have never agreed, the view that what was lost in original sin was simply what was never due to nature, for although I do not accept that view and think F. H. misinterprets the condemnation of Baius[4] & the Jansenists,[5] it is a view which you may not only hold, but hold in very good company. The Jansenists and Baius held that both original justice and what is called the integrity of nature, were in the state of innocence due to nature, or that original justice & integrity were both natural, and in fact confounded them, under the name of integral nature. In that sense only as I understand it was natura integra defined to be not due to nature as nature. In the condemnation of the propositions taken from Baius by St. Pius V,[6] the Holy Pontiff says [that] although [they] may in sense be true, yet in the sense of the *Assertors,* they are false, heretical, &c. Hence it is only in the sense of the Assertors that they are condemned, and the Augustinians who hold that God could not have created man in the beginning without integral nature, though he might have created him without the supernatural justice in which he constituted him, have never been condemned. Consult Berti[7] and Berleli,[8] the Augustinian theologians of Benedict XIV.[9] Neither my opinion nor yours has been condemned, and neither can assert his own opinion as of Catholic faith. I believe mine is the sounder opinion, & you believe yours is the better opinion. The only fault I find on this point is that he gives the opinion of the school he follows as Catholic doctrine, which I humbly submit it is not. It is Sententia in Ecclesia, not yet Sententia Eccles*iae.*[10]

But the points on which I find fault are that Adam was only the representative or putative head of the race, not its natural head in the order of generation, and that genera & species are not real. In both respects he seems to be inconsistent with himself, and to escape Calvinism which imputes the sin of Adam by virtue of a convenant stipulation to his posterity, or else to deny original *sin* altogether. I cannot understand how Father H. who asserts the unity of the species, and defines the Church to be "the human race in the highest sense,["] should treat the reality of the species as a fiction. Nor can I understand how if in the human [race] nothing is real but individual men, original sin positive or negative can be transmitted by natural generation. Nor can I understand how if we were not in Adam as the race individualized in him his sin could be ours, or how we could be born in sin, and children of wrath, except putatively. In a word Father H. seems to me really to deny original sin, or that the race really sinned in Adam. We are born, according to my understanding of his doctrine, in consequence of Adam's sin under great disadvantages, but not as the Catechism says "born in sin." To my understanding F.H. really by his [e]xplanations denies original sin,[11] and recognizes no sin of the race in the person of Adam, and in fact only actual sins. How is original sin properly sin in us, or only the effect of sin and the forfeiture incurred by the prevarication of Adam?

I pray you and F.H. to forgive me the freedom of these strictures. It is never without much misgiving [that] I differ from you or from him. It may be he is right & I am wrong, but I have given what appears to me a just criticism.

In my article[12] I have avoided as much as possible all direct collision with his view, as you will see. As you read me you will find one passage that may be considered as designed to modify his view. If you think best you can strike it out. The hiatus left will not be noticed.

I have worried much over the article, and worked myself into a fit of the gout, from which I am slowly recovering. I care little for the article itself, only if rejected on account of its doctrine, I must give up writing on the philosophy of religion for the C.W. which I should [be] sorry to do. For although I may never wish to write another on the subject, it would, if debarred from doing it, so operate in spite of my will and my better sense, so operate on my crotchety and sensitive nature as to render me unable with all my endeavors to write on any thing else. Yet you exercise ful[l]y your own judgment, cut out, cut down, alter, amend, or reject altogether at your own sovereign pleasure.

I am reading Draper.[13] He is simply a Positivist, and by no means the ablest of his school. I will try and treat him civilly, but I must have time.

I have not been able to read a single article in the last C.W.[14] but a glance at the contents and at a few pages inclines me to believe it is a very superior number.

Will you relieve my suspense as to the Church & her Attributes as soon as you have decided? Perhaps its rejection will not discontent or trouble me beyond a few hours.

With a thousand heartfelt thanks for all your goodness, kindness, consideration and patience in my behalf, and with respectful regards to the Fathers of the Community, believe me

Most truly & affectionately
Your obliged Friend

O. A. Brownson.

V[ery] R[everend] I T. Hecker.

P.S. I have read most of the art[icles] in the last C.W. It is a capital number. In two of my articles[15] of which I did not see the proofs the proofreader has been much at fault. They are full of grave errors. I have relaxed and read the Comedy. It is well done.

1. "The Church and Her Attributes," *CW*, VI (March 1868), 788–803.

2. *CW*, IV (February 1867), 655; for Brownson's reference, see *CW*, VI (March 1868), 789.

Hewit's articles in the *CW* on "Problems of the Age" ran from May 1866 through February 1867 and were gathered into a book *Problems of the Age*

(New York: CPS, 1868). Brownson's critique of Hewit's understanding of original sin (see n. 3 below) apparently had an effect, for Hewit wrote in the Preface to his book *Problems of the Age* the following statement: "I have also added to the chapter which treats of original sin some further explanations of the exposition I have given, derived from the works of standard theologians."

3. On original sin, see "Problems of the Age," *CW,* IV (January 1867), 519–33, and *Problems of the Age,* chapter X. On the Church, see *CW,* IV (February 1867), 654–58, and *Problems of the Age,* chapter XII.

4. Baius, or Michel de Bay (1513–1589), professor of Sacred Scripture and theologian at the University of Louvain; for his condemnation, see n. 6 below.

5. The followers of Cornelius Jansen (1585–1638), Dutch theologian and eventual bishop of Ypres, Belgium. Seven Jansenist propositions were condemned by Pope Innocent X on 31 May 1653.

6. Pope Pius V, Dominican philosopher and theologian, papal reformer who reigned from 1566–1572; he condemned seventy-nine of Baius's statements from his writings on 1 October 1567. Pope Gregory XIII reaffirmed these condemnations in 1580.

7. Giovanni Lorenzo Berti (1696–1766), Italian Augustinian priest whose writings on St. Augustine, especially *De theologiciis disciplinis* (1739–45), were accused of Jansenism.

8. Fulgenzio Bellelli (1675–1742), Italian master general of the Augustinians, author of two polemical works against Baius and the Jansenists.

9. Benedict XIV, who reigned from 1675–1758, declared Berti's writings (see n. 7 above) to be orthodox.

10. *Sententia ecclesiae* ("an opinion of the Church") comprises an official Catholic consensus on a doctrine of faith; *sententia in ecclesia* ("an opinion in the Church") comprises an individual or group opinion on a doctrinal issue still open to debate among theologians.

11. See n. 2 above.

12. See n. 1 above.

13. John William Draper (1811–1882), historian and scientist at the University of New York.

14. *CW,* February 1868.

15. Possibly "Nature and Grace," *CW,* VI (January 1868), 509–27 and "The Reign of Law," *CW,* VI (February 1868), 595–606.

103

BROWNSON TO HECKER • 29 JANUARY 1868

Eliz. Jan. 29th, 1868.

Rev. & dear Father,

I did not mean to convey the idea that you had grieved or pained me; all I meant was that I had worried over the question, till I have brought on, as worrying always will, a fit of the gout. What you did and said is perfectly right. An Editor is and always should be [an] autocrat. The whole responsibility is on you, and your power should be absolute. Yet having been myself an autocrat for thirty years, I have some difficulty in making my mind work freely, if while I am writing, I am in doubt whether what I write will be accepted or not. I always write with the public before my eyes, and when you veil that public from my sight, I lose both my freedom & power of thinking and expression. It is a weakness, but the habits of thirty years' standing are too strong for me now to overcome.

I am far from wishing to injure the C.W. In all I have written for it I have done my best, not as well as I could have done once, but as well as it is in my power to do now. I am not what I was. In the article on "An Old Quarrel"[1] I contradicted without knowing it the doctrine of Father Hewit on genera & species, and differed from him as to intuition of God, at least in [e]xpression, and you found no fault with me. The very slight difference between the view I actually [e]xpressed in the article just sent, from some of his views, which I must regard as heterodox, I thought might be suffered to pass. I do not complain, but I think you are demanding a unity of thought that cannot be maintained where you have a diversity of writers. My rule as Editor was to exclude no article on account of its doctrine, if it accorded with the generally received Catholic Theology. I am aware of no school that my article contradicts, and I do not think that there is any school of Catholic [theology] that holds Fr. Hewitt's [*sic*] opinion, namely, that all men as the race did not sin in Adam. The reality of the species or race being denied, it seems to me undeniable that the race did not & could not sin in Adam, & therefore that there is and can be no original sin, and what is called original sin is simply an original damage or misfortune. I deem the point important, as it strikes at the whole Christian faith as I have been taught it, & understand it, & do really hope that Fr. Hewit whom I profoundly reverence & tenderly love will review it. To me, in the language of a Bishop, "he explains away the whole mystery of original sin." But enough of this.

Will you be so good as to tell Kehoe when he sends the proofs to send also the copy, so I can see not only what is struck out, but whether the hiatus is properly co[n]cealed. I wish also to know what opinions I am in

[the] future to avoid expressing. Do not imagine that I am hurt or grieved at any liberty of alteration or omission you have [e]xercised. My only grief is that C.W. should be committed irrevocably to a doctrine that if not heterodox comes so near heterodoxy that there is no fun in it. Will you also oblige me by asking Kehoe to get and send me The American Quarterly Church Review for this present month. It is the Episcopalian Review published [at] New Haven, and is said to have a sharp criticism upon [me] as a philosopher.

I forgot to thank you for the value [*sic*] present of the five excellently bound volumes of the Cath. World. I am greatly obliged to you for them. But in handling them I could not but think if you made the magazine three instead of two volumes a year it would be a convenience to the reader. It would make three volumes a year large[r] than Brownson's Quarterly.

The first article[2] in the February No.[,] I set down to Father Hewit, and like it very much. The Old Religion[3] is well done, and an admirably written article. Am I right in ascribing it to Father Young? Who writes Magas; or long ago?[4] Where did he learn that "the soul is divine?" For my part I have always regarded the soul as human, and created. To make the soul divine is a species of pantheism. Is the writer he who wrote Domilitilia?[5] The Bishop[6] of Orléans's Discourse[7] is Frenchy, & wants substance. The Prehistorical Congress of Paris[8] is interesting, witty, but wants firmness of tone. Why do not the Jesuits take up these great questions that the Savants are grappling with, master them, and refute the scientific infidels on their own ground? Are they overawed by great names? Have they no confidence in faith? Is their own physical science of the same character? or do [they] think persiflage the best way to answer them? If I were not more than fifty I would try & master the so-called sciences, and expose them. Alas! I am too old now, and must die without having done anything, even without saving my own soul. My whole life has been frittered away, & nothing has come of it. Yet with all the fault I find, I like the last number very much. It is the most readable number throughout that has appeared. The Article[9] on Father Lacordaire makes one regret [that] so pure, so gifted, so noble a man was comparatively thrown away. But I have bored you long enough, & too long. I cannot doubt your generous friendship, and I pray you to be[lieve me]

Most truly & affectionately

Yours, O. A. Brownson.

V[ery] R[everend] I T. Hecker.

1. *CW*, V (May 1867), 145–59.

2. "Paris Impious–And Religious Paris," *CW*, VI (February 1868), 577–86.

3. "The Old Religion; Or, How Shall We Find Primitive Christianity?" ibid., pp. 622–38 by Rev. William Lockhart (1820–1892).

4. "Magas; Or, Long Ago. A Tale of the Early Times," ibid., pp. 666–80.

5. "The Two Lovers of Flavia Domitilla," written under the pen-name 'Clonfert,' was serialized in the fifth volume of the *CW* from June through September 1867.

6. Félix Antoine Phibbert Dupanloup (1802–1878), bishop of Orléans, educational theorist, and leader of the anti-infallibilist forces at the First Vatican Council; he addressed the Third Catholic Congress of Malines, Belgium, in September 1867.

7. "Bishop Dupanloup's Speech At The Catholic Congress of Malines," *CW*, VI (February 1868), 587–94.

8. "The Pre-Historical Congress of Paris," ibid., pp. 703–8.

9. "Father Lacordaire," ibid., pp. 689–700.

104 Draft

BROWNSON TO HECKER • [c. 1 FEBRUARY 1868]*

[*Undated*] [1]

Very Rev. Father

Having in my two letters[2] sufficiently cleared myself of the bile stirred up by the Editor of the C.W. I want now to touch more particularly on the theologica[l]-philosophical question at issue. Neat systems of theology which *aprimis* [= *assume*] that *aprimis* the *status naturae purae*[3] to be or to ever have been a real state and supposes that man such as he is or ever has been could have a natural beatitude I do not accept, and I am not obliged to accept it by Catholic doctrine. A natural beatitude is a created, finite beatitude, and man has been created for God, & naturally, according to St. Thomas, desires to see God in the beatific vision, that is, his natural desire for happiness can be satisfied with nothing less.

But the point I make with Fr. Hewit is that he really denies original sin, not because he makes it consist simply in the loss of what was never du[e to nature. . . .]

*Microfilm, roll eight (unaddressed, calendared [187?]).

1. This undated, incomplete rough draft, found among the Brownson Papers (UNDA), is not a draft of any *extant* letter from Brownson to Hecker. We have assigned the date c. 1 February 1868 because the two letters men-

tioned (see n. 2 below) presumably are those in which Brownson further clarified his critique of Father Hewit's understanding of original sin.

2. Very probably Brownson's two letters of 24 January 1868 (Letter 102) and 29 January 1868 (Letter 103).

3. Brownson consistently maintained that humankind was under "a supernatural Providence," that is, that God had given humankind the supernatural means (through the Church of Christ and the sacraments) to attain a supernatural end; hence humankind had never been destined for a purely natural beatitude or happiness, or for a purely natural end (even from the beginning, *a primis*).

105

BROWNSON TO HECKER • [c. 4 FEBRUARY 1868]*

[*Undated*][1]

Very Rev. & dear Father

I return the proofs and copy.[2] The proofs are very foul, and I hope you or Father Hewit will examine the revise. It is the least you can do after the slaughter of the innocents. Hereafter I pray you to return my articles, when they do not suit you, with the objectionable passages marked. I can bear the rejection of an article, but I find I cannot bear its mutilation by any hand but my own. I am too old a writer and too old an Editor to be treated as a schoolboy writing his themes for his master.

I think you have much injured the article, but let it pass. I suppose I shall get over both my anger and mortification; yet it is a little trying, after devoting some two month's hard labor to an article to have it spoiled. The readers of the C.W. generally recognize my articles and I have to share with you their responsibility. If you want me to write for the Magazine you must allow me a reasonable freedom, and also try and not make me feel that my articles are accepted only as a favor to me. I think I have helped the Magazine as much as it has helped me.

With your purposes and general views I heartily sympathize, & I wish to coöperate with you to the best of my ability, but I can no more sink my individuality in another's than you can yours. I would not knowingly interfere with any of your plans, nor come in conflict with the opinions of the Paulists, published or unpublished, but if you wish me to aid[,] you must let me feel that I am at home in the C.W. and welcomed. I must feel that I am free to work in my own way or I cannot work at all. I say this simply, and in no ill humor.

I shall as soon as my eyes permit attack Draper. In the meantime, believe me, though hurt, as ever,

Yours truly

O A. Brownson

Very Rev. Father Hecker.

*Ryan, *OAB,* p. 680 (dated as late 1867 or early 1868, with omissions).

1. Dated c. 4 February 1868 since Brownson's article "The Church and Her Attributes" (see n. 2 below) was not yet revised when he wrote his letter of 24 January 1868 (Letter 102) and was not mentioned in his letter of 12 February 1868 (Letter 106). Since this article appeared in the March 1868 *CW,* it had to be sent to Hecker before mid-February when the March 1868 *CW* appeared. Hence, a date between Brownson's letters of 24 January 1868 and 12 February 1868 is feasible, and 4 February 1868 is an estimate.

2. Of "The Church and Her Attributes," *CW,* VI (March 1868), 788–803.

106

BROWNSON TO HECKER • 12 FEBRUARY 1868

February 12, 1868.

Very Rev. & dear Father,

My gout never makes me more amiably or better able to appreciate the virtues of others. I am one of those who never profit by suffering. I never murmur against Providence, for I know I deserve all I suffer & more too, but I get mad at myself, for my folly, & when mad at myself, I am in good humor with nobody. The gout did not make me feel more kindly to you, but your letter did, while it pained me to learn that you have been suffering.

I received the Church Review yesterday. Will have, I hope [,] my reply[1] to it ready, so as to send it by Monday or Tuesday next. The Catholic World, not Dr. Brownson, replies. The Reviewer is very ignorant, very weak, very conceited, and understands not even himself.

I can't make anything of the Monks of the West, for the Catholic World. Indeed I am not at present in the mood of writing on the subject, and am engrossed with Draper, and another class of subjects. If your Dominican[2] will relieve me of the Monks I shall be greatly obliged.

I hope you are quite well now. My regards to the Fathers and the Levites, and believe me

Yours truly

O A. Brownson

Very Rev. I. T. Hecker.

1. "The Church Review and Victor Cousin," *CW*, VII (April 1868), 95–113.
2. Bernard Chocarne, O.P. (see Letter 100, n. 6).

107

BROWNSON TO HECKER • 10 MARCH 1868

Eliz. March 10, 1868

Dear Father Hecker,

I hope the article on Draper's Works[1] will pass. It is not what I wish it was, but as good as I could make it. There is much more in his works to criticize, but he is really a very superficial man, and by no means an honest writer.

Have you anything else for me to do? I am afraid to undertake of my own accord, anything else, for I fear I shall be led into trains of thought that will be unacceptable to the Magazine. The harsh word of Father Hewit said to me on the article that was rejected disturbed me, and feeling that I must meet his views as well as yours, I lack that confidence that enables [me] to put my whole soul into what I write.

I have some dozen subjects on which my mind is running, and which I could six months [ago] have written with interest to myself, but now I do not dare broach [them]. I would go & see you, and compare notes again, but I am held a prisoner by my old enemy. Just now my mind is more than usually active, but I am afraid not active in your direction. The truth is I am beginning to be once more an *oscurantisti,* and can hardly be said to belong to the Catholic Movement. I am become a convert to the Encyclical,[2] and am almost beginning to despair of the success of the American [e]xperiment. I never had a spice of real radicalism in my composition, and all my radicalism was always fortititous [*sic*] or spasmodic. There is no use in denying I have my eyes in my hindhead, and regret more than I hope. I think I am turning Paddy. I have lost confidence in my countrymen, & become ashamed of them. But too much of this.

What say you to an article criticizing Cousin's doctrine of human liberty, which I reserved in my article on him? Or to an article on the different kinds of pantheism and refuting pantheism ex professo? Or an article on materialism refuting it and the sensist philosophy; or on monasticism, showing the moral and social influence of the three vows? Or on modern literary tendencies? Or the National Debt, the Currency? Finance? I must do something, or I shall stagnate & die. Tell me frankly, if you want me to write for you or if you would rather I would write no more. If the latter I must resume by book,[3] & endeavor to complete it. Pray answer me, and

believe me Very truly
and affectionately yours

O. A. Brownson.

Very Rev. I T. Hecker
Superior of the Paulists.
New York.

1. "Professor Draper's Books," *CW,* VII (May 1868), 155–74; besides *Human Physiology, Statical and Dynamical . . .* (New York, 1856), Brownson reviewed three of Draper's historical works.

2. Pope Pius IX's encyclical *Quanta Cura,* with its attached *Syllabus Errorum,* promulgated in December 1864. Under some eighty headings, the *Syllabus* condemned as errors the belief that God was not distinct from the universe (pantheism); that all religious truths were derived from human reason; that divine revelation was imperfect and subject to progress; that all religions were equally good; that civil power could define the limits of church authority; that church and state be totally separated; that the Church had no prerogatives in the temporal order; that the pope be reconciled to political liberalism, democratic movements, and modern civilization.

3. A projected book on the relationship between reason and revelation, which evolved into the *Essay in Refutation of Atheism* (1873–74).

108

HECKER TO BROWNSON • 14 MARCH 1868*

NY. March 14, 1868

My Dear Friend,

Your note is dated the 10th which I received only last evening. Am sorry that your health is so poor, and prevents your coming to N.Y. and making us a visit. Were not my hands so full I would have started off to see you to day.

The article on Draper was crowded out of the April number but will be in the March.[1]

An article *on Modern literary tendencies,* or on Pantheism—ditto on Materialism. These, either or all, would be welcome. It is likely that the Church Review will give you another opportunity to write on Cousin.

In the April number of the Atlantic there will be an article[2] treating of Catholic matters, and which will not be unfavorable to us, but containing opinions which your pen might take up & refute. If it does appear I shall send you a copy of the Atlantic which is out about the 20th. The idea is that the Catholic Religion is the best going, but a more perfect religion is coming. It is the old idea of the Church of the Future. I have not seen the article.

The Tract "Is it Honest?"[3] has created great excitement—called forth several sermons & newspaper articles. How would it do for you to take up some of these in the Tablet? If you have not seen any of these, let me know and I will get copies and have them sent to your address.

F. Tillotson[4] is confined to his room, Young bad throat, & Hewit languid, feeble.

Our students are doing well—12—except Cavanagh[5] who is out west, but is doing better.

You cannot be very far gone into oscurantism [*sic*] or you would not be willing to confess the fact. God is calling on our nation to exert its national conscience *and it will do it.* This is His way of educating us *as a people.*

With sincerest and most affectionate Regards.

Yours faithfully,

I. Th. Hecker

Dr O. A. Brownson.

*Brownson, *BLL*, pp. 517–18 (with omissions).

1. Hecker meant May.

2. "Our Roman Catholic Brethren," *The Atlantic Monthly*, XXI, (April 1868), 432–51.

3. *Is It Honest?* (CPS, 1868), possibly written by George Deshon, C.S.P. This tract was polemical in character, defending Catholic teachings on the sacrament of confession, the use of the Bible, indulgences, veneration of the Blessed Mother and the saints. For the text, see Walter Elliott's *Life of Father Hecker* (1894 ed.), pp. 352–54.

4. Robert Beverly Tillotson (1825–1868); while visiting Dr. John Henry Newman in England, he converted to Catholicism from the Episcopal Church c. 1850; ordained priest of the Birmingham Oratory 1856; first recruit to the Paulist community 1859.

5. Eugene Tobias Kavanagh (d. 1870), joined Paulists 1865; apparently a sickly person, he died as a Paulist seminarian. The other eleven seminarians were: Augustine Michael Brady (b. 1848), John Francis Donaher (b. 1844), William Ignatius Dwyer (b. 1846), Walter Elliott (1842–1928), Benjamin Denis Hill (b. 1842), Henry Stephen Lake (1846–1875), Thomas Verney Robinson (1840–1903), Adrian Aloysius Rosecrans (1849–1876), George Mary Searle (1839–1918), Francis Aloysius Spencer (b. 1845), James Mary Stone (b. 1840).

109

BROWNSON TO HECKER • 17 MARCH 1868

Eliz. March 17, 1868

Very Rev. & dear Father,

The article I sent you on Draper was not intended for the April number, but for May. I shall wait for the Atlantic before commencing an article for June. I have not seen or noticed any comments on the Tract Is it honest? Send them, and I will do them for the Tablet.

I really am becoming an oscurantisti, but perhaps not of the blackest sort, as you will see if you read for a week or two to come The Tablet. I have been made a little savage by Father Hewit's article on New England Protestantism,[1] & the embarrassing position in which it places us, and the advantage it gave to Dr. Bacon.[2] If these old Puritan Ministers were in good faith, and if we have no just reason to doubt that they are saved, I cannot see what is the use of preaching or writing against heresy of any sort.

It was that article and your striking out from my articles whatever implies that nature suffered only positive moral injury by the Fall, and refusal to allow me to war on the modern spirit or spirit of the age, which I hold is the spirit of Satan, false & mischievous in its essence, not merely an abuse or misapplication of a truly Christian tendency [that] are at the bottom of my uneasiness and doubt of my ability to cooperate in the policy of the C.W.

I do not want to dictate the course of the C.W. but I want, if I write for it[,] to approve its policy, and enter into it heart and soul. Your policy may be far better than mine, but not being what *I think* the best, I am always in fear that I shall do something that will cross it, and injure it, & this fear to a certain [e]xtent paralyzes myself, and greatly restricts the number of subjects on which I feel I may venture to write. I cannot write well unless I feel that you repose confidence in my judgment, as well as my good intentions, or [I cannot write well] without confidence in myself. Indeed there is not that perfect sympathy in our methods that renders it easy for us to work together. All I want is to feel that you have confidence in me, that I will [not] knowingly cross your policy, and that I may be to some extent trusted. I shall take care not [to] abuse your confidence.

I have resumed work on my book, which I shall labor to complete according to the original plan.

I regret to hear of the illness of F[ather] Tillotson, that F. Young has a bad throat, & Father Hewit is falling back where he was before his voyage. My health is now pretty good, and hope to be able to visit you soon. My kindest regards to all the Fathers, & to [the] students.

Yours truly

O A. Brownson

Ver Rev. I T. Hecker
Paulist Convent.

1. "The Catholic Doctrine of Justification," *CW,* VI (January 1868), 433–41. This article was a follow-up to one entitled "Dr. Bacon on Conversions to the Catholic Church," *CW,* V (April 1867), 104–19; the latter article was in turn a response to an article written by Dr. Bacon (see n. 2 below) entitled "A Roman Philosopher . . ." in the January 1867 number of *The New Englander*, which critiqued a *CW* article "The Philosophy of Conversion," IV (January 1867), 459–71.

Brownson judged Hewit's article to contradict his own belief that Protestants needed to convert to the Catholic faith in order to be saved.

2. Leonard W. Bacon (1802–1881), Congregationalist minister, founder of *The New Englander,* professor of theology at the Yale Divinity School.

110

HECKER TO BROWNSON • 19 MARCH 1868*

N.Y. March 19, 1868

Dear Dr,

I send you the enclosed, and when done with them please return them. The same calumnies return again and again. The "Tract"[1] has done some good in calling the attention of the public to the doctrines of the Church.

I send you another "What Does the Bible Say?"[2] We have the advantage in putting them on the defense. They feel it too.

It gives me pleasure to hear that your health is better and of your visiting us soon. I shall be glad to have the opportunity of settling the difficulties which have recently sprung up. Our opinions on the effect of the Fall, and what is the best policy?[3] undoubtedly do differ; but not to an extent that we cannot work together. This I think can be made evident when we talk it over together. I shall expect to see you at your earliest convenience.

Your article on "The Church Review"[4] is in my opinion, one of the best of its kind which has ever come from your pen. All think so who have read it in our community.

The Atlantic is out about the 20th. to-morrow or next day.

faithfully yours,

I T Hecker

Dr O. A. Brownson.

*Brownson, *BLL,* p. 514 (with omissions).

1. *Is It Honest?* (see Letter 108, n. 3).
2. Published by the CPS, 1868.
3. In apologetics and convert work.
4. "The Church Review and Victor Cousin," *CW,* VII (April 1868), 95–113.

111

HECKER TO BROWNSON • 22 MARCH 1868

March 22, 1868

Dear Dr

I have just read the article in the Atlantic entitled "Our Roman Catholic

Brethren." The present one is very fair and favourable, and will do a great deal of good. The author[1] honestly avows his skepticism and the next article[2] which he promises, may afford a subject for an article.

But I send you the second sermon[3] of Mr Bacon[4] on "Is it Honest?". I am not sure that he will publish another on this tuesday. If so I shall send it to you immediately.

I shall esteem it a favour if you will take up the sermons and refute their errors etc. An article[5] in ten days will be in time.

I send you the enclosed thinking it might not come under your eye.

The April number is not all that I desired to make it;–some articles were crowded out–among others one on "The Catholic aspects of Tennyson"[6] by an english pen which would have improved it.

The notices of the Non-Catholic press are most encouraging.[7]

faithfully yours,

I T Hecker

Dr O. A. Brownson.

1. James Parton (1822–1891), author and biographer, free-religionist.
2. *The Atlantic Monthly,* XXI (May 1868), 556–74.
3. Three "Sermons in Answer to the Tract 'Is It Honest?' " appeared in the *Brooklyn Times* on 9, 17, and 24 March 1868.
4. Leonard Woolsey Bacon (1830–1907), Congregationalist pastor in Brooklyn; son of Leonard W. Bacon (see Letter 109 above, n. 2).
5. "Is It Honest?," *CW,* VII (May 1868), 239–55.
6. "Tennyson in His Catholic Aspects," *CW,* VII (May 1868), 145–54.
7. See, for example, Letter 112, nn. 7, 8.

112

HECKER TO BROWNSON • 27 MARCH 1868*

March 27, 1868

Dear Dr.

Mr Kehoe tells me that he sent to you Bacon's third and last sermon which I have just read. I suppose that you have Bp. England's[1] Works[2] in your library & you remember that he has refuted at length the calumny about the Chancery in Rome.[3] Let me call also your attention to his treatment of the testimony of "Arnobius"[4] in Vol 2, p. 313.

I feel a great interest in the reply to Bacon, and satisfied it is in the right hands. Your article on "Rome and the World"[5] has been translated into French & published in the "Revue Generale"[6] of Brussels.

"The Nation"[7] and "The Round Table"[8] have very good notices of the April number of the C.W.

I trust that your health is good. F[ather] Tillotson is somewhat better this week. F. Young is at work again.

When you have the leisure we shall all be glad to see you and especially

yours faithfully

I T Hecker

Dr O A Brownson.

*Brownson, *BLL,* p. 518 (with omissions).

1. John England (1786–1842), Irish-born author and Catholic apologist, became first bishop of Charleston, S.C. 1820, founded *The United States Catholic Miscellany* 1822.

2. *Works of the Right Rev. John England, first bishop of Charleston,* five volumes (Baltimore, 1844–49), edited by Bishop Ignatius Aloysius Reynolds (1798–1855), bishop of Charleston, S.C., 1844.

3. It had been alleged that tariff prices were posted at the Chancery Office in Rome for the pardon of all sorts of sins; see *CW,* VII, 252.

4. Arnobius the Elder or Arnobius of Sicca (d. c. 327), a pagan turned Christian, author of *Adversus nationes* (c. 311), which refuted paganism and served as an indirect apologetic for Christianity.

5. "Rome and the World," *CW,* VI (October 1867), 1–19.

6. "Rome et Le Monde," *Revue Generale,* n.s., VII (February 1868), 113–34.

7. *The Nation,* VI (March 1868), 255–56.

8. *The Round Table,* VIII (28 March 1868), 202.

113

BROWNSON TO HECKER • 30 MARCH 1868

Eliz. March 30, 1868.

My dear Father Hecker,

I have sent to-day the Reply. It is not as good as I wished to make it, for the time you allowed me was short, and I could not wait for the last sermon before beginning it. Moreover, I have to prepare it while suffering severely from the gout in my head which rendered me unable to sleep except in my chair. If you on reading it, should judge it as I do, and are willing to let it lie over till the June number, you might return [it] with any suggestions you please, and [I] will rewrite it.

I have Bishop's [*sic*] England's Works, and know the answer to the Chancery question, but I could not recollect whether it was Bishop England's [*sic*] or some other writer who had refuted the charge, and I found it so painful to move that I disposed of the question without consulting any authority. If you take the article as it is, it may be well where Bacon speaks of "Penitence & Cash[''] as quoted to add a note giving the substance of the refutation[,] prefacing it with the remark, Dr. Bacon gives what purports to be the tariff of prices posted up at the Chancery Office in Rome for the pardon of all sorts of sins from the highest to the lowest. The explanation in the text that the learned doctor is amply confirmed by ———. Or if there is time, let me know and I will prepare the note, though you or Father Hewit can do it without much trouble if you think more needs to be said on the point than I have said in the text.

I know nothing about Mr. Bacon, but his sermons prove him very weak, very vain, ver[y] conceited, very ignorant, very disingenuous, very hostile to Catholicity, and very anxious to prove that he is not. He affects candor & freedom from the prejudice, only that his attacks may be the more effective. He has some of the traits of Dr. Bacon of New Haven.[1] I have tried to preserve the character of the C.W. in my answer. I think, however imperfect my article may be, that it fully sustains the Tract, and proves that Mr. Bacon and the Journals have not cleared Protestants from the serious charges it prefers against them, & which they feel to be serious. I think we shall hear from them again.

I am glad to hear Rome & the World is translated & published in Belgium. I think it the best article I have written for you. I wrote it *con amore.*

My health is such that, unless you resume Is it honest? for June[,] I shall not be able to furnish you an article for that month. While the gout remains in my feet it troubles, but does not alarm me, but I do not like its getting into my neck & head, and feel that will not do to do much brain work. I have for the last five or six weeks been working very hard, having resumed labor on my book, The Great Problem, or Reason & Revelation. Indeed, I have been doing too much. I am glad to hear that F[ather] Young is well, and th[at] F. Tillotson is better. I attributed Canada Thistles[2] to F. Young. It is a capital article. Père Chocarne, who has paid me a visit and is a charming man, has done scant justice to The Monks of the West.[3] Your last number[4] was the best you have got—for the Irish. I am very Irish—when I do not listen to their own defences of themselves, for they are really a most remarkable people—a wonderful people, and they are the mainstay, under God, of the Church with us.

I am reading Père Chocarne's life of Père Lacordaire. It is beautifully written, with a loving & really filial tenderness toward the author's spiritual father. But somehow I have no special taste for tracing the interior life of individuals, any more than I have for the psychological analysis of one's own feelings. Père Lacordaire seems to me to have been a very eloquent man, an eminently humble & holy man, but not a deep thinker or a very wise man. He was brite [*?*] within, but seldom failed to blunder without. So it seems as far as I have read, but I reserve my final judgment till finishing the book.

My regards to all the Fathers, and believe me,

Yours truly,

O A Brownson.

Very Rev. I T. Hecker.

1. Brownson refers to Bacon's father; see Letter 109, n. 2.
2. "Canada Thistles," *CW*, VI (March 1868), 721–31.
3. *CW*, VII (April 1868), 1–10.
4. *CW* (April 1868).

114

HECKER TO BROWNSON • 22 MAY 1868

NY. May 22, 1868

Dear Dr.

I returned this morning after a long tour through the west[1] –lecturing in the principal cities–with more or less success.

Everywhere your friends inquired about you with great interest and were glad to hear about your health and labours.

I am making up a list of articles for the C.W. for the month of July and will you supply one for that month? I hope that your health will permit. If so, can you give me its title? & how many pages?

My Kindest Regards to Mrs Brownson & Sarah.

faithfully yours

I T Hecker

O A Brownson LLD

1. Detroit and Ann Arbor, Mich.; Chicago; St. Louis.

115

HECKER TO BROWNSON • 6 NOVEMBER 1868*

Nov. 6, 1868

Dear Dr

If you can look at this Vol. of Porter's,[1] and give an article, or a notice of it for the C.W. please do so. If you are not able please return it.

I trust that your health has improved.

I could not find Ewer's[2] articles[3] and requested Kehoe to procure them and send them to you.

faithfully yours

I T Hecker

O A Brownson L.L.D.

*Brownson, *BLL*, p. 518 (with omissions).

1. *The Human Intellect* (New York, 1868) by Noah Porter (1811–1892), Congregationalist clergyman, president of Yale College, known for his anti-Unitarian and anti-positivist stances.

2. Ferdinand Cartwright Ewer (1826–1883), ordained Episcopalian priest 1858, author, became rector of Christ Church in New York City 1862.

3. Four discourses on the *Failure of Protestantism, and Catholicism the Remedy* (1868), delivered at Christ Church. Ewer saw Anglo-, not Roman Catholicism as the remedy for the failures of Protestantism.

116

BROWNSON TO HECKER • 22 NOVEMBER 1868

Elizabeth. Nov 22, 1868

Very Rev & Dear Father

I have nearly finished and shall [send] you about the middle [of next week], D[eo] V[olente][1] an article[2] on Dr. Ewer's Failure of Protestantism, chiefly devoted to a consideration of the "Catholicism" which he proposes as a remedy.

I had it written a week ago, but I took it into my head to rewrite it, by which it has probably lost more than it gained, for in rewriting my head got confused, worked on spoiling white paper & accomplishing not much. It will make as I estimate from 10 to 12 pages. Parts of the Essay I think you will like, for I like them myself.

Professor's Book on the Human Intellect I hope to be able to review in an article[3] for the February no. It is a book I do not like to review without reading, but to read it is a task I would not impose upon my bitterest enemy. I have got over a hundred pages or so, but have as yet no suspicion of what the professor would be at. If you [have] any more such books come to you, I am willing to review them, but I should be obliged to you if you would read them for me.

My health is slowly improving. I can walk out in the yard with my crutches, and can even take two or three steps without them, but my head is still weak, as well as my knees.

I wish to thank you & Father Hewit for the very generous reference to me in the Hypnotics.[4] I am glad Father Hewit forbore to call me erudite, which I am not, & never pretend to be. If I had had any thing like the learning of Father Hewit, I could have introduced a far greater variety into my Review, and made it far more interesting & serviceable to the public.

The article on Galileo[5] as yet leaves the only point I care about in the controversy. Did the Sacred Congregation condemn the Heliocentric theory as a heresy or did they not? If they did how defend the infallibility of the Congregation?

But enough. I hope you & the Fathers are well, & that the Institute is flourishing.

I am very truly
Your friend & obedient servant in X

O. A. Brownson

V. Rev. I. T. Hecker, Superior of the Paulists.

1. *Deo volente*, a pious Latin expression meaning "God willing;" hereafter it will not be expanded.
2. "Protestantism A Failure," *CW*, VIII (January 1869), 503–21.
3. "Porter's Human Intellect," *CW*, VIII (February 1869), 671–86.
4. "Hypnotics," *CW*, VIII (December 1868), 296–97.
5. "Galileo-Galilei, The Florentine Astronomer," *CW*, VIII (December 1868), 321–39, and (January 1869), 433–53.

117

BROWNSON TO HECKER • 23 JANUARY 1869

Eliz. Jan. 23, 1869.

Dear Father Hecker,

I send you an article which I entitle the Old & the New.[1] If it suits, or if you think it suitable to your Magazine, I could add one or two additional conversations, & need to do so in order to carry out my original design. Will you be kind enough to signify your wishes at your earliest convenience? I presume the article, if you accept it[,] is too late for the March Number.

My son[2] told me you had something you wanted me to do. If you have, will you tell me what, & set me about it. I want to see you very much, & though my health is much improved, my understanding is too uncertain & too feeble to permit me to venture to visit just at present, & fear that I cannot do so till after Easter. My head is however tolerable clear [*sic*], & I can work as well as I ever could, providing the work I have to do does not require me to cram for it. I wish you would come & spend a day with me. I will be on my good behavior, and I think a visit from you would be of great service to me, both physically & morally, & give me trust & serenity.

If you have anything you want translated from the Italian, pray, send it to Maj. H[enry] F[rancis] Brownson, U.S.A., Detroit, Michigan. He told me he gathered from something you said to him, that you had something you wanted him to do. He claims to know all the languages of Europe, except the Slavonic & Turkish, though I suspect his knowledge is limited to the Italian, French, Spanish, & Portuguese, German, Swedish, Danish, the Flemish & Hollandish. From any of these languages he can translate. He is struggling hard to correct his former faults; marriage has done him good, & I shall be obliged to you, if you find it your way to encourage him. The darkness is leaving his countenance & his soul.

Let me hear from you, & come to see me as soon as you can make a day.

Yours truly & affectionately

O. A. Brownson.

Very Rev. I. T. Hecker.
New York.

1. This piece was not published in the *CW*, but served as the basis for Brownson's book *Conversations on Liberalism and the Church* (New York, 1870).

2. Henry F. Brownson.

118

HECKER TO BROWNSON • 26 JANUARY 1869

NY. Jan 26, 1869

Dear Dr.

This morning before your note reached me, I requested Mr Kehoe to send you the two last numbers of Harper's, which contain two articles—"The Pope of Rome".[1]

You have shown time and again that [in] the conflict[s] between the popes & kings, the popes were always on the side of morality, liberty & true progress. You might take up Harper's articles on this point. If you wish to make this a 2d. in the series of conversations,[2] do so. If you prefer to make it a separate article—all right. This will not task you as you are familiar with the matter. Could you enumerate the popes, and the causes, it would increase the value & interest of the article.

The art. "The Old & the New", I received only last evening, and I shall read it today, and send you a line if called for.

I would be glad to make you a visit this week if possible and will. My trip out west has left so much on my hands that I hardly know how to stir. But I will come, if it be only for a few hours.

Dear Dr. I shall in the future, starting with the April number, pay you four instead of three dollars a page. Try and manage it, that an article does not exceed 10 pages—say 12.

This afternoon I shall visit Benzingers[3] to examine some German books which if the critics do not mislead me, it would be well to translate for the C.W. and I shall put them in the hands of Major Brownson.

On friday last I received from the holy father[4] a letter in which he expresses his joy at the success of our religious community, Catholic World, Publication Society, and my Lectures to protestants etc. ending with "Caelestis vero favoris auspicem, et paternae nostrae benevolentiae testem Apostolicam Benedictionem tibi tuaeque Missionanorum familiae peramanter inspertimus[")] —with his own signature.[5]

The endorsement is complete for all works we are engaged in.

faithfully yours,

I T Hecker

O A Brownson L.L.D.

1. Actually "The Bishops of Rome," *Harper's New Monthly Magazine*, XXXVIII (January 1869), 222–38.

2. Brownson's submitted article "The Old and the New" (see Letter 117, n. 1) was written in a series of conversations.

3. Benziger Brothers, a New York Catholic publishing firm, begun in 1860 under the direction of the Austrian-born J. N. Adelrich Benziger (d. 1878) and Louis Benziger (d. 1896).

4. Together with a 5 January 1869 letter from Cardinal Barnabò, this 30 December 1868 letter from Pope Pius IX was published in *CW*, VIII (March 1869), 721–23.

5. "And as a token of the divine favor, and an evidence of Our paternal good will, We impart most affectionately to you, and to your congregation of missionaries, Our apostolic benediction." (It is interesting to observe that the expression *benevolentiae testem* reappeared in the 22 January 1899 encyclical of Pope Leo XIII—*Testem benevolentiae*—which condemned Americanism.)

119

BROWNSON TO HECKER • 4 FEBRUARY 1869

Feb. 4th, 1869

Ver[y] Rev. Father Hecker,

I have done the best I could with Harper,[1] according to my judgment, & yet I am not at all satisfied. Articles of that sort are calculated to do much harm, but it is no easy matter to reply to them.

I cannot judge accurately of the length of the article, for I have written on differently ruled paper, and I cannot tell how much in the Magazine a page of my manuscript will make, but I estimate that it will make slightly less than half a page. I shall know better next time. I have been better pleased with my second article on Porter,[2] which I have just read in the proofs[,] than I expected to be.

I shall give you one or two more parts of the Old & the New, & I wish you would make the title of the one you have,

The Old & the New Part I.

If I get my courage up to the striking point I shall visit you on Saturday, but it is uncertain. If I do I shall spend two or three days in the City.

I send you the No of Le Correspondent you wanted.[3] I will ask you to be kind enough to preserve it, & return it when you are through with it.

I hope what I have said of St. Gregory VII[4] will not seem to you too bold to be prudent. If you tame me down too much, you will make me weak & insipid, deprive me of my masculinity. I must be allowed to work a little in my own way or I cannot work at all. Pegasus[5] could never be made to draw in harness. I approve your object, but I must be allowed to feel that it is mine also, and to serve it as if it were my own. If I do not feel that I am working for a purpose of my own, my mind is no better than a dried stick. What I do I must do *con amore.*

My kindest and most respectful regards to Father Hewit, & the other Fathers, & believe me

Yours truly

O. A. Brownson

1. "The Bishops of Rome," *CW*, IX (April 1869), 86–97.
2. "Porter's Human Intellect," *CW*, VIII (March 1869), 767–84.
3. The article "Influence of Locality on the Duration of Human Life" was translated from *Le Correspondant* in the *CW*, IX (April 1869), 73–85.
4. Pope St. Gregory VII (c. 1020–25–1085), papal reformer against simony, lay trusteeism, and royal control of bishops; for Brownson's remarks, see *CW*, IX (April 1869), 94–97.
5. In Greek mythology, a winged horse which caused Hippocrene, the fountain of the Muses, to issue from Mount Helicon.

120

HECKER TO BROWNSON • 26 FEBRUARY 1869

Feb. 26, 1869

Dear Dr.

I am home, and would be glad to receive a visit from you anytime your health and convenience will permit.

My Kindest Regards to your family,

faithfully yours,

I T Hecker

O A Brownson L.L.D.

121

BROWNSON TO HECKER • 5 MARCH 1869

Elizabeth March 5, 1869.

Very Rev. & dear Father Hecker

I am threatened with an attack of the gout, though I hope to throw it off without any long delay, but I cannot visit you as I hoped to do this week.

I sent on Wednesday the two Parts, II & III of the Old & the New, and an article on the Woman Question.[1] The article on the Woman Question I hope will meet your approbation. The Question is becoming a serious one & involves most fearful consequences. You are *seemingly* less conservative than I, & believe more in catching radicals by disguising your bate [*sic*], or by guile than I do, but I cannot believe you favor Women's Suffrage, or are unwilling that the C.W. should oppose it. I look upon the present movement as the most dangerous that has ever been attempted in our country.

I have not carried out my original intention in the Old & the New. From some remarks you made, I saw I could not without crossing some of the views of the C.W. I have therefore given a different tone [to] the Conversations, & really made them more commonplace than I intended. Yet I think they have their interest & value. The truth is, dear Father, you restrain my freedom, or at least make me feel that I am restrained, when I touch any practical question, & this takes away my nerve, & prevents me from putting forth my strength. I say this, not by way of complaint, but by way of apology for being so tame & commonplace. You do not get what is best & strongest in me, but what is weakest & dullest.

If you accept the Woman Question, I think you would do well to put it [in] the same Number with the castigation of Harper, of which I have just read the proof, and not begin the Old & the New till the May Number, for Harper & Part I will be too much of me for one Number.

Kehoe sent me paper ruled very differently from that which I have been using, & have not till now been able to estimate how much my writing would make. Hereafter I will endeavor that the long article shall not exceed 12 pages, & the short 8 or 9.

I have the gout in the fingers of my right hand, which makes writing difficult, but I hope my fingers will grow limber again. Do not consider that I either complain of you & want to dictate the course of the Magazine. I want to aid you in your purpose, and serve to the best of my ability the cause you have at heart, but I am fractious when you apply the curb. I go best with a loose rein. Give kind regards to Father Hewit, & the other Fathers, & believe me truly and affectionately

Your Old Friend

O. A. Brownson.

P.S. Who wrote the vigorous article on the Progress of Nations?[2] It is very well written, especially the first half, but I do not recognize the hand.

O. A. B.

1. "The Woman Question," *CW*, IX (May 1869), 145–57.
2. "The Progress of Nations," *CW*, VIII (March 1869), 724–33.

122

HECKER TO BROWNSON • 8 MARCH 1869*

NY. March 8, 1869

Dear Dr.

The article on "The Woman Question"[,] two on "The Old & the New" with your letter of the 5th. have been received.

These 10 months past I have been thinking on the Woman Question—and taken some steps in the way of discussing it in the pages of the C.W. I read the Revolutionist,[1] and have several "Tracts"[2] published on the subject. My intention was to send these tracts to you. Your article on the subject is most welcome, and your treatment of it most satisfactory to my judgment. If you wrote the article under any restraint Dear Dr, in my opinion you never wrote better in your life. I say this with all sincerity.

I regret that I cannot get it into the April number. Several other articles for insertion had to be left out. Yet I will try and get it in if possible, because it would attract attention.

Might not the Tracts be tacked on at the foot note with "The Revolutionist"?[3] I will send the Tracts to you, as the subject will require further discussion, & your article will call out replies.

The two articles entitled "The Old & the New" I have not had time yet to read. They will be all right.

I send you a book by Epes Sargeant entitled Planchette.[4] Its subject is "Spiritism". I see he quotes you, & me on the subject. Evidently Spiritism is not dead; and S[argeant] gives the best side of it. The dark side he conceals.

With this book I send you a pamphlet "Spiritualism unveiled"[5] and one from Judge Edmonds.[6]

Please return the pamphlets when of no further use.

I should like to have an article from your pen on this matter.

Hassard[7] wrote the article on "The Progress of Nations".

Mr Spenser[8] will be ordained, next saturday by the ABp.[9] in the cathedral. Say a "Hail Mary" for him.

I am cogitating about starting an "Illustrated Boys & Girls Paper".[10] Sarah can be of great service, if she will, in that enterprise.

I am yours as old in friendship if not in years,

faithfully

I T Hecker.

*Brownson, *BLL*, pp. 519–20 (with omissions).

1. *The Revolution*, the weekly paper of the women's rights and suffrage movement, published at New York from 1868 to 1872.

2. Including an address by George William Curtis, *Equal Rights for Women*, given at Albany, N.Y., on 19 July 1868; and one by Thomas Wentworth Higginson (1823–1911), *Ought Women to Learn the Alphabet?*

3. The tracts are named in a footnote to "The Woman Question," *CW*, IX (May 1869), 145.

4. *Planchette, or the Despair of Science, Being a Full Account of Modern Spiritualism, its Phenomena, and the Various Theories Regarding It* (Boston, 1869), by Epes Sargeant (1803–1880), journalist, poet and dramatist, leading advocate of Spiritualism.

5. Elder Miles Grant, *Spiritualism Unveiled, and shown to be the Work of Demons* . . . (Boston: The Crisis Office, [1866]).

6. John Worth Edmonds (1799–1874), spiritualist writer and lecturer; author of *Interesting Facts in Relation to Spirit Life and Manifestations* (New York: Spiritual Magnetic Telegraphic Agency, n.d.).

7. John Rose Green Hassard (1836–1888), journalist and historian, Catholic convert from Episcopalianism 1851, editor of the *CW* and critic for the *New York Tribune.*

8. Francis Aloysius Spencer (1845–1913), Scripture scholar and church musician, Catholic convert from the Episcopal Church 1866, ordained Paulist priest 1869, entered the Dominicans 1872.

9. Archbishop John McCloskey.

10. *The Young Catholic: An Illustrated Magazine for Young Folks* (later *The Leader* 1904), a monthly magazine founded by Hecker and edited in New York by Josephine Hecker (Mrs. George Hecker); its first issue appeared in October 1870.

123

BROWNSON TO HECKER • [c. 12 MARCH 1869]*

[*Undated*][1]

Very Rev. & Dear Father

I am glad you like the article on the Woman Question, the ugliest and most dangerous question that could possibly be raised.

As you take no interest in my articles on the Old & the New, & probably do not wish to publish them, unless to oblige me, will you have the kindness to return them to me? I will make another use of them. I am sorry to put you to so much trouble, but perhaps you will take for old friendship's sake.

I am a little disappointed in having only my short article on Harper in your April number, for I understood you to say when here that you would accept two articles a number from me, one long, & one short one; but I am very glad that you have so many better and abler writers than I.

I proposed to you some two years ago to discuss the subject of Spiritism, but you did not accept the proposal, & the subject has since passed from my mind. It is an unpleasant subject to deal with, and I have no confidence in my ability to treat it to your mind. You allow that it has a good side, I think it bad, Satanic, on all sides. I see in it no mixture of good, & if it strikes a blow at materialism, it introduces that which is worse. Yet, if you say treat it my own way, according to my own mind, I will do it.

What do you say to an article on Professor Huxley's Physical Basis of Life?[2]

I like your idea of an illustrated Magazine for the young folks, but if you want my daughter to write for it, you must write to her & tell her so. I suspect she thinks your folks hardly gave her a fair price for the story she sent you, & she will not accept me as a negotiator. You have raised my pay, but have more than balanced it by the reduction of the number of pages you allow me to write, & she thinks that the Brownsons are not in good odor with you. It is her mistake, but only you can convince her of it. You must tell her what you want her to do, & what you allow her to [e]xpect in return.

Do not forget to return me the Old and the New.

I shall send you a short article, entitled Pope or People,[3] in a few days. My health is only so so, & I am threatened to be attacked as I was a year ago. I hope, however[,] to be able to throw it off in a few days. If I write the article on Spiritism,[4] I shall require time to study up the question afresh.

I do not mean you to understand that I wrote under [any] other restraint than that of being restricted to a very few questions on which I can write freely according to my own mind, & that I had to be on my guard lest I should unwittingly write something not in accordance with your views or policy. I am an old man, & probably approaching my second childhood, & very likely I am oversensitive, as well as silly. But it goes hard with me not to be trusted, & to be regarded by my dearest friend as the world has always regarded [me,] as a man without judgment.

Very truly, your old friend,

O. A. Brownson.

Very Rev. I. T. Hecker. Paulist Convent.

*Microfilm, roll nine (calendared [May 1869]).

1. Dated c. 12 March 1869 because it implies that Brownson was aware of the contents of the April 1869 *CW*, which appeared around the middle of March. It is probable that it was written soon after Hecker's of 8 March (Letter 122) but before Brownson's of 16 March (Letter 124).

2. Thomas Henry Huxley (1825–1895), *New Theory of Life. Identity of the Powers and Faculties of All Living Matter,* noticed in the *New York World,* 18 February 1869.

3. "Pope or People," *CW*, IX (May 1869), 212–21; written in response

to the Boston-based Unitarian paper *The Congregationalist and Boston Recorder*, 4 March 1869.

4. "Spiritism and Spiritists," *CW*, IX (June 1869), 289–302.

124

BROWNSON TO HECKER • 16 MARCH 1869

March 16, 1869.

Rev & dear Father,

Since I wrote you last I have looked over Planchette, & I hasten to say that in the extract from you there appears to be no difference between your views of Spiritism & my own. I was led to think the contrary from what must have been an incorrect report of your lecture of your subject in one of the city papers.

But from what point of view do you wish me to treat the subject? Shall I simply review Sargent's book from the point of view of philosophy or theology, showing the antagonism of Spiritism to Christian faith & morals? Or shall I open the whole subject, & endeavor to show that the order of facts, as far as not juggling or [e]xplicable on natural principle, are of Satanic origin? That is, give you an essay on Satanophany? Or finally shall I discuss it in its bearing on the materialistic philosophy? I do not suppose Spiritism affords us any evidence of the immortality or future [e]xistence of the soul, for the facts do not prove that departed spirits do really communicate with the living, for the pretended spirits may be simply personated by Satan or other fallen angels.

I am willing to treat it from either of these points of view. Which shall I select? Pray communicate to me your wishes.

I repeat my request for the return of the Old & the New.

My health is not good. I am affected as I was a year ago, only then the pain was in the back of my neck, while now it is under my left shoulder blade. I hope, however, that I shall be able to throw it off.

Very truly yours in X

O. A. Brownson.

Very Rev Father Hecker.
Superior of the Paulists.

125

HECKER TO BROWNSON • 18 MARCH 1869*

NY. March 18, 1869.

Dear Dr.

In the matter of Spiritism between us there is no difference of opinion. The thesis—"The order of facts as far as not jugglery or explicable on natural principles, are of satanic origin"—which you suggest, seemed to me the best.

What is real in Spiritism is satanic, and leads finally to either insanity or immorality. Sargeant knows this, but conceals its effects designedly and culpably. Spiritism is the revenge of neglected catholic truth.

"The Woman Question" will be the first in the May number, and the one "Pope & People" is terse, pointed, perfect. This will also appear in the May No.

In reading your letter again, it strikes me as a new and most important point to show that Spiritism does not "afford any evidence of the immortality, or future existance [*sic*] of the Soul." It certainly does not, and yet this is their main stay.

No one can regret more than I do your ill health, & were my prayers answered, your health would be restored, and your life preserved for the glory of God and the advancement of His Holy Church in our land, "ad multos annos". To-morrow is St Joseph's feast, and you will have a special memento in my Mass.

It seems to me Dear Dr. that there is an awakening in the public mind in regard to Catholic Questions, and the Church, that has no precedent in our country. The Catholic question is a live one in almost every thinking mind.

The School question will be brought before the NY. Legislature this winter. A bill[1] will be presented in the Senate this week. Its object is to pave the way for denominational schools. It is broad, & unsectarian, that is, it demands no exclusive privileges for catholics. The future of the Church is involved in our success in this matter. It may take several years to obtain success.

Father Deshon has an article[2] in the April No.—"Comparative morality of Catholic & Protestant Countries."—His first.

My kindest remembrance to your wife & Sarah—with my sincere prayer that God may bless you & them with His choicest gifts & blessings.

faithfully yours

I T Hecker

O. A. Brownson L.L.D.

*Brownson, *BLL*, pp. 520–21 (with omissions).

1. On 26 March 1869 a bill was presented in the New York State Senate by William Marcy Tweed (1823–1878), state senator and head of Tammany Hall, who advocated financial aid to private schools (including Catholic parochial schools) meeting certain enrollment and other requirements.

2. "Comparative Morality of Catholic and Protestant Countries," *CW*, IX (April 1869), 52–62.

126

BROWNSON TO HECKER • 17 MAY 1869

Monday. May 17, 1869.

Dear Father Hecker,

I was quite unwell all last week, but I shall send, D.V. to-morrow an article on Lecky's Morals.[1] I have devoted the article almost [e]xclusively to the preliminary chapters "On the nature & foundation of Morals." I wish to follow it by another,[2] principally on the Conversion of Rome & the triumph of Christianity in the Empire. The author is an able Pagan, & his subject I think will bear two articles.

The article I send to-morrow is short, from ten to twelve pages, probably not over ten. I hope it will be in season for the July Number. I shall see you as soon as I can wear a shoe.

Yours truly & affect.

O. A. Brownson.

1. William Edward Hartpoole Lecky (1838–1903), English historian, scientist, philosopher of history, author of the two-volume *History of European Morals, from Augustus to Charlemagne* (London, 1869). Brownson reviewed the work in "Lecky on Morals," *CW*, IX (July 1869), 529–40.

2. "The Conversion of Rome," *CW*, IX (September 1869), 790–803; reviewing Lecky's *History of the Rise and Influence of the Spirit of Rationalism in Europe* (New York, 1868).

127

HECKER TO BROWNSON • 19 MAY 1869

NY. May 19, 1869

Dear Dr.

I am at home only a few days from a lecturing tour in the East. Two of these my headaches have laid me up.

In the July number the articles on "Spiritualism & Materialialism"[1] & "The Physical Basis"[2] will appear.

The two on Lecky will be most acceptable.

I will send for your notice, or an article, just as you prefer, "Primeval Man" by the Duke of Argyle [*sic*].[3] A small Vol. If an article,—do it at your leisure, if a notice only, by the first of next month if convenient.

Rogers the convert is staying now with us. He intended to call on you on his way to Baltimore but was prevented.

Last evening I received into the Church Dr. Hammond.[4] A couple of weeks ago, a descendant of old General Stark,[5] a graduate of Harvard, by name C. Stark Newell[6]—a lawyer, about 50 years of age, I received him into the Church.

Lecky's Morals has this moment reached me.

I hope that "toe" will come in shape to permit you to make us a visit—all will be glad to see you again.

faithfully

I T Hecker

Dr O. A. Brownson

1. "Spiritualism and Materialism," *CW,* IX (August 1869), 619–34.
2. "The Physical Basis of Life," *CW,* IX (July 1869), 467–76.
3. George Douglas Campbell, *Primeval Man. An Examination of Some Recent Speculations* (New York, 1869).
4. William Alexander Hammond, M.D. (1828–1900), neurologist, author, became surgeon-general of the U.S. Army 1862.
5. John Stark (1728–1822), Revolutionary War general.
6. Charles Stark Newell (1814–1876), graduate of Harvard 1835, lawyer, commissioned major in the Union Army during the Civil War 1862.

128

BROWNSON TO HECKER • 22 MAY 1869

Eliz. May 22, 1869

Very Rev. Father,

Permit me to suggest if it would not be better to insert in the July No. The Physical Basis &c., & Lecky on Morals, & leave Spiritualism &c. for August. Spiritualism & Material[ism] is really only the pendant of the Physical Basis, & I think should come in after it.

The 2d article on Lecky you will receive before the middle of June. The author affords matter for any amount of comment. He is perhaps the ablest representative of his school that we have in English, & the most dangerous.

I shall be glad to receive the Primeval Man, of the Duke of Argyll, & will do my best with it.[1]

The operation on my toe brought back an attack of gout, but I am getting better of that, & hope in a couple of weeks to get to the City, & to see my tailor, for I have no clothes in which I am fit to appear.

The June Number of the C.W. was a very able number. I do not think much of your "English Catholic,"[2] who writes as if [he/she] presumed we Americans were savages with no literary culture. Cesare Cantu[3] is able, but too diffuse. Daybreak[4] has a Catholic body with a non Catholic soul. The author's conversion has reached only the scarf-skin. Yet you have gathered around you a class of able writers, who put my contributions, especially as to style & finish[,] to shame. I feel while reading the articles, "I cannot write like this. Here is a culture & refinement, & a knowledge which I lack." But it is to mend. I am getting decidedly superannuated. My articles all seem to me coarse & tame, with no literary merit at all. Surely I must be getting into my dotage [*?*], or I heretofore [have] been vastly overrated.

Remember me to all the members of the Community, & believe me

Yours truly

O A. Brownson.

Rev. I T. Hecker.

1. "Primeval Man," *CW,* IX (September 1869), 746–56.

2. "Good Old Saxon, by an English Catholic," *CW,* IX (June 1869), 318–22.

3. Cesare Cantù (1807–1895), Italian historian and poet; author of

Storia universale, thirty-five volumes (Turin, 1837–). Cantù's article, "The Supernatural," was translated from the Italian *Rivista Universale* of Genoa, *CW,* IX (June 1869), 325–42.

4. "Daybreak," *CW,* IX (June 1869), 303–17; this article, which appeared in six installments from April through September 1869, was written by Mary Agnes Tincker (1831–1907), novelist, Civil War nurse, Catholic convert c. 1851.

129

HECKER TO BROWNSON • 7 JUNE 1869*

NY. June 7, 1869

Dear Dr.

The suggestions which you made were carried out, & the art. "Spiritualism & Materialism" was laid over for Aug. Two of yours are in the July No.[1]

If you have an article ready or are engaged in one, please let me know, as I am engaged in making up the Aug. number.

Your high opinion of the writer[s] of the C.W. surprises me, no less than that of several others which I have heard from good judges. There must be something in it. But your opinion of your own articles is not just—if I be any judge you never wrote more finished articles than those on the Woman Question & Spiritism. The first took me quite by surprise—its gentle tone and polish did not at all abate your usual strength. The ABp.[2] of N.Y. expressed his complete satisfaction with these articles, and said you never had written better. He is not alone in this opinion.

I have daily expected your visit, & should have written earlier, & would have done so, but for my absence in Philadelphia.[3]

We shall all be glad to see you and the earlier the gladder we shall be.

You have heard that I have received Dr Hammond into the Church.

My kindest regards to your family.

faithfully yours

I T Hecker

O. A. Brownson. L.L.D.

*Brownson, *BLL*, p. 521 (with omissions).

1. "Physical Basis of Life" (pp. 467–76) and "Lecky on Morals" (pp. 529–40).

2. John McCloskey.

3. Hecker was engaged in a lecture tour.

130

BROWNSON TO HECKER • 9 JUNE 1869

Wednesday. June 9, 1869

Rev & dear Father,

I sent with the returned proof of the Article Lecky on Morals, the article I promised on The Conversion of Rome, which I hope is not lost. I am preparing a brief article on Primeval Man, which I will send you in the course of next week. It will not exceed 8 or 10 pages.

I want to write a third article on Lecky,[1] if agreeable to you, defending Christian Morals from Constantine to Charlemagne, that is, during the barbarous ages.

The article on the Duke of Argyll's work,[2] I intend to go along with one of the longer articles you have in hand. You would [have] had [it] before this but for my illness. I hope to be able to see you in a couple of weeks or so. My toe is recovering, slowly.

I thank you for the flattering opinion you [e]xpress of my articles, yet in smoothness, fluency, & finish I hold them below most of your writers. They seem to me, also, to be wanting in freshness, vividness, energy, & true eloquence. I think they mediate something of old age. I need to get out & see folks, & to renew my broken connections with the literary world of to-day. I live without seeing any body with whom I can interchange thought, and the last time I heard Mass was in your Church.[3] Twice only in nearly two years have I received Holy Communion, & then only in my own house. I hope that I soon shall be able to go to Church.

Write to let me know if the second article on Lecky[4] came safe to hand.

My affectionate regards to your whole conventual family, & believe me

Yours truly

O. A. Brownson

*Microfilm, roll nine (calendared 9 January 1869).

1. Intended as a sequel to "Lecky on Morals" and "The Conversion of Rome" but never published.

2. "Primeval Man," *CW*, IX (September 1869), 746–56.

3. The Church of St. Paul the Apostle, West Fifty-ninth Street at Columbus Avenue, New York City, was opened in 1859 and twice enlarged, in 1861 and 1865. The present edifice was opened in 1885.

4. "The Conversion of Rome" (see Letter 126, n. 2).

131

HECKER TO BROWNSON • 18 JUNE 1869*

NY. June 18. 1869

Dear Dr.

With this note you will receive the July No. of Putnam which contains an article entitled "Our Established Church."[1] The ArchBishop of N.Y.[2] has made corrections etc. on the margin,—that is he promised me he would.

I send also an art. from the Journal of Commerce, & one from the Express on one of the points—the school question.

To-morrow or Monday I will send comparative statistics from the State, and the City, of grants received by protestants and catholics.[3]

You would be aiding the good cause and doing me a favour by writing an article[4] for the Aug. No. of the C.W. in reply to the Putnam.

The ABp. remarked that you were the one to write the art. and said, he liked your way of treating the School question. The common Schools were a pet of the American people, & it was not good policy, to run a tilt against them.

He also suggested leaving out entirely the point of political offices. Let those whom this concerns attend to that.

Could the article be got ready by the first of July, it would serve us well.

These fellows have been fattening on public pap, & the moment a spoonful is put in our mouths, they cry out: "Church & State!".

It is a fixed fact, my going to the Council.[5] The Bishop[6] of Columbus, Ohio, has appointed me his procurator,[7] which will rank me with the Episcopate in the Council.

I hope your health is improving.

Kindest regards to your family.

faithfully yours

I T Hecker

O. A. Brownson L.L.D.

*Brownson, *BLL*, pp. 518–19 (dated 8 June 1869, with omissions).

1. "Our Established Church," *Putnam's Monthly Magazine,* n.s., IX (July 1869), 39–52. This article contended that the Roman Catholic Church would become the established church in New York if it received subsidies from the state (see Letter 125, n. 1).

2. John McCloskey.

3. *Putnam's* article (n. 1 above) contained such data.

4. "Our Established Church," *CW,* IX (August 1869), 577–87.

5. Hecker departed for the First Vatican Council (1869–70) at Rome in October 1869 and returned in June 1870.

6. Sylvester Horton Rosecrans (1827–1878), Catholic convert 1845, ordained priest 1853 and consecrated bishop 1862, became first bishop of Columbus, Ohio 1868.

7. In canon law a procurator is an agent who has been delegated by another to handle his affairs in juridical matters such as attending councils.

132

HECKER TO BROWNSON • [19 JUNE 1869]*

Sat. 19th[1]

Dear Dr

I tried to get the Documents[2] & have not succeeded as yet. I am promised them on tuesday. Perhaps on Monday.

The ABp. has not notated as explicitly as I expected. He said he marks some as exaggerations.

The articles received are those in the July & the proof of the one for Aug., which you have read. None other.

faithfully yours,

I. T. Hecker

*Mircofilm, roll five (calendared [186?] Sat. 19).

1. Though the month and year are not given, this letter is most feasibly dated 19 June 1869 since it was a Saturday, and the letter's contents are obviously a follow-up to Hecker's of 18 June 1869 (Letter 131).

2. The documents mentioned in Letter 131.

133

HECKER TO BROWNSON • 29 JUNE 1869

N.Y. June 29, 1869

Dear Dr

Next Sunday we celebrate the festival[1] of our Patron, St Paul. The Abp.[2] assists at the Mass, and dines with us. Dr Hammond[3] will also dine with us.

You will give us all a great pleasure if you will come and pass the day in our house and be our guest.

faithfully yours

I T Hecker.

O. A. Brownson L.L.D.

1. In the Western Church the principal feast of St. Paul occurs with that of St. Peter; the feast of Sts. Peter and Paul is 29 June. It seems that the Paulists were planning a special celebration on Sunday 4 July 1869.
2. John McCloskey.
3. William A. Hammond, M.D., a convert.

134

BROWNSON TO HECKER • 26 JULY 1869

Eliz. July 26, 1869

Very Rev. & Dear Father,

I enclose you a brief correction of the misstatement[1] in my article on Spiritualism & Materialism,[2] which I wish you to insert, with such alterations, additions, or retrenchments as you see proper.

I have aimed in the correction to separate the writer as far as possible from the Magazine, & to cast the blame where it belongs. I exceedingly regret my blunder and would have shown more humility, if I had written in my own name. Pray, let me hereafter write in the first person singular, except where to do so would be improper, both for you & me.

I am writing the anti dualistic essay we agreed on, under the title "An

Imaginary Contradiction.["][3] By the way, I sent you the Article on The Primeval Man. I think it is due me, seeing the doctrine is mine rather than his, that you should insert it before you insert any thing on the same subject[4] from your Philadelphia friend.[5] I beg you to scan my article closely, for, if I am not mistaken, it contains systematic views not generally received, placing progress in the second cycle,[6] & holding it to be by virtue of the moral law instead of the natural law is a novelty, & has considerable reach, & I should be sorry to entrap you with publishing views which may not be in accordance with your own mind. You will perceive that I am working a lead that runs deep into the earth. While I reject traditionalism,[7] I hold man is under a supernatural Providence, & is always more or less than nature. Look closely after me.

Yours truly

O. A Brownson

Ver. Rev. Father Hecker.

1. "Correction of a Mistake," *CW*, IX (September 1869), 855. See Brownson to A. F. Hewit, 22 July 1869 (APF); microfilm, roll nine.

2. *CW*, IX (August 1869), 619-34.

3. *CW*, X (October 1869), 1-12; the supposed contradiction, posed by an article entitled "The Spirit of Romanism" in the Cincinnati-based journal *The Christian Quarterly* (July 1869), involved a Catholic's yielding his reason and free will to the teaching authority of the Catholic Church.

4. During this period a three-part article entitled "The Immutability of the Species"–arguing an anti-development thesis–appeared in the *CW*, X (November 1869), 252-67; (December 1869), 332-46; (February 1870), 656-73.

5. Possibly James Keogh, D.D. (1834-1870), Irish-born, Roman-trained priest of the Pittsburgh diocese, theologian and lecturer; moved to Philadelphia and became professor of dogmatic theology at St. Charles Seminary, Overbrook, Pa., 1865-68; first editor of the Philadelphia *Catholic Standard* 1866.

6. Believing all history to be under God's supernatural providence, Brownson insisted that progress was not merely the result of the natural evolution of human nature but depended instead on God's free gift of grace. Thus the "second cycle" (divine grace) presupposed and perfected the "first cycle" (human nature and activity).

7. The fideistic theological doctrine that unaided individual reason cannot know metaphysical, moral, and religious truths with certitude. Such truths were made known to the human race through a primitive revelation and then communicated through tradition, which is safeguarded by the authority of the Roman Catholic Church.

135

HECKER TO BROWNSON • 21 AUGUST [1869]

NY Aug. 21.[1]

Dear Dr.

Have you an article in preparation?

There is a regret that springs up in my mind in reading your articles, and that is, the apparent estimation of them is so far below their real value. However this may be there are those who do appreciate them now, and a larger number will appreciate them in the future.

Every day the C.W. is exerting a wider and more important influence on a large class of minds. It would baffle me to say how my time and strength as a missionary could be more efficacously [*sic*] and beneficially spent than in the C. World. In this work you are first among those who have the largest share.

Let no doubt enter your mind regarding the good that you are doing with your pen.

Nothing worth while has come to hand suitable to your pen, or you would have heard from me sooner. Have you received the pamphlet[2] giving an account of "The Free Religious Association"[3] in Boston last May? Perhaps that might give you a good subject.[4]

My trip to Lake George[5] has done me a great good, F[ather] Hewit who is now there, says the same.

Were there any chance of my getting off, I would come to see you. We are only two priests at home.

Kindest Regards to your Wife & Sarah.

faithfully [y] ours

I. T. Hecker.

1. Even though the year was omitted, it was 1869 because the meeting of the Free Religious Association (see n. 2 below) took place in May of that year, and Brownson's article about that gathering was included in the November number of the *CW* for 1869 (see n. 4 below).

2. *Proceedings at the Second Annual Meeting of the Free Religious Association, held in Boston, May 27th and 28th, 1869* (Boston, 1869).

3. A group comprised mostly of dissatisfied Unitarians and social reformers, the Free Religious Association (1867–97) was organized "to promote the interests of pure religion, to encourage the scientific study of

theology, and to increase fellowship in the spirit." The Association was founded by Octavius B. Frothingham (see Letter 91, n.2) and Francis Ellingwood Abbot (1836–1903), Unitarian clergyman and philosopher, editor of *The Index* 1869–80.

4. "Free Religion," *CW*, X (November 1869), 195–206.

5. The Paulist community maintained a summer home—St. Mary's of the Lake—on French Mountain, Lake George, New York. The tract of land was a gift from Charles O'Conor (1804–1884), Irish-born, prominent Catholic spokesman, New York lawyer and jurist.

136

BROWNSON TO HECKER • 24 AUGUST 1869

Eliz. NJ. Aug 24, 1869.

Very Rev & dear Father,

I sent you yesterday a notice of Beecher's *Norwood,*[1] a rather long article[2] of about 8 or 9 pages.

I am as much opposed as you are to articles continued, but you insist on my making my articles short which is hardly possible! if I am to do justice to the subjects I am discussing. The range of subjects I am at liberty to discuss in your pages, without running athwart your plan, is very limited, and they are subjects which it is impossible for me to treat in a light & superficial manner, if I would. I am not and cannot be what is called a popular writer, and you must take me for what I am, or not take me at all.

In every article I write for you, I do my best within your boundaries. They are toned down, I admit, and somewhat tame, for if I ventured to write in a higher key, and to give further play to my natural tendencies, & study to make them more animated & interesting, I should most likely say something that would jar on the mild & conciliatory tone of the Magazine; I cannot let my hand, except in particular subjects, run in its natural channels, & am obliged to suppress all visaging[?] and all feeling. If you permitted me to write in the first person singular, & under my own name, as I have done all my life, I could write for more body & serve you better, or evise[?] under a *nom de plume*.

But I think even my dull and heavy articles are of service to the C.W. They add to its character for solidity & thoroughness, and help give it weight with the public.

I had intended to give you another article on Lecky, and you told me to do so, but after your letter I cannot without a renewal of your permission. I have not seen the pamphlet you refer to.[3] The fault you find with my articles is[,] I suppose[,] that they are too much on the same subject or subjects, & therefore have the appearance of being for the most part only parts of one and the same article. This is to some [e]xtent, no doubt true, but how am I to avoid it? I write with a general philosophical and theological doctrine in my mind, & cannot help discussing all philosophical & theological questions in its light. If you would send popular historical or literary works, novels & the like to review, or not require me to attach my articles to some publication, I could avoid it. But you usually send me works in one particular line. But I have said enough to prove that the operations of my mind are not suited to your purpose as the Editor of a Magazine, and I am too old to undergo a new literary training, or to get out of my old ruts.

I am very glad to learn the C.W. is prospering, doing great good, & very thankful for the rank, so far above my merits[,] which you assign me among those engaged in the good work. You have forty or fifty better Magazine writers than I, who have a grace, a vivacity, a finish of style that I cannot aspire to, & who can tell their whole thought on a subject in a single article, in other words, who can restrict their purpose to what they are able to effect in a single article. Alas for me, the writing of an article suggests matter for a dozen articles, & is only the least part of my thought that I seem able to get into a single article. It is a deplorable defect in a Magazine writer.

I have now no article in preparation, and no subject on which I dare write, for any subject which I should venture to take up would be kindred to those I have already discussed. Your letter, which is very kind, very appreciative, & intended to encourage me has had the effect [of] discouraging me, & making me despair, [e]xcept by accident, of ever being able to satisfy the Editor of the C.W. If you want an article from me, send me the subject, & tell me how you want it treated.

Forgive me for boring you with so long a letter, & believe me as always,

Yours truly

O. A. Brownson.

Very Rev I. T. Hecker.
Superior of the Paulists.
Paulist Convent 59th Street
New York.

1. *Norwood; or Village Life in New England* (New York, 1868) by Henry Ward Beecher (1813–1887), prominent Congregationalist preacher, theologian, and author; pastor of the Plymouth Church in Brooklyn, N.Y.

2. "Beecher's Norwood," *CW*, X (December 1869), 393–401.

3. On the meetings of the Free Religious Association; see Letter 135, n. 2.

137

HECKER TO BROWNSON • 26 AUGUST 1869*

Aug 26, 1869

My Dear Dr.

My last note was a blunder. Yours of the 24th shows me clearly that I failed entirely in communicating my thought. My intention was to express to you what I have done by word of mouth on many occassions [*sic*], my most sincere appreciation of the value and high importance of the contributions of your pen. Any other thought than this was not present to my mind.

The second article on Lecky I shall be glad to receive. The pamphlet on the "Free Religious Association" I will send with this mail.

You will find a passage in Emerson's speech[1] which I have marked. He professes to find a contradiction between "the without" and "the within" —an imaginary one—as between faith and science, or revelation and reason. I had marked this on reading the pamphlet.

The making of articles in the C.W. personal, would involve a change, which at present at least, does not seem to me advisable.

Believe me yours

faithfully

I T Hecker.

O. A. Brownson. L.L.D.

*Brownson, *BLL*, pp. 521–22.

1. Ralph Waldo Emerson's "Speech at the Second Annual Meeting of the Free Religious Association, at Tremont Temple, Friday, May 28, 1869." Brownson quoted from this address in his article, "Free Religion," *CW*, X (November 1869), 198–99.

138

HECKER TO BROWNSON • 18 OCTOBER 1869

NY Oct 18, 1869

Dear Dr

The cars on my return from Baltimore were behind time five hours, and this hindered my stopping and making you a visit.

On the 20th I leave,[1] and till then I have hardly the time to say my soul is my own.

Whatever in regard to articles or books for your pen, occurs to me when abroad, I will communicate to you.

My Kindest Regards to Mrs Brownson & Sarah.

Yours ever faithfully

I T Hecker

O. A. Brownson L.L.D.

1. For the First Council of the Vatican in Rome.

139

HECKER TO BROWNSON • 30 JANUARY 1870*

Rome, Jan. 30th, 1870[1]
Piazza di Spagna 9

My Dear Dr.

Nothing is more surprising to an American, than the increased interest and appreciation of men of all schools and parties in Europe, of the principles of our free institutions & the state of things existing in our country. They are becoming aware of the fact, that the light to be derived from our experience, would remove serious difficulties existing in their own and many other minds in Europe. At this moment, no greater service can be rendered, than to give to Europe, the explanation of the relations of the Church to our free institutions.

You have in your article on "Church and State" C.W. April 1867 treated this subject, and touched upon it again in "Rome and the World". But do not hesitate to repeat what you have said, for the attention of Europe is especially directed now to the subject[,] and what you will write, will find a fresher and fuller appreciation.

The principal aim of the article[2] *should be to enlighten*, its advice put in the form of suggestion, and its entire tone moderate. The existance [*sic*] of the Vatican Council should not be mentioned.

I regret not being able to see you and having a talk on the subject. To supply the place of this on my part, I have penned down some thoughts for your perusal, and which are intended only as suggestions.

The present condition of things in Europe is not unlike that of the 16th century. The discoveries and other important events at that epoch created a desire for amelioration and reforms in society & the Church. The impatience for reforms in the Church was the occasion of a deplorable separation and heresy. Recent discoveries and a more general education has given rise in different populations in our day to the demand for changes in matters both political & religious.

In political matters

It is evident that among other causes, the existing success in political self-government in the U.S., exerts a great influence on the entire populations of Europe. From this has arisen the demand on their part, of a larger share of action in the direction of the interests and destiny of their own countries. If concessions of this kind be not granted, the nations of Europe run a great risk as in 1789 and 1848 and 9, to be overthrown by revolutions.

England has taken the lead in this direction, & has prudently enlarged the basis of political suffrage; Napoleon[3] has followed suit, and retained his imperial crown by changing the government of France from absoluteism [*sic*] to constitutional monarchy. Italy and Spain have made changes but too sudden and too sweepingly to last; Austria has acted with her wonted caution, & Prussia, despotic as she is, cannot maintain herself against the inevitable. If she pushes repression too far, a Republic will be proclaimed as in 1849, over her head.

It is therefore the dictate of political wisdom in the present crisis in Europe, to prevent revolutions by a wise concession of greater political power to the people. If capable, why should not the people have a larger share in the direction of the destiny of their own country?

This extension of political power to the people, is in no way hostile to the spirit and dogmas of the Catholic Religion. For the more the responsibility in the direction of a nation is shared by those who compose it, provided they rightly fulfill its duties, the greater their dignity and merit, & the greater the glory of God.[4] And if Kings derive their right to govern from God through the people, which is the common opinion of Catholic theologians, why should not the people exercise that right in proportion to their ability of self-government?

This concession of greater political power to the people, will call forth fresh zeal in the Church to educate and direct the people in order properly to fulfill their new responsibilities. This will extend her influence, and a new title of gratitude for her services, and show in a new light the absolute necessity of Religion to sustain civil society and good government. For nowhere is the directing or restraining influence of Religion felt to be so necessary as there w[h]ere the people and the Govt. under the external restraints of political power—as in a free government.

Regarding therefore from this point of view the changes which are now taking place in the political governments of Europe, Religion has nothing to fear. If rightly understood, and met on the part of religion with a friendly eye, they may be the providential means of her regaining the good will and the affections of the populations of Europe and renewing her ancient glories on their soil.

In religious matters.

It is also evident that a change between the Church and State in Europe is impending. The union that had existed has been undergoing a change for some time past, and to meet these changes concordats were invented and adopted. As long as the political power was in the hand of the King or a few individuals, and stationary, such arrangements served their purposes. The present changes render them almost a nullity. What the King or Kaiser thinks is no longer the standard of right or wrong for the people; their decisions serve no longer for the basis of political action. Public opinion and the vote of the people is now the practical rule of all political action. The concordats made with [the] Emperor of Austria, the King of Italy and the Queen of Spain are set aside by a power greater than that of the throne. The one made with France needs only a change in the ministry, & which may take place at any moment, to render it of no more value than so much waste paper.

The changes in those relations which have existed in many states in Europe, between the Church and State, whatever may be our opinion, whether we deplore or desire them, are taking place, and further ones are pending. These changes will eventually necessitate the Church to assume her own independance, [*sic*] and throw herself upon the offerings of her children for support.

These changes will be consummated only by overcoming great difficulties and by great sacrifices. But by a willingness to foresee them, and to prepare for them, they may be greatly lessened.

It will demand on the part of the Episcopate and the priesthood a closer following of the Apostolic example of living; a more earnest and direct manner in preaching the Gospel; and this will produce a closer union of sympathy and interests between the priesthood and the people. It will tend to place the foundations of Religion where our Maker intended they should be, on the convictions of each individual soul and on personal sacrifices.

The loss sustained by the Church by the withdrawal of state support, will not be without its compensation. It will leave her her national freedom so necessary to her true existance [*sic*] and advancement. The freedom to choose her own ministers, freed from the control of state dictation. Is not this exemption of state control in a matter of such vital importance to the Church sufficient to compensate for the many great sacrifices which she will have to make?

Who knows but that the Church[,] no longer confiding in princes, and trusting to Him who alone is her great strength and support, her life will be renewed, her influence extended over all Europe, and in a near future, Europe will be reconstructed on a basis more in harmony with the principles of Christianity.

For Europe is now engaged in the act of a partial and temporary separation of the union between Church and State, a form of union inherited from a time when the state of things and the conditions of society, where [*sic*] quite different from those which now exist. This partial and temporary separation is precedent and necessary to a transition to a more perfect union. For scarcely anyone who has made this subject a serious study, will pretend that an entire separation of Church and State can be maintained[,] were it possible, as the normal and more perfect condition of society. It is a truth established by the best of ancient and modern writers of all schools, on the philosophy of political governments, that religion is the basis of all society, and its dogmas the foundation of political principles. Sooner or later an intelligent people must recognize this connection, conform their political legislation accordingly, and thus bring about naturally an union between the Church and the State.

Of the ability of the Church to maintain herself independently of her connection[,] without support* from the state while Europe is passing through this crisis of transition, no one can entertain a doubt, unless he is prepared to affirm the decadence of the nations of Europe[,] like those of Africa and Asia, and shuts his eyes to the light of the example of the Church in Ireland, England, Prussia, Australia, and above all, that of the United States of America. (*Not to be [mis]understood by our readers, when we speak of the support which the Church derives from the State, it should be known, that this support is but a very small part of the restitution which the State owes to the Church for the property unjustly taken from her during the revolutions in 1789 in Europe.)

In our own country, where the Church exists in her entire independance [*sic*] from State control, yet all her rights acknowledged and protected by the laws of the country, where her right to hold property, of establishing colleges, schools, charitable associations, etc. and to govern and administer her affairs according to her own laws and customs; it is here she is putting forth an energy and making conquests which vie with the zeal & success of the early ages of Christianity.

So strong were the Irish hierarchy in the conscious[ness] of the ability of the Church to triumph in her own strength, and maintain herself by the voluntary offerings of the faithful, that when the English government recently offered to grant to the Church State support, they rejected it unanimously. In both Ireland and England, as the State abolishes its oppressive and august laws, the Church in the might of her own power, recovers herself, and bids fair to regain her lost supremacy.

In Belgium and Switzerland, where the separation is only partial, as Catholics learn that the price of faith is constant vigilance, action, and self-sacrifice, they will conquer opposition, assert their rights, and exercise their legitimate influence in making the laws and in the direction of the State. A lesson which it appears they have been slow in learning, being as it were the first nations to be placed in this new position. This lesson however, once learned, they will stand forth as an example to the Catholics of surrounding nations and to future Europe.

Conclusion

Thus by timely opening this door to a larger share of political power to the people, by wisely accepting the changes of the relations between the Church and State, two of the greatest evils that can befall the Church and State can be avoided, namely revolution and apostasy. This at the same time will make a transition possible and open up to both Church and State a new career and a brighter future.

There Dear Dr. I have penned down my thoughts, and I repeat they have been written with the simple intention of expressing views which would have been expressed with you in conversation.

In what you have formerly written you have always been cautious in giving it to be understood that our understanding of the liberty of the Church is not what the radicals of Europe understand by it. This distinction is necessary, not to be misunderstood and misinterpreted. Please make it in your article.

This letter will reach you about the 20th of this month. Could you get your article ready for the April number, it would render great service. Please drop a line to F. Hewit and inform him whether it be possible.

Monseigneur Mermillod[5] of Geneva has just called to make me a visit. I gave him the two articles[6] on Abbé Martin's[7] book,[8] which he will send to him. He agrees with your criticism that protestantism as such will cease to exist. He said he had written to the author that in this he was inexact in his letter of approbation.

Of matters concerning the Council my mouth is of course shut. Some of the schema which were previously proposed are now under discussion. No one can conjecture what will be accepted or what rejected. The question of infallibility at present, is quiet.

The article I have proposed to you is one in my judgment of great importance, and your pen is the one to write it. Should you however, from ill health or any other cause not be able to write it, please send these notes as early as possible to F. Hewit.

My kindest regards to Mrs. Brownson and Sarah.

Ever yours faithfully

I. T. Hecker

*HP, APF; omitted from microfilm.

1. This letter was enclosed in a letter from Hecker to Hewit, 2 February 1870 (APF). The following pencil notation occurs at the top of this letter: "The article [see n. 2 below] cannot go into the Apr. No. A[ugustine] F[rancis] H[ewit]."

2. "Church and State," *CW*, XI (May 1870), 145–60.

3. Napoleon III, Louis Napoleon Bonaparte (1808–1873), Emperor of France 1852–70.

4. Another pencil notation by Hewit occurs here: "I dissent from this. A. F. H."

5. Gaspard Mermillod (1824–1892), Swiss author, leader in Catholic education and social movements, auxiliary bishop of Lausanne for Geneva 1864, named cardinal 1890.

6. "The Future of Protestantism and Catholicity," *CW*, X (January 1870), 433–48 and ibid. (February 1870), pp. 577–89.

7. Abbé François Martin (1814–1877), French priest at Ceyzériat, author and historian.

8. *De l'avenir de protestantisme et du catholicisme* (Paris, 1869).

139 Draft

HECKER TO BROWNSON • [30 JANUARY 1870]*

[*Undated*] [1]

THE PRESENT CONDITION OF THE CHURCH & STATE IN EUROPE– 1870

My Dear Dr.

It seems to me that an article[2] from your pen on the present general aspect of things in Europe would be of great service to the true interests of the Church. From our point of view, from experience in the U.S., we can shed light on their actual difficulties political & religious in Europe, which will aid in their peaceable solution, and greatly assist the Church in passing through this crisis of transition.

For the convenience of conveying some of my thoughts on the subject, I will divide the problems of Europe in two points:

1st political. It is evident that the success already obtained in political self-government in the United States exerts a great influence at the present on the whole people of all Europe. Creating a demand of a larger share of action in the direction of the destiny of their own country. This demand must be satisfied by concession of greater political action to the people[,] or Revolution. England has taken the lead in enlarging the basis of suffrage. Napoleon the third has preserved his crown only by recent concessions. Austria, Prussia, Italy, Spain, etc. will have to follow.

The dictates of political wisdom in Europe consist in preventing revolution by a wise concession of political action to the people. The preparation of the people to use concessions made, to the advancement of the general well being is the work of the Church. The extension of political liberty is not in any way necessarily hostile to Religion. On the contrary, the more the responsibility is shared and rightly fulfilled by the individuals comprising a nation, the greater the glory to God & merit to the individual. Intellig[ence] & liberty are necessary to every act of virtue. If kings derive their right to govern through the people, why should not the people exercise their rights in proportion to their ability to govern themselves? This extension will necessarily call out fresh energy of the Church in instructing the people to fulfill properly their new duties. Giving to her wider influence, and adding a new title of gratitude for her services, and showing in a new form the necessity of Religion. For as countries become less dependent on the authority of Kings in directing their destiny, the more the people have need of virtue and personal direction from on High. It is the office of Religion to supply this.

Regarding therefore this political change that is inevitable in Europe, & which has already taken its start, the Church has nothing to fear, but if rightly understood and in due season, and regarded with no unfriendly eye, the government may be the providential means of her regain[ing] the good will & affection of the people of Europe & renewing their ancient glories on their soil.

Religious. It is no less evident that a change between the Church relations and the State is becoming inevitable in Europe. The perfect union that heretofore existed was no longer possible, and to modify their relations concordats were invented and adopted. As long as the government of the Nation was in the hands of the King or a few individuals, such arrangements served their purpose. The political changes of to-day render them a nullity. The question is no longer, as at other times, what does the Kaiser or King think, as a sufficient reason; or his decision as the rule of right or wrong; the question is what is the public opinion, the vote of the people. The people in one way or another begin to make their opinions and convictions the ruling power, and Kings & Emperors to hold their crowns must obey them. Hence the concordats made with crowned heads, such as the Emperor of Austria [,] are set aside by a power greater than his own, & on which it depends. Those made with Italy and Spain either has ceased or soon will do so. The one with France needs only a change in the Ministry to render it of no more worth than so much waste paper.

The separation of that relation of the Ch. with the State, which has hitherto existed in Europe among some nations, is inevitable, what ever may be our opinion about its necessity, or the desirableness, or the contrary.

The Church will necessarily, by this change, be called upon to assume her independence, and look for her chief support to the voluntary offerings of her faithful children.

A change of this kind will undoubtedly be effected by no little difficulty and great sacrifices. But by a willingness to foresee this difficulty and to make preparations for the event, these may be greatly lessened.

It will demand on the part of the priesthood and Episcopate a return to a closer following of the Apostolic example of living. A more earnest and direct manner of preaching the Gospel. A closer union of the priesthood & people. A greater freedom of action in following the authority of the Church and in keeping those laws which she regards as necessary to the salvation and well being of her children. It will place more completely the lines of religion in the position of the early times of Xty, in the conviction of each individual soul and with personal sacrifice.

The losses sustained by the Church by this separation, will be not without some compensation. It will have to [give] to her that freedom which is so necessary to her existance [*sic*] & progress. The freedom to choose her own ministers without the control of political authority. Is not the example of state control alone sufficient to compensate for making great sacrifices?

Who knows but that the Church[,] and once more depending on Him alone who is her strength, & withdrawing her confidence also from princes, may be the means under Providence of renewing her life in Europe, and extend her influence over the people of Europe, and bring about its reconstruction on a basis more perfect, more in harmony with the true principles of Christianity than that established in the middle ages?

Of her ability to meet the present religious crisis, by standing on her own strength & self-support, no one can entertain a doubt, unless one who gives up European peoples as inevitably lost to the Church as nations, and shuts his eyes to the light of the example of Ireland, England, the United States, Belgium and Australia.

In the U.S. where the independence of the Church is recognized, and most complete, there in the midst of opposing sects, she is putting forth an energy and making conquests which vie with the conquests of the Church in the early ages of Christianity.

In Ireland and England as the oppressive state laws are abolished by her own strength she recovers, and bids fair to recover her position by the zeal and voluntary offerings of the faithful.

In Australia the Church is in her infancy, but shows already that the faith of the Ch. has lost none of its early power by being transported to the antipodes.

In Belgium, as the catholics begin to learn that the price of faith is vigilance, action, and sacrifice, they will vanquish infidelity and opposition, and assert their rights and exercise their legitimate power in the direction of the State. A lesson tho slow in learning, being as they were the first on the continent to be placed in this new position, now learned they will be an example to all catholics of future Europe.

By opening the doors to a larger share of political power to the people, by accepting the changes of the relations of the Church and State, two [of] the greatest evils which can befall the State & the Church, Revolution and Apostasy[,] will be avoided, & a new career, and a brighter future [will] be opened up to the State and to Religion.

The light to be derived from the position of the Church in our Republic, its entire independance [*sic*] of State control and freedom to do her work, and the protection of her rights etc. would remove the difficulties existing in many minds in Europe. You have in your article on Ch. & State—April 1867—C.W. treated this subject, and also touched upon it in Rome & the World. Do not hesitate to repeat what you have already said, for as the attention of Europe is now especially directed to it, & what you say will find a fresh appreciation.

Nothing is more surprising than the increased attention and appreciation in Europe & from men of all schools and parties, of the principles and state of things existing in the U.S. At this moment no greater service can be rendered them than to give to Europe the light of our experiences, and the explanation of the condition of the Church in her relation to our Institutions. You have the thesis in your article on "Church & State."[3]

The aim of the article should be to enlighten, its advice only suggestive, and its tone moderate.

I regret not being able to see [you] and having a talk on the subject. I have penned down some of my thoughts for your inspection to supply the place of a conversation, which are only intended as suggestions.

Scarcely anyone who has made the study one of serious study will pretend that separation of Church and State can be maintained as the normal and more perfect condition of Society. Religious dogmas are the basis of political principles whether we recognize the fact or no and sooner or later an intelligent people will see they harmonize, and seek a union. Europe is now in the act of a temporary separation, (Ignore the continuing of the Vatican—make no mention of it) from a form of union inherited from a quite different state of things [then] existent. This partial separation is necessary to a transition to a more perfect union, for altho we cannot help seeing that a change of the relations of between Church & State is taking place throughout Europe and which will likely end in the entire independance [*sic*] of the Church.

The present condition of things in Europe is not unlike that of the 16th century. The discoveries made then, in printing, of America, and navigation etc. the renewal of classic literature etc. created a desire for amelioration and reforms both in Society and the Church. The impatience for reform in the Church caused a deplorable separation and heresy. The Council of Trent, tho it made all the changes and reforms which were found necessary, was not able to heal the wound which had been made by the separation, and which we have still to deplore.

Fortunately for our time, the Vatican Council by the inspiration of the Holy Ghost and the wisdom of the Sovereign Pontiff, has been called in time to meet the emergencies of our epoch. For the new discoveries of steam and its application to machinery, to steamboats & railroads; of the application of electricity to telegraphic communications; the diffusion of education and the press; has caused in different populations the desire for change and reform in matters political & religious.

In political matters

It is evident that the obtained success in political self-government in the

U.S. exerts a great influence on the entire population of Europe. This has created a demand on the part of the population of each country [for] a larger share of action in the direction of the interests and destiny of their own country. Either this demand must be satisfied, or the nations of Europe will again as in 1798 [*sic*], and in 1849, be overthrown by revolutions.

England has taken the lead in this direction of enlarging the basis of political suffrage; Napoleon has followed suit and retained his imperial crown by changing from absolutism to a constitutional government; Austria, Prussia, Italy (how much too sudden!) and Spain will be compelled to follow unless they would have a Republic proclaimed over their heads.

It is therefore the dictate of political wisdom[,] in the present crisis in Europe, to prevent revolutions by a wise conception of a larger field of political action to the people in the direction of the interests and destiny of their own country.

It is the work of the Church to prepare the people for a wise use of these concessions in order that the new power may be directed to the well being of the nation. For the extension of political suffrage and places of power to the people is in no way hostile to the dogmas of the Catholic Religion. On the contrary, the more the responsibility is shared by the individuals who compose a nation, in its direction, the greater their merit and the greater the glory of God. Intelligence & liberty are the conditions of the right use of all power, as well as the conditions of all acts of virtue.

And if Kings derive their right to govern from God through the people, why should not the people exercise that right in proportion to their ability to govern themselves?

This concession, will necessarily call forth from the Church a fresh zeal to instruct the people to fulfill properly their new responsibilities. Thus giving an extension to her influence, adding a new title of gratitude for her services, and showing a new light the absolute necessity of Religion for civil society & good government, for nowhere is the voluntary government and influence of Religion felt to be so necessary as there where the people are the best under the restraints of political power.

Dear Dr.[4] An article on the present aspect of things in Europe from your pen would throw light on some difficulties existing in the minds of many persons. The light to be derived from the position of the Church in our country, would be, if properly presented, of great value.

*HP, APF; omitted from microfilm.

1. This undated draft is an interesting variant of Hecker's letter of 30 January 1870.

2. *CW*, XI (May 1870), 145–60.

3. The following erasure occurs here: "But we should not find nothing to disagree about. The tone of the article should be moderate, its character suggestive, and its aim to enlighten."

4. This erasure occurs here: "I have put down on paper a few thoughts for yr perusal in view of your writing an [article . . .]."

140

HECKER TO BROWNSON • 4 FEBRUARY 1870*

Rome Feb. 4, 1870

Dear Dr.

I send by mail Caesare Cantu's article on "Chiesa e Stato,"[1] which may serve, if you choose, as a basis for the Article[2] on Church and State, which I suggested for your pen.

Should you not have received my letter on this subject, which was sent by Bp. Bacon[3] who returned a few days ago to his diocese, you will in a day or two as he said he would go directly to NY. by way of Havre on the first steamer.

Caesare Cantu stands high in the esteem of the Pope and all sound Catholics of all parties. I formed his acquaintance here, he resides in Milan, and has returned home.

The Council is in the via purgativa of discussion, and from appearances it will be some time before it will enter upon the via illuminativa.

"L'homme se meut, mais Dieu regit"[4] are the words of Bossuet,[5] & applicable to men in the Council even with more force than men without.

Light will come, and action will follow in due season.

I trust you will write the article suggested. You shall be remembered at the altar for help from above from today forward. Your pen and experience make it a duty.

[*no signature*]

O. A. Brownson L.L.D.

*Brownson, *BLL,* p. 522 (with omissions).

1. *Chiesa e Stato . . . , dall Rivista Universale* 1867.

2. "Church and State," *CW,* XI (May 1870), 145–60.

3. David William Bacon (1813–1874), ordained priest 1838, became first bishop of Portland, Maine, 1855.

4. Best rendered as "Man proposes, but God disposes."

5. Jacques-Bénigne Bossuet (1627–1704), French Catholic author and eminent orator, literary apologist, bishop of Meaux 1682.

141

HECKER TO BROWNSON • 15 JULY 1870*

NY. July 15, 1870

Dear Dr.

I send the Mercersburg Review[1] –with a [*illegible*][2] "Where is the Church?"[3] and told Mr Kehoe to obtain the other[4] noticed in the article "Union with the Church".[5]

An article on the subject of *Union with the Church*[6] would come apropos of the meeting of the Holy Alliance[7] in this City in September. The article would appear in the October Number.

I hope that your health is improving, mine has been remarkably good since my return.

With Kindest Regards to Mrs Brownson and Sarah, believe me

Yours faithfully

I T Hecker.

*Brownson, *BLL*, p. 538 (with omissions).

1. *The Mercersburg Review*, a quarterly theological journal founded in 1849 at the German Reformed seminary at Mercersburg, Pa., by its first editor John Williamson Nevin (1803–1886), who together with Philip Schaff (1819–1893) promoted therein the Mercersburg Movement.

2. Henry F. Brownson renders this illegible text as "leader" (*BLL*, p. 538).

3. *Where Is the City?*, second edition (Boston, 1868).

4. Henry Harbaugh, D.D. (1817–1867), *Union With the Church the Solemn Duty and Blessed Privilege of all who would be saved*, 4th ed., revised (Philadelphia, 1867).

5. "Union With the Church," *The Mercersburg Review*, n.s., July 1870, pp. 373–401.

6. "Union With the Church," *CW*, XII (October 1870), 1–16.

7. A group of Christian European monarchs formed in 1815 by Tsar Alexander I of Russia for the purpose of infusing politics with a religious dimension and to urge monarchs to rule as Christians.

142

BROWNSON TO HECKER • 25 AUGUST 1870

Elizabeth Aug. 25, 1870

Dear Father Hecker

I send an article[1] on the Great Commission by Dr. Harris,[2] a book sent me by Kehoe. There is nothing very orig[inal] in the article, but I think it proves that Protestants have no commission, no authority, & no ability or capacity to evangelize the world, & that no one is bound or has the right to listen to their preachers. My aim has been, without any defense of Catholicity, to turn the arguments Protestants use against themselves, and show that their charges against her and their boasts over her prove conclusively that "they are of the world, speak of the world, & the world heareth them."[3]

My belief is that we should attack rather than defend, or rather, that we should defend the Church by attacking and disproving the pretensions of her enemies. They never heed what we say in our own defense, or heed it only to misrepresent it.

If you have something more for me to do, pray inform me, for till we can meet and prepare notes I am uncertain alike of your present position on the range of topics you will permit to be discussed in the C.W. In a word, I do not know your present purpose or how far we are in perfect sympathy. For myself, I neither indulge the hopes nor cherish the tendencies I did some six or eight years ago. I am really once more an old fogie in my views and sympathies. I defend the republican form of government for our country, because it is the legal & only practicable form, but I no longer hope anything from it. Catholicity is theoretically compatible with democracy, as you and I would [e]xplain democracy, but practically, there is, in my judgment, no compatibility between them. According to Catholicity all power comes from above and descends from high to low; according to democracy all power is infernal, is from below, and ascends from low to high. This is democracy in its practical sense, as politicians & the people do & will understand it. Catholicity & it are as mutually antagonistic as the spirit & the flesh, the Church and the World, Christ & Satan.

Instead of regarding the Church as having advantages here which she has nowhere else, I think she has here a more subtle and powerful enemy to combat than in any of the old monarchical nations of the world. Say what we will, we have made little impression on our old American population, & what we have made we owe to the conviction that [the] Church sustains authority, demands government, is anti-radical, anti-democratic. There is every a subtle influence at work, which undermines the authority alike of the parent & of the magistrate, with Catholics as well as with non-Catholics. Catholics as well as others imbibe the spirit of the country, imbibe from infancy the spirit of independence, freedom from all restraint, unbounded license. So far are we from converting the country, we cannot hold our own. And the most lawless & rowdyish and even criminal portions of the population are Catholics or their offspring, who make saints of the Florence Scandals,[4] and martyrs of the Riels.[5] The scandal is fearful. See not where are we to look for a remedy: We cannot keep our Catholics, either in faith or practice, even under evidence they nominally [show] they adhere to the Church, go to confession, & receive Holy Communion.

I have no idea that one Catholic in twenty believes of the Catholic laity the recent decree of the Council,[6] or that one in a thousand of them is prepared to accept the Schema de Ecclesia,[7] which only embodies the doctrine of the Syllabus.[8] How many Catholics can you find born & brought up in the country that do in reality hold the Church to be higher than the people, or who do not consider her voice authoritative only when it coincides with that of the people?

These considerations make me feel that the whole influence of democratic ideas & tendencies is directly antagonistic to Catholicity. I think the Church has never encountered a social & political order so hostile to her, & that the conversion of our republic will be a far greater victory than the conversion of the Roman Empire. You can see how this convi[c]tion must modify many of the views in which we formerly held in common. I have supposed that you believed, which I do not. I hate it, under any form it can assume in practice, as I do Satan. I do not want to say so publicly, but I do not want to be obliged to maintain [e]xplicitly or implicitly the contrary.

I have defended Catholic education as in duty bound, but I hope little from it, for it will prove impotent against the spirit of the Country. I have heretofore wished to effect a harmony of the American & the Catholic idea, but I believe such harmony impracticable except by sacrificing the Catholic idea to the National.

You see, dear Father, where I stand. Can we work together or can we not. If not it is useless to try; if you think we can, I will do the best I can for the C.W. & cease to grumble. Pray, let me know your view of the matter.

I have seen nothing in the C.W. for a long time that has pleased me so much as your last article on the C[ouncil] of [the] Vatican.[9] Your argument against Gallicanism is conclusive & unanswerable, & remarkable alike for its dignity & vigor. The other articles[10] I have not yet read.

I expect to be in Brooklyn a week from Sunday, but I fear my engagements with [the] Tablet will not permit [me] to visit you. I wish then for you would write me [e]xpressly in answer to my question, or what is better, come & see me. I want, if possible, to identify myself with the C.W. & give it my best thoughts and my best labors, but if that is impossible, I wish to know it, but I trust even in that case our old friendships will remain undiminished.

Yours truly

O A Brownson.

Very Rev Father Hecker.

1. "The Great Commission," *CW,* XII (November 1870), 187–200.

2. John Harris, D.D. (1802–1856), *The Great Commission; or, The Christian Church Constituted and Charged to Convey the Gospel to the World* (Boston, 1870). The first edition was published in 1842.

3. 1 John 4:5.

4. The secret Convention of the Fifteenth of September (1864) in Florence, wherein the Italian statesman Count Camillo di Cavour offered to make Florence instead of Rome the capital of a united Italy if Napoleon III of France would remove from Rome his troops protecting the pope.

5. Louis Riel (1844–1885), Canadian leader of the 1869 Manitoba Insurrection by the *Métis* or "Half-Breeds" (persons of both European and Indian descent).

6. Brownson probably means *Pastor Aeternus* (18 July 1870), the declaration of the doctrine of the primacy and the infallibility of the pope at the First Vatican Council.

7. The *Schema de Ecclesia* was not promulgated as a separate document at Vatican I but integrated into the constitution *Pastor Aeternus* (see n. 6 above).

8. The Syllabus of Errors, attached to Pius IX's encyclical *Quanta Cura,* December 1864 (see Letter 107, n. 2).

9. "The First Oecumenical Council of the Vatican," *CW,* XI (September 1870), 838–47.

10. A series of eight unsigned articles on the Vatican Council appeared in the *CW,* X–XI, between February and September 1870; they were jointly authored in Rome by Bishop Gibbons and Bishop Lynch. James Gibbons (1834–1921), pre-eminent churchman and apologist, vicar apostolic of North Carolina 1868, archbishop of Baltimore 1877, second American cardinal 1886. Patrick Neeson Lynch (1817–1882), Irish-born Roman-educated editor and author, bishop of Charleston, S.C., 1857.

143

BROWNSON TO HECKER • 30 AUGUST 1870

Eliz Aug. 30, 1870

My dear Father Hecker,

I received your kind answer to mine yesterday. Whatever difference time has effected in our views on the question of democracy as the people practically understand it, there is, judging from your statement of your views, aims, & purposes [agreement] as to the mode or means of remedying the evils which we alike see & deplore. Indeed I feel from your letter that your convictions are substantially[,] or at least so far as they can have any practical bearing on our work[,] the same with mine, and also feel that there is a deeper & more perfect sympathy between us than I have felt there was for years.

I am not great on self-denial, nor have I much pious fervor, but I feel that I can willingly & freely coöperate with you, in my feeble way, in what you propose, both in the Tablet & writing for the Catholic World, if you wish. What you want is what I want.

I will see you on Monday next if possible, though on second thought, I will, D.V. go over and stay with you at the Convent on Friday. Expect me about 5 o'clock P.M.

Yours truly

O. A. Brownson.

Very Rev. Fr. Hecker.
New York.

144

HECKER TO BROWNSON • 8 OCTOBER 1870

Oct. 8 .1870

Dear Dr

I enclose this note[1] to you as it gives one an idea, and a very fair one, of the state of mind of a class of persons in our day.

There are one or more good points to be made from it, The true & false idea of progress; The true and exaggerrated idea of science; The distinction between Salvation & perfection etc.

The treatment of these in a familiar way, would meet the writer of this note and many others, and be useful to all the readers of the C.W.

Do not be afraid of going over the ground again. Remember the saying, and a true one, the most powerful figure in rhetoric is that of repetition.

An article of 10 pp. for the Nov. number which will go on with the one on Steps of Belief.[2] The letter[3] would be published as the text of your article.

I hope your health is good.

faithfully yours

I T Hecker

O A Brownson L.L.D.

1. Addressed to Hecker, this unsigned note was dated 6 October 1870, New York. Although it is no longer extant, it was published as the foreword to Brownson's essay "Answer to Difficulties," *CW,* XII (December 1870), 328–40.

2. *CW,* XII (December 1870), 289–304. This was Brownson's review of *Steps of Belief; or, Rational Christianity, maintained against Atheism, Free Religion and Romanism* (Boston, 1870) by James Freeman Clarke (1810–1888), Unitarian minister and Transcendentalist author.

3. See n. 1 above.

145

HECKER TO BROWNSON • 25 OCTOBER 1870

NY. Oct. 25, 1870

Dear Dr

Three Vols. of H. W. Beecher's sermons,[1] and "Our Seven Churches" by T. K. Beecher[2] are on hand for a notice.

The B[eecher]s have a hold on the popular mind, and if you were to show the abyss to which they are leading it, your pen would do a good & great service.

They show an entire absence of all positive Xty, and the idea of the Church, and are the pioneers of our country of the orthodox Protestantism in its route to naturalism and nihilism.

Shall I send them to you for an article?[3]

I am on Retreat this week but write this note not to delay if you are willing to take these for an art.

faithfully yours

I T Hecker.

1. *The Sermons of Henry Ward Beecher in Plymouth Church.* First, Second, and Third Series, from September 1869 to March 1870; three volumes (New York, 1870).

2. *Our Seven Churches* (New York, 1870), by Thomas Kinnicut Beecher (1824–1900), Congregationalist clergyman; pastor of the Independent Congregational Church, Elmira, N.Y.; son of Lyman Beecher.

3. "Beecherism and Its Tendencies," *CW,* XII (January 1871), 433–50.

146

BROWNSON TO HECKER • 26 OCTOBER 1870

Eliz. Oct. 26, 1870.

Dear Father Hecker,

I have not yet received the Beecher Books, but when they come, I shall be happy to pay respects to [them]. The Beechers are fast men, and are rapidly squandering what [is] their religious patrimony.

I have written an article[1] on Lady Georgiana Fullerton's *Mrs.* Gerald's Niece[2] in which I have passed strictures on modern novels in general, & feminine novels in particular, and expressed some views on religious novels so called, with some suggestions to our Catholic novel writers, as to what a Catholic novel should be. I shall send or bring the article this week. Will the *Answer to Difficulties* go in the December No.? I ask, because I have some arrangements which may be affected by the fact.

The November No. is a superb No. English Translations of the Bible[3] is learned, able, grand, & to the purpose. Did Bishop Lynch[4] write it? I like the article[5] on *The Invitation Heeded,*[6] & especially the one from the German on Prince Metternich.[7] I have some doubts as to Rachel.[8] She was not only a Jewess, but I have always understood, a denizen of the Demi-Monde. Neither you nor I worship genius divorced from religion or truth & virtue. Look out for Ma'am Ellet.[9] I have no confidence in her. The falling off in the circulation of the Magazine was caused by the neglect of your canvassers.

Very truly yours

O. A Brownson.

Ver. Rev I T. Hecker.

1. "Mrs. Gerald's Niece," *CW*, XII (January 1871), 546–57.

2. Lady Georgiana Charlotte Fullerton (1812–1885), English convert from Anglicanism, author and novelist; *Mrs. Gerald's Niece. A novel . . .* (New York, 1870).

3. "English Translations of the Bible," *CW*, XII (November 1870), 149–70.

4. Patrick N. Lynch, bishop of Charleston, S.C.

5. "The Invitation Heeded," *CW*, XII (November 1870), 250–61.

6. *The Invitation Heeded; Or, Reasons for a Return to Catholic Unity* (New York, 1870) by James Kent Stone (1840–1921), educator, missionary, theologian; ordained Episcopal minister 1866, Catholic convert 1869, ordained Paulist priest 1872, transferred to the Passionist community 1878.

7. "Prince Clement Von Metternich," *CW*, XII (November 1870), 239–50; translated from the German journal *Der Katholik.*

8. "Rachel," *CW*, XII (November 1870), 200–207.

9. Elizabeth Friest Lummis Ellet (1818–1877), historian of women's roles in American history, poet and translator; Catholic convert.

147

HECKER TO BROWNSON • 27 OCTOBER 1870

NY. Oct 27, 1870

Dear Dr

I subscribe to every one of your criticisms on the articles in the C.W.

Gilmery Shea[1] wrote the art. on the Bible.

To-morrow Kehoe will send you the Vols of the Beechers. When done with them you would do me a favour by returning them as they will be useful to our Library.

Very glad to see you. I shall be out of my retreat Saturday morning.

Both of your articles will be in the December number.[2]

The one on Catholic novels is very important. Lady F[ullerton]'s last is no novel, a poor work in my opinion, and a dry one on controversy.

Perhaps the canvassers[*?*] were at fault. I have a new one out.

Great trust in God & earnest work for God is my reliance.

God bless you, your wife & children.

faithfully yours

I. T. Hecker.

1. John Dawson Gilmary Shea; see Letter 75, n. 20, and Letter 146, n. 3.

2. "Steps of Belief" (pp. 289–304) and "Answer to Difficulties" (pp. 328–40).

148

HECKER TO BROWNSON • 28 JANUARY 1871

NY. Jan 28, 1871

Dear Dr.

I have seen the ABp.[1] about Senator Wilson's[2] article in the Atlantic.[3]

The political question is one which strikes at the genius of our political system.

The educational question strikes a blow at Religion, at Catholicity. It is the union of Protestantism and the State.

Secretary Boutwell[4] tells us in his speech in Washington the Church is incompetent to give any adequate education!

What is Education? To aid a man to secure his true destiny. Now if God has made man [an] immortal being, and gave him a law by observing which he secures his destiny, that will require one's education to be in harmony with that law.

If man be developed out of a monkey, and when he dies goes back to his original elements, & ceases to exist a personal consciousness. That will require quite another education. One would not apply the 10 commandments to a monkey! It is not fair, it would cheat him out of many gratifications for no reason.

The Question is, What is Education?

Let the state say what it requires to make good citizens, and make that compulsory, if it pleases.

They talk about Prussia, there is in Prussia denominational freedom.

Denominational freedom with compulsion is not objectionable. Such is Prussia. It would aid us in getting our own children to our schools.

In my mind Wilson is at the head of a set of fanatics who are in a conspiracy to destroy our political system of government and religious freedom.

I send you the enclosed as evidence of a concerted action and there is a bill to come up before Congress next week on the subject.

Please write the article for the April number—the present one is nearly all "up."

faithfully yours

I. T. Hecker

1. John McCloskey.
2. Henry Wilson (1812–1875), Republican senator from Massachusetts, became U.S. vice-president 1873 (under Ulysses S. Grant).
3. "New Departure for the Republican Party," *The Atlantic Monthly,* XXVII (January 1871), 104–20.
4. George Sewall Boutwell (1818–1905), congressman during Reconstruction; secretary of the treasury 1869–73; and U.S. senator from Massachusetts 1873–77.

149

BROWNSON TO HECKER • 30 JANUARY 1871

Eliz. N.J. Jan 30, 1871.

Dear Father Hecker,

I have received to-day yours of Saturday. You do not say in it whether the Archbishop permits the question in its political aspect to be taken up or not. As a question between existing political parties I do not wish to treat it, but as repugnant to the genius of our political institutions, and destructive of the federal element of our government, & therefore revolutionary in its character[.] I should like to protest against Wilson's doctrine,[1] as well as against a union of the State & Protestantism.

Wilson is the tool of the fanatics, but he is leaky, & it is easy from him to ascertain the purpose & plan of the Evangelicals.[2] It is evident to me that the purpose is to outlaw the Church; & the plan of proceeding is to absorb all legislation touching the rights of persons and conscience in Congress, to make education national & compulsory, and it is hoped by the aid of female suffrage, an essential part of the plan to succeed. Yet I trust in God that the plan will fail.

I have written to Kehoe to send me the No. of the Atlantic Monthly, & as soon as I receive it, I will set about preparing the article & follow out your hints. If I hear nothing from you to the contrary, I shall touch briefly the political question.

I have an article[3] more than half written on the Origin of Civilization,[4] reviewing Sir John Lubbock. It will contain no [e]xtracts, & will be short, about 12 pages of the Magazine. I would like to have Fr. Hewit read the Ms. before it goes to the printer, & correct any errors he may detect in it. I am quite well [e]xcept the gout in my teeth. Regards to all you companions.

Yours truly

O. A. Brownson

Very Rev. I. T. Hecker.
59 Street, New York.

1. Senator Henry Wilson's proposal that the U.S. be unified through national compulsory education in public schools (even for Catholic children attending parochial schools). In Brownson's view, such a proposal not only spelled the end of Catholic education but also allied Republicans as the party of wealth with evangelical Protestants against the poorer Catholic immigrants. See Letter 148.

2. Under the term 'Evangelicals,' Brownson included Congregationalists, Presbyterians, Dutch Reformed, Baptists, and Methodists.

3. "The Origin of Civilization," *CW*, XIII (July 1871), 492–504.

4. *The Origin of Civilization and the Primitive Condition of Man: Mental and Social Conditions of Savages* (New York, 1871) by Sir John Lubbock (1834–1913), first baron of Avebury, English historian and scientist, eldest son of the prominent mathematician and astronomer Sir John William Lubbock (1803–1865).

150

BROWNSON TO HECKER • [c. 15 FEBRUARY 1871]*

[*Undated*] [1]

Dear Father Hecker,

The article on Wilson's National Unification & Education[2] is written, and will be sent this week. I simply keep it by me a day or two in order to read it over and correct it. It is about the same length as this, shorter, if any difference. I send you both in season for April, but you will publish them, if at all, when you see fit. They are placed at your discretion, only suffer nothing to pass that you disapprove, or will censure me for hereafter.

I have another article for you, more than half written, The Church Accredits Herself,[3] appropos [*sic*] of Archbishop Manning's[4] Vatican Council,[5] to which, however, I give only a single paragraph.

My regards to all the community, especially to Father Hewit.

Yours truly

O A. B.

*Microfilm, roll nine (calendared [Feb. 1871]).

1. This undated letter was written about midway between Brownson's of 30 January 1871 (Letter 149), wherein he proposes to write his article on Wilson's plan of unification, and c. 1 March 1871 when the article probably went to press, since it appeared in mid-March 1871 when the April 1871 *CW* came out (see n. 2 below). A date c. 15 February 1871 thus appears feasible.

2. "Unification and Education," *CW*, XIII (April 1871), 1–14.

3. "The Church Accredits Herself," *CW*, XIII (May 1871), 145–58.

4. Henry Edward Manning (1808–1892), English Catholic convert from Anglicanism 1851, apologist and author; became archbishop of Westminster 1865; named cardinal 1875.

5. *The Vatican Council and Its Definitions* (New York, 1871); the American edition was published by Sadlier.

151

HECKER TO BROWNSON • 29 MARCH 1871

NY. March 29, 1871

My Dear Friend.

The answer to your note you will find in Chap. XXXII, "Authority".[1]

Whatever I would write in reply to the note would be only a repetition what that Chapter contains.

If the gentleman is interested sufficiently to call, I should be glad to see him and have a talk on the subject.

Let me know when you would make the visit.

The leading article[2] in the *May* number of the Cath. World will have something which will interest your friend. It is on the Church.

With Kindest Regards believe me

yours faithfully

I T Hecker.

1. A reference to chapter 32 of Hecker's *Aspirations of Nature* (New York, 1857), pp. 297–311.
2. "The Church Accredits Herself," *CW*, XIII (May 1871), 145–58.

152

HECKER TO BROWNSON • 3 APRIL 1871

NY., April 3, 1871

Dear Dr.

I send you the Vol. on Italian Unity[1] –for an article[2] from your pen.

Every day my admiration increases at the attitude of the Holy Father[3] in his defense of those principles which underlie the political order and natural morality. Is it not astonishing that men can not see this! He is resisting the destruction of all human society. The only power on earth that has had the courage to stand up against violence and injustice in the political order. Wonderful mission for God's Church!

Dana[4] sent me his letter separately. How weak in its conclusion!

Had I time it would give me great pleasure to visit you at Elizabeth. Holy Week is a busy time, & I have not a moment of leisure.

F[ather] Hewit has been quite feeble for several weeks past. Now he is improving in strength.

My Kindest Regards to your wife & daughter.

faithfully yours

I T Hecker

O. A. Brownson L.L.D

In my opinion, your article on Unification was one of the most finished that ever came from your pen. While its force was equal to its finish.

When done with the book please return it.

1. *The Unity of Italy. The American Celebration of the Unity of Italy, at the Academy of Music, New York, Jan. 12, 1871; with the Addresses, Letters, and Comments of the Press* (New York, 1871).

2. "Sardinia and the Holy Father," *CW*, XIII (June 1871), 289–304.

3. Pope Pius IX, reigned 1846–78.

4. Charles Anderson Dana.

153

HECKER TO BROWNSON • 18 APRIL 1871

NY. April 18, 1871

Dear Dr.

Tomorrow evening I lecture in Meriden, Conn. I leave here in the morning of the same day 19—& return in the afternoon of Thursday.

If I should not see you before your going to Detroit please make us a visit on your return.

The Unity article[1] is in the hands of the printer also a former article.[2]

F[ather] Hewit is reading the art. on Philosophy.[3]

With my best wishes & prayers for a pleasant visit to your son[4] at Detroit and with my Kindest Regards to him, believe me

Yours faithfully

I T Hecker.

1. "Sardinia and the Holy Father," *CW*, XIII (June 1871), 289–304.

2. Probably Brownson's article on Lubbock's *Origin of Civilization*; *CW*, XIII (July 1871), 492–504.

3. "Ontologism and Psychologism," which was eventually published in *BrQR*, July 1874, pp. 357–76.

4. Henry F. Brownson.

154

HECKER TO BROWNSON • 2 JUNE 1871

NY. June 2, 1871

Dear Dr

Your two articles[1] have reached safely. The proof of the 1st. you have received before this time.

The enclosed[2] speaks for itself. The articles from the Radical[3] I had laid aside for future use, but the same question is started by the lawyer, and an article[4] from your pen on this matter for the C.W. would help a great number of intelligent persons on the path of truth.

Dr McCosh[5] has published a book on "Xty. & Positivism."[6] I will order Mr Kehoe to send you a copy that you may judge whether it is worth a review from your pen in the C.W. Did you see a notice[7] of it in the last number of the Liberal Xtian, evidently by O. R. Bellows?[8]

You remember your articles[9] on that french Abbé[10] who became a greek—your task was a hard one—it paid. I heard of the conversion of an episcopal minister who is now a catholic priest, in consequence of those articles.

My health has been poorly this month or so, and to-morrow I leave for Lake George[11] for several weeks.

Please preserve those articles from the Radical.

faithfully yours

I T Hecker

P.S. If you Review McCosh, it would be better to write that first.

1. Very likely "The Secular Not Supreme," *CW*, XIII (August 1871) 685–701, and "The Reformation Not Conservative," (September 1871) 721–37.

2. Though the original letters are not available, Hecker sent Brownson the correspondence exchanged between him (or perhaps Hewit) and a New York lawyer concerning the question of the infallibility of the Church. This lawyer was Dwight Hinckley Olmstead (1827?–1901), a subjectivistic thinker. Excerpts from the correspondence ("the editor's note" and "the lawyer's note") were contained in Brownson's article (see n. 4).

3. "Notes," *The Radical,* VIII (March 1871), 147–49; (May 1871), 306–12; (June 1871), 377–78; and "The Ethics of the Will" (May 1871), 233–41.

4. "Authority in Matters of Faith," *CW,* XIV (November 1871), 145–57.

5. James McCosh (1811–1894), Scottish-born Presbyterian clergyman, a philosopher of the school of Scottish common-sense realism, president of the College of New Jersey, Princeton, 1868–88.

6. *Christianity and Positivism. A Series of Lectures to the Times, on Natural Theology and Apologetics* (New York, 1871).

7. *The Liberal Christian,* XXVI (27 May 1871).

8. Henry Whitney Bellows (1814–1882), Unitarian writer, pastor of All Souls Church, New York City, editor of *The Liberal Christian.*

9. "Guettée's Papacy Schismatic," *CW,* V (July 1867), 463–79; (August 1867), 577–93.

10. Abbé François Guettée became a Greek Orthodox (see Letter 97, n. 1).

11. Location of the Paulists' summer retreat.

155

BROWNSON TO HECKER • [c. 1 JULY 1871]*

[*Undated*][1]

Dear Father Hecker,

I send you the article[2] on McCosh. In spite of all I could do it would assume the shape of a criticism on the author, who is intense[ly?] egotistical & pretentious, promising liberally & performing sparingly. His book is bosh, & fit only to rhyme with McCosh.

I have read Fr. Rosmini[3] and Fr. Kleutgen[4] and have [e]xamined as well as I am able to do the propositions of the Louvain professor[s] and of Branchereau[5] censured by the Holy See.[6] Some of the inferences drawn by the Jesuit Fathers from the propositions censured I do not accept, but there is not one of the propositions censured that I have not always condemned, and certainly avoided in the article Father Hewit was afraid of. The Holy See has condemned *ontologism,* but not *ontology* as a part of philosophy, & ontologism I have never since I was a Catholic I have never defended. The ideal formula has an ontological element, but asserts in the fact that it is *ideal* that it is held by intuition under the form of a universal

& necessary idea, and is not identified with Ens, or known to be Ens by intuition any more than Ens is intuitively known to be God.

The propositions condemned are of two classes, the one censured as pantheistic, & the other as asserting ontologism, or the direct & immediate cognition or intuition of God, an objection you will remember I made to F[ather] H[ewit]'s first article on the Problems of the Age[7] at the time of publication.

You will see in reading the article on McCosh, that I have avoided in my defense of the argument from necessary & universal ideas for the [e]xistence [of God] the censure of the Holy See, & frankly assert that I have never understood the ideal formula as imply[ing] direct & immediate intuition of God, or even of Ens itself. An intellectual or reflective process was always necessary to identify the ideas in Ens as well as Ens with Deus.

I own, however, that I have not always been explicit enough to avoid being misunderstood by those who hated Gioberti & have never believed that any body but one of "Our Fathers"[8] could know any thing either of philosophy or theology, though "Our Fathers" differ widely from another with regard to both. I consequently propose to rewrite my article on Ontologists & Psychologists, taking the two books you gave for a text, inserting in the article the propositions censur[ed] by the Holy See, show what is censured & what is not censured, in their censure, explain more carefully what is given by intuition, & point out the ground on which the two schools may harmonize, & psychology be saved without psychologism and ontology without ontologism[,] & submit it to you & Fr. Hewit, who I am sure has misapprehended both Gioberti & me, & supposed we agreed with him when we did not. The censures of the Holy See strike him, but not me.

In the meantime I must write an article[9] on the Correspondence[10] & the Radical[11] you sent me. But I wish you to inform [me] at your earliest convenience, whether you wish me to insert the Correspondence in the article, or simply reply to the Lawyer's objection? If left to myself I shall take the latter course, not as the easiest for me, but as probably the most satisfactory to the readers of the Magazine. But in either case I do not think that I can treat in the same article the subject you mentioned to me, Christus Creat Ecclesiam.[12] The Correspondence presents two subjects. The infallibility of the Church, which depends on the Christus Creat Ecclesiam, & the impossibility of an infallible belief even on infallibility, presented by the Lawyer in his long letter, or note. Which shall I treat first? The first seems to me too difficult for this bruising weather.

I hope you are rewriting. My respects to all the community, & believe me

Yours truly

O A. Brownson

Very Rev. Father Hecker.

*Microfilm, roll nine (calendared [Sept. 1871]).

1. Dated c. 1 July 1871 because its contents indicate that it was written after Hecker's of 2 June 1871 (Letter 154) and before Hecker's of 16 July [1871] (Letter 156).

2. "Christianity and Positivism," *CW*, XIV (October 1871), 1–15.

3. Antonio Rosmini-Serbati (see Letter 75, n. 10). Brownson may have read Rosmini's *Nuovo saggio sull'origine delle idee* (Rome, 1830), or possibly part of his five-volume *Teosofia* (Turin, 1859–74), or *Teodicea* (Milan, 1845).

4. Joseph Kleutgen, S.J. (1811–1883), German theologian and scholastic philosopher; played an influential role in revising the schema of the relationship between faith and reason (*Dei Filius,* 24 April 1870) at the First Vatican Council. Brownson may have read his two-volume *Die philosophie der vorzeit* (Munster, 1860–63).

5. Louis Branchereau (1819–1913), French Sulpician priest whose book *Praelectiones Metaphysicae* was extensively used in French Catholic seminaries.

6. Pope Pius IX condemned seven propositions of Louvain ontologists on 18 September 1861 (see Letter 93, n. 8), while fifteen of Branchereau's propositions were condemned in 1862.

7. *CW,* III (May 1866), 145–50; see Letter 93 for Brownson's objection.

8. Most probably a reference to the Jesuits who vigorously opposed Gioberti.

9. "Authority in Matters of Faith," *CW,* XIV (November 1871), 145–57.

10. See Letter 154, n. 2.

11. See Letter 154, n. 3.

12. "Christ creates the Church."

156

HECKER TO BROWNSON • 16 JULY [1871]*

Lake George July 16.[1]

Dear Dr.

I write at once to say that in regard to the article on The Correspondance [*sic*], answer the questions in the way you deem best.

As my note has nothing in it on the question[,] it had best be left out.

As to the article on philosophy[,] [2] give me time to consider.

My health is not so good, and I have been suffering from severe headaches.[3]

I write this in haste to reach the next post.

faithfully yours

I. T. Hecker

*Microfilm, roll six (calendared 16 July 1869).

1. The year was omitted, but the mention of the correspondence between

Hecker and Dwight H. Olmstead as well as the philosophy article situate this letter within 1871.

2. "Ontologism and Psychologism" (see Letter 153, n. 3).

3. Elliott observed in *LFH,* p. 371: "From severe colds, acute headaches, and weakness of the digestive organs Father Hecker was a frequent sufferer. But towards the end of the year 1871 his headaches became much more painful, his appetite left him, and sleeplessness and excitability of the nervous system were added to his other ailments."

157

BROWNSON TO HECKER • 28 JULY 1871

July 28, 1871.

Very Rev. & dear Father,

I had begun my article on the Correspondence before I received your Letter.[1] If you think your note had better be left out, you can strike it out, without having to change only a very few words in the article. Yet I think upon second tho't that it had better stand,[2] for you open in the conclusion a train of thought that will bear developing. I have made a slight alteration in your letter, which you can accept or not, as you think best. You say, the infallibility comes from the Holy Ghost to Christ & from Christ to the body. I propose to read from the Holy Ghost through Christ to the body or Church. My reason is that the alteration preserves the idea of Christ as the Medium or Mediator, & excludes the notion that Christ is not personally infallible, & receives his infallibility from the Holy Ghost, which is hardly compatible with his [Christ's] equality.

I am not very well satisfied with the article in reply to the Lawyer's Note. I have [e]xperienced a difficulty, that of making the answer complete without plunging deeper into philosophy & scholastic theology than would be desirable in a Magazine article, a fault I some times commit. I have done the best I could, but it seems to me that the several links of the logical chain are not as closely attached to one another as they should be, and that the article does not have on the reader the impression of an indissoluble whole. In truth the question I have had to treat is a difficult one to treat in a popular manner, and to leave nothing unsaid that is essential to a full and complete understanding of it. If the article strikes you as defective, pray, correct it, or send it back & let me rewrite it. Perhaps I can improve it.

I wish you would let me know if the article on McCosh[3] is accepted, that I may know what course to take in reference to future articles. I have been, unless I deceive myself, in a better mood for writing, at least much more disposed to labor, than I have been for years in summer weather, & I am sorry that you are suffering so much. I hope this will find you much better. You must not let the disappointments you have met with prey upon you. He who aims well & does the best he can, may leave the rest to Providence. Men enter the religious life for the sake of sacrifice.

Did Father Hewit write the article on Infallibility.[4] It does not sound much like him, but I know not who else could have written it. It reads as if written by an Englishman & a disciple of Newman.[5] I do not quite like it, especially what it says about our obligations to act on probabilities as if they were certainties. Nevertheless the article displays rare ability.

The New York Observer, I am told, for I have not received my copy, is out on "The Secular Not Supreme."[6] If I think it important enough I shall send you a brief reply for the C.W. If not I shall content myself with responding to it in The Tablet.

I shall finish writing & send you my article on Ontologism & Psychologism, but I shall not ask you to publish it, unless it meets your and Father Hewit's approbation, for I shall have an opportunity for publishing it in a volume of Essays which I am preparing for Sadlier to bring out, perhaps, next Spring.

Have you seen the new *Syllabus* of the Pope, as the *Herald* calls it?[7] Of course the Herald's account is incorrect, but I think it very likely that it goes far enough to warrant the doctrine asserted & defended in *The Secular Not Supreme.* I am anxious to see it.

Have you any other work marked out for me? I must do what I can & work as hard as I can for the day is short, & the night cometh in which no man can work. I have at best but a short time to remain in this world, & my work is not done, either for the world or for my own soul. Make my kind and respectful regards to all the Fathers of the Community. Pray for me, & believe me

Yours truly

O. A. Brownson.

Very Rev Father Hecker.

1. See Letter 156.
2. The note was included; see *CW,* XIV (November 1871), 145.
3. *CW,* XIV (October 1871), 1–14.
4. "Infallibility," *CW,* XIII (August 1871), 577–94. The dogma of papal infallibility had been proclaimed at the First Vatican Council (July 1870).

5. John Henry Newman.

6. "The Secular Not Supreme," *CW,* III (August 1871), 685–701.

7. On 28 July 1871 the *New York Herald-Tribune* noted an address by Pope Pius IX after certain Eastern Catholic prelates had assented to the proclamation of the dogma of papal infallibility; in his address the Pope noted that papal infallibility did not imply the power to depose sovereigns, but he still maintained his prerogative as supreme judge on the moral dimensions of the spiritual and temporal orders.

158

HECKER TO BROWNSON • 9 AUGUST 1871

Lake George Aug 9. 1871

Dear Dr.

All your articles are accepted and will appear in the C.W. as soon as possible.

Were I at home as it was my intention to be, and my head in working order, it would be less difficult for me to suggest some subjects for articles from your pen.

The recent events in France is a live subject[1] and which you are familiar with. What think you?

Then the recent riots[2] treated from a common sense point of view. To me it seems that orangeism is an outrage on every feeling of both american and irish manhood. It is the triumph of religious persecution & political tyranny.

But you undoubtedly have thoughts on the subject, and if you feel so inclined[,] write an article on the subject. Since I left N.Y. I have not seen the Tablet.

F[ather] Hewit who is now here expresses great satisfaction at your publishing a volume of your articles, & says he has no doubt they will do a great good.

I am highly gratified to learn that your health this summer is so robust.

F. Hewit wrote the article on Infallibility.

The Syllabus you speak of I have not heard of, if it reaches me in any official shape you shall have it.

The article on Philosophy I shall read with great interest.

My health is improving, somehow my strength is slow in coming.

I stay here until the 17th then go to Boston, & hope to be in N.Y. about the 23d.

Please let me know of any subject for your pen which occurs to you.

faithfully yours.

I T Hecker.

F. Hewit & the members of the community wish to be remembered to you.

1. A reference to the rise of the Paris Commune against Napoleon III (March 1871) and to the events and consequences of the Franco-Prussian War.

2. On 12 July 1871 there occurred in New York City a clash between Catholic Irishmen and Protestant Irishmen who were celebrating the Battle of the Boyne (1690) with a parade.

159

BROWNSON TO HECKER • 12 AUGUST 1871

Eliz. Aug. 12, 1871.

Very Rev & dear Father

I have half written, & will send you the article on the Orange Riots[1] next week, probably by the 17th. It will make about 10 pages. The other article you suggest on the Recent Events in France,[2] I will, D.V. write & send as soon as you will need it.

I am sorry to learn your strength is slow in coming, but the weather will soon be seen favorable. I have been uncommonly well *in my head*, & very able to sit at my desk & write in these hot summer days, but I find myself otherwise weak, & a very little bodily [e]xertion overcomes me.

I have changed my mind about the philosophy article. I shall not send it to this Magazine, but shall reserve it for my volume,[3] which I intend shall be composed of original Essays, not heretofore published. I think it will be best to begin with an original Volume, as it will meet a reading sale, and serve as an introduction to those [volumes] to come after it, made up from my previous writing. The philosophy article will be [e]xtended to an Essay, as long as two or three articles in the C.W. The other questions to be discussed I have not yet determined on in my own mind, but they will be of popular interest, unless I finally conclude to [e]xpand my Essay on philosophy into a volume, if not a regular treatise.

Very respectfully yours,

O. A. Brownson.

1. "The Riot of the Twelfth," *CW*, XIV (October 1871), 117–26.

2. "The Recent Events in France," *CW*, XIV (December 1871), 289–304.

3. Eventually Brownson's projected volume became his "Essay in Refutation of Atheism," *BrQR*, October 1873, pp. 433–65; January 1874, pp. 1–37; April 1874, pp. 145–79.

160

HECKER TO BROWNSON • 31 AUGUST 1871

NY. Aug 31, 1871

Dear Dr.

General Marcy[1] of Orange Mountain requested me to ask you whether you could call on Mrs Sherman[2] who will make him a visit the early part of next week. Mrs S. had expressed the desire to see you. I suppose there are trains from Elizabeth to Newark—and from Newark to Orange there are quite a number.

My Brother George will have a carriage at the Depot to take you up the mountain, and should you wish to stay over night, he offers you the hospitality of his house.

I shall try to be there. You shall have timely notice, if you decide to come, when Mrs Sherman arrives.

I returned home on friday evening last. My strength is slowly increasing. The cold weather in the fall will set all right again. My mind is made up to cut off next winter lecturing; not to work quite so much.

The article on "the Riots of the 12th." is the most vigorous and able article from your pen. You will receive the proofs to-day or tomorrow.

Now once more home, I shall look around for material & subjects for your pen.

I hope your mental vigor holds out, and trust that your body also may be equal in strength to your mind.

Kind regards to your wife & daughter.

faithfully yours

I T Hecker.

1. Randolph Barnes Marcy (1812–1887), Civil War brigardier-general 1861–63, later major general.

2. Eleanor Boyle Ewing Sherman (1824–1888), prominent Catholic, active in Catholic charities; married General William Tecumseh Sherman of Civil War fame in 1850.

161

BROWNSON TO HECKER • 1 SEPTEMBER 1871

Eliz. NJ. Sept. 1, 1871.

My dear Father Hecker

I regret that it will not be convenient for me to accept Gen. Marcy's invitation, for I should much like to meet both him and Mrs. Sherman, especially Mrs. Sherman, for whom I have the highest regard; but my wife & daughter are both absent in the Allegheny Mts.[1] & I cannot well leave home, for I do not like to leave my servant girl alone. Be so obliging as to make them my regrets, & also my thanks to your brother for his proffered hospitality.

I am glad you like my article on the Riot. It seems strange to me that nobody seems to have understood the law in the case, or comprehended that the Orange procession as celebrating [something] wholly foreign to American nationality can be *only* by sufferance, not by right.

I will endeavor to give you the French article[2] in season for your December No.

I shall not publish a volume [of] Essays from the Review, but shall attempt to carry out & revise [*?*] plans, comprising three or four separate works. The first work, already begun, is to be an "Essay in Refutation of Atheism & Pantheism." In which I shall refute the Cosmic Philosophers,[3] both by showing [that] their science is nescience, & by proving by reason the [e]xistence of God, creation & Providence, the fundamental principles of Christianity. Into this work, which will contain nothing unacceptable to so called orthodox Protestants, I shall be able to work in my philosophy.

If this work takes, I shall follow it by another on the principle of ethics & aesthetics; that by another on the Christian Mysteries, & concluding by another on the Church, though I may not follow the order here indicated. Into these volumes I shall endeavor to compress the essence of all I have published in separate articles bearing on these subjects, worth retaining. The volumes will not be much larger than that on Liberalism & the Church.[4]

I hope to get the first work completed in three or four months, but it will depend on the state of my health & my eyes. My eyes are bad just now, but are getting better. My health otherwise is as good as usual, but my head is a little muddy, & I have to rest it. I wish you would make the sacrifice of coming to spend the day with me.

By the way tell Mr. Kehoe that I have used up all the paper he sent me, and that I wish him to send me more, & also Herbert Spencer's *Principles of Philosophy,*[5] the second volume of Spencer's *Biology*. I have the First Volume, & also Spencer's Principles of Psychology, as I combat him in my proposed Essay.

With high respect & affection
I [am] yours truly

O A. Brownson.

Very Rev. I. T. Hecker.

1. At Loretto, Pa., where Brownson's daughter Sarah was doing research for her biography, *Life of Demetrius Augustine Gallitzin, Prince and Priest,* (New York, 1873).

2. "The Recents Events in France."

3. Brownson particularly means John Fiske (1842–1901), American historian and popularizer of evolutionary theory; Herbert Spencer (1820–1903), British evolutionary philosopher; and Auguste Comte (1798–1857), French positivist philosopher.

4. *Conversations on Liberalism and the Church* (New York, 1870).

5. *First Principles of a New System of Philosophy,* 2nd ed. (New York, 1871).

162

HECKER TO BROWNSON • 4 SEPTEMBER 1871

THE WESTERN UNION TELEGRAPH COMPANY[1]

Dated: Orange N.J.   Sept. 4, 1871
Received at: Central R.R. Depot[2]
To: Dr Brownson

Received no answer. Mrs Sherman will be on Mountain[3] on Monday only. Will you come?

I.T. Hecker

1. Since this was written on a telegram form, it obviously is not an autograph letter.
2. Elizabeth, N.J.
3. Orange Mountain, N.J.

163

BROWNSON TO HECKER • 26 SEPTEMBER 1871

Eliz.   Sept. 26, 1871.

Rev. & dr. Father Hecker,

I send you an article[1] on Herbert's Spencer's First Principles. I wrote the article because [my] mind was occupied with [the] question involved. I have to travel over the same ground in my Essay Against Atheism & false Theism.

I will try to get you the article[2] on Frank Matters in season for the December No. or in the fore part of October.

Hodge[3] is able, yet vulnerable, but I want time. I shall attack, not defend, or defend only by way of attack. I protest against the C.W. being put on the defensive.

Professor Bascom's book[4] is superior to McCosh's. It represents the best phase of the philosophy of Protestant N[ew] England, & is vulnerable only through its misapprehension of intuition. He makes ideal intuition, or intuition of ideas the [*?*] furnished by the mind prior to all experience, from its [the mind's] own nature or constitution,–the innate ideas of Descartes, does not understand that the ideal is real & necessary being on its intelligible side or side facing the human intellect, any more than do our own Jesuit philosophers. The good Fathers Liberatore[5] [and] Tongeorgi,[6] and others thought they have got the ideal philosophy condemned, and their own doctrine built on abstractions confirmed by the Holy See, but they got only the doctrine of the Ontologists that we have immediate intuition of God condemned, & a few pantheistic propositions, which escaped the Louvain professors, not the proposition that we have immediate intuition of the ideal along with & as the necessary condition of empirical intuition. I shall make Professor Bascom's Book the text for discussing the whole doctrine of ideal intuition in the light of the recent decisions of the Holy See, which decisions Fathers Ramiere[7] & Kleutgen are very far from understanding. Indeed it is very necessary that their interpretations should be shown to be untenable. The Society must learn that they are not the Church, & cannot restrict philosophy to their ignorance of St. Thomas, & to their psychological abstractions which they substitute for the teachings of the Angel,[8] of the Schools. I condemn the condemned propositions, but I condemn equally the Jesuits' inference as from their condemnation. I have already written the article[9] in part, and shall have it finished D.V. for the February or March No. of the C.W.

Yours truly

O A B.

1. "The Cosmic Philosophy," *CW,* XIV (February 1872), 633–45.

2. "Authority in Matters of Faith," *CW,* XIV (November 1871), 145–57.

3. Charles Hodge (1797–1878), Old School Presbyterian, systematic theologian, author and professor at Princeton Theological Seminary. Brownson intended to critique the chapter "The Protestant Rule of Faith" of the first volume of Hodge's *Systematic Theology* (New York, 1872).

4. *Science, Philosophy, and Religion* (New York, 1871) by John Bascom (1827–1911), Presbyterian, professor at Williams College; he became president of the University of Wisconsin 1874, later a Social Gospel theologian.

5. Matteo Liberatore, S.J. (1810–1892), Italian Thomist philosopher and theologian, co-founder of *Civiltà Cattolica* 1850.

6. Salvatore Tongiorgi, S.J. (1820–1865), Italian conservative theologian, professor at Rome's Gregorian University, contributor to the textbook or "manual" tradition of Catholic scholastic philosophy.

7. Henri Ramière, S.J. (1812–1884), French Thomist theologian, author of *The Unity of Philosophy* (1862), especially directed against ontologism.

8. St. Thomas Aquinas was often called the "Angelic Doctor."

9. On Bascom's book (n. 4 above), but this article was never printed in the *CW*; see "Bascom on Intuition," *BrQR*, July 1873, pp. 301–22.

164

BROWNSON TO HECKER • 9 OCTOBER 1871

Eliz. N.J. Oct. 9, 1871.

Dear Father Hecker,

I send you the French article.[1] It is bold & independent, but I think not rash, or likely to startle *much.* I have written & rewritten it, & worked over it till I am utterly unable to judge whether it amounts to anything or not. It is longer than for your sake I could wish, but with all my endeavors I could not make it shorter without leaving the question very partially treated. If you publish it, I think it would [be] best to publish [it] in the December No. & let the Cosmic, I was about to write comic, Philosophy article lie over till January. But I beg you or Father Hewit to [e]xamine it carefully so that nothing may escape that will compromise the C.W.

I will try & do up Hodge for your February Number,[2] & Bascom on intuition for March.[3] But I must take a little rest, for I have overworked myself, & my head is not as clear as it was last summer. The labor on my back is a little too much; but a week's rest will set me all right again. I shall hope to visit the Convent on Saturday. My family have returned.

My regards to all the Fathers, and believe me

Yours faithfully,

O A. Brownson.

Ver Rev. I. T. Hecker
Paulist Convent

1. "The Recent Events in France," *CW,* XIV (December 1871), 289–304.
2. "The Protestant Rule of Faith," *CW,* XIV (January 1872), 488–503.
3. "Bascom on Intuition" (see Letter 163, n. 9).

165

HECKER TO BROWNSON • 17 OCTOBER 1871

N.Y. Oct 17, 1871

Dear Dr

I received your note last week informing me that you would make us a visit on Saturday.

To be home I delayed a visit to Orange.

I fear that you are ill. Please let me know how you are and when you will make your welcome visit and believe me yours

faithfully

I T Hecker.

166

HECKER TO BROWNSON • 6 DECEMBER 1871

Dec 6, 1871

Dear Dr

I send Owen's[1] Book to you in advance sheets.[2]

Do as you please about noticing it–give it a long or a short article; or if you think it is worth the while, two or more short articles, to be published in succeeding months.

I send also Bp. Potter's[3] book[4] as coming in the scope of your own. Also to be noticed as you deem best.

faithfully yours

I T Hecker.

1. Robert Dale Owen (1801–1877), radical social reformer and communitarian socialist, freethinker, served as American diplomat to Naples (Italy), turned to spiritualism 1856.

2. *The Debatable Land Between This World and the Next* (New York, 1872).

3. Alonzo Potter (1800–1865), Episcopal clergyman and educator, professor at Union College in New York, became Episcopal bishop of Pennsylvania 1845.

4. *Religious Philosophy; or Nature, Man, and the Bible Witnessing to God and to Religious Truth* (Philadelphia, 1872), basically four courses of lectures delivered before the Lowell Institute 1845–53 and published posthumously.

167

BROWNSON TO HECKER • [c. 12 DECEMBER 1871]

[*Undated*] [1]

Dear Father Hecker,

I send you the promised article on Reason & Revelation.[2] Neither it nor the one on Papal Infallibility[3] is precisely what I intended, but I hope both will be suffered to pass.

I have necessarily had to touch on the effects of origin[al] sin, but I hope I have stayed clear of any collision with Father Hewit. I have aimed to do so, and have done all I could, with what I consider to be the relation of the natural & supernatural orders.

I send you the article on Ontologism, but I forgot to send Fr. Kleutgen's book from which certain extracts are to be made. I send it now. Perhaps I may bring that & the article myself, to-morrow.

Yours truly,

O. A. Brownson.

I wrote this on Friday, but I was too unwell to visit you Saturday. My principal difficulty is with my eyes. I am at present almost wholly unable to use them, but I apprehend no protracted trouble.

I send the two books you request me to return. The extracts are from Father Kleutgen alone. Father Hewit I thin[k] will see that I escape any censure that has been yet published by the Holy See.

Yours truly

O A. B.

1. In all probability this undated letter was written shortly before Brownson's of 18 December 1871 (Letter 168), wherein he asks Hecker if the articles on "Reason and Revelation" and "Ontology and Ontologism" (mentioned in this letter as just having been sent) have reached him; see also Hecker's of 8 January 1872 (Letter 169).

2. Not published in the *CW*, but later under the title "What Is the Need of Revelation?" *BrQR*, January 1873, pp. 85–95; see Brownson's own note to this effect, ibid., p. 85.

3. Not published in the *CW*, but later under the title "Papal Infallibility," *BrQR*, July 1873, pp. 322–40.

168

BROWNSON TO HECKER • 19 DECEMBER 1871*

Elizabeth. NJ Dec. [*?*] 19th, 1871[1]

Very Rev. & Dear Father,

I do not take or see the Dublin Review.[2] I have ordered it, but it has not yet come. I will thank you to send me the Number you mention,[3] as also Wendell Phillips's Speech or Address,[4] and I will do my best, though I confess, while I have decided views with regard to the Internationals, I am not a little undecided on the Labor Question. I have not made up my mind on the question whether as between labor & capital, & sink from the question of monopolies & that of the credit system which places a mortgage on the future and converts debt into capital. The laborer here or abroad upon an average receives his proportion of the joint proceeds of capital & labor. Are not our laboring class really the most independent & least suffering class among us? Give me any book on the subject that [you are able*?*] to get.

I will write the article[5] as soon as I can but I do not think I can possibly have it ready before Epiphany[6] or before in season for your March Number.

Have you received Ontologism & Ontology? Will it pass? Has *Reason & Revelation* come to hand? Does Father Hewit regard it as clashing with his views on original sin?

I have an article partly written on Owen.[7] I am rather tickled with his curt recommendation to Protestants to avail themselves of the aid of the spirits, that is of the Devil[,] in order to be able to maintain the struggle against the Church. Yet as the Devil has been their fast friend from the first, and done his best for them, I do not well see how the spirits can help them. Yet Owen's book is instructive from the light it throws on the great Gentile Apostasy, of which Protestantism is a reproduction.[8] It enables one to see how the Devil succeeded in getting himself worshipped as God, and it also [enables?] one to realize the truth of the Scriptural assertion, "All the gods of the Gentiles are devils" or daimons.

I have received the Jan. No. of C.W. I have read only the continuation [of] the H[ouse] of Y[orke].[9] The Lady[10] who writes it is highly gifted, writes with power & frequently with rare beauty and grace, but her heart & soul have been so saturated with Transcendentalism & she adopts so much of the Transcendental cant which formerly so disgusted me, that she is far from stirring me. She has spoiled her heroine by suffering her while betrothed to Dick to fall in love with Carl, as if love is fatal, & not under the control of reason & duty, the most damnable error of modern popular literature. The author needs conversion; her soul is not yet Catholic, even if her intellect is. She is in reality one of the strong minded and is sadly deficient in feminine grace & delicacy.

I am sorry to learn that you are suffering from your head. Mine, which has been very muddy for the last three months[,] shows signs of clearing up. I have been suffering very much from weakness in my eyes, having abused them [by] my night reading; but they are growing so worn.

My engagement with the Tablet has been renewed, at an advance from $15. to $20. a week. So I have little time to work on my book, hardly a day in the week.

I hope Father H[ewit] is well, and all the Community. By the way, is anything likely to come of the Catholic Union?[11] The Tablet is likely to be less satisfactory than ever. Young Frank Sadlier is likely to be as [*illegible*] as jejune [*?*]. To my hurt I shall be swampt [*?*]. It is humiliating to have to write almost wholly for the sake of money. My kind regards to the Community, and believe me

Yours truly

O. A. Brownson

Very Rev. I. T. Hecker.
Paulist Convent. New York.

*Microfilm, roll nine (calendared 19 October 1870).

1. Brownson's difficult handwriting here could be read as 19 October 1870 or 1871. But Hecker's of 8 Janaury 1872 (Letter 169), as well as the internal evidence of the letter (i.e., the mention of the January [1872] number of the *CW*), date it as 19 December 1871.

2. *Dublin Review* (later *The Wiseman Review*) was a Catholic literary quarterly founded in London in 1836 by Rev. Nicholas Patrick Wiseman

(1802–1865), who was named archbishop of Westminster and cardinal 1850. From 1863 to 1878 the magazine was edited by William George Ward (1812–1882), theologian and author, Catholic convert 1845.

3. "Article IX, The International Society," *The Dublin Review,* n.s. XVII (October 1871), 447–64.

4. "The Labor Movement," delivered c. 6 December 1871 at Steinway Hall, New York City by Wendell Phillips (1811–1884), ardent abolitionist and lecturer.

5. "The International Association," *CW,* XIV (February 1872), 694–707.

6. A Church feast celebrated on 6 January, commemorating the adoration of the Magi, or the Three Kings (Mt. 2:1–12).

7. "Owen on Spiritism," *CW,* XIV (March 1872), 803–12.

8. See ibid., pp. 809–10; Brownson refers to the Scripture text, "All the gods of the Gentiles are demons." (Ps. 96:5; 1 Chron. 16:26).

9. "The House of Yorke," *CW*, XIV (January 1872), 473–87; this piece was serialized in the *CW* from April 1871 through June 1872.

10. Mary Agnes Tincker (see Letter 128, n. 4).

11. A Catholic lay movement organized in May 1871 primarily by Henry James Anderson (1799–1875); the Union advocated a daily Catholic newspaper, a national Catholic university, a Catholic Congress, lectures, and religious celebrations.

169

HECKER TO BROWNSON • 8 JANUARY 1872

NY. Jan 8, 1872

Dear Dr.

The duties of the holydays with poor health has [*sic*] hindered me from replying to your letter of Dec. 19th. My mother has been at the point of death, but thank God! is recovering.

Today is the first leisure I have had for several weeks. F[ather] Hewit writes the enclosed[1] on the article on ontologism etc.

How I have read & reread your article on the necessity of Revelation, and consulted with F. Hewit, and in answer to your question whether it clashes with views held by him, I frankly say it does, as well as those maintained always by myself. In my judgment it would seriously impair the influence of the C.W. to bring out in its pages conflicting views on such important subjects.

You ask my opinon [*sic*] about the Catholic Union? It is this, that within the period of my knowledge there has been no movement promising to be of so great an importance as it does. There is a large body of men connected with it who mean work. Among their first efforts, will be that of starting a Daily Newspaper. Other important subjects are before it, such as an University, Catholic Congress etc. I confess confidence in the movement.

If your health and the weather permits, I would be gratified if you could favour us with a visit towards the end of this month. Mr Marshall[2] returns to the City then, and he with some other gentlemen are desirous of making your acquaintance. As soon as I can fix the time I will let you know.

Tho your relations with the Tablet are not in many respects satisfactory, still I was glad to hear from you that you had made a new engagement, and pecuniary [*sic*] more favourable. Your criticism on Bellows[3] met with hearty appreciation. It was a capital hit.

Hepworth's[4] new departure may prove serious to the Unitarians.

F. Hewit's health is middling. Today he is unwell.

From the depths of my heart I wish you a Happy New Year, and beg the blessings of God upon you and all who are dear to you.

faithfully yours

I. T. Hecker.

The article on Owen will be in time for March?

1. See A. F. Hewit to Brownson, 7 January 1872 (BP, UNDA). Microfilm roll seven.

2. Thomas William Marshall (1818–1877), Englishman, Anglican priest and Catholic convert 1845, controversial theologian and author; visited the U.S. 1870–72.

3. Henry W. Bellows. See *CW*, XIII (August 1871), 685–701.

4. George Hughes Hepworth (1833–1902), Unitarian author and preacher, minister at the Church of the Messiah in New York City 1869–71; in early 1872 he left his Unitarian connections to become an evangelical and to establish an ecumenical "Church of the Disciples."

170

BROWNSON TO HECKER • 10 JANUARY 1872

January 10, 1872.

Dear Father Hecker,

You are the judge [,] not I [,] of what is suitable for your pages. [I] only regret that my philosophy & my theology are under [the] ban of the

Catholic World. I will be greatly obliged to you, if you will return me the two rejected articles.[1]

I have read Fr. Hewit's criticism [of my] ontology article, and though it has surprised me, but I beg you to give him my thanks for it.

I thank you for the invitation. I should like to see Mr. Marshall.

With profound respect
Yours Affec [tionate]ly,

O A. Brownson

Very Rev. Fr. Hecker.

1. "Ontologism and Psychologism" and "Bascom on Intuition."

171

BROWNSON TO HECKER • 12 JANUARY 1872

Eliz. N.J. Jan. 12, 1872.

Very Rev & Dear Father Hecker,

I was in a great hurry and pressed for time, & also a little perturbed, when I wrote my brief & abrupt note[1] to you on Wednesday. I have thought over the matter since, and as there is a manifest difference between me & the Catholic World on the two important subjects of philosophy & theology, the best thing will be for me, & probably for it, to discontinue my articles for its pages, and with a friendly mutual understanding. I am not willing, indeed, it would deeply grieve me, to have our long continuous friendship interrupted or grow cold, & I trust it will not.

I have several books that should be returned to you, and some writing paper, which as soon as I can find the leisure I will box up & send to the office.

Understand, my dear Father, that I do not withdraw in a pet, or with the slightest unkind feeling. The labor was too much for me, & as Sadlier pays me enough with my annuity to enable me to live, I think it better that the time—about three weeks a month upon an average—which I spend in writing & correcting proofs for the C.W. should be spent in preparing the series of works you are aware I have in hand, & which I could not prepare, if I continued my connection with the C.W. I am growing old, & I could not continue long to work as I have done for the last two years, and must have some relief.

I hope our intercourse will continue as friendly as ever; yet I shall not dare accept your kind invitation, unless it is renewed. I have written to Father Hewit.[2] I am sure he does not understand me, probably through my fault; but I love & reverence him as [a] true friend & a loyal soul.

I am glad to hear that your mother is recovering. Remember me kindly to the members of the community, & believe me

Gratefully yours

O A. Brownson

Very Rev. I. T. Hecker.
St. Paul's Convent.

1. Brownson's of 10 January 1872 (Letter 170).
2. O. A. Brownson to A. F. Hewit, 11 January 1872 (APF). Microfilm, roll seven.

172

BROWNSON TO HECKER • 24 JANUARY 1872

Jan. 24, 1872

Rev. & dear Father,

I very much regret that the illness of my Wife,[1] & effects of a recent touch of the gout from which I am not yet wholly recovered will deprive me of the pleasure of dining with you tomorrow & meet Dr. Marshall,[2] whom I am very anxious to meet. Pray assure him of my regret, and the pleasure he would give me, if he would honor me with a visit at Elizabeth.

Yours very truly

O. A. Brownson.

Very Rev. I. T. Hecker.
Superior of the Paulist
Community. 59 Street
New York.

1. Sally Healy Brownson caught a severe cold in her lungs in early January 1872, and she died the following April at the age of 68.

2. Thomas William Marshall (see Letter 169, n. 2).

173

HECKER TO BROWNSON • 30 JANUARY [1872]*

New York Jan 30, 1871[1]

Dear Dr.

I greatly regret that you were hindered in coming to dine with Dr Marshall and other gentlemen on the 25th inst. More so, because it would have given, I am sure, the occassion [*sic*] of our coming to a satisfactory understanding.

It seems to me that if you would continue to write such articles as you have done the last two years or more in refutation of the calumnies of the enemies of the Church, in applying Catholic principles to the social and political questions of the day, in directing the young Catholic mind how to judge and act in the midst of existing difficulties, which never were greater or more threatening, and in boldly confronting and silencing the leading advocates of heresy and error, you would promote to the greatest degree Catholic interests, give the highest satisfaction to the hierarchy, and interest most the readers of the Magazine.

Believe me Dear Dr. you can have no idea of the great good which you have done by your pen employed in this direction. I who am in more direct contact with the readers of the Catholic World hear the satisfaction expressed on all sides and by all classes for articles of this nature, all rejoicing that in you they have found a champion of their faith and a master who teaches them how to harmonize their duties as Catholics with the best interests of Society and the state.

Whatever value you may attach to my judgment, or sincerity to my friendship for you, believe me, that this is a matter of most serious consideration in the presence of God, before you leave this great field of doing good, and give up the privilege of leading and directing the Catholic minds of our Country.

I have never known you to falter in what you considered to be your duty, and whatever may be your deliberate conclusion in this matter, the high esteem and sincere friendship which I have borne for you now nearly forty years, will be none the less or in no way affected.

As ever

Yours faithfully & affectionately

I T Hecker.

O A Brownson L.L.D.

*Brownson, *BLL,* pp. 564–65 (dated 30 January 1871); McSorley, *FH&F,* pp. 292–93; Ryan, *OAB,* pp. 685–86 (dated 30 January 1871). Microfilm, roll seven (calendared 30 January 1871).

1. Though the year 1871 was written, Hecker meant 1872, since the dinner with Dr. Marshall took place in January 1872.

173 Draft

HECKER TO BROWNSON • [30 JANUARY 1872]*

[*Undated*][1]

Dear Dr.

I regret greatly that you were hindered in coming in to N.Y. to dine with Mr. Marshall and others. My notice was short on account of Mr. Marshall's [*illegible*] not certain before I sent the telegram.

Your visit would have given I am sure the occassion [*sic*] of our coming to a better satisfactory understanding. It seems to me that if you would consent to write a class of articles for the *C.W.* in refutation of the more unpopular attacks and by Protestant enemies of the Church such as you have done mainly these couple of years past, you would promote greatly Catholic interests and give the highest satisfaction to the hierarchy, and interest most all the readers of the magazine.

Whatever value you may attach to my judgment or sincerity to my friendship for you, believe me that you will best serve the Church for which you have devoted your abilities & energies by considering seriously before God, before you give up this great field [of] doing good and the privilege of leading & directing the Catholic minds of our Country.

Believe me Dear Dr. you can have no idea of the great good which you have done by your pen employed in this direction. I who am in more direct contact with the readers of the magazine, hear satisfaction expressed on all sides by all classes, for articles of this nature, all rejoicing that in you they found a champion of their faith, a master who teaches them how to harmonize their duties as Catholics with the best interests of society & the state.

It seems to me that if you would continue to write such articles as you have done these last two years or more

1–In refutation of the calumnies of the enemies of the Church

2–In applying Catholic principles to the social and political questions of the day

3–in directing the Young Catholic mind how to judge and act in the midst of existing difficulties

4–in boldly confronting & silencing the leading advocates of heresy and error.

*HP, APF; omitted from microfilm.

1. This undated draft of Hecker's letter of 30 January 1872 (173 above) differs little from the actual letter, except in the placing of its paragraphs.

174

BROWNSON TO HECKER • 31 JANUARY 1872*

Eliz. NJ. Jan. 31, 1872.

Dear Father Hecker

The rejection of my two articles may have been the occasion of my withdrawal from the Catholic World, but not the cause or reason. I was a little vexed I admit, but I could & should have soon got over that. But I found neither my head, nor my eyes, nor even my hand would allow me to write so much as I was writing. I was decidedly breaking down. If I continued to write for the Cath. W. I must abandon the works I had under way, which I might have consented to do, perhaps, if I could have published some things, on which my heart was set, in the C.W. but that was henceforth out of the question. I therefore concluded to withhold my contributions.

The *Tablet* pays me more than I could make by writing for the C.W. and at one fourth of the labor. What it pays me, so long as my connection with its lasts[,] with my annuity enables me to support my family, and secures me three weeks, instead of one out of four, to devote to my work, Atheism Refuted & Theism Demonstrated. I judged it best therefore to drop the C.W. to which I had devoted upon an average about three weeks a month of hard labor.

I think you overrate the importance of my articles, and if you did not I could not be expected to keep up articles of equal merit, month after month, & year after year, at my age. Then you do not need me. You have better and far more popular writers than I am. The writer of the 1st article in the last number,[1] the writer of the article on Calumnies Refuted,[2] & Fr. Preston's[3] article on the Episcopal Convention,[4] as well as Col. Meline's[*?*][5] far surpass me in freshness & freedom of style. My withdrawing will also enable you to bring forward younger men, and develop fresh genius and talent.

If I was convinced that it was my duty to continue my contributions, I would at once withdraw my resolution, but I think I can serve Catholic interests more effectually in completing the series of works I have in contemplation than in any other way that I can employ the few days I may yet remain on the earth. At any rate, it will be no disadvantage to you to let matters remain for the present year as they are.

I thank you for the many proofs of your friendship you have given me, and I assure you that my feelings towards you have undergone no change. And I trust our intercourse is not to be interrupted, but is to continue as cordial and friendly as ever.

Yours truly

O. A. Brownson

Very Rev. I. T. Hecker.

*McSorley, *FH&F,* pp. 293–94.

1. "Who Is to Educate Our Children?" *CW,* XIV (January 1872), 433–47.

2. "Several Calumnies Refuted; Or, Executive Document No. 37," ibid., pp. 665–82.

3. Thomas Scott Preston (1824–1891), ordained Episcopalian priest 1848, Catholic convert 1849 and ordained priest 1850, author and rector of St. Ann's Church in New York City, became vicar-general of the Archdiocese of New York 1853, co-founder of the Sisters of the Divine Compassion.

4. "The Late General Convention of the Protestant Episcopal Church," *CW,* XIV (January 1872), 506–20.

5. Brownson most probably means James Florant Meline (1811–1873), journalist, historian, colonel U.S. Army.

Appendix

1

JOHN HECKER TO BROWNSON • 7 JANUARY 1843*

New York January th7. [*sic*] 1843

My Dear Friend

I received your letter last week. It gave me a great deal of satisfaction to hear you had taken such an interest in my brother's afflictions. They are such I think you will be able to give him that advice and encouragement which he needs. He has since he has become acquainted with you always thought more of what you said than any one of his family. His disease I always have thought arose from to[o] much exercise of mind and in my telling him so[,] doing my best to check that tendency[,] it has made him keep all his feelings and thoughts to himself. Therefor [*sic*] I think you will be able to do us a favour if it is not asking to[o] much. You can get out of him more of his feelings than we can. In his last letter he asks us to give him our advice. He says he wants to go to Brook Farm and study one or two Languages. If I had not already felt that his disease was brought on him by to[o] much study I would gladly give him that advice. I should like to hear from you in regard to it. The letter we received from him when we received yours would have given us a great deal of uneasiness if we had not received at the same time one from you explaining the condition he was in when he wrote it. I shall feel ever thankful to you for it. The last letter we received from him we found a decided improvement which I fear if he follows out his own desires will call those nervous spells to return more frequently. In the whole course of his sickness he has had much his own way [and] he was always better when he was expecting something or was about to undertake a journey[,] any thing like Physical labour mentioned to him had a very disagreable [*sic*] effect upon him. When he got what [he] expected or finished what he undertook he would get such spells of despair that he would make us all feel bad for his sake. Anything he undertook we found it necessary not to cross him but give him encouragement hoping for the better[,] thinking some unknown circumstances would restore him to us as he once was. The Physician he had, thought if he could have his mind employed in some Physical employment where the mental could be united[,] he would get better. I have thought so to[o], but to get him to feel so and do it we could not. He says himself he thinks it would do him good. I hope you will be able to discover some better remedy or cure for him being you can get a better explanation from him than we can. Mother thinks he is under a severe religious change or under peculiar convictions which she thinks all persons must have before they are Christians in a more or less degree. The only thing she thinks he is looking for or wants is a giving up of his whole mind to Christ and then he would be relieved. If any such thing should exist, I think he must have already explained to you. If so we would be glad to hear. She often says she hopes Mr Brownson will be a spiritual guide or Father to him. If my Brother wants anything I know you will assist him and if it lays in our power to repay you, it shall not be wanting on our part. He may let you know more of his pecuniary wants than he would us. If so be so kind and let us know. There is no person I could have selected for him to stay with sooner than yourself and if you think it would do him no harm to stay at Brook Farm and study, I will be satisfied and I will do for him what is necessary. I am sorry to have to trouble you so much with our Family affairs but it has in this case been necessary.

I have been this last week to hear Bishop Hughes lecture in the Tabernacle. His subject was on civilization. He gave a very interesting lecture.[1] He spoke two hours long and interested his audience the whole time and now and then he received bursts of applause. He undertook to show that it was Christianity alone [which] advanced civilization. He showed it in so plain a manner that it was very interesting. The Incidents he hit upon where [*sic*] so descriptive of the Brotherhood of the race and the Perfection of the Idea of Humanity [that] I thought sometimes I was hearing you. The house was crowded to overflowing so that many had to leave with out hearing him. I have written this letter while my wife is to Church. I have had to rock the child and if you find in some places not much connection you must look over it.

Yours Truly

John Hecker

Mr O A Brownson

*Brownson, *BEL,* pp. 501–3.

1. "The Influence of Christianity upon Civilization," given on 5 January 1843 before the Catholic Library Society.

2

JOHN HECKER TO BROWNSON • 20 AUGUST 1843

New York August th20. [*sic*] 1843

Mr Brownson

Dear Sir

I have mentioned to a few of my friends that you would be willing to write an address for a meeting to be called by the citizens of New York in favour of John C Calhoun for President of the United States.[1] We have concluded [,] that is [,] many of the friends of John C Calhoun [,] to call a meeting in the Park as soon as possible. Our Legislature in the close of the last Session reccommended [*sic*] a convention of the state to be held at Syracuse for to take in consideration or to adopt the primary action for the delegates to the Baltimore Convention [;] in the different Wards of our city they did not seem to understand the object or reason for this convention [,] but it was explained before we got through [;] at these meetings it showed there had been a design to force by surprise upon us none but Van Buren men. When this was understood by us to force Martin Van Buren as candidate for President we objected and run [*sic*] a Calhoun ticket [,] and in all the Wards where they [*sic*] was any one to take lead for Calhoun [,] which I believe was five Wards [,] the Calhoun ticket was elected. To have so many Wards without any concerted action surprised all the Calhoun men themselves [;] therefore we think a movement like this will have great effect upon that question and be the means of calling us together for a better disciplining of our forces. I must relate a circumstance of our Ward of the unwillingness of the Van Burenites to alow [*sic*] the voice of the people to be heard [;] that after they found we had elected Calhoun delegates to the convention, [it] being late and [a] great many had left the meeting [,] they passed resolutions instructing the delegates to go for Van Buren [,] which was one of the old tricks of the agency of Van Buren by which they expect to effect his nomination. It was recommended by both Parties by resolution to adopt the district system [,] but we think if the Van Buren delegates in the convention are in the majority [,] they will not allow it. If they should [,] I think we may send Calhoun delegates to the Baltimore Convention from this City. We intend to call this meeting before this convention meets [,] that is the 15th of this next month. If you feel like writing it [,] we would like to hear from you as soon as possible. In the mean time they say if you can do justice to the address and make it short it will please his friends here. My Brother Isaac has arrived home and feels like taking hold of business again. His health is somewhat improved[,] but I think your Boston Transcendentalists have had to[o] much influence on his mind[,] which I am in hopes will wear off. I want you to write him if you find time to disabuse his mind of these errors. He intends to write you soon. You must except [*sic*] this imperfect letter from one who don't [*sic*] write often.

Yours Respectfully

John Hecker

1. See Letter 5 and notes.

3

GEORGE V. HECKER TO BROWNSON • [c. 25 SEPTEMBER 1845]*

[*Undated*] [1]

Dear Mr Brownson

We received a letter from Isaac yesterday and he wished me to write to you that he had arrived in very good health in 25 days[;] he had a very pleasant passage and he would write to you when he arrived at St Trond which would be a few days. He feels that it is the goal that he has for years secretly wished for. I hope you will write as often as you can for I think the advice you would give him would be of great benefit to him.

His leaving has come very severe upon mother[;] she can hardly overcome it. If you have any Catholic news if it will not be asking too much[,] would you be so kind as to send them on to me[;] I shall be grateful to you for it.

From Your Friend

George V Hecker

*Microfilm, roll two (calendared [1845]).

1. Dated c. 25 September 1845 on the basis of a letter George Hecker received from Isaac written from London and dated 29 August 1845. Isaac Hecker's letter probably took four or five weeks to reach George.

Index

I

J

K